HIKING
CONNECTICUT AND
RHODE ISLAND

HIKING
CONNECTICUT AND
RHODE ISLAND

A GUIDE TO THE AREA'S GREATEST HIKING ADVENTURES

SECOND EDITION

Rhonda and George Ostertag

FALCONGUIDES

GUILFORD, CONNECTICUT

FALCONGUIDES®

An imprint of The Rowman & Littlefield Publishing Group, Inc.
4501 Forbes Blvd., Ste. 200
Lanham, MD 20706
www.rowman.com

Falcon and FalconGuides are registered trademarks and Make Adventure Your Story is a
trademark of The Rowman & Littlefield Publishing Group, Inc.

Distributed by NATIONAL BOOK NETWORK

British Library Cataloguing in Publication Information available

Library of Congress Cataloging-in-Publication Data available

ISBN 978-1-4930-3996-8 (paperback)
ISBN 978-1-4930-3997-5 (e-book)

∞™ The paper used in this publication meets the minimum requirements of American National
Standard for Information Sciences—Permanence of Paper for Printed Library Materials, ANSI/
NISO Z39.48-1992.

Printed in the United States of America

CONTENTS

ACKNOWLEDGMENTS   ix

INTRODUCTION   1

   WEATHER   3

   FLORA AND FAUNA   4

   WILDERNESS RESTRICTIONS/REGULATIONS   6

   TRAIL NAVIGATION   7

HOW TO USE THIS GUIDE   9

HOW TO USE THE MAPS   10

TRAIL FINDER   11

MAP LEGEND   14

WESTERN CONNECTICUT   15
Northwest Connecticut Trails   16

   1. Mount Frissell   16
   2. Appalachian National Scenic Trail   23
   3. Falls Brook Trail, Tunxis State Forest   29
   4. Windsor Locks Canal State Park Trail   34
   5. Enders Falls Trail   39
   6. Peoples State Forest   43
   7. Great Pond State Forest   48
   8. Burr Pond State Park   53
   9. Mohawk Mountain State Forest   58
  10. Metacomet Trail, Talcott Mountain   64
  11. Macedonia Brook State Park   70
  12. Sessions Woods Wildlife Management Area   75
  13. Ragged Mountain Preserve Trail   80

   Honorable Mentions, Northwest Connecticut   85
   A. Farmington Canal Heritage Trail, Granby to Simsbury   85
   B. McLean Game Refuge   85
   C. Northwest Park   86
   D. Sharon Audubon Center   86
   E. Roaring Brook Nature Center   86

  F. White Memorial Foundation, Nature Trails   87
  G. White Memorial Foundation,
       Mattatuck-Five Ponds Hike   87
  H. Mount Tom State Park   88
   I. Farmington River Trail   88
   J. Hill-Stead Museum Trails   89
  K. Shade Swamp Sanctuary   89
   L. Pratt Nature Center   90
  M. Lovers Leap State Park   90

Southwest Connecticut Trails   *91*

  14. Lillinonah Trail   91
  15. Southford Falls State Park   96
  16. Kettletown State Park   101
  17. Zoar Trail   107
  18. Farmington Canal Heritage Trail,
       Cheshire to New Haven   113
  19. Sleeping Giant State Park, Tower Hike   118
  20. Sleeping Giant State Park, White Trail to
       Violet Trail Loop   122
  21. Mattabesett Trail: Millers Pond to
       Coginchaug Cave; Bluff Head   127
  22. Cockaponset State Forest   133
  23. Collis P. Huntington State Park   139
  24. Regicides Trail   144
  25. Devil's Den Preserve   150

Honorable Mentions, Southwest Connecticut   **155**
  N. River Highlands State Park   155
  O. Larkin State Park Trail   155
  P. Wadsworth Falls State Park   156
  Q. Millers Pond State Park Reserve   156
  R. Tarrywile Park   157
  S. Saugatuck Valley and Aspetuck Valley Trails   157
  T. Chatfield Hollow State Park   158
  U. Cockaponset State Forest, Weber Tract   158
  V. Roy and Margot Larsen Wildlife Sanctuary   158
  W. Greenwich Audubon Society   159
  X. Westwoods Preserve   159

 Y. McKinney National Wildlife Refuge,
  Salt Meadows Unit 160

EASTERN CONNECTICUT 161
Northeast Connecticut Trails 162
 26. Bigelow Hollow State Park 162
 27. Mashamoquet Brook State Park 168
 28. Case Mountain Recreation Area,
  White Carriageway Loop 173
 29. Nipmuck Trail, Fenton River 178
 30. James L. Goodwin State Forest 183

Honorable Mentions, Northeast Connecticut **188**
 Z. Shenipsit Trail, Soapstone Mountain 188
 AA. Major Michael Donnelly Land Preserve 188
 AB. Risley Pond 189
 AC. Hop River State Park Trail 189
 AD. Trail Wood, Edwin Way Teale Memorial Sanctuary 189
 AE. Bafflin Nature Sanctuary 190
 AF. Gay City State Park 190
 AG. Mansfield Hollow State Park 191

Southeast Connecticut Trails 192
 31. Air Line National Recreation Trail,
  East Hampton to Columbia 192
 32. Salmon River Trail 198
 33. Pachaug State Forest, Pachaug-Quinebaug Loop 203
 34. Devil's Hopyard State Park 211
 35. Green Fall Pond, Narragansett-Nehantic-
  Pachaug Hike 217
 36. Hartman Recreational Park, Heritage Trail 222
 37. Nayantaquit Trail/Uncas Pond 227
 38. Bluff Point State Park and Coastal Reserve 232
 39. Barn Island Wildlife Management Area 237

Honorable Mentions, Southeast Connecticut **243**
 AH. Shenipsit Trail, Great Hill Hike 243
 AI. Hurd and George Dudley Seymour State Parks 243
 AJ. Machimoodus State Park 244

AK. Poquetanuck Cove Preserve   244
 AL. Gillette Castle State Park   244
AM. Selden Creek Preserve   245
 AN. The Oswegatchie Hills Nature Preserve   245
 AO. Haley Farm State Park   246

RHODE ISLAND   247

40. George Washington Management Area,
    Walkabout Trail   249
41. George B. Parker Woodland   255
42. Tillinghast Pond Management Area   259
43. East Bay Bike Path   264
44. Breakheart Pond–Mount Tom Loop,
    with Ben Utter Spur   269
45. Great Swamp Management Area   275
46. Sachuest Point National Wildlife Refuge   280
47. Vin Gormley Trail   285
48. Ninigret Conservation Area, East Beach Hike   290
49. Trustom Pond National Wildlife Refuge   294
50. Block Island, North Island Hiking   299

Honorable Mentions, Rhode Island   **304**
AP. Blackstone River Bikeway   304
AQ. Lime Rock Preserve (Aust Family Preserve
    at Lime Rock)   304
AR. Pachaug Trail   304
AS. Browning Mill Pond   305
AT. Chafee Nature Preserve   305
AU. Norman Bird Sanctuary   306
AV. Carolina Management Area   306
AW. Francis C. Carter Memorial Preserve   307
AX. Ninigret National Wildlife Refuge   307

CLUBS & TRAIL GROUPS   308

ABOUT THE AUTHORS   309

ACKNOWLEDGMENTS

We would like to acknowledge the hard work of the region's nonprofit trail and conservation associations, with a special nod to the Connecticut Forest and Park Association for its leadership, and the many dedicated volunteers who help blaze and maintain the trails. We thank the preservationists who work to save the area landscape and its history and the landowners who generously have allowed these trail systems to grow and endure.

We would like to thank the individuals who have helped with our research, volunteered their ideas or faces, and guided this book through production. We offer up enormous thanks to our family who freed us to do this work.

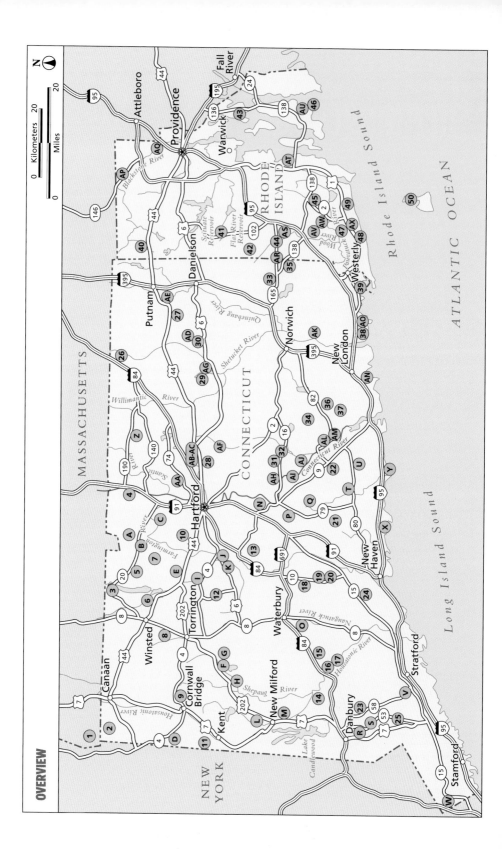

OVERVIEW

N

0 Kilometers 20
0 Miles 20

MASSACHUSETTS

NEW YORK

CONNECTICUT

RHODE ISLAND

ATLANTIC OCEAN

Rhode Island Sound

Long Island Sound

Canaan
Winsted
Cornwall Bridge
Kent
Torrington
New Milford
Waterbury
Danbury
Stratford
Stamford
New Haven
Hartford
New London
Norwich
Putnam
Danielson
Providence
Attleboro
Warwick
Fall River
Westerly

Housatonic River
Shepaug River
Naugatuck River
Housatonic River
Lake Candlewood
Farmington River
Still River
Stanton River
Willimantic River
Shetucket River
Quinebaug River
Connecticut River
Scituate Reservoir
Flat River Reservoir
Blackstone River
Pawcatuck River
Wood River

INTRODUCTION

When pondering the nation's great places to hike, it might take you a while to rattle off Connecticut and Rhode Island. But don't let their size fool you.

Despite their small geographic footprint, the combined lands of Connecticut and Rhode Island roll out an intriguing tapestry for exploration. Hundreds of miles of trail entice you to lace on the hiking boots and experience firsthand the bounty that ranges from short nature walks to rugged ridgeline hikes to wilderness beach strolls. You will meander through appealing natural areas and extensive forested reaches, and you will rejoice in a rich geologic and cultural history.

The featured trails showcase premier parks, forests, ponds, peaks, traprock ridges, coastal flatlands, bluffs, swamps, and beaches as well as private reserves and sanctuaries. You'll hike past charming waterfalls and commanding cliffs and revel in summit views and, yes, wilderness solitude. You will shuffle across crackling carpets of autumn-colored leaves and dig your toes into clean white sand. Turtle, salamander, deer, raccoon, osprey, bald eagle, hawk, gull, and warbler will number among your co-travelers. There will likely be encounters with needling mosquitoes, too, but the visual rewards and spiritual benefits are worth seasonally slathering on some yucky, smelly armor.

This guidebook pulls together a region-wide sampling of short nature walks, day hikes of varying length and difficulty, and backpacking trips, where available. Surprisingly, you may puff and sweat to earn your rewards. Even we, the authors, have felt the physical tug of the land despite having strengthened our lungs and legs in the high country of the West. Terrain, gradient, cumulative elevation, distance, and design all figure in a trail's workout and its delivery of a sense of accomplishment.

A legacy of glacial deposited rock graces this land and riddles trails. Glaciers sculpted the face of both Connecticut and Rhode Island, grinding down ridges, broadening valleys, and gouging out river courses and brooks. The resulting landscape of ledge and boulder outcroppings, traprock ridges, cascading and plummeting waterfalls, and excavated lowland swamps is a welcome mat that any hiker could salute.

While traveling the trails, you will flip through the pages of history. You'll rub shoulders with such historical figures as Governor Winthrop, Roger Williams, and General Rochambeau and maybe even with the legendary Sherlock Holmes. You'll discover Indian and colonial graves and unravel the story of war and settlement and the Industrial Revolution. When your boots are worn and your soul is primed, you will truly know Connecticut and Rhode Island.

At the heart of Connecticut's trail system are the famed blue trails of the Connecticut Forest and Park Association (CFPA), the state's oldest private nonprofit conservation group, organized in 1895. These trails are part of a long-standing tradition and commitment to trails tracing back to Reverend Edgar Laing Heermance, the father of the blue trail system and first chairman of the CFPA. He was an advocate of healthy living

Hardwood forest, Macedonia Brook State Park, Connecticut

and finding the spiritual in nature. The signature light-blue blaze was his selection—he deemed it the most visible color when viewed in dusk lighting.

In 1929 the CFPA moved to establish the long-distance trunk lines known as the blue trails. The Quinnipiac Trail, which passed through Reverend Heermance's land at Rocky Top in Hamden, led the way in 1930. Because several of the longer blue trails require bridging segments of road travel, we typically spotlight only sections of them, preferring our boots connect with the good earth and our air be exhaust-free. A host of federal, local, and private organization and land-trust trails complete the state inventory.

Rhode Island's trail system is an eclectic pool of public and private lands and their respective trail systems. The best central source for finding trails to date is the ExploreRI partnership of the Rhode Island Blueways Alliance (paddle) and Rhode Island Land Trust Council (hiking trails), www.exploreri.org. The groups' inventory is not yet complete but they hope to add the state Department of Environmental Management (DEM) trails in the future. So far, locating good source information on the conditions and lay of DEM trails remains a hunt.

Both Connecticut and Rhode Island have fine rail and canal trail offerings. Do not dismiss the natural merit of these linear routes—they are vital greenways for wildlife. A black bear shared our morning ramble on Connecticut's Farmington River Trail.

A fine and willing volunteer constituency keeps the trails passable for us all and helps protect each state's hiking resource. As beneficiaries of the fine work, we should support the organized groups through membership and support individual volunteers by doing our part to keep the trails clean and clear. In the recreation dynamic, we trail users have an obligation to use the land responsibly, respect private ownership, and protect and preserve trails and the landscapes we traverse. Respecting switchbacks, contours, and other design features helps retain the integrity of the land. Our adventure should not come at the cost of the land or the enjoyment of future trail users.

Although the following trail collection is by no means exhaustive, it does launch you into the foot-trail possibilities of this two-state area. The rest of the discovery is up to you.

WEATHER

Connecticut and Rhode Island offer reliable three-season hiking, with days of no or minimal snow extending the activity into winter. Some trails double as winter cross-country ski or snowshoe routes. Spring and fall offer the preferred mix of mild temperatures and low humidity levels, while summer can bring both high temperatures and high humidity. Generally speaking, the climate for both these states falls in the humid continental zone. Seaward reaches experience coastal effects and flirt with humid subtropical climate conditions.

Thunderstorms, some violent, are a fairly regular occurrence in summer. Hurricane season can bring tropical storm conditions to the region.

Like much of the East, Connecticut and Rhode Island endure a mosquito and blackfly season. Spring and summer hikers should come prepared for biting insects. Less troublesome in dry years, the insects can be annoying in wet years.

For hiking safety and proper preparation, it's a good idea to seek out current weather forecasts for the area of your chosen trail. This is especially true for long hikes and overnight outings.

Whatever your information source, though, it's always good to keep an eye on the sky.

Awareness of the weather forecast to prepare and travel by is helpful, but do not discount the unexpected. These reports are only forecasts. Pack on the side of caution, and know what to do if the weather turns bad.

FLORA AND FAUNA

Both Connecticut and Rhode Island are more than 60 percent forested. Nearly 1.9 million acres of forest clad the Connecticut countryside. Rhode Island, the Ocean State, is another 14 percent water.

Before colonization, this two-state area was nearly 90 percent forested. Stands had a parklike quality at that time because the native peoples would burn away the brush. Agriculture removed great numbers of trees, but the manufacturing era nearly denuded the eastern states of forest, as wood was sought for the production of charcoal.

The forest of today is not the forest of yesteryear. When the Europeans arrived, white pines grew tall and straight, desirous traits for ship masts and building. The multitrunk pines that were passed over for cutting became the genetic base for the white pines seen today. The demands for timber and charcoal along with invasive infestations and disease have influenced the mix.

In both states hardwood forests predominate, but the canopy will vary. Rhode Island's primary complex is oak-hickory, but fifty-one tree species vegetate the state. Connecticut's lower reaches blend compositions of beech, birch, tulip magnolia, sweet gum, hickory, maple, and oak, while red maples favor its swamps. Sugar maples support a maple-sugaring industry in Connecticut and provide clues to property lines of long-ago homesteads.

Viburnum, sarsaparilla, bunchberry, baneberry, Solomon's seal, azalea, rhododendron, and mixed ferns shower the forest floor and midstory. Mountain laurel, the Connecticut state flower, is a common adornment in its wooded realms. Rhode Island's common blue violet seeks out lime-based soils and woods. All sorts of lichens, mosses, mushrooms, and conks decorate the woodlands.

Mountain laurel along Mohawk Trail, Mohawk State Forest, Connecticut

The meadow plains and abandoned fields of Connecticut and Rhode Island

parade out such species as goldenrod, black-eyed Susan, Queen Anne's lace, milkweed, butterfly weed, joe-pye weed, and blackberry bramble. Wetlands bring together cattail reeds, rushes, purple phragmites (a nonnative species), and sweet pepperbush. The kaleidoscope of shape, color, and texture fashions a visually and sensory rich backdrop to the pathways of both states.

Populating the two states' niches and habitats are hundreds of species of mammals, birds, reptiles, fish, and amphibians and tens of thousands of species of invertebrates. The common large mammal sighting for each state is the white-tailed deer. Beavers or, more likely, their waterway enhancements are familiar sightings. The large rodent's industry improves fisheries and water quality. Moose, unexpected sightings, are not as rare as they once were. Black bears, too, can be spied.

More common encounters would include woodchucks, gray squirrels, chipmunks, mice, rabbits, raccoons, and muskrats. Songbirds, hawks, woodpeckers, ducks, shorebirds, and wild turkeys engage bird watchers. Rhode Island's Sachuest Point National Wildlife Refuge records sightings of 250 bird species, and an Australian ornithologist we met in Florida touts Connecticut's Bluff Point as ideal for warblers. Turtles, frogs, toads, efts, newts, salamanders, crabs, and slithering snakes can disturb the water or part the grasses. While most snakes are harmless, copperheads and timber rattlesnakes find limited habitats. Fish populations claim fresh, brackish, and saltwater environments.

Even when the two-state menagerie goes unseen, we can rejoice in the songs, tracks, rustles, splashes, and subtle clues of life around us. As stewards of the flora and fauna, we need to minimize both our own trace and that of our pet companions when we hike the trails.

WILDERNESS RESTRICTIONS/REGULATIONS

Although this book concentrates primarily on public land offerings, trails across private, trust, conservancy, and sanctuary lands extend the hiking opportunities. To continue this privilege, you must assume full responsibility for your own well-being whenever you cross onto privately held land. Heed all posted rules and exercise your best no-trace wilderness manners. Keep to the trail, leave gates as they were found, and police your actions and those of your animal, if indeed pets are allowed. "Pack it in, pack it out."

The text will indicate if and where trails travel onto these lands. But, occasionally, ownership changes or a landowner may withdraw the privilege of through travel. Respect such closures. At private preserves and nature centers, fees or suggested donations may be requested for the use of the facility's trails.

The Nature Conservancy (TNC), a nonprofit organization devoted to the protection of biodiversity, opens its trails to the public for hiking, nature study, and photography. Please note that straying from the trail, hiking with pets, collecting, smoking, picnicking, camping, building fires, swimming, and bicycling are forbidden activities in these preserves. With a mission to conserve and preserve the land and its habitats and inhabitants, TNC extends us hiking privileges only where and when such access is compatible with the primary objective. Donations help defray the cost of both maintaining existing preserves and acquiring new ones.

National and state Audubon facilities and sites, with a guiding directive of wildlife protection and habitat preservation, restrict usage to foot travel and nature study. Picnic only at established sites, leave pets at home, no mountain bikes, and no collecting. Heed all posted rules regarding use, times, and closures. Membership in the society or the payment of a modest entry fee keeps these properties operating and the trails and facilities maintained.

The White Memorial Foundation in Litchfield, Connecticut, maintains a remarkable 4,000-acre gift from a farsighted brother and sister committed to preserving nature and its tranquility, and to providing future generations the opportunity to enjoy and explore the land. The site promotes conservation, research, education, and compatible forms of recreation within this natural arena. Heed trail-use restrictions and no collecting. The Conservation Center museum, the educational programs, and the campgrounds are fee-based. The 35 miles of trail and center grounds picnicking are free, but donations and memberships are welcome.

Trails traversing lands managed by state, county, water district, and federal agencies shape the core of this book. Of the state-operated properties, state parks typically show greater grooming and development and possess more facilities. Beginning in 2018 Connecticut residents will no longer be charged a parking fee at Connecticut Parks and Forests. Parking fees will apply for nonresidents. Currently, Rhode Island charges a seasonal entry fee only at its state beaches and imposes an in-state/out-of-state pricing tier.

For many of us nonresidents who avidly hike and use the Connecticut outdoors, the purchase of the state's seasonal pass can pay for itself, awarding us flexibility and convenience besides access. For the calendar year of purchase, the pass allows unlimited vehicle access to any state park or recreation area where parking fees are charged. Passes can be purchased at regional headquarters, at entry stations to the individual parks or forest recreation areas (during times of operation), or by mail (or online) from the Connecticut Department of Energy and Environmental Protection—DEEP Store, 79 Elm St.,

Hartford, CT 06106-5127; www.ct.gov/deep. For current fees and payment instructions, call (860) 424-3555.

State forests and management areas account for much of the region's open space. These minimally developed woodland sites typically offer a wilder experience, with few or even no facilities. Those with campgrounds charge camping fees.

State wildlife management areas and federal national wildlife refuges primarily promote and sustain waterfowl and wildlife populations, with hunting and fishing, bird watching, and hiking variously allowed as compatible recreations. Trail parking and use are generally free, although some nature centers and day-use areas may require fees.

For backpack camping along Connecticut's long-distance blue trails, you must apply for a permit by application form (available online) two weeks in advance of your trip. For detailed rules and regulations, go online to www.ct.gov/deep and look up backpack camping under "Outdoor Recreation."

Along the Appalachian National Scenic Trail, the lean-tos are available first come, first served. Remember, you must share these shelters with other parties.

TRAIL NAVIGATION

With the predominance of leafy forests in Connecticut and Rhode Island, look for some manner of blazing—paint, diamond, or disk—to guide you through your travels. On some private lands, blaze patterns may exist for one-directional travel only; therefore, be sure to consult a map board or flier before plotting your course of exploration. Cairns and stakes are other manners of marking a route. A double-blazing pattern typically

Forest trail near Tri-State Point, Litchfield County, Connecticut

warns of a change in direction. Examine the top blaze: An offset to the right or left cues you to the direction you should turn.

Several multistate long-distance routes crisscross these states, each with a signature blaze color or emblem disk. The Appalachian Trail is marked by a signature white blaze. The North–South Trail through Rhode Island is dark blue, and the New England Greenway Trail has its own emblem.

The Connecticut Forest and Park Association marks more than 825 miles of its forest, park, and private land trails with a light-blue paint blaze. Side trails typically bear a colored dot within the blaze or a 50/50 blue and color-coded blaze.

While the Connecticut blue trails have a predictable standard of blaze size, placement, and spacing, not all trails are as precise, and trees can fall and paint can fade. It's a sound practice to familiarize yourself with the blazing frequency on the trail you are walking. An uncommonly long lapse between blazes may indicate that you have strayed off-course, in which case you should backtrack to the last known marker and look again. If reasonably short searches do not turn up the next marker and the line of the trail, the wise course of action is to turn around and return to the trailhead. Autumn adventures require special vigilance because fallen leaves can completely conceal even well-tracked paths.

For any backcountry travel, know there are unavoidable risks that you assume and must be aware of and respect. In all cases, know yourself and your abilities and let independent judgment and common sense be your ultimate guide to safe travel.

BE TRAILHEAD SMART

Unattended hiker vehicles are vulnerable to theft and vandalism, but the following steps can minimize your risk:

- When possible, park away from the trailhead at a nearby campground or other facility.
- Do not leave valuables in the vehicle. Place keys and wallet in a button-secured pocket or remote, secure compartment in your pack, where they will not be disturbed until your return.
- Do not leave any visible invitations. Stash everything possible in the trunk, and be sure that any exposed item advertises that it has no value.
- Be suspicious of loiterers, never volunteering the details of your outing.
- Be cautious about the information you supply at the trailhead register. Withhold information such as license plate number and duration of stay until you are safely back at the trailhead. Instead, notify a trusted friend of your trip details and notify them promptly upon return.

HOW TO USE THIS GUIDE

Each region begins with a **section intro,** where you're given a sweeping look at the lay of the land. After this general overview, you'll find chapters presenting the specific hikes within that region.

To aid in quick decision-making, each hike begins with a **summary** that provides a taste of the hiking adventure to follow. You'll learn about the trail terrain and what surprises the route has to offer. Next, you'll find the hike specs, the quick, nitty-gritty details of the hike: where the trailhead is located, hike length, approximate hiking time, difficulty rating, elevation change, type of trail terrain, best hiking season, the other trail users you may encounter, canine compatibility, land status, the nearest town, usage fees, trail schedule, maps, and trail contact (for updates on trail conditions), plus any special considerations that may affect your safety or enjoyment.

The approximate hiking times are based on a standard hiking pace of 1.5 to 2 miles per hour, adjusted for terrain and reflecting normal trail conditions. The stated times should get you there and back, but be sure to add time for rest breaks and enjoying the trail's attractions. Although the stated times offer a planning guideline, you should gain a sense of your personal health, capabilities, and hiking style to make this judgment for yourself. If you're hiking with a group, add enough time for slower members. The amount of carried gear will influence hiking speed, as will the weather and actual conditions found on the ground. In all cases, leave enough daylight to accomplish the task safely.

The **Finding the trailhead** section gives you dependable directions from a nearby city or town right down to where you'll want to park your car. It also gives the trailhead Global Positioning System (GPS) reading. **The Hike** is the meat of the chapter. Detailed and honest, it's our researched, firsthand impression of the trail. Although it's impossible to cover everything and conditions can and do change, we make every effort to address what's important—the good and the bad. In **Miles and Directions** we provide mileage cues to key junctions, switches to new trails, and points of interest. The selected benchmarks allow for a quick check on progress and serve as your touchstones for staying on course. At the end of each hike, you'll find **Hike Information,** which offers up local information sources for learning more about the area and may suggest things to do nearby or places to camp.

Lastly, at the end of each region, the **Honorable Mentions** section identifies hikes that didn't make the cut, for whatever reason. In many cases it's not because they aren't great hikes, but because they are overcrowded, have limited parking, or are too environmentally sensitive to handle heavy foot traffic. Others appear here because we had a lot of choices for this book. Be sure to read through the entries—a jewel might lurk among them.

HOW TO USE THE MAPS

As a hiker aid, you may wish to copy or take cell phone picture of the Miles and Directions and map for the selected route to carry with you while hiking. Or, just slip the whole book into your pack and take it along with you to make the most of your time in the outdoors.

Route Map

This gives you the layout of each hike, with the selected route highlighted. It shows the accessible roads and trails, water, landmarks, towns, and key navigational features. It also distinguishes trails from roads, and paved roads from unpaved roads. While never intended to replace the more-detailed agency maps, road maps, state atlases, or topographic maps, each basic route map will help you to visualize and navigate the described hike.

Trail Finder

	BACKPACKERS	YOUNG CHILDREN	OLDER CHILDREN	DOGS (LEASHED)	NATURE LOVERS	HISTORY LOVERS	WATERFALLS	PEAK BAGGERS	VISTAS
1. Mount Frissell	•		•	•	•			•	•
2. Appalachian National Scenic Trail			•	•	•	•	•	•	•
3. Falls Brook Trail, Tunxis State Forest			•	•	•		•		
4. Windsor Locks Canal State Park Trail		•	•	•	•	•			
5. Enders Falls Trail			•	•	•		•		
6. Peoples State Forest			•	•	•	•			•
7. Great Pond State Forest		•	•	•	•				
8. Burr Pond State Park		•	•	•	•				
9. Mohawk Mountain State Forest	•		•	•	•	•		•	•
10. Metacomet Trail, Talcott Mountain			•	•	•	•		•	•
11. Macedonia Brook State Park			•	•	•			•	
12. Sessions Woods Wildlife Management Area		•	•	•	•				
13. Ragged Mountain Preserve Trail			•	•	•			•	•
14. Lillinonah Trail			•	•	•				
15. Southford Falls State Park		•	•	•	•		•		
16. Kettletown State Park			•	•	•				•
17. Zoar Trail			•	•	•				
18. Farmington Canal Heritage Trail, Cheshire to New Haven		•	•	•	•	•			

	BACKPACKERS	YOUNG CHILDREN	OLDER CHILDREN	DOGS (LEASHED)	NATURE LOVERS	HISTORY LOVERS	WATERFALLS	PEAK BAGGERS	VISTAS
19. Sleeping Giant State Park, Tower Hike			•	•	•	•		•	•
20. Sleeping Giant State Park, White Trail to Violet Trail Loop			•	•	•				
21. Mattabesett Trail: Millers Pond to Coginchaug Cave; Bluff Head			•	•	•	•		•	•
22. Cockaponset State Forest			•	•	•	•			
23. Collis P. Huntington State Park			•	•	•	•			
24. Regicides Trail			•	•	•	•		•	•
25. Devil's Den Preserve		•	•	•	•	•			•
26. Bigelow Hollow State Park		•	•	•	•				
27. Mashamoquet Brook State Park			•	•	•	•			•
28. Case Mountain Recreation Area, White Carriageway Loop		•	•	•	•	•		•	•
29. Nipmuck Trail, Fenton River			•	•	•	•			
30. James L. Goodwin State Forest			•	•	•				
31. Air Line National Recreation Trail, East Hampton to Columbia		•	•	•	•	•			•
32. Salmon River Trail			•	•	•	•	•		
33. Pachaug State Forest, Pachaug-Quinebaug Loop			•	•	•	•			
34. Devil's Hopyard State Park		•	•	•	•	•	•		

	BACKPACKERS	YOUNG CHILDREN	OLDER CHILDREN	DOGS (LEASHED)	NATURE LOVERS	HISTORY LOVERS	WATERFALLS	PEAK BAGGERS	VISTAS
35. Green Fall Pond, Narragansett-Nehantic-Pachaug Hike					●				
36. Hartman Recreational Park, Heritage Trail		●	●	●	●	●			●
37. Nayantaquit Trail/Uncas Pond		●	●	●	●				
38. Bluff Point State Park and Coastal Reserve		●	●	●	●	●			
39. Barn Island Wildlife Management Area		●	●	●	●	●			
40. George Washington Management Area, Walkabout Trail		●	●	●	●	●			
41. George B. Parker Woodland		●	●		●	●			
42. Tillinghast Pond Management Area		●	●	●	●	●			
43. East Bay Bike Path		●	●	●	●	●			●
44. Breakheart Pond–Mount Tom Loop, with Ben Utter Spur	●		●	●	●		●	●	●
45. Great Swamp Management Area		●	●	●	●				
46. Sachuest Point National Wildlife Refuge		●	●		●				●
47. Vin Gormley Trail			●		●				
48. Ninigret Conservation Area, East Beach Hike		●	●		●				
49. Trustom Pond National Wildlife Refuge		●	●		●				
50. Block Island, North Island Hiking		●	●		●	●			●

MAP LEGEND

═══ 81 ═══ Interstate Highway	✗ Airport
═══ 460 ═══ US Highway	▬ Bench
─── 362 ─── State Highway	⇌ Boat Ramp
─── 613 ─── County/Forest Road	⏝ Bridge
─────────── Local Road	■ Building/Point of Interest
= = = = = = = Unpaved Road	▲ Campground
┣━┿━┿━┿━┫ Railroad	⌒ Cave
•─•─•─•─• Power Line	🗼 Lighthouse
▬ ▬ ▬ ▬ ▬ Featured Trail	℗ Parking
─ ─ ─ ─ ─ Trail	▲ Peak/Summit
·······🔺······· Appalachian Trail	⊞ Picnic Area
─ · · ─ · · ─ State Line	🛈 Ranger Station
‖‖‖‖‖‖‖ Boardwalk/Steps	🚻 Restrooms
⌇⌇ Small River or Creek	🖼 Scenic View/Viewpoint
⸮⸮ Marsh/Swamp	🏛 Tower
⬭ Body of Water	○ Town
▭ National Forest/Park	① Trailhead
▭ National Wilderness Area	❓ Visitor/Information Center
▬ State/County Park	💧 Water
	⋛ Waterfall

WESTERN CONNECTICUT

As a natural divide, the Connecticut River slices Connecticut into east–west halves. In the far western part of the state, you will find the rugged, steep, and hilly terrain of the Litchfield Hills, part of the ancient Appalachian Mountain chain, and the geologic and cultural region known as the Berkshire Hills. Connecticut's highest hills are found here, and they bear rocks akin to those found in the Taconic Range, dating back 450 million years ago.

At the eastern extreme of this region is the volcanic trough of the Connecticut River, whose origin traces back to the birth of the Atlantic Ocean about 200 million years ago. Here the region's western traprock ridges face off with their eastern counterparts. Together these volcanic ridges shape the highland of the Connecticut River Valley. A flatter coastal plain greets Long Island Sound to the south, and throughout the region is rolling forested expanse.

Southern hardwoods, eastern hemlock groves, naturally growing white pines, and red and white pine plantations cloak the western hills and countryside. Tulip poplar is a showy woodland resident, both in size and bloom. Red maples splash autumn fire onto lowland swamps, while bushes of mountain laurel (the state flower) grow with abandon across the region, heralding in spring and early summer. The midstory at the state's western extreme straddles a transition zone between the milder mountain laurel belt to the east and the colder uplands to the west where hobblebush and striped maple prevail.

Twisting the imagination, dinosaurs once walked Connecticut. Native Americans lived, fished, hunted, and managed the forests through the use of fire before the European settlers arrived. Early settlement brought farming and shipping. Large tracts of forest were cleared for settlement, but the land was nearly denuded of trees to fuel the Industrial Revolution. Stone walls are the legacy of early farms, pastures, and animal pens. Mills and dams record the efforts at industry. Western Connecticut was a producer of weapons, tools, and other ironwork. Textiles, too, were an important output of the region.

This region encompasses the state's populated urban centers and rural enclaves. Some view western Connecticut as New York City's big backyard. Tucked away along the curving mountain roads of western Connecticut are many who have slipped the bonds of the city for a quieter existence.

The region's trails explore forests, hilltops, rocky ledges, ponds, brooks, waterfalls, and swamps. The famed Appalachian National Scenic Trail advances along the western edge of Connecticut. Paths explore along both the free-flowing and the captured waters of the Housatonic River, while others breathe new life into former rail and canal routes. In western Connecticut you can roam a giant's anatomy and hide with the exiled British judges who ordered the execution of Charles I.

NORTHWEST CONNECTICUT TRAILS

Northwest Connecticut, composed of Litchfield and Hartford Counties, stretches from the state's wooded high country to the historic factory belt along the Connecticut River. This corner is a land of lofty views, romantic woods, welcoming lakes, and working rivers turned recreational. As in much of the state, history abounds, and the trails celebrate all.

1 MOUNT FRISSELL

You must hit the road to tag the highest point in Connecticut because, at 2,372 feet, it is not a peak but a point on the southern shoulder of Massachusetts's Mount Frissell. It sits just below the summit and east of Tri-State Point, the shared boundary of New York, Massachusetts, and Connecticut. The more civil approach, featured here, is by either New York's South Taconic Trail or the trails of Massachusetts's Mount Washington State Forest. Connecticut serves up a short, but steep approach over Round Mountain. But, however you get there, the accomplishment is all Connecticut.

Start: South Taconic/Bash Bish trailhead in New York's Taconic State Park, or headquarters trailhead in Massachusetts's Mount Washington State Forest

Distance: 17 miles out and back via South Taconic Trail, or 10.2 miles out and back via Massachusetts's Alander Mountain and Ashley Hill Trails (the latter has the option for a loop return with a spur to Alander Mountain for a total of 14 miles).

Hiking time: 8 to 11 hours, depending on choices along the way.

Difficulty: Strenuous

Elevation change: The South Taconic Trail starts at 800 feet and then rolls between 1,500 and 2,300 feet as it travels the Taconic Crest. There is 900 feet of change on the out-and-back Alander Mountain–Ashley Hill Trail and its return loop option.

Trail surface: Earthen foot trail and woods road

Best seasons: Spring through fall

Other trail users: Hunters, snowmobilers, cross-country skiers

Canine compatibility: Leashed dogs permitted

Land status: New York state park and Massachusetts and Connecticut state lands

Nearest town: Copake Falls, NY, with gas in Copake, NY, or Sheffield, MA

Fees and permits: Entrance fee at New York's Taconic State Park; permit and fee for designated backcountry camping spots in Massachusetts (preregister at state forest headquarters)

Schedule: Year-round, sunrise to sunset, with registered backcountry camping at designated spots in Massachusetts

Maps: Taconic State Park map (available online at https://parks.ny .gov/parks), Mount Washington State Forest trail map (online at www.mass .gov/locations/mount-washington-state-forest), and New York–New Jersey Trail Conference Trail Map, South Taconic Trail (available at traditional and online bookstores or from the conference: www.nynjtc .org)

Trail contacts: Taconic State Park, Route 344, PO Box 100, Copake Falls, NY 12517; (518) 329-3993; https://parks.ny.gov/parks. Mount Washington State Forest, 143 East

Street, Mount Washington, MA 01258; (413) 528-0330; www.mass .gov/locations/mount-washington-state-forest.

Special considerations: It is best to avoid the trails during deer season (Nov–Dec), but if you do hike, wear orange or other bright-colored clothing.

FINDING THE TRAILHEAD

For the South Taconic Trail, from Copake Falls, NY, go 0.7 mile east on NY 344 to reach Taconic State Park's South Taconic/Bash Bish trailhead on the right. Trailhead GPS: N42 07.047' / W73 30.494'

For the Mount Washington State Forest approach, from the junction of MA 23 and MA 41 in South Egremont, take MA 41 south for 0.1 mile and turn right on East Street. At its junction with Jug End Road in 1.7 miles, a sign indicates to stay on East Street for Mount Washington State Forest. In another 6.8 miles, turn right for the headquarters and trailhead. Trailhead GPS: N42 05.183' / W73 27.738'

THE HIKES

If you must run for the border, at least you have two nice hikes from which to choose.

NEW YORK'S SOUTH TACONIC TRAIL

This gateway to Connecticut's high point traces the Taconic Mountain spine southward. You begin following white blazes down the limited-access cabins road to a bridge crossing and the foot-trail ascent. Passages in mountain laurel, a hemlock stand, a high-canopy maple forest, and pine-oak woods carry you to the ridge and a junction. Here a short blue spur leads to a 180-degree western perspective, with Washburn Mountain prominent.

Southbound, you hike past a second blue trail. As the trail hugs the ridge, views flip east. On a flat exposed outcrop on Alander Ridge (just before the old lookout site, in case you missed it), a painted blue marker indicates the trail to Massachusetts's Alander Mountain and Mount Washington State Forest. Stay on the South Taconic Trail, which soon rewards with a 270-degree three-state highline/western valley view. Wavy-patterned schist creates the opening. The wooded trail then drops away. After a left on woods road, you pass color-coded trails, fragments of stone wall, and waist-high ostrich ferns. Mountain laurels close rank for a picturesque passage.

Back on the ridge, a crescent spur veers right for a western vantage. Past Massachusetts's Ashley Hill Trail, the road grade eases and you reach the red trail descending left toward Mount Frissell and Connecticut's high point. Past the monument for Tri-State Point, reach the quested high point on the south ridge of Mount Frissell. It sits 740 feet south and 80 vertical feet below the top. Look for piled rocks on an outcrop near an unassuming survey state line geologic marker. A site box holds a notebook for journaling about the experience. Good luck! Return as you came.

MASSACHUSETTS'S ALANDER MOUNTAIN AND ASHLEY HILL TRAILS

From the information board, follow signs for Alander Mountain Trail, passing through field and conifer-hardwood forest. After the footbridge crossing of Lee Pond Brook, you'll pass the Charcoal Pit Trail, coming to a trail junction (the loop junction). Follow the Ashley Hill Trail left. The Alander Mountain Trail ahead is the optional loop return.

View from Mount Frissell near Connecticut high point, Litchfield County, Connecticut

On a woods road, the trail ascends, contouring the slope above rushing Ashley Hill Brook, a beaver-enhanced 10-foot-wide stream. Blue triangles and paint blazes point the way. Continue past a trail descending right to campsites. Black oaks join the mix as a fern sea holds eyes transfixed. Again walk past the Charcoal Pit Trail, cross a side drainage, and ascend parallel to Ashley Hill Brook. After crossing the brook, the Ashley Hill Trail bears left, becoming more trail-like. Mountain laurels wrap it in bloom mid-June through early July. Azaleas write their signatures a few weeks earlier.

Past a Massachusetts–New York state line marker, reach a red-blazed trail. Turn left toward Mount Frissell and Connecticut's high point (a right here begins the loop return via the South Taconic Trail). You pass through low-stature woods, ascending over bedrock. Past the 1898 Tri-State (Connecticut–Massachusetts–New York) monument, the climb steepens. Continue east to tag the highest point in Connecticut. Again, it sits 80 vertical feet below, 740 feet south of the Mount Frissell summit. Rocks on an outcrop and a survey pipe quietly mark the spot. Vicinity views sweep from South Brace Mountain in New York to Mount Plantain in Massachusetts, with Connecticut's Round, Gridley, and Bear Mountains. Although Frissell summit is within 0.1 mile, it's viewless. Backtrack to the Ashley Hill Trail junction.

For the simple out-and-back, backtrack the Ashley Hill and Alander Mountain Trails to the state forest headquarters. For the loop return, follow the red-blazed rock-studded trail, ascending to meet the South Taconic Trail, and then follow the white blazes right (north). The open, rolling ridge extends looks across rural New York. Past a blue trail, the South Taconic Trail briefly veers left from the woods road for limited western views. On its return, laurel, rock walls, and waist-high ferns decorate the way. After the woods road bottoms out at a rocky drainage, follow the white blazes right on a steeply charging foot trail.

Atop Alander Ridge, past the concrete platform of a former lookout tower, keep an eye out for an open flat rock with a blue-paint blaze (which may be faint). This signals where you descend right on the Alander Mountain Trail for the headquarters return. You quickly come to a saddle and rustic cabin. The loop descends past the cabin. A spur east tops Alander Mountain (2,250 feet) for an open view. The descent's well-trampled trail parallels a small drainage, crossing feeder streams. Knitted overhead is a rustling canopy.

Later, a milder gradient and a defined woods road ease travel. Continue forward past a trail heading right to campsites. You'll cross Ashley Hill Brook, upstream from its confluence with Lee Pond Brook, to ascend to the initial loop junction. Remain on the Alander Mountain Trail, returning to headquarters.

MILES AND DIRECTIONS

SOUTH TACONIC TRAIL

0.0 Start at the west end of Bash Bish trailhead parking. Descend south on the limited-access road toward the cabins, following the white-blazed South Taconic Trail. *Option:* The closed service road heading east, upstream, offers a 1.5-mile out-and-back hike to Bash Bish Falls, an energetic tumble over bedrock.

1.1 Reach a ridge junction. Continue your ascent on the white-blazed South Taconic Trail. *Option:* The 0.1-mile blue spur leads to a vantage point.

3.0 Reach a notch.

3.5 Reach a blue-trail junction on Alander Mountain ridge (it's north of a former lookout site). Continue south on the white trail. *Option:* For an Alander Mountain detour, descend left on the blue trail, coming to a saddle, a rustic cabin, and a blue-trail fork in 0.1 mile. The prong descending past the cabin traverses Massachusetts's Mount Washington State Forest, eventually reaching backpacker campsites and the forest headquarters. The prong ascending east tags Alander summit in 0.2 mile for views.

5.2 Pass the red-blazed Robert Brook Trail.

6.7 Follow the foot trail veering right for a crescent spur to a western vantage. The spur returns to the woods road ahead.

View from Mount Frissell near
Connecticut high point,
Litchfield County, Connecticut

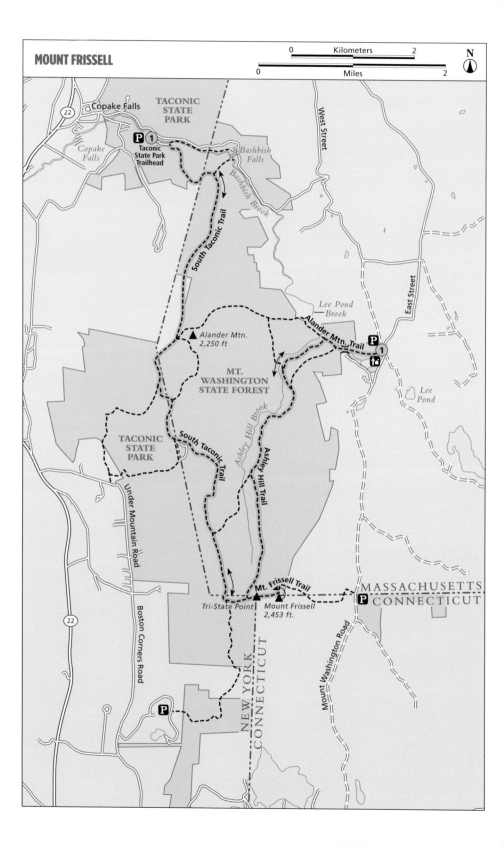

MOUNT FRISSELL

Kilometers
0   2
0   2
Miles

N

Copake Falls

(22)

TACONIC
STATE
PARK

West Street

P 1
Taconic
State Park
Trailhead

Copake
Falls

Bashbish
Falls

Bashbish Brook

South Taconic Trail

East Street

Lee Pond
Brook

Alander Mtn. Trail

Alander Mtn.
2,250 ft

P
1

MT.
WASHINGTON
STATE FOREST

Lee
Pond

Ashley Hill Brook

TACONIC
STATE
PARK

South Taconic Trail

Ashley Hill Trail

Under Mountain Road

Mt. Frissell Trail

MASSACHUSETTS

Tri-State Point

Mount Frissell
2,453 ft.

P

CONNECTICUT

(22)

Boston Corners Road

Mount Washington Road

NEW YORK

CONNECTICUT

P

6.8   Hike past the Ashley Hill Trail (blue).

7.6   Reach the red-blazed Mount Frissell Trail; follow it left. **Option:** Proceeding straight on the white South Taconic Trail leads to Brace Mountain, its 5-foot-tall stone cairn, and views in another 0.6 mile.

8.1   Reach Tri-State Point. Continue hiking east and up Mount Frissell.

8.5   Reach Connecticut's high point. It sits 80 vertical feet below and 740 feet south of the summit. Return as you came. **Option:** The red trail tops Mount Frissell in another 0.1 mile, but the oak-crowned summit offers no views.

17.0   Arrive back at the Bash Bish trailhead.

ALANDER MOUNTAIN AND ASHLEY HILL TRAILS

0.0   Start at the forest headquarters trailhead. Follow the signed Alander Mountain Trail.

0.8   Reach the loop junction. Turn left on the Ashley Hill Trail. **Note:** The Alander Mountain Trail straight ahead is the optional loop return.

1.5   Reach a trail junction. Keep left to continue on the Ashley Hill Trail. **Note:** The trail to the right leads to backcountry campsites and the Alander Mountain Trail.

2.4   Continue upstream along Ashley Hill Brook.

3.0   Cross a side brook and keep left on the Ashley Hill Trail. **Note:** Straight leads to the South Taconic Trail.

4.5   Reach a red-trail junction. Turn left to follow the red trail to Mount Frissell and Connecticut's high point. **Note:** The red trail to the right leads to the South Taconic Trail for the optional loop return.

4.7   Reach the Tri-State Point monument and continue east up Mount Frissell.

5.1   Reach Connecticut's high point. Return as you came to the 4.5-mile junction. **Option:** Forward on the red Mount Frissell Trail tops Mount Frissell (elevation 2,453 feet) in 0.1 mile, but there are no views.

5.7   Reach the 4.5-mile junction. For the out-and-back hike, retrace the Ashley Hill and Alander Mountain Trails to the state forest headquarters at 10.2 miles. **Option:** For the loop return, follow the red-blazed trail ahead to reach the South Taconic Trail (6.0), and turn right (north) to continue the loop. (**Note:** Brace Mountain sits 0.6 mile south.) On the loop, reach the blue Alander Mountain Trail junction, a blazed flat outcrop past the onetime lookout site (10.3). Turn right on the blue trail. Reach a saddle cabin and trail junction (10.4). Ascend east for views from the Alander Mountain summit (10.6) and return to the saddle (10.8). Follow the blue trail past the cabin to descend to the Mount Washington State Forest headquarters. Reach a trail junction for the backcountry campsites (12.3); proceed forward. Close the loop (13.2) and continue back on the Alander Mountain Trail to the headquarters at 14.0 miles.

HIKE INFORMATION

LOCAL INFORMATION

Columbia County Tourism Department, 401 State St., Hudson, NY 12534; (518) 828-3375; https://columbiacountytourism.org or www.travelhudsonvalley.org.

    Southern Berkshire Chamber of Commerce, PO Box 810, 362 Main St., Great Barrington, MA 01230; (413) 528-1510 or (800) 269-4825; http://southernberkshire chamber.com.

Western Connecticut Convention and Visitors Bureau, PO Box 968, Litchfield, CT 06759; (860) 567-4506; http://litchfieldhills.com.

LOCAL EVENTS/ATTRACTIONS

The Harlem Valley Rail Trail—built on the old railroad bed that connected New York City, the Harlem Valley, and Chatham—extends a paved discovery route to hikers and cyclists. You'll find accesses in Ancram, Copake, and Copake Falls/Taconic State Park. Contact the HVRT Association at (518) 789-9591 or www.hvrt.org.

ACCOMMODATIONS

Taconic State Park Campground, open early May through Oct, has more than 100 sites (serving both tent and trailer campers) and 3 cabin areas. Reservations are through ReserveAmerica, (800) 456-2267 or www.reserveamerica.com.

ORGANIZATIONS

New York–New Jersey Trail Conference, 600 Ramapo Valley Rd. (Route 202), Mahwah, NJ 07430; (201) 512-9348; www.nynjtc.org.

2 APPALACHIAN NATIONAL SCENIC TRAIL

This nearly 2,200-mile-long hiker filament strings along the Appalachian mountain chain from Mount Katahdin, Maine, to Springer Mountain, Georgia. More than 50 miles of prime Connecticut countryside advance the trail, including 5 uninterrupted miles on the west bank of the Housatonic River—one of the longest river-paired stretches on the entire Appalachian Trail (AT). Connecticut travel takes you through low-elevation mixed forest and past stunning ledges and outcrops. You'll discover multistate views, waterfalls, and historic stone walls, canals, and towns. Between the drive-to trailheads at Under Mountain and Bulls Bridge, you can hike 48 miles of the Connecticut AT.

Start: Massachusetts-Connecticut border north of Connecticut's Bear Mountain

Distance: 51.6 miles one way through Connecticut

Hiking time: 5 to 7 days

Difficulty: Strenuous

Elevation change: Travel between a low point of 250 feet along the Housatonic River and a high point of 2,316 feet atop Bear Mountain.

Trail surface: Earthen and rocky paths, woods roads, developed roads

Best seasons: Spring through fall

Other trail users: Snowshoers, cross-country skiers, hunters (on lands where allowed)

Canine compatibility: Leashed dogs permitted (Be sure to carry adequate food and water for your dog when through-hiking.)

Land status: This national park linear trail crosses multiple public lands with a few private sections; heed postings.

Nearest towns: Cornwall, Salisbury, and Kent, CT

Fees and permits: None

Schedule: No time restrictions

Maps: Appalachian Trail Conservancy (ATC), Appalachian Trail maps (available at traditional and online bookstores or from the ATC online store: www.atctrailstore.org)

Trail contact: ATC, PO Box 807, 799 Washington St., Harpers Ferry, WV 25425-0807; (304) 535-6331; www.appalachiantrail.org

Special considerations: The AT is for foot-propelled use only; no bikes, no vehicles, and no horses, llamas, goats, or other pack animals. In places the terrain can be rugged, rocky, and steep. You need to work out the logistics for carrying and obtaining food and supplies, have a plan for emergencies, and arrange for transportation at the end of the trail. As campfires are not allowed on the Connecticut AT, bring a stove for your cooking needs. Do not rely on the availability of a lean-to; a tent is standard equipment. Pitch tents in established sites. Be sure to safely pack and store all food. Rodents have identified the lean-to bonanza.

AT thru-trail and day hikers should contact the ATC for its official maps and guides. Their work is worth supporting, and they have the inside track on current conditions and trail changes. Strong map and compass skills will ease travel. Stay alert for the AT's white blazes, which occur at regular intervals. If you have hiked 0.25 mile without spying one or another trail clue, backtrack to the last-seen blaze and reassess. If the trail still does not reveal itself, you may have to backtrack. As with any long-distance trail, keep your senses and exercise judgment about proceeding. Be alert for temporary changes or reroutes, and keep to the narrow protected greenway to avoid trespassing.

Use caution at ledge outcrops, especially when burdened with a heavy pack, and be cautious when hiking during hunting season. Dress to be seen and be sure your pet is in protective colors, too, or safe at home. Wet, frosty, icy conditions can steal footing. Be aware of ticks and the possibility of copperheads and rattlesnakes.

FINDING THE TRAILHEAD

The AT crosses many Connecticut state routes and traverses several state parks and state forest lands. Find Connecticut's northernmost drive-to trailhead, the Under Mountain trailhead, west off CT 41, 3.2 miles north of Salisbury. The parking lot can fill because this is the gateway trailhead to Bear Mountain, the tallest peak in the state, a rite of passage for Connecticut hikers. Trailhead GPS: N42 01.727' / W73 25.736'

For the Bulls Bridge trailhead, from the junction of CT 341 and US 7 in Kent, drive south on US 7 for 3.8 miles to Bulls Bridge and turn right on Bulls Bridge Road. Find parking on the south side of the road in 0.1 mile, additional parking on the north side of Bulls Bridge Road in 0.2 mile, and the AT itself at the Bulls Bridge Road–Schaghticoke Road intersection in 0.4 mile. Trailhead GPS: N41 40.525' / W73 30.490'

THE HIKE

Conceived in the early 1920s and the first trail to win national scenic trail distinction, the Appalachian Trail (AT) passes through the mountain wilds of fourteen eastern states. More than 50 miles trace Connecticut's scenic northwest corner, touring forest, field, and mountaintop. Here you'll find opportunities for round-trip, shuttle, and thru-trail hiking. The white-blazed AT advances primarily via foot trail, with sections on abandoned woods road. Where necessary, it travels developed roads.

During its Connecticut sojourn, the AT rolls along the Housatonic River Valley, up and down the state's highest peaks, and through the forests of the southern Berkshires. Ledges and clearings regularly reward with views. Swamps, fields, streams, ponds, the Great Falls, and inviting villages complement travel. Revolutionary and Civil War figures, mill sites, and a canal that leaked the dreams of forward-thinking citizens seed travel.

View from Bear Mountain, Appalachian National Scenic Trail, Connecticut

Arriving from Massachusetts, you follow the AT south and begin bagging Connecticut peaks, starting with the highest peak (not point) in Connecticut, Bear Mountain. The summit's stone pyramid, now stabilized rubble half its original size, lifts you above the treetops, but far better views are secured from the schist outcrops on the mountain's shoulder. It took local mason Owen Travis three years to haul 350 tons of stone to this roadless summit to erect the pyramid, 20 feet square at its base and 22 feet tall, tapering at the top. The stone tablet placed in 1885, now

Housatonic River, Stanley Works Cooperative
Wildlife Management Area, Connecticut

faint, declares Bear Mountain the highest ground in Connecticut, though modern measures have disproved this statement.

On descent from Bear Mountain, the wavy schist bedrock common throughout the Taconic Range opens views and shapes fine seating. As the AT travels the southern extreme of this mountain range, it tops Lions Head and Prospect Mountain to reach and trace the Housatonic Valley floor. After pairing up with the Housatonic River for views of the aptly named Great Falls, a river-wide tumult that has both harnessed and natural features, the AT takes you across the restored 1903 steel bridge into Falls Village. Falls Village offers up the beauty, history, and industry associated with the river and falls.

The AT then returns to ridge travel, overlooking the river, traversing Sharon Mountain, and passing through Housatonic State Forest. It then follows the west bank of the Housatonic River for a 5-mile stretch—one of the longest river-paired segments on the entire national scenic trail. Where the trail comes out at South Gate on River Road, you follow the lightly used access road downstream before turning west into woods.

At St. Johns Ledges, the ridge climb remains rugged despite ninety stone steps placed by the Appalachian Mountain Club. Attracting rock climbers, the Ledges' smooth and steep-faced cliffs fashion a striking vertical relief in the enfolding leafy woods and carve out rim views. The AT crosses Calebs Peak and more ledges that afford a raven's-eye view of the river. It then dips briefly back to the valley. At Schaghticoke Mountain, the AT flirts with New York travel but returns to Connecticut, following Schaghticoke Road to its intersection with Bulls Bridge Road.

Thru-hikers continue south, crossing Bulls Bridge Road and entering woods on foot trail. For those with vehicles spotted at Bulls Bridge Road, turn left (east) for the parking areas. The AT sashays between New York and Connecticut before committing to New York past Hoyt Road.

MILES AND DIRECTIONS

0.0 Start at the AT junction at the north end of Paradise Lane in Massachusetts. Proceed south on the AT into Connecticut.

0.7 Top Bear Mountain.

1.6 Reach Riga Junction; continue south on the AT. To the left is the Under Mountain Trail.

4.0 Top Lions Head.

6.7 Reach CT 41.

10.7 Reach Rands View.

12.6 Top Prospect Mountain.

13.4 Cross the steel bridge at Falls Village.

17.5 Reach US 7 parking with a Housatonic River bridge crossing.

20.7 Reach Sharon Mountain Camp.

30.7 Reach the River Road stretch along the Housatonic River.

35.4 Reach South Gate. Round the gate and follow the lightly used road downstream to where blazes turn west into forest.

35.9 Reach St. Johns Ledges.

36.6 Top Calebs Peak.

40.1 Reach CT 341.

43.3 Reach Schaghticoke Mountain Camp.

47.9 Reach the intersection of Schaghticoke Road and Bulls Bridge Road. Thru-trail hikers enter the woods south of the intersection. *Option:* For those who spotted a vehicle at Bulls Bridge Road, turn left (east) on Bulls Bridge Road to reach the parking lots near the bridge spans.

51.6 Reach the New York leg of the AT at Hoyt Road.

Option: At Bear Mountain, a loop is possible stitching together the Under Mountain, Paradise Lane, and Appalachian Trails. From the Under Mountain trailhead north of Salisbury, follow the wide, well-designed, well-paced blue trail striking west uphill. Along the trail you'll see mountain laurel as well as hobblebush and striped maples. The latter are more common to the high country farther west.

At 1.1 miles reach the Paradise Lane Trail and follow it right for a counterclockwise loop, approaching Bear Mountain from the north. You will glimpse your summit destination before reaching the AT at 3.2 miles. At the AT, turn left (south) to top Bear Mountain and to thru-hike the Connecticut leg of the AT.

The summit of Bear Mountain (3.9 miles) is one of the most popular destinations in Connecticut, but not because of its view. It's the loft that counts. In 1885 mason Owen Travis raised a summit pyramid here, which over time has crumbled. However, the stabilized rubble still allows an eastern survey toward the Twins Lakes—Washining (East Twin) and Washinee (West Twin)—and the surrounding farms, woods, and rises. More open views await you on the mountain's south shoulder.

From the open schist outcrops, you'll view both Connecticut and New York. Southbound, the AT traces the ridge, passing through densely clustered, head-high sassafras, chestnuts, pitch pines, and oaks. At Riga Junction (4.8 miles), loop travelers turn left on the Under Mountain Trail for the return descent. Close the loop back at the Paradise Lane Trail junction at 5.6 miles, and continue the descent to end at the trailhead at 6.7 miles.

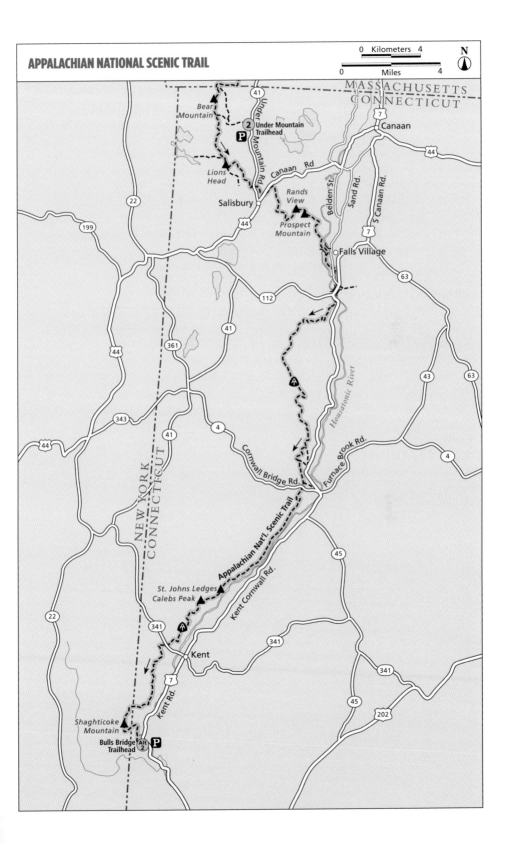

HIKE INFORMATION

LOCAL INFORMATION

Western Connecticut Convention and Visitors Bureau, PO Box 968, Litchfield 06759; (860) 567-4506; http://litchfieldhills.com.

LOCAL EVENTS/ATTRACTIONS

Fly fishing the Housatonic River is a popular regional pastime. Local outfitters offer guided trips and instruction. For more information, contact the Western Connecticut Convention and Visitors Bureau.

Beckley Furnace Industrial Monument, c/o Burr Pond State Park, 385 Burr Mountain Rd., Torrington 06790; (860) 482-1817; www.ct.gov/deep. Beckley Iron Furnace Industrial Monument in East Canaan, on the National Register of Historic Places, is considered one of the best-preserved relics of Connecticut's industrial period. It operated from 1847 to 1919 and produced iron for railcar wheels.

ACCOMMODATIONS

Macedonia Brook Campground, (860) 927-4100; **Housatonic Meadows Campground,** (860) 672-6772; www.ct.gov/deep. Thru-trail hikers will find established campsites and shelters regularly spaced along the length of the AT. Day hikers will find seasonal camping at area state parks, Macedonia Brook (51 sites) and Housatonic Meadows (61 sites). To reach Macedonia Brook State Park, heading west on CT 341 from US 7 in Kent, go 1.7 miles, turn right, and follow signs. Housatonic Meadows, in the town of Sharon, is east off US 7, about 3 miles south of West Cornwall Covered Bridge and 2 miles north of CT 4.

ORGANIZATIONS

Appalachian Mountain Club (AMC), Connecticut Chapter, www.ct-amc.org.

3 FALLS BROOK TRAIL, TUNXIS STATE FOREST

The challenge with this Tunxis State Forest hike is the timing. You want to view the waterfalls at their charged best, while still being able to ford the brook for the hike's loop. Fortunately, this is a hike that calls you back again and again, so ultimately the fates are bound to align. Whether spilling in tinsel shimmer and charm or racing white, the serial cascades of Falls Brook win you over. When hiking in the wet season, you should watch your step because salamanders and red efts can part the leaf mat.

Start: CT 20 trailhead
Distance: 1.8-mile lollipop with spur
Hiking time: 1 to 1.5 hours
Difficulty: Moderate due to trail footing, but high water can bump it to strenuous, or even impossible to complete in its entirety because of the fordings on the loop
Elevation change: 300 feet
Trail surface: Earthen path, rooted and rocky and at times streaming water
Best seasons: Spring through fall
Other trail users: None
Canine compatibility: Leashed dogs permitted
Land status: State forest with metropolitan water district land adjoining; heed signs at boundary
Nearest town: Winsted, CT

Fees and permits: None
Schedule: Year-round, from a half hour before sunrise to a half hour after sunset
Map: Connecticut Forest and Park Association (CFPA) *Connecticut Walk Book, West* (available from CFPA, www.ctwoodlands.org)
Trail contact: Department of Energy and Environmental Protection, State Forests, (860) 424-3200; www.ct .gov/deep
Special considerations: Wet, frosty, or icy conditions can cause slipping. Do not insist on making a fording if conditions do not warrant it. The danger of wet rocks and fast water should not be dismissed lightly. Use common sense.

FINDING THE TRAILHEAD

From the junction of CT 179 and CT 20 in East Hartland, follow CT 20 west around the north end of Barkhamsted Reservoir. In 5.3 miles find the Falls Brook Trail and its roadside parking on the left. Look for the blue oval, the characteristic road signage for the Connecticut Forest and Park Association (CFPA) blue trail system. Eastbound on CT 20 from its junction with CT 181 (0.8 mile west of West Hartland), drive 3.3 miles to the trailhead. Trailhead GPS: N42 01.304' / W72 57.137'

THE HIKE

This hike explores that part of Tunxis State Forest drained by the East and West Branches and main stem of Falls Brook. The trail follows the east bank of the main stem down-stream to its waterfall plummet and then loops back crossing the feeder branches. It packs a lot of beauty in its short distance. Falls Brook and its branches captivate with their stepped waters and wending pools and their wooded complement.

THE EMERGENCE OF THE CONSERVATION MOVEMENT AND THE CFPA

The Connecticut Forest and Park Association (CFPA), the nonprofit organization that defends and advocates for the Connecticut outdoors and works hands-on in the field, formed in 1895. Like other conservation and hiking associations of that time, it emerged in response to an awakening interest in the outdoors. The first meeting of the CFPA pulled together like-minded people concerned about the welfare of the state's forests.

Throughout the nation, conditions were ripe for nature to be viewed in a new light. Industrialization had shifted populations to cities, regional forests had been battered down by unchecked use and the spread of fire, and the raw landscapes of the American West were capturing attention and imagination. Transportation, too, was improving, easing travel to distant and outdoor places. There was both a want and a need for the outdoors.

Several historians credit the sportsmen of the day with ushering in this awareness. The nation's leading thinkers, writers, artists, and political leaders then fanned the flames of enthusiasm. The nation was primed to embrace the benefits of nature and outdoor recreation, and for the first time, the natural world had intrinsic value. A conservation movement was born.

This early movement emphasized protecting lands as public parks, forests, refuges, and reserves. It also endorsed both the responsible use and the scientific management of water, mineral, soil, forest, fish, and wildlife. The outdoor resource we enjoy today had entered its formative years.

In Connecticut the CFPA took the helm and has become a model for like organizations in other states. It coaxed and guided the state's outdoor resource into the first-rate offering that it now is, and the work continues. Under the CFPA, Connecticut has gone from being 20 percent forested to being 60 percent forested, and it has one of the best planned and managed trail systems in the nation. As a facilitator, the group has overseen the addition of some one hundred parks and forests to the state coffer, notably Gillette Castle, Talcott Mountain, Rocky Neck, and Sherwood Island State Parks and Peoples and Mohawk State Forests.

In 1929 the CFPA conceived of its blue trail system, a network of paths that crisscross the Connecticut landscape, traversing public and private land. This trail system now encompasses more than 825 miles of trail, incorporating nearly ninety communities. An army of volunteers makes the blue trail system work. Keeping this resource blazed, cleared, and growing commands a whopping annual commitment of more than 25,000 volunteer hours. The CFPA volunteer effort is exemplary. Hundreds of volunteers commit to classes and workshops on how to blaze, clear, and care for the land. And, how many groups can claim a waiting list of volunteers willing to step in as project managers?

The CFPA workplace isn't always out in the fresh air, however. The group also toils in stale rooms, mitigating between interest groups. The CFPA worked diligently throughout the 1960s to help the state craft an important landowner responsibility law with adequate protections and flexibility to encourage private landowners to open their land willingly to recreational use and through-trail travel. The CFPA earned the trust of landowners and works to hold it. The law, which passed in 1971, has given the trail system a great avenue for growth.

So, the next time you walk past the sky blue 2-by-6-inch blaze, know that it is more than a familiar guide, pointing the way. See it as a standard representing the good work of the CFPA.

Falls Brook along Falls Brook Trail,
Tunxis State Forest, Connecticut

The trail descends into a hemlock–mixed hardwood forest, with some good-size trees. Only showings of young mountain laurel, a few ferns, or smatterings of ground cedar pierce the leaf mat with its overlay of decaying birch logs and limbs. As the descent accelerates, the trail becomes rockier. Mosses color the rocks of the woodland floor.

Although deer can be seen, wildlife viewing along the trail is often at boot level. Stoop to see red efts (or red-spotted newts), salamanders, frogs, and caterpillars. The first three are especially lively after a rainfall. The colorful red eft has three life stages: larval, terrestrial eft, and adult aquatic. In its terrestrial stage it is bright orange to brown, with granular skin and black-ringed spots along its sides. The red eft thrives here in the Connecticut highland forest, away from urban centers.

At the loop junction, marked by a Trail Junction sign and the branching of blue blazes, you first glimpse the brook. Proceed forward downstream, trending closer to its flow. You gather tree-filtered images of the stepped water, cascades, and boulders. Where the brook comes into tighter view, bedrock ledges and rocks animate the water, especially after heavy rain.

At the junction where the loop swings right to follow along the brook, the path straight ahead takes you along and down the brook canyon slope, serving up overlooks of a long chute. The brook drops away faster. If you continue on this spur, you eventually reach the forest's border with the Metropolitan District public water supply (no trespassing).

Keeping to the loop, you reach a short spur to an upper falls overlook, just where the primary trail turns upstream. The waterfall is about 20 feet high with a divided flow at its head and a pretty canyon departure as it wends toward Barkhamsted Reservoir. In full glory, it creates its own breeze, as it races white. A leafy bower and boulder assembly complete the winning image.

From the refreshment of the falls, hike upstream to where the trail hooks left to the first fording at a rock ledge. This clockwise tour ends the hike closer to the water, with fine upstream views of the spilling cascades. Once across, you follow the west bank upstream, scrambling along shore and closely paired with the charming brook. At the confluence of the East and West Branches, you must ford the West Branch. Initially you hike upstream along the West Branch before turning away to cross the wooded divide between the two branches. You then descend to the East Branch for its fording. At the branch crossings, stones may keep feet dry in low water.

At the East Branch crossing, the water is more meandering and flat, effusing serenity. Cross and follow the blazed path downstream to the point where you leave the brook, ascending to the loop junction. Close the loop and backtrack to the trailhead.

Red eft, Tunxis State Forest, Connecticut

MILES AND DIRECTIONS

0.0 Start at the CT 20 trailhead. Follow the signed and blue-blazed path west and downhill.

0.3 Reach the loop junction. Head forward for a clockwise loop; the return is on your right.

0.6 Reach a junction. The main waterfall overlook and loop are to your right. First follow the unblazed trail heading down-canyon.

0.7 Reach the end of the state forest and overlook the lower waterfall canyon. Return upstream to the 0.6-mile junction.

0.8 Turn left toward Falls Brook to continue the loop and reach the main waterfall overlook—a boulder outcrop just off the trail. View the 20-foot falls and then briefly hike upstream on the blue trail to where it hooks left for the fording. Cross and continue upstream.

1.0 Reach the West Branch fording site. Cross and follow the blue blazes through woods.

1.4 Reach the East Branch fording. Cross and follow the blue blazes downstream.

1.5 Close the loop; backtrack left uphill to the trailhead.

1.8 Arrive back at the trailhead.

HIKE INFORMATION

LOCAL INFORMATION

Western Connecticut Convention and Visitors Bureau, PO Box 968, Litchfield 06759; (860) 567-4506; http://litchfieldhills.com.

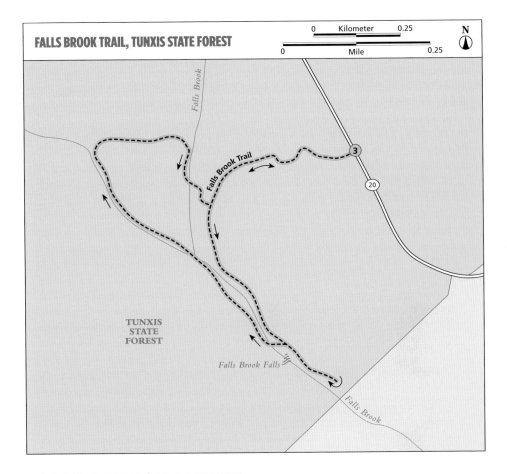

LOCAL EVENTS/ATTRACTIONS

Granville State Forest, 323 W. Hartland Rd., Granville, MA 01034; (413) 357-6611; www.mass.gov/locations/granville-state-forest. North of the border in the southern Berkshires, Massachusetts's Granville State Forest offers 2,426 acres of wooded wild to explore, hike, fish, and ride mountain bike or horse. This was once the hunting and fishing grounds of the Tunxis Indians. Here the Hubbard River spills fast and collects in pools passing through rocky confines.

ACCOMMODATIONS

Granville State Forest in Massachusetts, reached by traveling north off CT 20 east of West Hartland on Milo Coe/West Hartland Road, has **21 campsites along Halfway Brook,** with toilet and shower facilities. The camp is open late May through mid-Oct and reservations are recommended. Sites can accommodate RVs up to 35 feet long.

ORGANIZATIONS

Connecticut Forest and Park Association (CFPA), 16 Meriden Rd., Rockfall 06481; (860) 346-8733; www.ctwoodlands.org.

4 WINDSOR LOCKS CANAL STATE PARK TRAIL

This 4.5-mile-long linear park serves up an unparalleled acquaintance with the Connecticut River and its companion canal built to bypass the river's Enfield Rapids. Carrying freight from the 1830s to the 1840s, until railroading supplanted its usefulness, the canal helped grow the nineteenth-century industries that sprang up along the Connecticut River. Today the canal's paved towpath serves hikers, cyclists, and bird watchers. During nesting season, bald eagles stake priority claim to the corridor.

Start: Northern trailhead
Distance: 9 miles out and back
Hiking time: 6 to 8 hours
Difficulty: Easy
Elevation change: Flat
Trail surface: Paved towpath trail
Best seasons: Apr through mid-Nov, when activity does not threaten the bald eagles
Other trail users: Mountain bikers, birders, anglers, cross-country skiers
Canine compatibility: Leashed dogs permitted. Because of the narrowness of the travel corridor and wildlife considerations, the leash should be shorter than 7 feet. Clean up after pets.
Land status: State park. (Private property adjoins southern trailhead; no trespassing.)
Nearest town: Windsor Locks, CT

Fees and permits: None
Schedule: Apr 1 to Nov 15, from a half hour before sunrise to a half hour after sunset, unless otherwise posted
Maps: Windsor Locks Canal Trail description and map (available online at www.ct.gov/dot/LIB/dot/Documents/dbikes/128.pdf)
Trail contact: Department of Energy and Environmental Protection, State Parks, (860) 424-3200; www.ct.gov/deep
Special considerations: Eagle nesting takes precedence over recreational access, so heed postings and gates. Pass at your own risk, carry water, and pack in/pack out. Redevelopment of the Montgomery Mills building at its southern end is underway.

FINDING THE TRAILHEAD

For the northern trailhead, turn east off CT 159 onto Canal Road, 4.2 miles north of Windsor Locks, 0.1 mile south of the CT 159–CT 190 junction. Drive 0.4 mile to the gravel parking lot at road's end. There are picnic tables and a chemical toilet at the trailhead. Trailhead GPS: N41 59.232' / W72 36.347'

THE HIKE

More relaxing, carefree travel would be hard to come by. This linear park unites river images, riparian-divide woods and tangles, and sleepy canal waters. Historically, it offers a peek into the industrial past of this working river and its companion canal. The corridor is open through a joint effort of The Nature Conservancy, Connecticut Department of Energy and Environmental Protection, and Windsor Locks Canal Company.

Towpath trail, Windsor Locks Canal State Park Trail, Connecticut

From the northern trailhead parking lot, you follow the paved path south along the riverside mesh fence to pass through a gate and cross the head lock to follow the towpath south. North from the trailhead is the bike path to Enfield, Connecticut.

The trail has a decided patriotic theme. Images of the American flag interweave trailhead mesh gates, and bald eagles, a national emblem since 1792, reign over the corridor each winter. The shallow waters at Enfield Rapids shape an ideal fishery for them. Despite forward strides in the bald eagle's recovery, the aerialist remains a threatened species in Connecticut. Nesting eagles returned to the state in 1993, with a successful nesting pair here in 2011. Since then, eagle chicks have fledged in the corridor every year but 2012 and 2013. Trail user cooperation contributes to that success.

As you travel the narrow towpath real estate, elm, silver maple, sycamore, locust, cottonwood, sassafras, dogwood, and wild grape contribute to the richly varied bower riverside and toward the canal. For Connecticut River viewing, this has to be one of the best trails in the state. The Connecticut River flows big, wide, and fast. Initially the CT 190 bridge is visible upstream. A sprinkling of gulls often rides the river.

Stonework of the 1829 canal often can be viewed along the murky green channel. Cross-canal views find cornfields, tobacco barns, woods, and, near the

From the northern woods near the Canadian border to Long Island Sound, the Connecticut River flows 410 miles, draining 11,000 square miles. It is an American Heritage River, recognized for its economic, environmental, cultural, and historical significance. In 2012, as part of President Barack Obama's America's Great Outdoors Rivers Initiative, the Connecticut River was named the first National Blueway for its recreational potential.

southern end of the trail, the railroad tracks that spelled the end for the canal. Window-like openings in the natural vegetation afford views, and benches suggest lingering. A few painted distances on the paved towpath can help you track progress.

Visually, there are long straightaways and gentle trends from the absolutely straight. With the open cathedral, the towpath trail can bake midday. There is an occasional plop of turtle or frog in the canal or a shuffle in the brush. Crows and vultures pass overhead.

Where Kings Island divides the river flow, you pass along the narrowed river channel and gain more open views toward the canal. Snags reflect in the canal waters. River views now stretch south downstream to a rail bridge. Train whistles carry to the site.

The towpath takes you past the Stony Brook Aqueduct, built for the Windsor Locks Canal Company. Here graffiti prophets have marred the pillars of the historic structure. A more noticeable bend carries the trail south. Although

Connecticut River shoreline, Windsor Locks Canal State Park Trail, Connecticut

the woods buffer toward the river fills in, big sycamores and ash engage the eyes.

Later the river and canal become close cousins, with only the towpath slicing between them. Length-of-canal views become a treat; previously, most of the viewing was cross-canal. You overlook the full river where the towpath crosses under the railroad trestle. Take a moment to admire the river and the repeating trestle piers because the woods ahead again isolate the river. Cardinals, blue jays, and rabbits visit the towpath corridor.

At the southern terminus, you can view the redeveloped factory buildings as they enter the next chapter.

MILES AND DIRECTIONS

0.0 Start at the northern trailhead. Follow the paved path south along the riverside fence to pass through a gate and cross the historic lock to hike the towpath south.

2.5 Reach the Stony Brook Aqueduct. Continue south on the towpath.

3.5 Pass under a train trestle and continue south. *Option:* Instead you may turn around here for a 7-mile out-and-back journey.

4.5 Reach the southern terminus; return as you came for the 9-mile out-and-back trip.

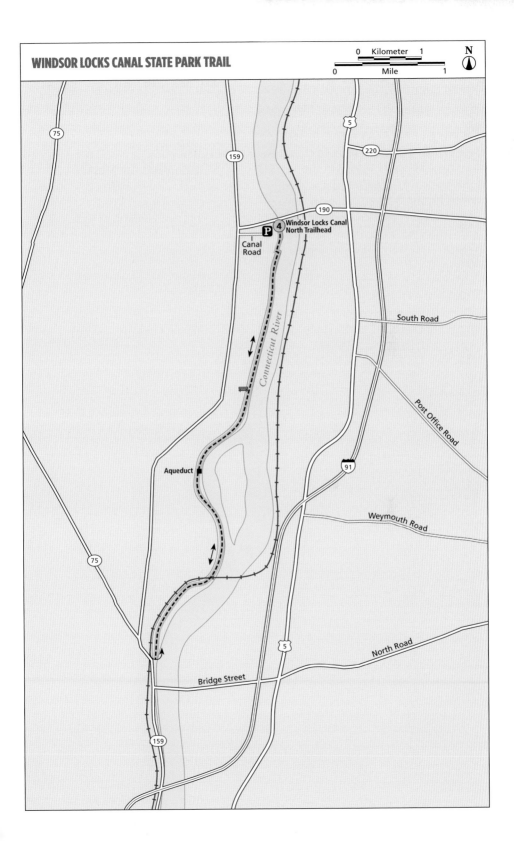

0   Kilometer   1

0   Mile   1

N

75

159

5

220

190

Windsor Locks Canal
North Trailhead

P 4

Canal
Road

Connecticut River

South Road

Post Office Road

Aqueduct

91

Weymouth Road

75

North Road

5

Bridge Street

159

HIKE INFORMATION

LOCAL INFORMATION

Central Regional Tourism District, 1 Constitution Plaza, 2nd Floor, Hartford 06103; (860) 787-9640; www.centerofct.com.

LOCAL EVENTS/ATTRACTIONS

Connecticut Fire Museum and **Connecticut Trolley Museum,** 58 North Rd., East Windsor 06088; (860) 627-6540; www.ct-trolley.org. **New England Air Museum,** 36 Perimeter Rd., Bradley International Airport, Windsor Locks 06096; (860) 623-3305; www.neam.org. A trio of transportation museums suggest area outings. The Connecticut Fire Museum and Connecticut Trolley Museum are associated attractions with seasonally changing hours and a single admission to access both. The New England Air Museum, with daily hours in summer (closed Mondays otherwise), is a separate fee attraction.

ORGANIZATIONS

Rails-to-Trails Conservancy, The Duke Ellington Building, 2121 Ward Ct. NW, 5th Floor, Washington, DC 20037; (202) 331-9696; www.railstotrails.org.

5 ENDERS FALLS TRAIL

Few long-distance trails can match the visual excitement of this short trail. Its nonstop, serial waterfalls turn a simple, less than half-mile trail into a party for the eyes. Stepped cascades, horsetail plummets, chutes, a 30-foot waterfall, plunge pools, potholes, and picturesque tannin waters transfix the eyes as you travel through dark woods of eastern hemlock, oak, and maple. The mossy ledges and canyon rock fashion an attractive stage for the flowing show.

Start: Enders State Forest trailhead
Distance: 0.8 mile out and back
Hiking time: About 1 hour
Difficulty: Easy, but wet footing along shore can be precarious
Elevation change: 150 feet between trailhead parking and lowest falls
Trail surface: Earthen path and woods road
Best seasons: Spring through fall
Other trail users: Birders
Canine compatibility: Leashed dogs permitted
Land status: State forest

Nearest town: Granby, CT
Fees and permits: None
Schedule: Daily, sunrise to sunset
Maps: None
Trail contact: Department of Energy and Environmental Protection, State Forests, (860) 424-3200; www.ct .gov/deep
Special considerations: Watch over children and use caution when hiking alongside waterfalls and negotiating rocks. Mist and wet or frosty conditions can steal footing. Pack in/ pack out.

FINDING THE TRAILHEAD

From US 202/CT 10 in Granby, head west on CT 20 toward West Granby. Drive 3.7 miles and turn southwest on CT 219. Continue 1.3 miles and turn left into the marked Enders Forest gravel parking lot. Trailhead GPS: N41 57.296' / W72 52.731'

THE HIKE

A truncated woods road that parallels Enders Brook is the gateway trail to this watery attraction. Side spurs descend from it to each of the serial cascades and falls on the brook's speedy descent. Footpaths closer to shore likewise stitch together the spurs, but be careful on this brook-hugging thread during wet and icy conditions. Roots and rocks can steal footing.

One of the last additions to the state forest system, Enders State Forest with its sparkling brook is a hidden prize. It came to the state as gift from the Enders family in 1970, and that gift was expanded by the family in 1981. The forest has since grown to cover 2,098 acres in the towns of Granby and Barkhamsted.

At the corner of the parking lot, you round the gate following the dirt management road/trail descending into the state forest toward the brook. The woodland engages with its cover of maple, birch, beech, and witch hazel. At the base of the slope where the grade turns left, the first spur descends by reinforced steps to the initial spill.

Enders Brook, a tributary feeding into the West Branch of Salmon Brook, is of good size with granite bedrock and boulders defining its plunges and mosses and ferns dashing

Hiking trail, Enders State Forest, Connecticut

color to its confines. Here the bedrock pinches the flow toward the far shore. As the water descends, it broadens and angles, reaching an island-divided plunge pool. The tannin water churns milky on the hurried descent.

Rainfall gives the brook a hearty voice, while low waters bring quiet charm. Lovely overhangs of birch and eastern hemlock complement the watercourse. Mountain laurels add seasonal bloom.

More eastern hemlocks darken travel as you descend with the brook. In a flash, you're at the next drop, with another hot on its heels and the original still visible upstream. Photographers find ample subject here. Rocks are as much a part of the story as the water, defining the flow and shaping the far shore.

Admire the alternating dark coffee and weak tea spills as the rocks pinch and free the water. Feathery ferns, conks reclaiming the decaying birch, and the black hemlock trunks add to the canyon setting. You don't rack up distance here, but you do rack up sights.

The third descent is a keyhole cascade that tumbles in steps. The next two falls are the genuine deal, spilling 20 to 30 feet. The early cascades were preshow; these are main events.

The first of these bigger falls slips over a bedrock lip, the width of the brook, to smack a plunge pool where a monument rock splits the falls in two. The resulting twin falls then hit a bubbling plunge pool that feeds into a gorge. The next major drop comes at the pinched gorge exit. Although downstream views show an easing of the brook's downhill intent, the canyon setting remains an engaging marriage of boulders and water.

After this canyon viewing, the return is upstream either by the woods grade or the footpaths along shore. By this point, the grade and brook have slipped apart, so there is a bit of a climb to return to the grade. Although young hemlocks narrow its bed, the grade still offers the easier upstream walk.

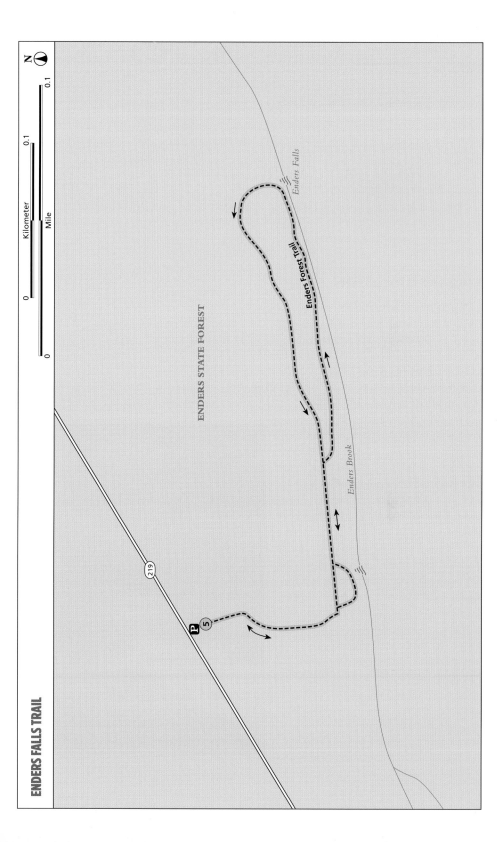

ENDERS FALLS TRAIL

ENDERS STATE FOREST

Enders Forest Trail

Enders Falls

Enders Brook

219

P 5

Kilometer
0   0.1   0.1

Mile
0   0.1

N

The canyon and flow are sights to see in all of their attitudes. But do not force views where shore conditions don't readily allow it.

MILES AND DIRECTIONS

0.0 Start at the Enders State Forest trailhead. Round the gate to descend on the old grade.

0.1 At the base of the slope, where the grade turns left, descend the first vista spur to the cascades. From this viewing, hike downstream via the worn brook-side footpath or on the grade above.

0.4 Reach the lowest falls and the end of the waterfall trail. Return upstream on either the hillside grade or the brook-side footpath.

0.8 Arrive back at the trailhead.

HIKE INFORMATION

LOCAL INFORMATION
Central Regional Tourism District, 1 Constitution Plaza, 2nd Floor, Hartford 06103; (860) 787-9640; www.centerofct.com.

LOCAL EVENTS/ATTRACTIONS
Old New-Gate Prison and Copper Mine, 115 Newgate Rd., East Granby 06026; (860) 653-3563; www.cultureandtourism.org. After a long absence, this site is again open and ready to tell its story. Old New-Gate Prison and Copper Mine, a National Historic Landmark, exemplifies historical repurposing—a bit unusual and perhaps inhumane, but no doubt intriguing. Here an early producing copper mine gone quiet was pulled into duty as Connecticut's first prison in 1773. At the time it was deemed more thoughtful than the day's public punishments. The underground tunnels held early wrongdoers, Revolutionary War political prisoners, and women prisoners beginning in 1824. It had its share of escapes before the prison closed in 1827.

Enders Brook, Enders State Forest, Connecticut

6 PEOPLES STATE FOREST

This 3,000-acre forest, purchased by public subscription in the 1920s, stretches east from the West Branch Farmington River in northwest Connecticut. It contains a diverse forest with stately trees, one of the best overlooks in the state, and "Barkhamsted Lighthouse," a historic Indian settlement. A splendid system of interlocking trails explores this forest of the people, by the people, and for the people. The described loop incorporates several of the trails.

Start: Matthies Grove Recreation Area trailhead
Distance: 6.1-mile lollipop, with option to extend the hike to Chaugham cabin
Hiking time: 3.5 to 4.5 hours
Difficulty: Moderate
Elevation change: 550 feet
Trail surface: Earthen path and old woods roads
Best seasons: Spring through fall
Other trail users: Anglers, hunters, youth-group campers, snowshoers, cross-country skiers, snowmobilers
Canine compatibility: Leashed dogs permitted
Land status: State forest
Nearest town: Winsted, CT, for full services, with gas available on US 44 in New Hartford
Fees and permits: Weekend/holiday parking fees for nonresidents, Memorial Day weekend through Columbus Day weekend
Schedule: Forest recreation areas open year-round, from 8 a.m. to sunset; all other forest areas open year-round, from a half hour before sunrise to a half hour after sunset. The Peoples State Forest Nature Museum (Stone Museum) open Friday through Monday from 10:30 a.m. to 4:30 p.m., Memorial Day through Columbus Day
Maps: State forest brochure (available online at www.ct.gov/deep and sometimes at trailhead); Connecticut Forest and Park Association (CFPA) *Connecticut Walk Book, West* (available from CFPA, www.ctwoodlands.org)
Trail contacts: Peoples State Forest, PO Box 1, Pleasant Valley 06063; (860) 379-2469. Department of Energy and Environmental Protection, State Parks, (860) 424-3200; www.ct.gov/deep
Special considerations: The trails are color-coded. The blazes either show the actual color or the specified color on a blue field.

FINDING THE TRAILHEAD

From New Hartford, go west on US 44 for 1.4 miles and turn north on CT 181. In 1 mile, turn right to cross the Farmington River. Upon departing the bridge, turn left on East River Road. You will pass Greenwoods Road on the right in 0.8 mile; it travels north through the heart of the forest, accessing trails and recreation areas. In another 0.2 mile, turn left off East River Road for Matthies Grove Recreation Area and its trailhead parking. Trailhead GPS: N41 55.532' / W72 59.961'

THE HIKE

The twentieth century rang in conservation awareness. Caught up in the current, Alain White and Jessie Gerard proposed the purchase of a true people's forest, where even folks of modest means could participate. For each $8 donation, an acre of this forest was purchased.

View from Chaugham Lookout, Peoples State Forest, Connecticut

This rolling hike fashions a loop through the relaxing woods and showers of mountain laurel, snaring prized overlooks and passing historic sites. You travel the Robert Ross, Jessie Gerard, Charles Pack, and Agnes Bowen Trails, all named for benefactors of Peoples State Forest.

From the information board at Matthies Grove Recreation Area, you cross East River Road to follow the blue-blazed Robert Ross Trail as it ascends an old grade through white pine–deciduous woods, coming out at the Nature Museum (Stone Museum). You skirt the museum, veering left across the gravel parking lot to resume the hike.

Beyond some head-tilting big trees, reach the loop junction with the Agnes Bowen Trail (the hike's return). Bear left, continuing on the blue-blazed footpath and still ascending in multistory forest. After a descent among laurel, the hike bears right on a woods road. At Kings Road, it angles left into forest.

At the upcoming fork, bear right, still chasing blue, for a similar rolling trek in relaxing woods. After crossing the Agnes Bowen Trail, a defined slope drops west to the Farmington River. Passing below the outcrop crest of rounded cliffs and sharp-edged breaks, the terrain grows rockier. With a brief steep descent, meet the yellow Jessie Gerard Trail. Descending left leads to "Barkhamsted Lighthouse" (the Chaugham cabin site) and an Indian settlement cemetery with primitive head- and footstones. Chaugham, a Native American, married the rebellious daughter of an American colonist. His night-lit cabin was a beacon that signaled stagecoach travelers 5 miles to New Hartford.

Loop hikers follow the shared Jessie Gerard/Robert Ross Trail uphill to the right, coming to the red Falls Cut Off Trail, which descends 299 Civilian Conservation Corps–installed stone steps beside a seasonal falls to visit the Chaugham cabin site. The loop climbs northward from the junction.

Where the blue trail departs right, follow the yellow Jessie Gerard Trail on a treacherously steep ascent over stone steps and canted outcrops to reach two overlooks. The first, Grand Vista, offers a mostly wild southern view out the Farmington Valley. When dressed in fall foliage, the landscape inspires. Top the ridge and hike north to Chaugham Lookout for a northwestern perspective with the rural charm of Riverton.

Pursuing yellow, you next descend among hemlocks and pass bookend multiton Veeder Boulders. Bear right on a woods road and again turn right on Greenwoods Road to follow the yellow Charles Pack Trail. It heads left just past the rustic Big Spring Youth Camp.

You descend along Beaver Brook in a hemlock-hardwood forest before crossing the brook via the Beaver Brook Road bridge. Pick up the trail, past the next youth camp. Watch for blazes along the lightly tracked path. After crossing dirt Pack Grove Road, you contour the hemlock slope above it before descending to cross it a second time. Rock walls and foundations add to forest viewing. At a fork, bear right to descend to a footbridge crossing of Beaver Brook.

Where the trail again ascends, it skirts Beaver Swamp, betrayed only by a change in lighting. The Charles Pack Trail then passes the baton to the orange Agnes Bowen Trail; go left. Its scenic rolling course finds greater concentrations of mountain laurel, skirts the James Stocking area, and descends beside a drainage before crossing over it to cross Greenwoods Road. Close the loop and backtrack the blue Robert Ross Trail to Matthies Grove parking.

MILES AND DIRECTIONS

0.0   Start at the Matthies Grove Recreation Area trailhead. From the information board, cross East River Road to hike the blue-blazed Robert Ross Trail, passing between a pair of posts.

0.1   Reach the Nature Museum (Stone Museum); when open, exhibits and information are available. The hike continues from the gravel parking area. Follow the blue blazes.

0.2   Reach the loop junction. Bear left (clockwise) on the blue trail. Your return is the orange Agnes Bowen Trail, to your right.

1.7   Reach the yellow Jessie Gerard Trail. For the loop alone, keep right, heading uphill on the shared Jessie Gerard/Robert Ross Trail. **Option:** Detour left to visit the Chaugham cabin site and Indian cemetery. If you remain on this trail, it reaches East River Road in 0.25 mile.

1.8   Reach the red Falls Cut Off Trail. Continue climbing on the shared blue and yellow trail. **Option:** The red trail descends along a seasonal waterfall on 299 stone steps placed by CCC and visits the historic Chaugham area before meeting East River Road in 0.2 mile.

2.0   Reach a trail junction. Stay on the yellow trail for the loop. The blue trail heads right to Warner Road.

2.1   Reach Grand Vista. Continue north on the yellow trail.

2.4   Reach Chaugham Lookout. Continue north on the yellow trail, descending.

2.7   Reach Greenwoods Road. Bear right to pick up the loop as it heads left via the yellow Charles Pack Trail, past Big Spring Youth Group Camp.

3.3   Cross Beaver Brook on road bridge.

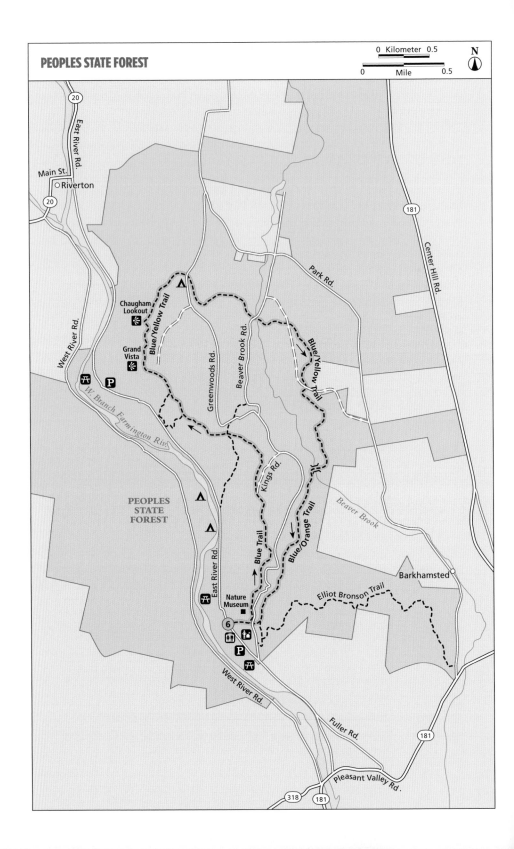

0 Kilometer 0.5

0 Mile 0.5

N

20

East River Rd.

Main St.
Riverton

20

181

Center Hill Rd.

Park Rd.

Chaugham
Lookout

Blue/Yellow Trail

Grand
Vista

Blue/Yellow Trail

West River Rd.

W. Branch Farmington Riv.

Greenwoods Rd.

Beaver Brook Rd.

P

Beaver Brook

PEOPLES
STATE
FOREST

Kings Rd.

Blue Trail

Blue/Orange Trail

Barkhamsted

Elliot Bronson Trail

East River Rd.

Nature
Museum

6

P

West River Rd.

Fuller Rd.

181

Pleasant Valley Rd.

318   181

4.6	Cross Beaver Brook to reach the orange Agnes Bowen Trail. Go left to close the loop.
5.8	Cross Greenwoods Road.
5.9	Complete the loop. Backtrack on the Robert Ross Trail to the trailhead.
6.1	Arrive back at the trailhead.

HIKE INFORMATION

LOCAL INFORMATION
Western Connecticut Convention and Visitors Bureau, PO Box 968, Litchfield 06759; (860) 567-4506; http://litchfieldhills.com.

LOCAL EVENTS/ATTRACTIONS
Farmington River Tubing, 92 Main St., New Hartford 06057; (860) 693-6465; www .farmingtonrivertubing.com. Tubing the Farmington River is a popular area recreation from Memorial Day weekend through Labor Day. From Satans Kingdom State Recreation Area, riders enjoy a 2.5-mile float marked by three sets of rapids that get the heart pumping.

For contained water fun, harnessed **Lake McDonough,** west off CT 219 south of Barkhamsted Reservoir, offers beaches, bathhouses, picnic areas, a boathouse and rowboat rentals, boat and shore fishing, and an all-ability nature trail that serves the blind. Metropolitan District Commission, 555 Main St., PO Box 800, Hartford 06142-0800; (860) 278-7850, ext. 3110, or (860) 379-3036 (in season for beach and boathouse information); http://themdc.org/recreation-areas.

ACCOMMODATIONS
Austin F. Hawes Memorial Campground along the West Branch Farmington River in American Legion State Forest has 30 sites. It is open mid-Apr through Columbus Day and operates under a tiered fee system for residents and nonresidents. For campground information, call (860) 379-0922. Reservations are through ReserveAmerica, (877) 668-2267 or www.reserveamerica.com.

ORGANIZATIONS
Connecticut Forest and Park Association (CFPA), 16 Meriden Rd., Rockfall 06481; (860) 346-8733; www.ctwoodlands.org.

7 GREAT POND STATE FOREST

This simple hike packs a lot of wallop. It unites a lovely vegetated pond active with beavers, ducks, geese, and croaking frogs with woodland that demonstrates James L. Goodwin's concept for and devotion to forestry. Goodwin was one of the nation's first professionally trained forest managers. A pocket grove of towering rhododendron and abundant mountain laurel urge hikers out in spring, pond lilies decorate the scene in summer, and colored leaves and their watery doubles beckon in fall. High water can cause soggy footing, and when the swamp-bridging boardwalks come up short, you may need to turn back.

Start: State forest trailhead
Distance: 1.8-mile lollipop
Hiking time: 1.5 to 2 hours
Difficulty: Easy
Elevation change: Essentially flat
Trail surface: Earthen path, boardwalk, woods road
Best seasons: Spring through fall
Other trail users: Birders, anglers, snowshoers, cross-country skiers
Canine compatibility: Leashed dogs permitted
Land status: State forest
Nearest town: Simsbury, CT
Fees and permits: None
Schedule: Year-round, 8 a.m. to sunset

Map: Massacoe State Forest, Great Pond Unit trail map (available online at www.ct.gov/deep and sometimes at trailhead)
Trail contacts: Massacoe State Forest, c/o Penwood State Forest, 57 Gun Mill Rd., Bloomfield 06002; (860) 242-1158. Department of Energy and Environmental Protection, State Forests, (860) 424-3200; www.ct.gov/deep
Special considerations: High water may prohibit loop travel, turning you back at swampy sites. A pit toilet and a few picnic tables are the lone amenities. Bring drinking water.

FINDING THE TRAILHEAD

From Simsbury, turn west off CT 10/US 202 onto Plank Hill Road (this turn is just north of the CT 167 junction). Drive 0.9 mile and turn right at the T-junction onto Great Pond Road. Continue 1.4 miles to find the state forest entrance on the right. Follow the forest's gravel entrance road 0.3 mile to trailhead parking at road's end. Trailhead GPS: N41 53.873' / W72 50.160'

THE HIKE

This hike explores the 280-acre Great Pond Block of Massacoe State Forest. The land was purchased in 1930 and managed for decades by Yale-trained forester/conservationist James L. Goodwin. Goodwin was a field secretary for and later president of the Connecticut Forest and Park Association (1958–1961). It was Goodwin's intent that this property perpetuate sound forest management. Through his generous gift, the state of Connecticut continues that mission.

A webbing of short interlocking trails serves recreationists, the most popular route being the one encircling Great Pond. For this hike, you start at the second rustic-pole gate to the right of the information board. It has the more trampled dirt lane leading into

Great Pond, Great Pond State Forest, Connecticut

Entrance sign, Great Pond State Forest, Connecticut

the forest. Here the white pine–hemlock–hardwood forest grows tall. Keep to the main travel lane, ignoring all foot trails to find the monument noting the forest gift at the pond's forested levee dam. The loop's return is the footpath to the left just before the monument.

In 1956 this property became Connecticut's very first recognized tree farm. White pines shading 35 acres south of the pond represent all ages, with specimens well over a hundred years old. Although the pines are noteworthy, the site canopy is diverse, with eastern hemlock, oak, and hickory and pond-residing black gum, birch, and swamp maple. Add in a varied tanglewood and you have a wonderful forest mix, creating food, habitat, and cover for wildlife. Birders have identified 182 bird species here, including wild turkey, common loon, warblers, birds of prey, dabblers, and waders.

Counterclockwise, the trail traces the levee, offering looks at the open-water swamp to the left and the treed swamp to the right. The hike's shortness is ideal for slow-touring and sightseeing, though the mosquitoes can hurry admiration. Lily pads, the seasonal white pond lilies, vegetated islands, a beaver lodge, and ringing woods add to pond views and reflections. An armada of Canada geese is a common sighting. Conchs give ruffled adornments to the dead and dying trunks. Colored leaves can pool in the blackwater puddles, and ever-widening rings on the surface record the escapes of frogs.

The clue is to keep left to remain as close to the pond as possible and to add any spurs. Some spurs to shore can be overgrown, so you may pick and choose which to include. The longest spur is on the east shore and travels a crescent through red pine plantation. It reaches a viewing bench before squeezing through a mountain laurel bonanza and hay-scented fern patch to return to the main trail at a four-way junction in a copse of tall rhododendron. The floral shrubs grow treelike, 15 to 20 feet tall, and sport a thick complement of radial leaves. Again, keep left for the loop.

At the northern end of the pond, swamp forest distances you from the pond's edge, and heavy rain can present soggy footing. Sassafras, ground cedar, mosses, and ferns add their signature shapes. Roots and rocks help keep feet dry, as do a pair of boardwalk spans, though superheavy rains may defeat the spans. But the puddles and brushy pockets are part of this forest's charm.

Younger pines with feathery needles frame travel as you continue to bear left, once again on easier trail beyond the swampy north shore. On the west shore return, you may find rustic (or decrepit) benches at the ends of a couple of pond spurs. The trail narrows to footpath width as it returns to the monument area. Close the loop and turn right, backtracking to the parking area.

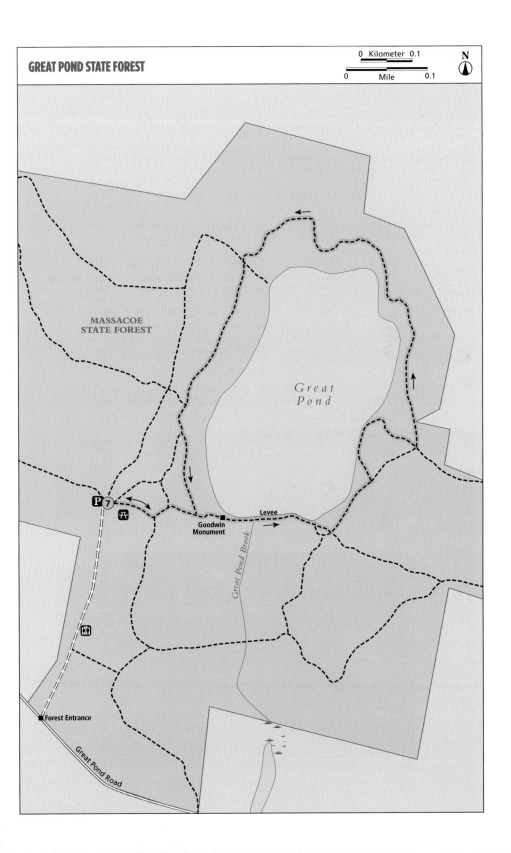

GREAT POND STATE FOREST

0 Kilometer 0.1
0 Mile 0.1

N

MASSACOE
STATE FOREST

Great
Pond

P 7

Levee

Goodwin
Monument

Great Pond Brook

Forest Entrance

Great Pond Road

MILES AND DIRECTIONS

0.0 Start at the state forest trailhead. Round the second rustic-pole gate to the right of the information board.

0.2 Reach the loop junction. Keep right (forward) for this counterclockwise loop. You'll soon reach the Goodwin Monument at the start of the forested levee dam. The foot trail to the left is the return.

0.5 Reach the crescent spur. Turn left to add this pond spur. *Option:* For the loop alone continue forward.

0.7 Reach the end of crescent spur and a four-way junction in a rhododendron grove. Continue left for loop. *Note:* You'd continue forward if you chose to forgo the spur.

1.6 Close the loop. Turn right to return to the trailhead.

1.8 Arrive back at the trailhead.

HIKE INFORMATION

LOCAL INFORMATION
Central Regional Tourism District, 1 Constitution Plaza, 2nd Floor, Hartford 06103; (860) 787-9640; www.centerofct.com.

LOCAL EVENTS/ATTRACTIONS
Simsbury Historical Society, 800 Hopmeadow St., Simsbury 06070; (860) 658-2500; www.simsburyhistory.org. The society owns and maintains 16 historical and modern buildings on a 2-acre site at the town center that relate to area history and are open for tours and study.

The Farmington River is a popular canoeing destination, with area liveries offering rentals and shuttles. **The Old Drake Hill Flower Bridge,** a retired wrought-iron and steel truss bridge decorated in memorial flower boxes and hanging planters, is one of the landmarks on this river paddle. Contact the Central Regional Tourism District or the town of Simsbury, www.simsbury-ct.gov.

Rhododendron with hiking trail, Great Pond State Forest, Connecticut

BURR POND STATE PARK

Centerpiece to this Connecticut state park, 88-acre Burr Pond dazzles travelers with its clear waters. In the 1850s this impoundment powered early industry, including the world's first condensed milk factory. Condensed milk was an important staple for the Union Army during the Civil War. The encircling Walcott Trail travels the pond's richly wooded rim and visits quiet coves, a peninsula, and a rock cave. The John Muir Trail extends the wooded journey south through Paugnut State Forest past Walnut Mountain to Sunny Brook State Park.

Start: Burr Pond State Park day-use beach area
Distance: 8-mile loop with out-and-back spur
Hiking time: 4 to 6 hours
Difficulty: Moderate
Elevation change: The pond loop changes less than 100 feet in elevation; the combined tour has a 400-foot elevation change.
Trail surface: Earthen path, woods road, plank stretches
Best seasons: Spring through fall
Other trail users: Anglers, joggers, snowshoers, cross-country skiers
Canine compatibility: Leashed dogs permitted; no pets on beach
Land status: State park and state forest
Nearest town: Torrington or Winsted, CT
Fees and permits: Parking fees for nonresidents at Burr Pond

Schedule: Year-round, 8 a.m. to sunset
Maps: State park and forest maps (available online at www.ct.gov/deep); Connecticut Forest and Park Association (CFPA) *Connecticut Walk Book, West* (available from CFPA, www.ctwoodlands.org)
Trail contacts: Burr Pond State Park, 385 Burr Mountain Rd., Torrington 06790; (860) 482-1817. Department of Energy and Environmental Protection, State Parks, (860) 424-3200; www.ct.gov/deep.
Special considerations: Off-season visits, when the high spirits and high numbers of summer wane, offer more tranquil pond strolls.The John Muir leg is always peaceful. CFPA cautions hikers to a re-route of the John Muir Trail, as well as a new blue/white connector between the Walcott Trail and the Muir Trail. Hikers should watch for signage.

FINDING THE TRAILHEAD

From CT 8, take exit 46 for Burrville. Head west on Pinewoods Road for 0.5 mile and turn left. In 1 mile, turn right on Burr Mountain Road for the park. Find the entrance on the left in 0.5 mile. Start this hike from the beach area. Trailhead GPS: N41 52.148' / W73 05.671'

THE HIKE

From the swimming beach, begin the counterclockwise tour of Burr Pond, entering the woods beyond the paddleboat/canoe rentals. At the lower edge of the picnic area, stillwater reflections of the treed rim and scattered boulders win admiring glances. Hemlock, birch, maple, beech, white pine, witch hazel, striped maple, and showy mountain laurel shape passage.

Burr Pond, Burr Pond State Park, Connecticut

Next to Burr Mountain Road, ash and basswood shadow the jewelweed drainages. From the boat launch, you reenter woods. Vultures, ducks, grouse, and kingfishers may cause you to reach for binoculars. A rock seat at water's edge suggests a stop.

At a boggy area, boardwalks and footbridges advance the trail. On a cabin-size boulder, find the Buttrick Memorial. Philip Buttrick, an area forester (1886–1945), led a Civilian Conservation Corps (CCC) camp here in the 1930s. The camp (like this trail) was named for Connecticut U.S. Senator Frederic C. Walcott, who spearheaded conservation and park acquisitions and was a strong supporter of the CCC.

A former beaver pond now stretches right. Past a utility line, the trail contours the slope above the pond. About midway around, you reach the west arm of the blue-and-white connector to the John Muir Trail. Keep to the pond loop. After a descent, look left to find Big Rock Cave, a skyward-tilted boulder with a blackened overhang.

Past the next shrubby corridor, you turn left for the peninsula spur. The point's outcrop nose offers open views and welcomes lazing in the sun. After resuming counterclockwise travel, you meet the re-route of the John Muir Trail, heading right (south). Keep watch for the blue blazes of the John Muir Trail, as the trailbed is still new. It swings over a rise and trends west rejoining its original southbound course where the blue/white trail arrives.

You pass through similar forest, weaving among glacial boulders. Chestnut, maple, and oak make appearances. The hike variously utilizes footpath and old woods road. Utility corridors open views to the woodsy neighborhood, while multitrunk white pines intersperse the hardwoods.

Descend to skirt a meadow and snags, likely a reclaimed beaver pond given the girdled trees in the area. The added light brings a burst of mountain laurel. Where the trail crosses Buttrick Road, find an open pine forest of evenly spaced trees, and later a scenic stand of beech.

With back-to-back crossings of a woods road and Guerdat Road, the trail remains well-blazed. Next ascend from the upper drainage of Walnut Mountain Brook and bear left on road grade. At the junction ahead, a right turn leads to Walnut Mountain, a left turn leads to Guerdat Road, and straight completes the Muir Trail.

Detour right, ascending a winding cobbled road. Trees frame a view overlooking the crowns of the immediate hardwood forest toward the next rise before the trail delivers you to a viewless, hemlock and oak enclosed grassy circle atop the hill (elevation 1,325 feet). Return to the Muir Trail, continuing south (right).

You now skirt the ridge of Walnut Mountain, tracking cairns along an outcrop. With a sharp descent, travel the boulder and rock slabs of the lower slope to cross Devaux Road. Beyond a beech grove, turn right to descend beside the cobbly East Branch Naugatuck River.

Past a memorial to an area trail builder, you'll ascend the rocky embankment of Newfield Road, cross the road bridge, and descend left into Sunny Brook State Park, a primitive park 2.5 miles northwest of Torrington. Backtrack north to Burr Pond to complete the counterclockwise loop.

You now explore the bay arm where the dam is located. At the dam and spillway, continue forward along the outlet, bearing left on closed Pond Road to cross a footbridge. Turn left, following the outlet upstream past the dam, to return to the picnic area near the restrooms.

MILES AND DIRECTIONS

0.0 Start at the beach area at Burr Pond State Park. Follow the blue blazes right (counterclockwise) around the pond.

0.3 Pass the boat launch.

0.8 Pass the Buttrick Memorial tablet.

1.4 Reach the blue/white connector to the John Muir Trail. Continue forward along the pond.

1.5 Pass Big Rock Cave.

1.8 Reach the 0.1-mile peninsula spur. Turn left for its view and then resume the pond loop.

2.0 Reach the re-route of the John Muir Trail. Follow its blue blazes south. **Option:** Proceeding forward on the pond loop, you'll come out at the picnic area at 2.7 miles for a satisfying short hike, perfect for young children.

2.5 Resume south (left), still on the blue John Muir Trail. **Note:** the blue/white connector arrives from the north.

3.0 Cross Buttrick Road.

3.5 Reach a four-way junction. Right tops Walnut Mountain, left leads to Guerdat Road, and straight continues the Muir Trail. Head right.

3.7 Top Walnut Mountain (no summit view).

3.8 Resume hiking south on the Muir Trail.

4.2 Cross Devaux Road.

4.8 Reach Sunny Brook State Park. Retrace the Muir Trail north to the pond loop.

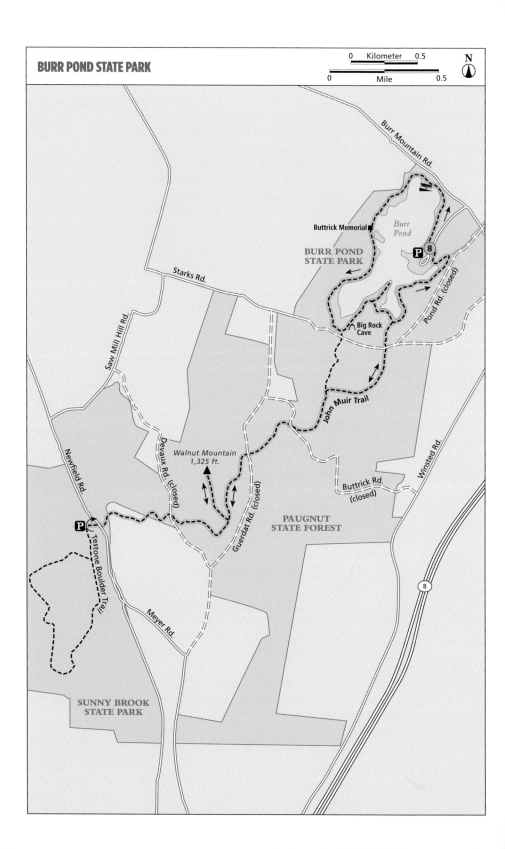

0   Kilometer   0.5

0   Mile   0.5

N

Burr Mountain Rd.

Buttrick Memorial

Burr Pond

BURR POND
STATE PARK

P 8

Starks Rd.

Pond Rd. (closed)

Saw Mill Hill Rd.

Big Rock
Cave

John Muir Trail

Newfield Rd.

Devaux Rd. (closed)

Walnut Mountain
1,325 ft.

Guerdat Rd. (closed)

Winsted Rd.

Buttrick Rd.
(closed)

PAUGNUT
STATE FOREST

P

Testone Boulder Trail

Meyer Rd.

8

SUNNY BROOK
STATE PARK

7.3 Resume counterclockwise pond travel, following the blue blazes to the right.

7.8 At the dam and spillway, proceed forward to cross a footbridge over the outlet.

8.0 Arrive back at the picnic/beach area.

HIKE INFORMATION

LOCAL INFORMATION

Western Connecticut Convention and Visitors Bureau, PO Box 968, Litchfield 06759; (860) 567-4506; http://litchfieldhills.com.

LOCAL EVENTS/ATTRACTIONS

Soldiers' Monument and Memorial Park, PO Box 322, Crown Street, Winsted 06098; www.soldiersmonumentwinsted.org. Atop Camp Hill an inspiring Gothic stone tower and assembly of flags honors the fighting men of Winchester during the War of Rebellion (1861–1865) and in the military actions since.

   Torrington Historical Society, 192 Main St., Torrington 06790; (860) 482-8260; www.torringtonhistoricalsociety.org. In Torrington the **Hotchkiss–Fyler House Museum,** a 1900s Queen Anne–style Victorian residence, offers a snapshot of life in that era and holds fine millwork and artwork. Open for touring, it sits next door to the Torrington History Museum.

ORGANIZATIONS

Connecticut Forest and Park Association (CFPA), 16 Meriden Rd., Rockfall 06481; (860) 346-8733; www.ctwoodlands.org.

9 MOHAWK MOUNTAIN STATE FOREST

Both the Mattatuck and Mohawk Trails, major arteries of the Connecticut blue trail system, weave through this state forest, unveiling its quiet beauty. You'll sleuth out a historic stone tower, a mountaintop panoramic view, a pond, and visually intriguing and ever-changing forest. Rustic Adirondack-style shelters serve thru-hikers. The forest trails brush past the summer-silent winter ski runs and lifts of the region's acclaimed Mohawk Mountain Ski Area.

Start: State forest entrance trailhead
Distance: 10 miles out and back
Hiking time: Most of a day or an overnight
Difficulty: Strenuous due to length and footing
Elevation change: This hike takes you from a trailhead elevation of 1,400 feet to a high point of 1,683 feet atop Mohawk Mountain, down to a low point of about 1,200 feet at Mohawk Pond.
Trail surface: Earthen path, mowed track, forest road
Best seasons: Spring through fall
Other trail users: Anglers and cross-country skiers
Canine compatibility: Leashed dogs permitted
Land status: State forest, with short stretch through state park
Nearest town: Cornwall, CT, with gas and services in Cornwall Bridge or West Cornwall
Fees and permits: No entrance fees, but camping permits for use of the shelters must be arranged in advance.
Schedule: Apr through Nov. Open dates depend on the end of the mud season and the arrival of the first snowfall. Gates are closed in winter. Forest recreation areas open 8 a.m. to sunset; forest trails open a half hour before sunrise to a half hour after sunset.
Maps: State forest map (available online at www.ct.gov/deep); Connecticut Forest and Park Association (CFPA) *Connecticut Walk Book, West* (available from CFPA, www.ctwoodlands.org)
Trail contacts: Mohawk State Forest, 20 Mohawk Mountain Rd., Goshen 06756; (860) 491-3620. Department of Energy and Environmental Protection, State Forests, (860) 424-3200; www.ct.gov/deep.
Special considerations: Can encounter soggy bottoms that complicate travel. No swimming allowed at Mohawk Pond.

FINDING THE TRAILHEAD

East of Cornwall Bridge, at the junction of CT 4 and CT 43, drive east on CT 4 for 1.2 miles and turn south into the state forest on Toumey Road. Make an immediate left, following the dirt access road to its end and trailhead parking. Trailhead GPS: N41 50.635' / W73 17.353'

THE HIKE

This state forest owes its start to the White Memorial Foundation, which in 1921 contributed 2,900 acres to its borders. The hike links two stars in the Connecticut blue trail system, the Mohawk and Mattatuck Trails, which dissect the forest.

Pick up the Mohawk Trail as it arrives from CT 4 and follow it west along the gravel trailhead road, turning left (south) into forest. You quickly pass a classic Adirondack shelter. Soggy reaches and rock-riddled stretches variously draw attention to your feet. Otherwise, the trail rolls out a pleasant conifer-hardwood ascent, where eyes and thoughts can wander.

A second shelter precedes Toumey Road. Here a trailside viewing bench and roadside parking overlook the rolling wooded expanse to the Connecticut high peaks in the north-northwest. Butterflies may animate the shrubs below the overlook.

You briefly pass along Toumey Road before turning right to resume the forest ascent. At a grassy aisle, part of Mohawk Mountain Ski Area, turn left, passing a couple of lifts and the associated buildings. Ahead is the signed junction with the Mattatuck Trail. Follow this new leader forward toward the summit; the Mohawk Trail turns right.

Mohawk Trail and Mattatuck Trail signs, Mohawk State Forest, Connecticut

The Mattatuck Trail reaches a rustic picnic area and follows alongside Toumey Road before turning right into woods for Cunningham Tower. Now gutted and ringed by forest, this 1915 30-foot-tall Italianate columnar stone tower was erected by Seymour Cunningham, who in this same period made a bid to gain ownership of Mohawk Mountain but was turned back by local opposition. The property was sold to Alain White, who

FLIGHTS OF FALL

Like the color change of the leaves, the fall migration of broad-winged hawks on the Atlantic Flyway is a New England call to enter the wild. It's a reason to celebrate and to walk with binoculars. All the excitement is about hawks—red-shouldered, red-tailed, sharp-shinned, Northern harrier, rough-legged, and Cooper's—as well as bald and golden eagles, ospreys, turkey vultures, peregrine falcons, kestrels, merlins, and kites.

Fall migration numbers top those of spring because of the success of the recent breeding season and because spring numbers reflect a natural winter attrition. Heads turn, fingers point, and the pages of bird identification books take flights of their own. At designated watch sites, spotters meticulously track species and numbers. The migration begins in August and strings into November, with September to early October holding peak numbers. The later migrants typically reside in the immediate states.

The masters of the sky are not the lone migrants, however. The exodus from the cooling north begins with the shorebirds, songbirds, and perchers, which are then followed by raptors and waterfowl. It is an exodus numbering in the millions.

Trail shelter along Mohawk Trail,
Mohawk State Forest, Connecticut

gave it to the state. The tower's eye to the sky and hexagonal red floor tiles hint it was
once a show-stopper.

Bearing east from the tower, the trail takes you among young birches and maples with
a few bigger beech trees. Mature pines join the forest highrises. Rusted artifacts, soggy
spruce patches, a wolf pine, stone walls, and midstory witch hazel, chestnut, striped maple,
and maple-leaf viburnum vary viewing. The trail's old stone steps were placed by the
Civilian Conservation Corps, which improved many of the nation's parks, woodlands,
and trails in the 1930s.

From an outcrop slot, the trail traces and then descends a ridge, coming to a narrow view stretching southeast. At the next height of land, you follow the gravel road
to Mohawk summit with its picnic tables, views, and communication towers. This is a
drive-to/hike-to summit.

History has it local tribes lit signal fires atop the mountain to warn friends of approaching Mohawks, who were feared raiders. A wander across the top assembles a 360-degree
view. Seasonal fog can mark Long Island Sound to the south and the Housatonic River
to the west. The Taconic and Berkshire Mountains rise north and northwest, and I've
been told clear-day views stretch to Mount Greylock in Massachusetts and the New York
Catskills. Fields, ponds, and thermal-sailing vultures can add to forest viewing.

At the shorter communication tower, you descend toward Mohawk Pond, traveling
atop ridge outcrops and passing through forest. Past a Volkswagen-size boulder, mountain
laurels partner with the trail. The trail next angles across Wadhams Road to roll between
mountain laurel slopes and oak rises. Where it next reaches Wadhams Road, follow the
blazes right. You continue along the mica-and-quartz-glinting road, turning left into
woods at some log parking barriers.

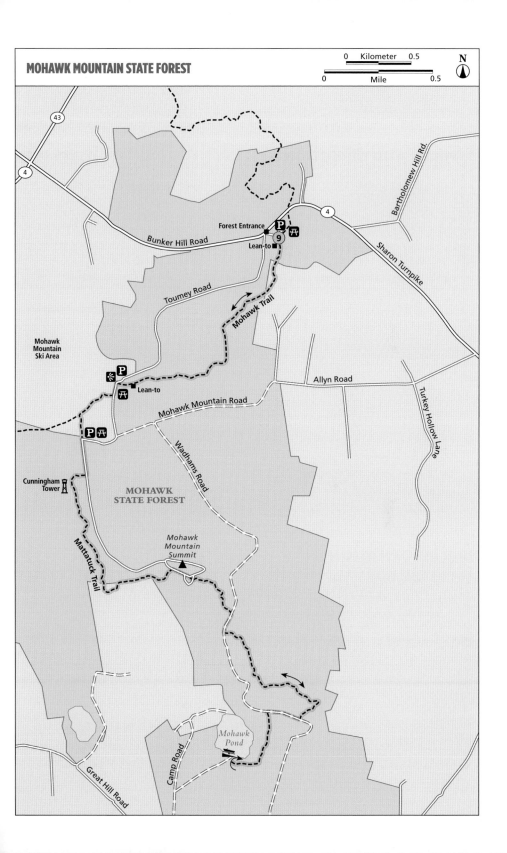

MOHAWK MOUNTAIN STATE FOREST

0   Kilometer   0.5

0   Mile   0.5

N

43

4

Bartholomew Hill Rd.

Forest Entrance

4

Bunker Hill Road

9

Lean-to

Sharon Turnpike

Toumey Road

Mohawk Trail

Mohawk
Mountain
Ski Area

P

Lean-to

Allyn Road

Turkey Hollow Lane

Mohawk Mountain Road

P

Cunningham
Tower

Wadhams Road

MOHAWK
STATE FOREST

Mohawk
Mountain
Summit

Mattatuck Trail

Great Hill Road

Camp Road

Mohawk
Pond

You now rub shoulders with mountain laurel, cross a brook on boxy boulders, and glimpse the pond's glare before emerging at boat launch parking. The Mattatuck Trail continues out the launch road but the selected hike ends here. Mohawk Pond is a 15-acre kettle pond stocked with trout, but ospreys and kingfishers may be the lone fishers. Return when ready.

MILES AND DIRECTIONS

0.0 Start at the state forest entrance trailhead. Pick up the southbound Mohawk Trail as it arrives from CT 4, and follow its blue blazes west and then south into forest.

0.2 Reach the lean-to shelter. Continue south uphill.

1.4 Reach a second shelter where the trail descends to cross Toumey Road at a viewpoint.

1.6 Reach the mowed tracks of the ski area (the state park). Turn left, hiking uphill past the lifts.

1.7 Reach the junction with the Mattatuck Trail. Proceed forward, now following the blue blazes of the signed Mattatuck. *Note:* The Mohawk Trail turns to the right here.

1.8 Reach a roadside picnic area. Hike uphill alongside the road to where the Mattatuck Trail turns right into woods.

2.1 Reach Cunningham Tower. Bear east past the tower, following the blue trail.

3.1 Reach the summit of Mohawk Mountain. Cross over the top to pick up the trail's continuation next to a communication tower building.

3.5 Cross a forest road (Wadhams Road).

4.3 Reach Wadhams Road. Turn right, hiking on the road.

4.5 Turn left off Wadhams Road onto forest trail.

5.0 Reach Mohawk Pond at its boat launch area. Return as you came.

10.0 Arrive back at the trailhead parking.

HIKE INFORMATION

LOCAL INFORMATION
Western Connecticut Convention and Visitors Bureau, PO Box 968, Litchfield 06759; (860) 567-4506; http://litchfieldhills.com.

LOCAL EVENTS/ATTRACTIONS
Fly fishing the Housatonic River is a popular regional pastime. Local outfitters offer guided trips and instruction. For more information, contact the Western Connecticut Convention and Visitors Bureau.

Litchfield History Museum, 7 South St., Litchfield 06759; (860) 567-4501; www .litchfieldhistoricalsociety.org. The museum unravels the story of life and society in this small New England town from settlement to present day through period pieces and art and changing exhibits.

ACCOMMODATIONS

White Memorial Foundation Family Campgrounds, 71 Whitehall Road, PO Box 368, Litchfield 06759; (860) 567-0089 (May through mid-Oct), (860) 567-0857 (mid-Oct through Apr); www.whitememorialcc.org. The White Memorial Foundation offers rustic, unspoiled camping for groups and families. Point Folly contains 47 sites on a Bantam Lake peninsula and is open early May through Columbus Day. Windmill Hill has 18 piney sites and is open Memorial Day through Labor Day. From these camps the foundation's 4,000-acre natural area and trails can be enjoyed. The Campground Store at 123 North Shore Rd. in Litchfield is open from early May until mid-Oct.

ORGANIZATIONS

Connecticut Forest and Park Association (CFPA), 16 Meriden Rd., Rockfall 06481; (860) 346-8733; www.ctwoodlands.org.

Mushrooms along Mohawk Trail, Mohawk State Forest, Connecticut

10 METACOMET TRAIL, TALCOTT MOUNTAIN

Talcott Mountain, a signature traprock ridge traced by the Metacomet Trail, offers you a chance to sample this long-distance trail that is now part of the greater New England National Scenic Trail, together with the Mattabesett and Monadnock Trails. Here the Metacomet rolls along the ridge and crest of Talcott Mountain, topping rock outcroppings and visiting Heublein Tower for prized vistas. Heublein Tower, a skyline adornment of locally quarried stone, can be spied from much of central Connecticut and is a must-see for anyone with restless feet and a need to climb.

Start: Metro District Hartford Reservoir No. 6 parking lot
Distance: 9-mile shuttle, passing through Talcott Mountain and Penwood State Parks to undeveloped Wilcox Park, with options to shorten
Hiking time: 5 to 7 hours
Difficulty: Strenuous
Elevation change: 650 feet
Trail surface: Earthen path and woods road
Best seasons: Spring through fall
Other trail users: Birders, joggers, cross-country skiers, snowshoers
Canine compatibility: Leashed dogs permitted on trails and in state park picnic areas
Land status: Water district and state park
Nearest towns: Avon or West Hartford, CT, with services along US 44
Fees and permits: None
Schedule: State parks open 8 a.m. to sunset; MDC land open sunrise to sunset; tower museum open 10 a.m. to 5 p.m., Thurs through Mon Memorial Day weekend through Sept and Wednesday through Monday Oct 1 through Oct 29
Maps: State park maps (available online at www.ct.gov/deep); Metropolitan District West Hartford Reservoirs and Reservoir No. 6 hiking trail map (available online at http://themdc.com); Connecticut Forest and Park Association (CFPA) *Connecticut Walk Book, West* (available from CFPA, www.ctwoodlands.org)
Trail contacts: Penwood State Park, 57 Gun Mill Rd., Bloomfield 06002; (860) 242-1158. Department of Energy and Environmental Protection, State Parks, (860) 424-3200; www.ct.gov/deep.
Special considerations: No food, drink, pets or walking sticks in Heublein Tower. Obey respective rules for MDC and state park lands. At the reservoir there is no swimming, fishing, camping, littering, collecting, or any activity that may disturb the water supply.

FINDING THE TRAILHEAD

Find the southern terminus (the primary trailhead) at MDC's Hartford Reservoir No. 6. Turn north off US 44, 2.2 miles east of CT 10. Trailhead GPS: N41 47.541' / W72 47.113'

Central to the hike, you will find Metacomet Trail access at the entrances to each Penwood and Talcott Mountain State Parks, located diagonal to one another off CT 185, 3 miles west of Bloomfield. Trailhead GPS: N41 50.310' / W72 47.091'

Undeveloped Wilcox Park offers another access. From the intersection of Terrys Plain Road and Wintonbury Road in Simsbury, turn east on Wintonbury Road, following it 0.3 mile to the dead end. The Metacomet Trail traverses the woods east of the barricade. Because the parking is limited and because the blazing here can sometimes be faint, this option is better for an end pickup arrangement. Trailhead GPS: N41 52.691' / W72 46.336'

THE HIKE

At Reservoir No. 6 you pick up the blue Metacomet Trail where it follows the reservoir road north along the impound's west shore. Mixed oak, hickory, spruce, pine, maple, beech, birch, dogwood, basswood, ash, and tulip poplar vary the tapestry. Fanning hemlocks filter all but the glare of the reservoir. Nearing the reservoir's end, you head left on a blazed footpath, settling into a meandering ascent.

The trail crosses woods roads and a shrubby power-and-gas line. A massive chestnut oak may catch your notice. Across a paved lane, you traverse Talcott Mountain ridge, skirt a radio tower, and gather views from the west rim outcrops. Oak, mountain laurel, and cedar prefer the rim. Below a picnic pavilion, views span the abrupt western slope to Simsbury.

Next is 165-foot-tall Heublein Tower. When open, its Observation Room extends a 1,200-square-mile panoramic view, stretching from Mount Monadnock, New Hampshire,

Farmington River valley view, Talcott Mountain State Park, Connecticut

Metacomet Trail, Penwood State Park

to the blue sliver of Long Island Sound. Historic displays and period rooms are other attractions. Fall adds flaming foliage and migrating broad-winged hawks.

Round west below Heublein Tower and briefly follow the Tower Trail, a descending woods road, before chasing the blue blazes right (north) to travel King Phillip Mountain. The Metacomet Trail rolls from laurel corridor to outcrop knoll to descend a grade through tall forest. Stay attentive for quick directional changes, traveling footpath, utility corridor, and woods road. Cross a brook and CT 185 to enter Penwood State Park.

Head north through the lower parking area and up the park road, skirting Gale Pond (no access). A foot trail then ascends left, returning you once more to the rolling ridge of Talcott Mountain. Keep to the blue-blazed trail.

After coming off a small rise, the trail zigzags and ascends in mountain laurel to trace the ridge north. Past a stone pedestal (to your right), the Metacomet Trail descends to the park road at Lake Louise, a dock, and tables. Bear right to round the shrubby east shore in marshy maple woodland. Past a retained scree slope, keep forward on the Metacomet. Left is the lake basin stroll.

Follow the foot trail and a steep stone stairway to top the ridge at a picnic flat and bear left. The Pinnacle extends western views of Simsbury, the Farmington River Valley, and haze-swallowed ridges. South is Heublein Tower. Keep north at the concrete remains of a lookout tower.

Past a red trail, the Metacomet rounds and tops rocky knolls and dips through sags, but gains no views. In places the blazed route may challenge you. A steep descent follows with a switchback and uneven footing. You then reach the closed dirt road in Wilcox Park, east of the barrier on Wintonbury Road. Here shuttle hikers turn west to end at Wintonbury Road; out-and-back hikers turn around.

Northbound, the Metacomet Trail ascends a cedar-deciduous slope to a birch flat, rolling toward an outcrop, which overlooks a utility corridor to the woods below and the Farmington Valley beyond. A tedious series of utility corridors next marks off progress. Track the blue blazes.

Beyond the utility lines, the trail again rolls between knoll features before passing from foot trail to carriage road. A short descent here leads to the Bartlett Tower ruins on the right. Its 40-foot-tall redbrick chimney, favored by swallows, and stone fireplace

New England National Scenic Trail marker on Metacomet Trail, Penwood State Park

recall a recreational development. From there a descent on the carriage road leads to Mountain Road at 11.2 miles, which descends to the intersection of CT 315 and CT 189, and more northern miles.

MILES AND DIRECTIONS

0.0 Start at MDC Hartford Reservoir No. 6 parking (the southern trailhead). Follow the blue Metacomet Trail north along the reservoir's west shore.

1.7 Reach the trail junction near the end of the reservoir. Ascend left, leaving the road. *Note:* An alternate red trail proceeds forward.

3.2 Reach Heublein Tower (elevation 1,040 feet). Continue on the blue trail.

4.8 Reach the junction with the alternate red trail. Keep left, following the blue Metacomet Trail.

5.6 Cross CT 185 to Penwood State Park. Continue on the blue trail.

7.4 Reach Lake Louise. Continue on the blue trail.

8.9 Reach Wilcox Park. Shuttle hikers turn left (west) here to reach Wintonbury Road at its closure for an arranged pickup ride.

9.0 End at Wintonbury Road.

HIKE INFORMATION

LOCAL INFORMATION

Central Regional Tourism District, 1 Constitution Plaza, 2nd Floor, Hartford 06103; (860) 787-9640; www.centerofct.com.

LOCAL EVENTS/ATTRACTIONS

Canoeing the Farmington River is a popular family summer pastime. Outfitters offer canoe rentals and shuttles for river trips of various lengths. **Old Drake Hill Flower Bridge,** a retired road bridge adorned in memorial floral boxes and hanging pots, is a colorful distance tracker on the paddle. Contact the Central Regional Tourism District

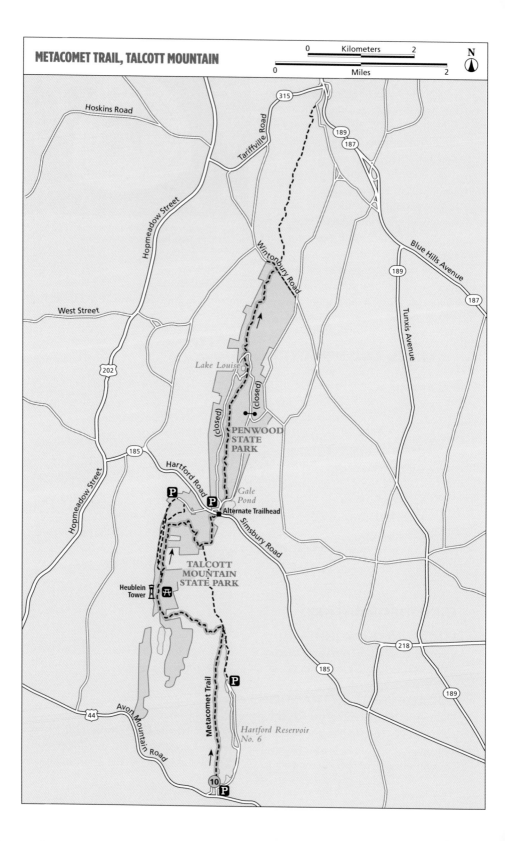

METACOMET TRAIL, TALCOTT MOUNTAIN

Kilometers

Miles

N

Hoskins Road

315

189

187

Tariffville Road

Hopmeadow Street

Wintonbury Road

Blue Hills Avenue

189

187

West Street

202

Tunxis Avenue

Lake Louise

(closed)

(closed)

PENWOOD
STATE
PARK

185

Hartford Road

Hopmeadow Street

P

P

Gale
Pond

Alternate Trailhead

Simsbury Road

TALCOTT
MOUNTAIN
STATE PARK

Heublein
Tower

218

185

189

Avon Mountain Road

Metacomet Trail

P

Hartford Reservoir
No. 6

44

10

P

or Huck Finn Adventures, PO Box 137, Collinsville 06022; (860) 693-0385; www.huck
finnadventures.com.

Hill-Stead Museum, 35 Mountain Rd., Farmington 06032; (860) 677-4787; www
.hillstead.org. The Hill-Stead Museum in Farmington offers an impressive 152-acre
grounds, with foot trails (see Honorable Mentions) and elegant buildings from a bygone
era. Housed here are French Impressionist paintings by the likes of Claude Monet and
Edgar Degas, as well as prints, photographs, ceramics, furniture, and historical books
and documents. On the Connecticut Art Trail, Hill-Stead is also a National Historic
Landmark.

ORGANIZATIONS

Connecticut Forest and Park Association (CFPA), 16 Meriden Rd., Rockfall
06481; (860) 346-8733; www.ctwoodlands.org.

11 MACEDONIA BROOK STATE PARK

Originating with a 1918 gift of land from the White Memorial Foundation of Litchfield, Connecticut, this 2,300-acre state park nudges the border with New York State. Split in half by the clear-skipping waters of Macedonia Brook, the park offers exciting ridgeline tours, vistas, and peaceful woods. Stonework and charcoal mounds hint at its ironwork past. During the Revolutionary War some one hundred Scatacook Indian volunteers attended signal fires atop these and other ridges in the Housatonic Valley.

Start: Lower bridge picnic area, 0.5 mile into the park
Distance: 6.8-mile ridge loop
Hiking time: 4 to 5 hours
Difficulty: Strenuous, with moderate East Ridge segment and rigorous West Ridge segment
Elevation change: 700 feet
Trail surface: Earthen path, old grade, and rock
Best seasons: Spring through fall
Other trail users: Anglers
Canine compatibility: Leashed dogs permitted on trails and in picnic areas; no pets allowed in campground. A difficult rock stretch on West Ridge may be inappropriate for dogs.
Land status: State park
Nearest town: Kent, CT
Fees and permits: Campsite fees
Schedule: Year-round, 8 a.m. to sunset

Maps: State park map (available online at www.ct.gov/deep); Connecticut Forest and Park Association (CFPA) *Connecticut Walk Book, West* (available from CFPA, www.ctwoodlands.org)
Trail contacts: Macedonia Brook State Park, 159 Macedonia Brook Rd., Kent 06757; (860) 927-3238. Department of Energy and Environmental Protection, State Parks, (860) 424-3200; www.ct.gov/deep.
Special considerations: Park trails are for foot travel only. A brief difficult rock descent and climb on West Ridge may be unsuitable for children and novice hikers, and may also be a concern when hiking with pets. Difficult footing can lead to scrapes.

FINDING THE TRAILHEAD

From the junction of US 7 and CT 341 in Kent, go west on CT 341 for 1.7 miles and turn right, following the sign for Macedonia Brook State Park. Go 0.8 mile, reaching the park at the junction of Macedonia Brook and Fuller Mountain Roads. Follow Macedonia Brook Road into the park, reaching the trailhead at the bridge in 0.5 mile, the headquarters in 0.9 mile, and the campground in 1.3 miles. Park at the small picnic area at the northwest corner of the bridge. Trailhead GPS: N41 45.662' / W73 29.633'

THE HIKE

This demanding loop travels the east and west ridges framing the Macedonia Brook drainage and offers two-state viewing. Sweeps west applaud the beauty of the Catskill and Taconic Mountains.

Follow the blue Macedonia Ridge Trail east (counterclockwise) from the south side of the bridge, making a steady assault on East Ridge, the milder of the two framing ridges. Travel a mixed-age, multistory forest with a wildflower-sprinkled floor. As you trace the ridgetop north, you pass among oaks. Encounters may include deer, gray squirrels, chipmunks, woodpeckers, scarlet tanagers, and honking geese. Veils of fog may rise from the drainages.

Pass the yellow trail, which descends left to the park core. Stone walls now intersect the path. Birch, maple, and hickory mix with the oaks. You next cross the green-blazed trail that links the campground (left) with Fuller Mountain Road (right). Watch your footing where the trail descends sharply, especially when rain-soaked or masked by leaves. A scenic fern floor claims the bottom.

The path then slabs the east slope, coming out on a woods road. Follow it briefly left, descending above a headwater of Macedonia Brook. You then cross the rocky brook adorned by false hellebore, skunk cabbage, and moss. The trail ascends and undulates at the western base of East Ridge in congested leafy woods. At Keeler Road (a dirt road), cross the road bridge and enter the woods on the other side of Macedonia Brook.

Follow the marked trail between the brook and a rock wall before turning left to pass through a gap in the wall. Yellow violet and jack-in-the-pulpit grow near the brook. The complement of big trees offers little clue that in 1848 the demand for charcoal fuel nearly denuded these slopes. Ahead enter a sharp descent marked by steep short pitches. Hemlocks cloak the moister slope.

You might glimpse Hilltop Pond, a privately held dammed water with rimming birch, before reaching and crossing Weber Road to follow a gated grassy road back into the park. The loop then takes you across dirt Chippewalla Road, briefly keeping to the grade before heading right on foot trail for a sashaying woods climb.

THE GIFT OF WHITE

If you hike in the Litchfield Hills of Connecticut, you are bound to come upon the names Alain and May White. Alain White was a Renaissance man: a sportsman, conservationist, botanist, scholar, and historian. As an international chess master, he is credited with helping to break the World War I German code based on chess moves. He and his beloved sister, May, were trailblazers in land conservation and planned giving. The pair purchased thousands of acres for preservation and donated blocks of land to the state of Connecticut for public recreational use.

What today is viewed as both forward-thinking and generous was less favorably viewed in 1913, when the 4,000-acre White Memorial was first set aside. Locals saw only that prized land was being bought up and removed from productive use, causing their region to lose tax revenue. White would later cover that loss.

Today Alain White receives recognition as the founder of the Connecticut state park system. From 1923 to 1928 he served as president of the Connecticut Forest and Park Association (CFPA). The family's generosity can be appreciated at Macedonia Brook, Kent Falls, Mohawk Mountain, and Campbell Falls State Parks, and Mohawk and Peoples State Forests.

Patches of mountain laurel precede the ridgetop. From a rounded bald outcrop tucked among low oaks, glimpse the neighboring ridges. Descend south along the west ridge to find an open view atop a steep slanted rock face. Here admire the Macedonia Brook drainage with its evergreen treetops piercing the leafy canopy and gain looks at Cobble and Chase Mountains. Be careful when descending because footholds are few and the rock surface is boot-polished.

At a thin drainage, a green trail descends left to the campground. Ahead lies a treacherous ascent. You trace a thin canted ledge along a tiny chasm and then enter a challenging rock scramble. Although the ascent is difficult, downhillers protest more loudly. A few scoot down on their backsides. Formerly this route tested the mettle of Appalachian Trail hikers, until designers rerouted the national scenic trail.

Hike across the lichen-mottled outcrop of Cobble Mountain for western views. The most expansive view is still ahead, overlooking a broad New York valley, the cliff-sided ridge below, and the distant Catskills and Taconics.

On your way down you meet a white trail that maintains the steep descent left to the campground. Bear right for the ridge loop. It rolls along the slope in mountain laurel and hardwoods. The descent again accelerates, and you will twice cross a side brook to end at the picnic area.

MILES AND DIRECTIONS

0.0 Start at the lower bridge picnic area. Hike east on the blue Macedonia Ridge Trail to ascend East Ridge for a counterclockwise circuit.

2.7 Cross the Keeler Road bridge.

3.7 Cross dirt Chippewalla Road to travel West Ridge.

4.9 Top Cobble Mountain.

6.8 Arrive back at the small picnic area.

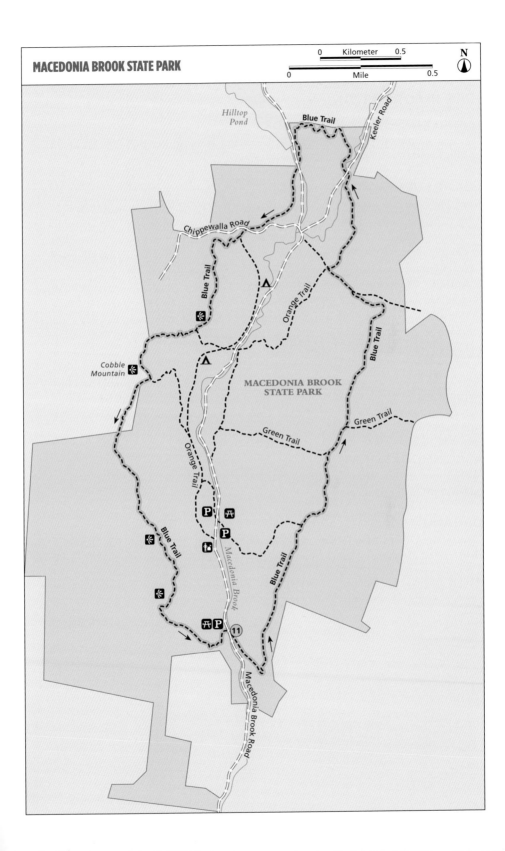

MACEDONIA BROOK STATE PARK

Hilltop Pond

Blue Trail

Keeler Road

Chippewalla Road

Blue Trail

Orange Trail

Cobble Mountain

MACEDONIA BROOK STATE PARK

Blue Trail

Green Trail

Green Trail

Orange Trail

Blue Trail

Blue Trail

Macedonia Brook

11

Macedonia Brook Road

0   Kilometer   0.5

0   Mile   0.5

N

HIKE INFORMATION

LOCAL INFORMATION

Western Connecticut Convention and Visitors Bureau, PO Box 968, Litchfield 06759; (860) 567-4506; http://litchfieldhills.com.

LOCAL EVENTS/ATTRACTIONS

Kent Falls State Park, c/o Macedonia Brook State Park, 159 Macedonia Brook Rd., Kent 06757; (860) 927-3238; www.ct.gov/deep. Kent Falls, tumbling 250 feet downhill to meet the Housatonic River, is one of the area's most popular draws, filling parking lots in summer. Reach Kent Falls State Park east off US 7, 4.5 miles north of the village of Kent. A summer parking fee is charged.

Antique Machinery Museum, (860) 927-0050, www.ctamachinery.com; **Eric Sloane Museum,** (860) 927-3849, www.cultureandtourism.org. Kent is also the home to this pair of museums. The Antique Machinery collection tracks early industry from the farm to the internal-combustion engine that powered the Industrial Revolution and advanced transportation. It also recounts when Connecticut was the "cradle of our country's mining industry." The Eric Sloane Museum re-creates the studio and displays the art and hand tool collection of Eric Sloane, a renowned landscape painter and historian of and writer about colonial tools. The museum property also holds the granite blast furnace from the 19th-century **Kent Iron Furnace.** All are at 31 Kent-Cornwall Rd., Kent 06757.

ACCOMMODATIONS

Macedonia Brook State Park offers 51 family campsites with rustic facilities from mid-Apr through early Sept.

ORGANIZATIONS

Connecticut Forest and Park Association (CFPA), 16 Meriden Rd., Rockfall 06481; (860) 346-8733; www.ctwoodlands.org.

12 SESSIONS WOODS WILDLIFE MANAGEMENT AREA

In its 700 acres this wildlife management area (WMA) demonstrates various land management and wildlife enhancement practices, which are explained on its self-guided trails. The featured Beaver Pond Trail is the site's longest and most popular trail. It explores mixed woods and small meadow clearings; brook, marsh, and vernal pond; laurel thicket; and a backyard wildlife habitat. Because sightings of deer, fox, beaver, wild turkey, cardinal, heron, and pileated woodpecker can enrich discovery, keep your binoculars ready.

Start: Trailhead on the right off the entrance road as you enter the education center parking lot
Distance: 3.3-mile loop with side spurs
Hiking time: 2 to 3 hours
Difficulty: Easy
Elevation change: 200 feet
Trail surface: Gravel and earthen path and management road
Best seasons: Spring through fall
Other trail users: Birders, mountain bikers on gravel roads only, snowshoers, cross-country skiers
Canine compatibility: Leashed dogs permitted (Keep animals leashed at all times.)

Land status: WMA land
Nearest town: Burlington or Bristol, CT
Fees and permits: None
Schedule: Year-round, sunrise to sunset
Map: WMA map, available online at www.ct.gov/deep (Wildlife Division) and usually available on-site
Trail contact: Sessions Woods Wildlife Management Area, PO Box 1550, Burlington 06013; (860) 424-3011; www.ct.gov/deep
Special considerations: No collecting and no feeding of wildlife. Beware of ticks and poison ivy.

FINDING THE TRAILHEAD

From the junction of CT 4 and CT 69 in Burlington, go south on CT 69 for 3.3 miles and turn right (west) to enter Sessions Woods WMA. Trailhead GPS: N41 44.001' / W72 57.336'

THE HIKE

The trails of this WMA welcome "Sunday" strolling, with seasonal discoveries bringing hikers to their knees and tilting heads skyward. Gravel or cinder-surfaced service roads host most of the travel. The long-distance Tunxis Trail briefly shares the Beaver Pond Trail.

A counterclockwise stroll begins off the entrance road to the north of the buildings and travels westbound. It offers a mildly rolling tour in a rich hardwood forest of maple, oak, hickory, black cherry, and birch. The shrub understory is a tumult of brambles, brier, sassafras, and chestnut. Almost immediately the blue Tunxis Trail arrives on the right. Interpretive signs introduce vegetation and explain management practices.

In clear-cut openings, wildflowers abound. In the forest and wooded swamps, mountain laurel, sheep laurel, azalea, and pond lilies up the ante. Benches dotting the route suggest pausing. Stillness often lets the wildlife come to you.

Ideal for short attention spans, side trails and attractions come rapid-fire. The Tree ID Trail heads left to follow along East Negro Hill Brook to Digger Dam, offering a shorter loop option. Keep to the Beaver Pond Trail. The next left offers a second chance to shorten the loop; it's the 0.4-mile Crosscut Trail through clear-cut woods. In a matter of strides, the Tunxis Trail departs to the right. Keep to the pond loop.

A few big pines may precede your reaching the star attraction, the beaver pond and its associated marsh. Water levels can fluctuate, depending on beaver activity or area management. A boardwalk spur leads to an island and waterfowl viewing site. The vast snag-filled pond particularly captivates when capped with pink and white pond lilies, when reflecting its autumn-tinted rim, or when a family of deer drinks at its edge. Overhead, ospreys may divert your attention with piercing screeches.

The American chestnut was a primary foodstuff for native peoples and colonial settlers. Before the 1900s this species accounted for one-quarter of the forest. But, sadly, a chestnut blight imported along with the Japanese chestnut virtually wiped out this susceptible indigenous species, attacking the tree as it reaches maturity. Saplings, though, still can be seen.

Past the main pond, a quick spur left leads to a vernal pond and its observation platform, rimmed by mountain laurel. Salamanders and frogs may be spied. More wetlands, some rock outcroppings, and hemlocks now mark the loop. At just over a mile, spurs branch right to a viewing blind and left to a 25-foot-tall observation tower (elevation 756 feet). The crow's nest of this three-story tower lifts you above the trees for a view stretching from Avon to Meriden.

Back on the loop, you come upon the trail's waterfall spur; it is on the right. Here you descend via footpath and earthen stairs to a cascade on Negro Hill Brook. The drainage features massive boulders and slabs with falling rivulets slipping through the rock crevices. After heavy rains a livelier falls courses over and through the rocks.

On the loop, you next find the returns of the Cross-cut and Tree ID Trails and see that Digger Dam on East Negro Hill Brook was actually a fish weir. The Beaver Pond Trail now remains mainly wooded, with occasional meadow openings. Still more spurs may divert you from course.

Beaver Pond water lily along Beaver Pond Trail, Sessions Woods Wildlife Management Area, Connecticut

Before the loop swings north, right spurs lead to Negro Hill Brook and a youth group camp. After trending north, a left leads to the Summer House, a covered pavilion with benches and a vista to the south. The next left holds an outdoor classroom, and a right leads to the backyard wildlife habitat, with identified plantings and a frog pond. Butterflies, dragonflies, and songbirds also animate the enclosure. With all of its asides exhausted, the trail returns you to the parking area.

MILES AND DIRECTIONS

0.0 Start at the entrance road trailhead. Hike the management road west into the WMA for counterclockwise travel of the loop.

0.2 Reach the Tree ID Trail, a 0.4-mile cut-across. Continue forward on the loop.

0.8 Reach the trail's namesake Beaver Pond and waterfowl blind. Resume loop travel, soon finding the left spur to a vernal pool and observation platform.

1.0 Reach and hike the spurs to a blind and the observation tower. Resume the loop.

1.2 Reach a waterfall spur. Detour right for its viewing before resuming the counterclockwise loop.

2.7 Reach the Summer House.

3.3 Close the loop back at the education center parking area.

Option: If time is short or you have little legs in your group, the center's flat 0.6-mile Forest Meadow Trail provides a snapshot of the site's natural offering and management theory. It starts to the left (south) of the education center. After rounding the gate, follow the service road right for a counterclockwise loop. True to its name, the trail passes through forest and meadow. Among its wildlife features are a bat shelter that can support 300 bats, bird nesting boxes and platforms, and brush piles that shelter wildlife. Interpretive plaques explain how each microcosm promotes wildlife.

SESSIONS WOODS WILDLIFE MANAGEMENT AREA

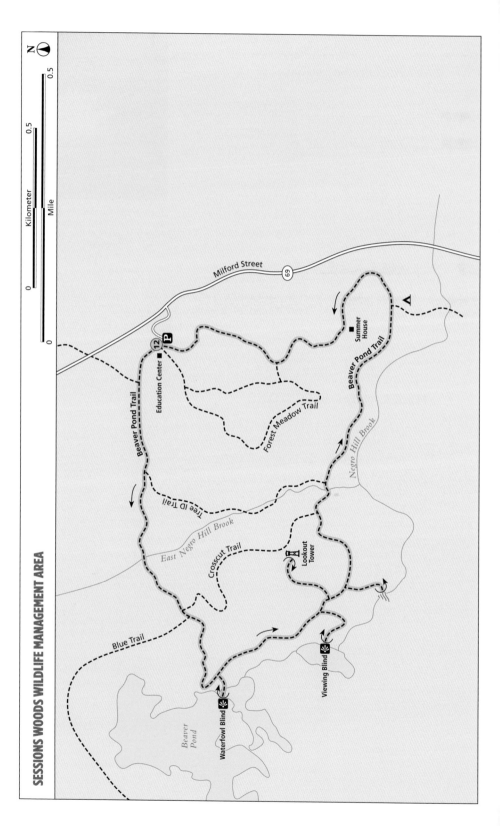

Interpretive boards along Beaver Pond Trail, Sessions Woods Wildlife Management Area, Connecticut

HIKE INFORMATION

LOCAL INFORMATION

Western Connecticut Convention and Visitors Bureau, PO Box 968, Litchfield 06759; (860) 567-4506; http://litchfieldhills.com.

LOCAL EVENTS/ATTRACTIONS

Burlington State Fish Hatchery, 34 Belden Rd., Burlington 06013; (860) 673-2340; www.ct.gov/deep. This, the oldest of Connecticut's fish hatcheries, off CT 4, offers an understanding of native fish species, their life cycles, and needs. The hatchery is open daily 8 a.m. to 3 p.m.

    Canton Historical Museum, 11 Front St., Collinsville 06019; (860) 693-2793; www .cantonmuseum.org. Historic Collinsville, off CT 179, calls you aside with its picturesque mill complex—the Collins Company Axe Factory, snugged to the Farmington River that powered it. Twenty-six of the original fifty buildings remain, now serving retail or housing. Industry was the thrust of many Connecticut communities in the 19th and early 20th centuries, and the Canton Historical Museum relates the story of it, Canton, and Victorian life and society.

    Lake Compounce Theme Park, 822 Lake Ave., Bristol 06010; (860) 583-3300; www.lakecompounce.com. Lake Compounce Theme Park almost insists on outside voices with its many rides and arcades. The park boasts Splash Harbor, Connecticut's largest water park, and Boulder Dash, a classic wooden roller coaster voted number one in surveys.

ORGANIZATIONS

Connecticut Forest and Park Association (CFPA), 16 Meriden Rd., Rockfall 06481; (860) 346-8733; www.ctwoodlands.org.

    Friends of Sessions Woods, Inc., PO Box 1550, 341 Milford St. (Route 69), Burlington 06013; www.fosw.org.

13 RAGGED MOUNTAIN PRESERVE TRAIL

Within this prized 563-acre open space, acquired through the Land and Water Conservation Fund, a demanding hiker loop rolls through restful mixed woods, skirts swamp, and travels a stirring cliff rim. Atop the cliffs you find trip-stalling reservoir-woodland views. This is one of the region's most popular climbing grounds, and you will often see experienced climbers clinging to the vertical rock faces. Wildlife sightings and fall foliage further recommend travel.

Start: West Lane/Wigwam Road trailhead
Distance: 5.5-mile loop
Hiking time: 3 to 4 hours
Difficulty: Strenuous
Elevation change: Travel from a trailhead elevation of 230 feet to a summit elevation of 761 feet atop Ragged Mountain.
Trail surface: Earthen path, rock outcrop, woods road
Best seasons: Spring through fall
Other trail users: Climbers, snowshoers, cross-country skiers
Canine compatibility: Leashed dogs permitted
Land status: Town of Berlin conservation land
Nearest town: Berlin, CT, with gas on Chamberlain Highway
Fees and permits: None
Schedule: Year-round (as weather allows), sunrise to sunset

Maps: Ragged Mountain (Preserve) park map (available online at www .town.berlin.ct.us); Connecticut Forest and Park Association (CFPA) *Connecticut Walk Book, West* (available from CFPA, www .ctwoodlands.org)
Trail contact: Conservation Commission, Berlin Town Hall, 240 Kensington Rd., Berlin 06037; (860) 828-7000; www.town.berlin.ct.us
Special considerations: Boots are recommended to protect ankles. Copperheads, although rarely spied, do dwell here, so be attentive when reaching, sitting, or stepping. Avoid cliff ledges during times of snow and ice, and use caution when conditions are wet. Weekend and summer parking is scarce. If a drop-off/pickup arrangement is possible, take it.

FINDING THE TRAILHEAD

At the junction of CT 372 and CT 71A in Berlin, go south on CT 71A for 1.2 miles and turn right (west) onto West Lane. Go 0.6 mile, reaching the trailhead where West Lane ends at Wigwam Road. Find roadside parking for up to a dozen vehicles. When arriving from the Berlin junction of CT 71 and CT 71A, go 1.1 miles north on CT 71A and turn left on West Lane to proceed to the trailhead. Trailhead GPS: N41 37.696' / W72 48.24'

THE HIKE

This loop through Ragged Mountain Preserve unites the blue/red preserve trail with the blue Metacomet Trail. Side trails to neighborhood streets and cross-trails that shortcut the loop are encountered along the way. The blue/orange and blue/white cuts-across put in place by volunteers shave distance off the north end of the loop. A blue/yellow cut-across shaves distance at the south end of the loop.

View from Preserve Trail, Ragged Mountain Preserve, Connecticut

Near the trailhead signboard, a boulder plaque commemorates the acquisition of Ragged Mountain Memorial Preserve. Enter the conservation land and follow the blue/red blazes, bearing left for a clockwise loop. Its narrow woods road conducts travel through ranks of hemlock, oak, maple, birch, and beech. Few plants pierce the leaf duff.

A footpath then takes over, for a slow gradual ascent. The regular interval of the blazes cues you to subtle direction changes. The trail grows rocky and rolling. Poison ivy caps the rocks and spirals up the tree trunks.

The trail next traverses outcrops and follows along the rim. As the low cliffs grade higher, gaps in the woods afford southeastern glimpses. Where the cliffs plunge 100 feet or more, views sweep Hart Ponds and the wooded terrain. Swans may ply the water. Rain clouds, fog, or excessive humidity can bring an uneasy aura of mystery.

Wild rose, blueberry, strawberry, and meadow grass accent the dark volcanic rock. The trail hugs the edge with brief lapses into woods. Red efts, toads, turtles, and spotted salamanders can detain the curious.

At the next rim height, look for a pull-apart section of cliff isolated from the main wall by a deep fissure. Low oaks dress the open rock. You survey Hart Ponds and the Hanging Hills of Meriden. Indian pipe and prince's pine lend a floral accent.

After the trail dips into fuller woods of maple, a fissure dishes up a southwestern view and offers a chance to admire the vertical-cliff profile. Here, too, you reach the Metacomet Trail, part of the 215-mile New England National Scenic Trail, traversing Connecticut and Massachusetts. Bear right on the Metacomet, now following blue blazes across the summit of Ragged Mountain. You'll find spurs of climb, some of which may require hand assists, and better views that trend west.

Rock climbers may shout instructions from the cliffs below, and a steep climber's trail descends left. Keep to the blue-blazed route. Midway through the loop a short detour left takes you to the rim above Wassel Reservoir for a dizzying look over the cliff. In the past a spotted turtle had chosen this forbidding site for laying her eggs. Grant all wildlife a wide comfort margin.

You then bid farewell to the blue Metacomet Trail and leave the ridge, once again following the blue/red blazes and once again following a woods road. Look for the trail to take a couple of turns, all well blazed. Mixed woods weave a relaxing tour.

After turning right off the woods road to follow a footpath through a dark stand of eastern hemlocks and oaks, you pass along the wooded edge of Panther Swamp. Here the trail rolls over low hilly bumps. Stay with the blue/red blazes, ignoring spurs to the neighborhood.

Forest floor plant, Ragged Mountain Preserve, Connecticut

Descend steadily, skirt a privately owned grassy flat, and enjoy changing woods before embarking on a foot-trail ascent of a rocky slope near an often-dry drainage. Under wet conditions, it hosts a seasonal falls. The trail tops out and a slow, broken descent follows. Blazes put you back on woods road to close the loop. Turn left to end at the trailhead.

MILES AND DIRECTIONS

0.0 Start at the West Lane/Wigwam Road trailhead. Follow the well-traveled aisle past the entrance sign/map kiosk into the conservation land.

0.1 Reach the loop junction. Bear left, following blue/red blazes.

0.8 Reach the blue/yellow cut-across (easily missed). Stay on the blue/red trail.

1.6 Reach the blue Metacomet Trail. Follow the blue blazes to the right.

2.5 Meet the blue/yellow cut-across. Stay on the blue Metacomet Trail.

3.2 Meet the blue/orange cut-across. Stay on the blue Metacomet Trail.

3.9 Reach the junction with the blue/red trail and the blue/white cut-across. Follow the blue/red trail to continue clockwise on the full preserve loop. The Metacomet Trail turns left.

5.4 Close the loop. Turn left to return to the trailhead.

5.5 Arrive back at the trailhead.

HIKE INFORMATION

LOCAL INFORMATION

Central Regional Tourism District, 1 Constitution Plaza, 2nd Floor, Hartford 06103; (860) 787-9640; www.centerofct.com.

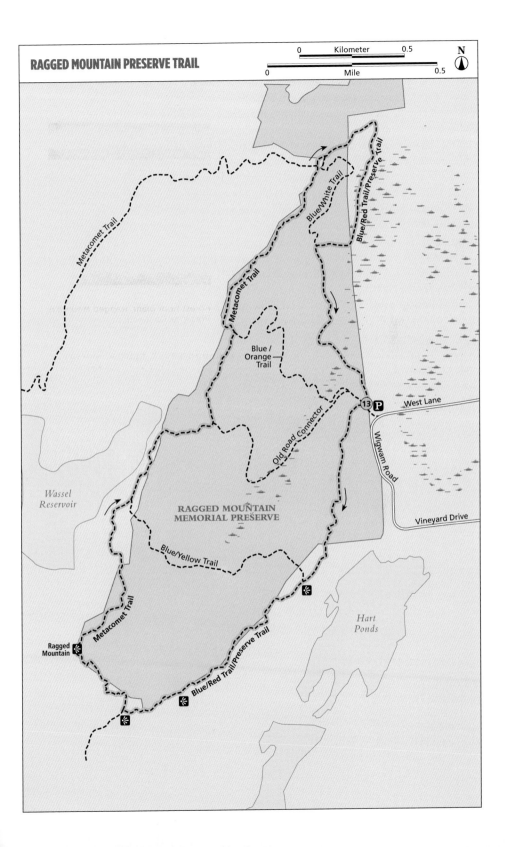

RAGGED MOUNTAIN PRESERVE TRAIL

Kilometer
0   0.5

Mile
0   0.5

N

Metacomet Trail

Blue/White Trail

Blue/Red Trail/Preserve Trail

Metacomet Trail

Blue /
Orange
Trail

Old Road Connector

West Lane

Wigwam Road

Vineyard Drive

Wassel
Reservoir

RAGGED MOUNTAIN
MEMORIAL PRESERVE

Blue/Yellow Trail

Hart
Ponds

Metacomet Trail

Ragged
Mountain

Blue/Red Trail/Preserve Trail

LOCAL EVENTS/ATTRACTIONS

Berlin Fair, 430 Beckley Rd., East Berlin 06037; (877) 828-0063; http://ctberlinfair
.com. A fixture for more than half a century and sponsored by the Berlin Lions Club, the
annual Berlin Fair is an old-fashioned harvest fair with exhibits, contests, farm animals,
food, and fun. It takes place the weekend of the third Sunday in Sept and runs Fri, Sat,
and Sun. Free continuous shuttle buses access the fairgrounds from off-site locations.

    New Britain Youth Museum at Hungerford Park, 191 Farmington Ave. (CT
372), Kensington 06037; (860) 827-9064; www.newbritainyouthmuseum.org. This
youth museum is an acclaimed natural history educational facility, where all ages can
learn. The site has farm and exotic animals, native wildlife, foot trails, ponds, gardens,
and exhibits. A picnic area and gift shop further serve visitors. This fee site is open
year-round, Tues through Sat from 10 a.m. to 4:30 p.m., with Saturday Public Animal
Programs.

    The town of Berlin has **other open spaces for hiking;** www.berlin.ct.us.

ORGANIZATIONS

Connecticut Forest and Park Association (CFPA), 16 Meriden Rd., Rockfall
06481; (860) 346-8733; www.ctwoodlands.org.

HONORABLE MENTIONS
NORTHWEST CONNECTICUT

A. FARMINGTON CANAL HERITAGE TRAIL, GRANBY TO SIMSBURY

This segment of the long-distance Farmington Canal Trail features the 8.5 miles south from Copper Hill Road to the parking area at Iron Horse Boulevard in Simsbury. The Canal Trail also continues north from Copper Hill Road. Although the southbound leg later closely pairs with roadways, its start is idyllic for walkers. The 1.5 miles to CT 20 offers a restful woodland stroll on a wide paved lane through swamp woodland, passing the outskirts of the 150-acre Great Marsh/Newgate State Wildlife Area. Until the late 1960s the aisle was used by Penn Central Railroad. Birch-oak hardwoods enfold travel, while benches invite lingering or wildlife watching. A variety of birds as well as raccoons, beavers, white-tailed deer, and even coyotes and bobcats have used the canal greenspace. East Granby Parks oversees this stretch. The canal trail is open sunrise to sunset. You can obtain a canal trail map online from the Farmington Valley Trails Council.

From US 202/CT 10 in Granby, turn east on CT 20. Go 1 block and turn north on Hungary Road. (It's a quick turnoff, so be alert.) Drive 1.8 miles and turn right on Copper Hill Road. Reach parking in 1 mile. The canal trail is 0.1 mile farther. Trailhead GPS: N41 58.445' / W72 45.438'. Trail contact: Farmington Valley Trails Council, PO Box 576, Tariffville 06081; (860) 202-3928; fchtrail.org.

B. MCLEAN GAME REFUGE

Senator George P. McLean gave to the people this 3,200-acre preserve that enfolds abandoned farmland, woodland, and ponds. McLean, an avid sportsman, hunted and fished here with US presidents Calvin Coolidge, William Taft, and Herbert Hoover and with Gifford Pinchot, who steered the US Forest Service. The refuge is free and open to the public from 8 a.m. to sunset (8 p.m. in summer) for hiking and nature study. Horseback riding is limited to yellow trails, spring through fall. Bicycles and camping are prohibited. A number of trails explore the refuge. Interlocking color-coded counterclockwise loops (blue, orange, and red) explore the main area, all returning via woods road. The blue loop is the longest at 2.1 miles; the red the shortest at 1.3 miles. The blue trail also allows connections to the purple North Trail and to the summit trail, which climbs to the top of East Barndoor Hill for views of West Barndoor Hill and overlooks of the neighborhood. Carry a map, available online.

For the main entrance, head north from Simsbury on US 202/CT 10 for 4.9 miles. Turn left (west) into the gated lot. Trailhead GPS: N41 56.446' / W72 47.616'. Trail contact: McLean Game Refuge, 150 Barndoor Hills Rd., Granby 06035; (860) 653-7869; www.mcleangamerefuge.org.

C. **NORTHWEST PARK**

This inviting Town of Windsor park adjacent Rainbow Reservoir encompasses nearly 500 acres of parklike grounds, woodland, field, bog, and ponds, with 12 miles of strolling lanes and paths, a nature center, tobacco barns, demonstration gardens, farm animal pens, and maple-sugaring exhibits. The trails are open to hiking, jogging, and cross-country skiing. Bicycles are restricted to roads, and dogs must be leashed. The park is open sunrise to sunset. Before 1972 much of the property was tobacco farmland, a once-thriving industry in the region. The John E. Luddy/Gordon S. Taylor Connecticut Valley Tobacco Museum (open mid-Mar to mid-Dec, Wednesday through Saturday, noon to 4 p.m. or call 860-285-1888 to schedule) explains the significance of this rapidly disappearing valley crop and industry.

From I-91, exit 38, go north on CT 75 (Poquonock Avenue) for 1.4 miles and turn west on Prospect Hill Road. Proceed 1.1 miles to the circle and take a right on Lang Road to reach the park at road's end in 0.4 mile. Trailhead GPS: N41 53.884' / W72 42.123'. Trail contact: Friends of Northwest Park, Inc., 145 Lang Rd., PO Box 773, Windsor 06095; (860) 285-1886; www.northwestpark.org.

D. **SHARON AUDUBON CENTER**

In northwest Connecticut, this 1,147-acre National Audubon Society wildlife sanctuary offers 11 miles of foot trails that meander past brook, pond, and bog; across wooded ridge; through unkempt fields of wildflowers; and past a maple-sugaring site. Stitching together named trails, you can craft loops of the sanctuary's east and west halves. In 2.5 miles you can explore two ponds and the woods and fields of the eastern sanctuary. Hiking 1.7 miles of rolling trail introduces the wooded serenity of the western sanctuary. Maps are available online or on-site. Either a per-person admission fee or National Audubon Society or Friends membership is required for entry. Obey posted rules. No pets. Trails are open sunrise to sunset, with the center open 9 a.m. to 5 p.m. Tues through Sat and 1 to 5 p.m. Sun.

From the junction of CT 4, CT 41, and CT 343 at the southern outskirts of Sharon, go east on CT 4 for 2.2 miles and turn right (south) to enter the sanctuary. From the CT 4–US 7 junction in Cornwall Bridge, go west on CT 4 for 5.2 miles to reach the sanctuary entrance. Trailhead GPS: N41 51.302' / W73 27.143'. Trail contact: Audubon Sharon, 325 Cornwall Bridge Rd. (CT 4), Sharon 06069; (860) 364-0520; http://sharon .audubon.org.

E. **ROARING BROOK NATURE CENTER**

This woodland and stream setting is representative of many small nature centers across the state that offer wending paths, quiet, and nature study. Its 5 miles of trail travel the center grounds and the adjacent state-owned 100-acre Werner farm property. Some 150 bird species, a butterfly garden, a replica Eastern Woodland Indian longhouse, and outdoor flight cages add to the learning experience. Trails travel ridge and brook and visit pond and quarry.

From the junction of CT 10 and US 44 in Avon, drive west on US 44 for 0.7 mile to Avon Center and continue west on US 44/US 202 for another 3.3 miles. Turn north on Lawton Road (where CT 177 arrives from the south, just east of Canton). Follow Lawton Road, bearing left at the Y-junction in 0.3 mile. At the cockeyed four-way junction 0.6 mile farther, you essentially follow the center option, which is Gracey Road, signed for the center. Reach the nature center on the left in 0.4 mile. Trailhead GPS: N41 50.485' / W72 52.898'. Trail contact: Roaring Brook Nature Center, 70 Gracey Rd., Canton 06019; (860) 693-0263; http://roaringbrook.org.

F. WHITE MEMORIAL FOUNDATION, NATURE TRAILS

Cradled in the Berkshire foothills of northwest Connecticut, this 4,000-acre private reserve offers the public 40 miles of trail and woods road to explore. The foundation is devoted to conservation, education, research, and compatible recreation and has set aside 600 acres as "natural area," where the land and habitats can change and prosper free from intervention. Ten acres of old-growth forest, a premier elevated boardwalk, observation platforms, Bantam Lake and River, mixed woods, marsh, and ponds entice visitors to explore. Bird and wildlife sightings recommend the Lake Trail and Little Pond Boardwalk, both easy. Standing water, pond lilies, tufted marsh grass, and cattails lend rich texture to the marshes. The museum/nature center is a fee attraction; trail access is free. Maps are available online or for purchase at the museum. Obey posted rules. Trails are open dawn to dusk. Museum hours are 9 a.m. to 5 p.m. Mon through Sat and noon to 5 p.m. Sun.

From the CT 63–US 202 junction in Litchfield, go southwest on US 202 for 2.1 miles. Turn left on Bissell Road, followed by a right on Whitehall Road to reach White Memorial Conservation Center and the nature trails in 0.5 mile. Trailhead GPS: N41 43.461' / W73 12.805'. Trail contact: White Memorial Conservation Center, 80 Whitehall Rd., PO Box 368, Litchfield 06759; (860) 567-0857; www.whitememorialcc.org.

G. WHITE MEMORIAL FOUNDATION, MATTATUCK-FIVE PONDS HIKE

This stretch of the Mattatuck Trail travels an isolated reach of White Memorial Foundation, a conservation land outside Litchfield, open to the public for hiking. With the help of spurs, a 6.7-mile out-and-back hike allows you to visit five ponds of individual personality and opens the gate to bird and wildlife sightings. Changing woodland images of big birch, huge pines, split snags, and mountain laurel lead you to acquaintances with Heron Pond, the aptly named Plunge Pool, Fawn Pond, Teal Pond, and lakelike Beaver Pond. Beaver lodges, woodpecker snags, frogs, ducks, and dragonflies add to pond viewing. Between Fawn and Teal Ponds, you'll pass the boulder monument honoring Alain and May White, the brother and sister whose love for nature prompted the saving of these quiet woods. Foundation maps are available online or for purchase at the site's museum/nature center off Whitehall Road (see the honorable mention above for directions). Trail access is free, with trails open dawn to dusk. Museum hours are 9 a.m. to 5 p.m. Mon through Sat and noon to 5 p.m. Sun.

From US 202 in Litchfield, turn south on CT 63 (Straits Turnpike) and go 2.2 miles to locate the trailhead on the left. Parking is on the right just south of the trailhead at the South Farm Entrance. Trailhead GPS: N41 42.894' / W73 11.187'. Trail contact: White Memorial Conservation Center, 80 Whitehall Rd., PO Box 368, Litchfield 06759; (860) 567-0857; www.whitememorialcc.org.

H. MOUNT TOM STATE PARK

Here, at one of the oldest Connecticut state parks (established 1915), the summit stone tower (repaired in 2011) is a siren song to hikers. This Mount Tom has a summit elevation higher than its better-known Massachusetts rival of the same name. The yellow tower trail climbs almost 500 feet and is less than 1 mile out and back. Rising 34 feet, the black stone tower extends a 360-degree view of the immediate Litchfield/Morris/Washington area. Looks stretch north to Massachusetts and west to New York. The park's spring-fed pond and picnic area appeal to summer fun seekers; weekend and holiday parking fees apply for nonresidents. Park hours are 8 a.m. to sunset.

From the junction of US 202 and CT 209 in Bantam, go west on US 202 for 3.1 miles and turn left (south) for the park, following signs through the park. In 0.5 mile you reach Tower Trail parking and picnicking, uphill on the right. Trailhead GPS: N41 41.723' / W73 16.806'. Trail contact: Contact the park office at (860) 567-8870 from Memorial Day to Labor Day. Otherwise, direct inquiries to Lake Waramaug State Park, 30 Lake Waramaug Rd., New Preston 06777; (860) 868-2592; www.ct.gov/deep.

I. FARMINGTON RIVER TRAIL

The Farmington River, a federal Wild and Scenic River known for its float trips and fishing, also boasts a fine companion rail trail. This rail-to-trail reclaims part of the Central New England Railroad for recreation and nature study. It serves hikers, cyclists, fitness walkers, wheelchair users, pushers of baby strollers, and dog walkers. A favorite segment stretches downstream from historic Collinsville, where the red-painted ax-factory complex recalls its heyday. The Farmington was a working river before it was a recreational river. The tree-lined paved path rolls out a comfortable travel lane, hugging the river course.

In historic Collinsville, the trail crosses over the river. Trailhead GPS: N41 48.611' / W72 55.404'. South of Collinsville, developed trailheads are located on CT 179. The first is on the left (east off CT 179) in 1.2 miles. Trailhead GPS: N41 47.664' / W72 55.518'. There's another south of the intersection of CT 179 and CT 4, 2.1 miles south of Collinsville in Burlington. Trailhead GPS: N41 46.882' / W72 55.314'. A third with off-road parking is 3.7 miles south of Collinsville. Trailhead GPS: N41 45.648' / W72

53.778'. Trail contacts: Farmington Valley Trails Council, PO Box 576, Tariffville 06081; (860) 202-3928; fchtrail.org. Burlington Town Hall, 200 Spielman Hwy., Burlington 06013; (860) 673-6789; www.burlingtonct.us/parks-recreation.

J. HILL-STEAD MUSEUM TRAILS

The Hill-Stead, acclaimed for its art and cultural offerings, also has attractive grounds to explore on historic farm roads and paths. The property consists of 150 acres. Centerpiece to the acreage is the 1901 Pope Riddle house, associated outbuildings, gardens, and what was an experimental dairy farm. Ponds, swamp lowlands, woods, fields, lawns, and rock walls contribute to the overall mosaic. The long-distance Metacomet Trail crosses the property. The white-blazed Woodland Trail is 1 mile long; the other colored paths are shorter. Walking here allows you to step back in time to a gentler era. The rolling acreage down to the farm pond is especially lovely when dressed in autumn red and gold. The grounds are open to hiking 7:30 a.m. to 5:30 p.m. Obey the no-trace rules. A donation for trail maintenance is suggested.

Rural view from Pope Riddle House, Hill-Stead Museum, Farmington, Connecticut

From the junction of CT 4 and CT 10 in Farmington, drive south on CT 10 for 0.3 mile and turn left onto Mountain Road, following the signs to Hill-Stead Museum. Travel the entry lane 0.4 mile to the parking lots and trailheads. Trailhead GPS: N41 43.281' / W72 49.138'. Trail contact: Hill-Stead Museum, 35 Mountain Rd., Farmington 06032; (860) 677-4787; www.hillstead.org.

K. SHADE SWAMP SANCTUARY

This 800-acre sanctuary, north off US 6 in Farmington, has parcels on either side of New Britain Avenue. The west side is traveled by white trail; the east side, by blue. The 1.5-mile Blue Trail, an Eagle Scout project, is representative. It begins beside a 1934 log-lattice picnic hut built by the Civilian Conservation Corps and on the National Register of Historic Places. The trail fashions a lopsided figure eight that takes you past remnant cages and the stone culvert dens of a onetime zoo. From 1934 up to the 1960s, the state ran a small zoo here, with native Connecticut game birds and animals. The dismal quarters vividly illustrate how zoos have matured and improved. The trail then takes you through native woods and past native and nonnative tangles, trickling drainages, and swamp-footed woods and marsh expanse. At one time the trail had fourteen stations; a few interpretive plaques remain, but no brochure. The trail rolls along slopes and atop a glacial meltwater ridge. It is easier to stroll going clockwise at loop junctions. The 2.5-mile White Trail visits a pond. Mosquitoes can annoy; come prepared.

From the junction of US 6 and CT 177, drive east on US 6 for 0.7 mile, turning north into the west trailhead parking space (the white trail). Trailhead GPS: N41 42.315' / W72 52.024'. Or continue 0.4 mile farther east, crossing New Britain Avenue, and turn north into the east trailhead parking space (the blue trail). Trailhead GPS: N41 42.259' / W72 51.550'. Trail contacts: Shade Swamp Sanctuary, c/o Penwood State Park, 57 Gun Mill Rd., Bloomfield 06002; (860) 242-1158. Department of Energy and Environmental Protection, State Parks and Forests, (860) 424-3200; www.ct.gov/deep.

L. PRATT NATURE CENTER

This nature center, open year-round, offers hiking in the surrounding 200 wooded acres. Color-coded trails guide you past Indian caves, wetlands, and meadows, and take you along streams and the East Aspetuck River and to the top of this area's Mount Tom (elevation 1,040 feet). The center staff warns that the site chickens may follow you, but that's fine with them. The land was once occupied by Native Americans and then farmed from the late 1700s to 1967, when the Pratts repurposed the land for an environmental education center. Travel is no-trace; leave dogs at home.

In New Milford at the junction of US 202 and CT 67, go north on US 202E for 3.5 miles and turn left onto Papermill Road. Parking is on the left in 0.1 mile; the center is on the right. A crosswalk links the two. Trailhead GPS: N41 37.424' / W73 23.838'. Trail contact: Pratt Nature Center, 163 Papermill Rd., New Milford 06776; (860) 355-3137; www.prattcenter.org.

M. LOVERS LEAP STATE PARK

This 160-acre walk-in park, parceled by the Housatonic River, takes its name from the ill-fated love story of Lillinonah, Pootatuck Chief Waramaug's beloved daughter, and her European suitor. One story has it her canoe was swept up in rapids and her lover leapt to her rescue but was swallowed up as well. A 0.2-mile trail leads to the rock formation that suggests the park's name. The park has a network of trails through the river-area woods, a red 1895 Berlin Iron Bridge (one of five remaining in Connecticut), ruins from the park's previous life, and interpretive panels along the bridge walk that tell the park story.

From the intersection of US 202 and CT 67 in New Milford, follow Grove Street south along the Housatonic River to reach the state park in 2.4 miles. Trailhead GPS: N41 32.597' / W73 24.503'. Trail contact: Lovers Leap State Park, c/o Squantz Pond State Park, 178 Shortwoods Rd., New Fairfield 06812; (203) 312-5023; www.ct.gov/deep.

SOUTHWEST CONNECTICUT TRAILS

Southwest Connecticut is represented by the vast sweeps of Fairfield and New Haven Counties plus western Middlesex County. Regional acclaims are the Housatonic River drainage, the traprock features shaping the Connecticut River highland, and the ports and shore of Long Island Sound. Wooded and rocky landscapes, captured and falling waters, a chesty giant, and a reclaimed canal towpath beckon exploration.

14 LILLINONAH TRAIL

In Upper Paugussett State Forest, this loop hike visits the wooded edge and slope along a confined stretch of the Housatonic River, Lake Lillinonah—a place of Indian lore and quiet beauty. An ill-fated love story has it that river rapids (now swallowed by the dam) snatched up a canoe paddled by Lillinonah, the beloved daughter of a Pootatuck Indian chief. When her European lover leapt to her rescue, he too fell victim to the water.

Start: Hanover Road trailhead
Distance: 6-mile loop
Hiking time: 4 to 5 hours
Difficulty: Moderate
Elevation change: Travel between a low point of 200 feet along Lake Lillinonah and a high point of 480 feet.
Trail surface: Earthen path, woods road, rock outcropping
Best seasons: Spring through fall
Other trail users: Hunters, anglers, mountain bikers on Brody Road (Lillinonah Trail is foot travel only), snowshoers, cross-country skiers
Canine compatibility: Leashed dogs permitted
Land status: State forest
Nearest town: Newtown, CT, with gas along US 6
Fees and permits: None
Schedule: Sunrise to sunset, mid-Mar to mid-Dec (closed during winter for nesting bald eagles)

Maps: State forest map (available online at www.ct.gov/deep); Connecticut Forest and Park Association (CFPA) *Connecticut Walk Book, West* (available from CFPA, www.ctwoodlands.org)
Trail contact: Department of Energy and Environmental Protection, State Forests, (860) 424-3200; www.ct .gov/deep
Special considerations: The Lillinonah Trail is open to foot travel only. Because bald eagles overwinter here, they have prior claim to the area Dec 15 to Mar 15. Hunting occurs within the state forest, so know the season and take precautions. Either avoid the area or dress in blaze orange for your safety. Consider, too, the safety of your pet during hunting season.

FINDING THE TRAILHEAD

From I-84, take exit 10 and follow US 6W as it heads south into Newtown. At 0.6 mile, turn right on The Boulevard and follow this road over the railroad track and back under I-84, where the name changes to Hanover Road. In 3.5 miles you reach the Pond Brook crossing on Hanover Road. Trailhead parking is on the right as you reach the bridge, and boat launch parking is on the right after crossing the bridge. Trailhead GPS: N41 27.517' / W73 19.546'

THE HIKE

This hike swings a 6-mile loop through 794-acre Upper Paugussett State Forest, traveling shoreline bluff and the wooded and bouldery rise above Lake Lillinonah.

Follow the blue blazes from Hanover Road parking, crossing flowing water via the road culvert before turning east into woods and uphill. You reach "Al's Trail," a yellow-blazed and placard-marked segment of the Newtown Trailway, which shares the way.

In a dip, find the loop junction. Keep left for clockwise travel. The trail has a defined earthen bed, sometimes rooted as it rolls along the foot of the slope above the Pond Brook inlet. The intermingled hemlock, birch, maple, and beech create a dark passage, parted by thin drainages. At the upcoming stone wall, a rustic sign indicates SCENIC TRAIL NEXT 3.1 MILES. It also communicates the winter closure for eagles.

The trail climbs to trace a woods plateau at times edged by stone wall. The glassy water of the big impound shines mirrorlike beyond the trees of the lower slope. In the fall, squirrels bombard passers with dropped hickory nuts. Where the trail first overlooks the primary lake, you pass a camp flat with rough lean-to and makeshift tables and benches.

The trail continues rounding to the right, following the bluff curvature to build a length-of-lake view. The flap of cormorants, the nag of crows, and the screech of an osprey signal you are not alone. Added light from the lake alters the plant growth and tree mix. View a giant oak, classic American beech trees, tulip poplars, at least five kinds of ferns, and a hodgepodge of fungi.

After a plank-spanned drainage crossing, the trail ascends beside the cascading drainage to the next point of crossing. The climb then continues, topping out beside the broken trunk of an ancient oak, whittled more by Hurricane Irene.

The trail rolls and drifts downhill, passing among granite outcroppings and boulders, patched with lichen, moss, and ferns. Mountain laurels favor this realm, showy in spring but attractive anytime. A couple of tricky descents follow. Wet conditions and leaf piles double the challenge. Mosquitoes are especially annoying in the soggy reaches.

The trail returns to trace Lillinonah's abrupt shore edge. But uphill travel again calls, with the area granite in all its shapes, sizes, and ledges adding beauty and workout. Then it's back at the water on this well-marked trail.

Woodpeckers, frogs, and spiders may divert attention before the final lake view toward the dam. Admire the big water, its even-height rim, and the long containing dam. Humidity may create an impressionistic view.

The trail now embarks on its return leg, leaving the lake and ascending a sunken grade through a network of stone walls. The Newtown Trailway goes its own way. Watch for blue blazes to point you right through an egress in one wall to follow the edge of another. Maple-sugaring lines stretch left, part of the 6-acre Sugarbush Demonstration Area. Reaching a two-track at some buildings, you follow the track to the right to Echo Valley Road parking.

The trail now rolls and meanders away from this access, crossing stone walls and settling into a fast stretch on woods lane. At a drainage the trail rolls up and over a rocky knoll to pass between boulder-riddled and ledge-capped hilltops.

Rockwall along Lillinonah Trail, Paugussett State Forest, Connecticut

Again, the trail rolls and descends. Where you pass through a stone wall, turn left on a woods road (Brody Road). A rusted old wreck sits off-trail. Afterward, blazes point you right onto a footpath to close the loop. From there turn left to return to parking. If you miss the turn, the woods road emerges at Hanover Road. Turn right and descend to parking.

MILES AND DIRECTIONS

0.0 Start at the Hanover Road trailhead. Follow blue blazes across a culvert and east into woods.

0.1 Reach the loop junction past Al's Trail. Bear left for clockwise travel. The return is to your right.

0.5 Reach the signed Scenic Area (the seasonal closure for overwintering eagles). You can proceed forward from March 16 through December 14. Otherwise, turn back or replot travel.

3.7 View the dam on Lake Lillinonah as the scenic area closure and lake travel come to an end. Follow the blue-blazed loop up sunken grade.

4.0 Reach Echo Valley Road parking. Follow blue blazes above and away from parking.

5.6 Reach a woods road (Brody Road). Turn left.

5.8 Reach a trail junction. Turn right off Brody Road onto a foot trail to close the loop. *Option:* If you miss the turn or choose to stay on the woods road, you'll come out on Hanover Road. Turn right to return to the trailhead.

5.9 Close the loop. Turn left to return to the trailhead.

6.0 Arrive back at the trailhead.

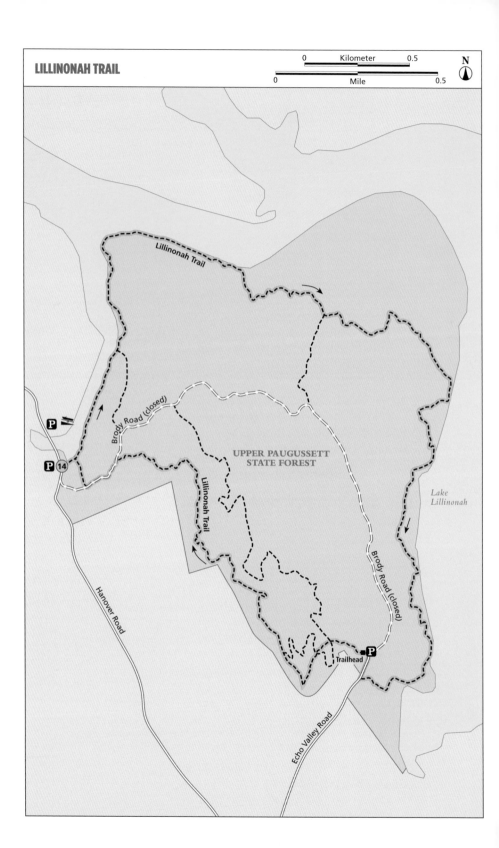

0   Kilometer   0.5

0   Mile   0.5

N

Lillinonah Trail

P

P 14

Brody Road (closed)

UPPER PAUGUSSETT
STATE FOREST

Lake
Lillinonah

Lillinonah Trail

Brody Road (closed)

Hanover Road

P

Trailhead

Echo Valley Road

BUILDING FENCES

The retreat of the Wisconsin Glacier at the end of the last ice age strew the land of Connecticut and Rhode Island with boulders, the building material of stone walls, pens, property lines, and cellars. Colonial settlers were agrarian, so clearing the land of this rock became a priority and stacking the rock became an expedient solution to removal. Stone wall building entered its peak from 1775 to 1825. In the nineteenth century, the need emerged for fence inspectors to settle liability disputes between neighbors when animals broke loose and damaged crops. Inspectors ruled on a fence's soundness, and a sound fence absolved its owner of responsibility.

In the early 1870s more than 20,000 miles of stone fencing webbed Connecticut. Today's hiking trails parallel and crisscross these stone records of bygone people and bygone land uses. That these walls stand after centuries of winter snow and ice and tumbled trees speaks to their soundness.

HIKE INFORMATION

LOCAL INFORMATION

Western Connecticut Convention and Visitors Bureau, PO Box 968, Litchfield 06759; (860) 567-4506; http://litchfieldhills.com.

LOCAL EVENTS/ATTRACTIONS

From early Dec through early March, Shepaug Hydroelectric Station hosts **eagle watching** from an observation area at Shepaug Dam on the Housatonic River in Southbury. For information and to secure the necessary advance reservation, phone (800) 368-8954, Tuesday through Friday, between the hours of 9 a.m. and 3 p.m.; www.h2opower.com/recreation/shepaug-hydroelectric-station.

Boating and fishing on Lake Lillinonah are popular pastimes. Boat launch parking is just north of the trailhead, across the bridge on Hanover Road. Consult Connecticut publications about boating and angling; www.ct.gov/deep.

Danbury Irish Festival, (203) 739-0010; www.danburyirishfestival.org. Danbury's annual Irish Festival may have you going green and dancing a jig. It takes place each Sept at Charles Ives Concert Park at Western Connecticut State University's campus in Danbury. The Danbury Ancient Order of Hibernians sponsors the event that celebrates Irish culture, music, dance, and food.

Mine Hill Preserve, Roxbury Land Trust, 6 Mine Hill Road, Roxbury 06783; (860) 350-4148; www.roxburylandtrust.org. The Trust's Mine Hill Preserve, on the National Register of Historic Places, interprets the site of a 19th-century iron mine and furnace complex, explaining the history and the iron-making process. Overlooking the Shepaug River, this 360-acre preserve also has 6 miles of hiking trails.

ORGANIZATIONS

Connecticut Forest and Park Association (CFPA), 16 Meriden Rd., Rockfall 06481; (860) 346-8733; www.ctwoodlands.org.

15 SOUTHFORD FALLS STATE PARK

At this charming Connecticut state park, you will find scenic picnic lawns with big shade trees, a cascading waterfall tumbling through a small gorge, a covered bridge, Papermill Pond, and the sparkling tannin-colored waters of Eightmile Brook—not bad for 120 acres. An efficient short trail offers a see-it-all hike. Historically, the racing falls powered various mills, including an early match factory.

Start: Papermill Pond trailhead
Distance: 1.6-mile loop with spur
Hiking time: 1 to 1.5 hours
Difficulty: Easy
Elevation change: 300 feet
Trail surface: Earthen path
Best seasons: Spring through fall
Other trail users: Anglers, snowshoers, cross-country skiers
Canine compatibility: Leashed dogs permitted on trails and in picnic areas
Land status: State park
Nearest town: Southbury, CT
Fees and permits: None
Schedule: Year-round, 8 a.m. to sunset
Map: State park map (available online at www.ct.gov/deep)

Trail contacts: Southford Falls State Park, Quaker Farms Road (CT 188), Southbury 06488; (203) 264-5169. Department of Energy and Environmental Protection, State Parks, (860) 424-3200; www.ct.gov/deep.

Special considerations: Southford Falls is a designated Trout Park. Its Papermill Pond is one of 11 sites across the state that receives regular trout stocking from the state fish hatcheries. The powerful wind storms of May 15, 2018, edited the woodland, taking down several big tulip poplars. Visitors might see evidence of the subsequent recovery.

FINDING THE TRAILHEAD

From I-84, take exit 16 and go south on CT 188, passing through Southford to reach the park on the left in 2.9 miles. Trailhead GPS: N41 27.529' / W73 09.902'

THE HIKE

With mostly gentle grades, this counterclockwise loop heads downstream along Eightmile Brook, ascends the hill rising east of the brook, and returns along Papermill Pond. Historical remnants—old millstones, a steam-engine foundation, and a sluice pipe—hint at a bustling era before the park.

From the parking at Papermill Pond, hike the wide gravel lane south along the pond's west shore toward the falls and core of the park. Papermill Pond reflects its wooded shore, but a wake from a muskrat can distort the watery duplicate. At the upper bridge, which signals the loop junction, forgo crossing. Proceed instead south (downstream) to Southford Falls viewing to begin counterclockwise travel.

Natural outcrop and attractive stonework configure the racing multidirectional cascades of Southford Falls. It is a beautiful juxtaposition of black rock and tiered white streamers. The longest drop of the 12-foot-high waterfall is 6 feet. From the falls, Eightmile Brook slips through a narrow rocky gorge, dropping in stages, exciting eye and ear.

Red Trail, Southford Falls State Park, Connecticut

At the covered bridge you find a gently riffling brook. Painted red with white trim, the Burr-arch bridge, built in 1972, replicates a circa 1804 design. Nearby rest stones and other evidence of the site's milling heritage. Pass through the bridge to the east shore and turn right, following the red blazes downstream along Eightmile Brook. For the falls loop alone, you would turn left, gaining new perspectives on the gorge and waterfall, before crossing at the upper bridge.

Rich woods of maple, birch, aspen, tulip poplar, elm, and hemlock enfold travel. Seasons alter the mosaic, with the bloom of laurel, the colors of fall, and the white of winter. Bypass a spur on your left that offers yet another loop option. Where a small boardwalk traverses moist bottomland, the tannin-tinted waters of Eightmile Brook flow within easy striking distance. Beyond the walk, look for the loop to head left uphill from the brook.

Mountain laurel, witch hazel, and tall oaks crowd the west-facing slope. As the trail rounds behind an outcrop knoll for a contouring ascent, the drone of CT 188 rides to the trail. With another uphill pulse, you top a small outcrop overlooking the wooded slope. Round left, coming to the tower junction. Go left to add a tower visit. A right continues the counterclockwise loop.

Following the tower spur, you ascend left in oak and laurel to the two-story platform. Trees enfold three sides, but you earn a southwestern glimpse of a neighboring ridge and a rural scene. Although a secondary trail crosses the summit to descend the east slope, for this hike, backtrack to the tower/loop junction and turn left.

You now travel the upper reaches of the eastern slope, with its cloak of oaks and tall mountain laurel. Below an outcrop crest, maples fill out the forest. At a hilltop depression, outcrops sweep up the sides of the bowl, and tulip poplar and aspen lend their leaf signatures to the canopy and floor. Veer right up the side of the bowl, coming to a plank walk and junction. Trail stretches left to Eightmile Brook for an alternative return. Bear right to complete the loop near the pond.

You arrive at the marshy end of Papermill Pond. Scenic boulders mark the far shore, while greenbrier, highbush blueberry, and sweet pepperbush crowd the immediate bank. Traverse the open lawn, rounding left and passing between a shelter and the pond shore to close the loop at the upper bridge. Pickerel hide among the aquatic vegetation, and often a heron stalks the shallows for shimmery minnows. Return north from the bridge.

MILES AND DIRECTIONS

0.0 Start at the Papermill Pond trailhead. Follow the gravel lane south along the west shore of Papermill Pond toward the falls and core of the park.

0.1 Reach the upper bridge and the loop junction. Continue south (downstream) to Southford Falls. The return is via the bridge.

0.2 Reach the covered bridge. Pass through the bridge to the east shore and turn right (downstream). *Option:* By turning left, you revisit the gorge and waterfall before returning via the upper bridge for a 0.3-mile waterfall loop.

0.3 Hike past the red trail, which heads left uphill to shorten the loop. Continue forward for the full red loop.

0.7 Reach the tower spur junction. Follow the spur left to the tower.

0.8 Reach the tower. Backtrack the tower spur and resume the counterclockwise loop.

1.3 Reach a trail junction. Proceed forward for the loop. *Option:* The left trail cuts across to Eightmile Brook for an alternative return. At the brook you turn right (upstream) to return to parking.

1.5 Complete the loop at the upper bridge. Pass through and turn right for the trailhead.

1.6 Arrive back at the trailhead.

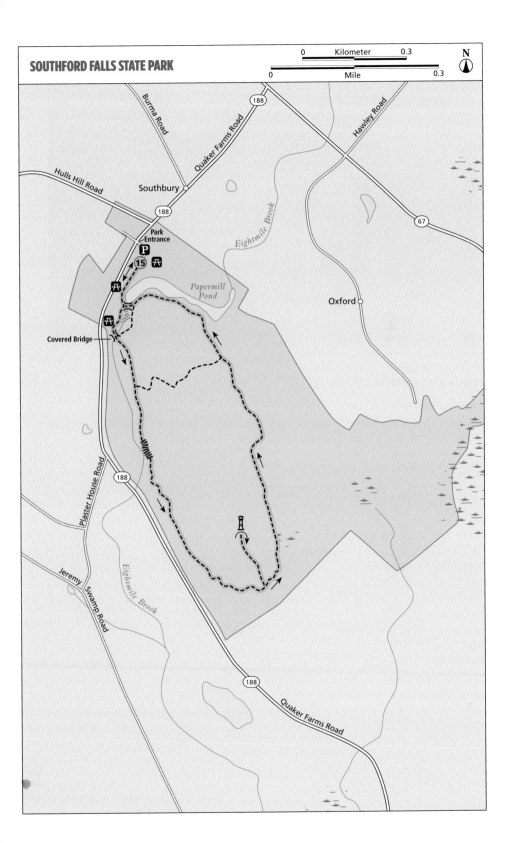

SOUTHFORD FALLS STATE PARK

0 Kilometer 0.3

0 Mile 0.3

N

Burma Road

188

Quaker Farms Road

Hawley Road

Hulls Hill Road

Southbury

67

188

Eightmile Brook

Park Entrance

P

15

Papermill Pond

Oxford

Covered Bridge

Plaster House Road

188

Jeremy Swamp Road

Eightmile Brook

188

Quaker Farms Road

Burr Arch covered bridge, Southford Falls State Park, Connecticut

HIKE INFORMATION

LOCAL INFORMATION

Western Connecticut Convention and Visitors Bureau, PO Box 968, Litchfield 06759; (860) 567-4506; http://litchfieldhills.com.

LOCAL EVENTS/ATTRACTIONS

Glebe House Museum, 49 Hollow Rd., Woodbury 06798; (203) 263-2855; www .glebehousemuseum.org. Here, docents in period costume guide you back to Woodbury in the years 1771 through 1786, when the Marshall family and their slaves lived in this 18th-century house. The garden by renowned landscape designer Gertrude Jekyll is the last example of her work in the United States.

Quassy Amusement Park, Route 64, Middlebury 06762; (203) 758-2913 or (800) 367-7275; www.quassy.com. For family fun, Quassy Amusement Park steps up, with a water-play area, wooden roller coaster and other rides, an arcade, a beach, food, and entertainment.

ACCOMMODATIONS

Kettletown State Park, 1400 Georges Hill Rd., Southbury 06488; (203) 264-5678, May through Sept (call Putnam Memorial State Park, 203-938-2285, Oct through Apr); www.ct.gov/deep. Kettletown State Park has 56 family campsites, with camping open Memorial Day weekend through Labor Day weekend. Reservations are through ReserveAmerica, (877) 668-2267 or www.reserveamerica.com.

16 KETTLETOWN STATE PARK

On the east shore of Lake Zoar, a long impoundment on the Housatonic River, this 605-acre Connecticut state park offers lake, brook, woods, and crest discovery. The park traces its name to the oral lore placing the sum the colonists paid to the Pootatuck Indians for the hunting and fishing rights here at one brass kettle. In 1919 the Stevenson Dam–raised water of Lake Zoar swallowed the site of the historic Indian village, erasing all record of this farming people, whose sophisticated drum talk could relay a message 200 miles in two hours.

Start: Trailhead parking for the William Miller Trail
Distance: 6.9-mile out-and-back, with two loops
Hiking time: 4 to 6 hours
Difficulty: Strenuous
Elevation change: 450 feet
Trail surface: Earthen path
Best seasons: Spring through fall
Other trail users: Anglers and snowshoers
Canine compatibility: Leashed dogs permitted on trails and in picnic areas, but no pets allowed on beach or in campground
Land status: State park, county park, private (brief stretch en route to Maple Tree Hill Road)
Nearest town: Southbury, CT
Fees and permits: Weekend/holiday parking fees for nonresidents at the state park, seasonal fee for day use at Jackson Cove Recreation Area; overnight camping fees for park campground

Schedule: Year-round, 8 a.m. to sunset
Maps: State park map (available online at www.ct.gov/deep); Connecticut Forest and Park Association (CFPA) *Connecticut Walk Book, West* (available from CFPA, www.ctwoodlands.org)
Trail contacts: Kettletown State Park, 1400 Georges Hill Rd., Southbury 06488; (203) 264-5678, May through Sept (call Putnam Memorial State Park, 203-938-2285, Oct through Apr). Department of Energy and Environmental Protection, State Parks, (860) 424-3200; www.ct.gov/deep.
Special considerations: Park trails are open to foot travel only. No trail camping and no fires. Kettletown was struck by the wind storms of May 15, 2018. Visitors might see evidence of the forest impact and recovery.

FINDING THE TRAILHEAD

From I-84, take exit 15 and head south on Kettletown Road, following signs for the park. In 3.5 miles turn right on Georges Hill Road to find the entrance on the left in 0.8 mile. Start at William Miller Trail parking, bearing right where the park road forks. Trailhead GPS: N41 25.562' /W73 12.566'

For Jackson Cove Recreation Area, forgo taking the right-hand turn onto Georges Hill Road at 3.5 miles. Instead, proceed south another 1.3 miles on Maple Tree Hill Road and continue on Jackson Cove Road for 0.2 mile more. Trailhead GPS: N41 24.693' / W73 11.410'

THE HIKE

This hike fashions a double loop exploring the ridge and slope above the east shore of Lake Zoar. It gathers area overlooks and finds limited lake access on the southernmost loop.

From Miller Trail parking, follow the blue/yellow trail descending toward the beach/bathhouse to take the surfaced lane along Kettletown Brook upstream. Cross the footbridge and bear left (upstream) continuing on the blue/yellow Brook Trail.

The trail meanders between boulders and alongside rushing Kettletown Brook. Hemlocks add a soothing darkness. Upon crossing the park road, you follow the blue Pomperaug Trail south, soon meeting the loop junction with the blue/white Crest Trail. Keep to the Pomperaug Trail for the clockwise loop. Blazes point out quick direction changes. The trail then settles into course, passing through hemlock-birch forest. It then grows steeper, putting you on a low ridge.

A rolling descent leads to the junction with the blue/red trail. Stay left on the Pomperaug Trail. It dips to a moist bottom with sweet pepperbush, then ascends. Outcrops and boulders riddle the woods, and mountain laurels add seasonal flourish. From the outcrop of Hulls Hill, find a framed view east.

Descend along a mica-sparkling outcrop and through woods to meet the southern end of the Crest Trail. To add the hike's second loop, continue south on the blue Pomperaug Trail. A steep 0.25-mile descent leads to the Lake Zoar shore, where the trail follows the shoreline south. Dogwood (showy in spring, dashing in autumn red), hemlock, maple, birch, and upper-canopy oak frame passage. Clearings extend lake views, but poison ivy suggests hesitation. Round a small cove to cross a brook and contour 30 feet above shore.

Kettletown Brook,
Kettletown State Park,
Connecticut

A steep pitch then leads to the crossing of Jackson Brook and your arrival at the boat launch at Jackson Cove Recreation Area. Cross the gravel parking lot, resuming the trail at the southeast corner. Reach the Oxford Loop junction at Cedar Mill Brook. Keep to the Pomperaug Trail as it heads left. This saves the shoreline passage on the blue/white Oxford Loop Trail for your return.

The Pomperaug Trail passes through hemlock and charges uphill along Cedar Mill Brook, where an 8-foot rock face disrupts the stream, seasonally hosting a waterfall. The trail's rocky high point offers a seasonal view, and you may notice garnets peppering the rock. Cross Wells Brook and pass a charcoal hearth site before meeting the blue/white Oxford Loop Trail.

Although the blue Pomperaug Trail continues south, for this hike you turn right, following blue/white blazes back to the park core. Switchbacks descend the slope, and

Pomperaug Trail, Kettletown State Park, Connecticut

you may glimpse an old millrace that washed logs down to the lake/river for milling. Cross back over cascading Wells Brook and trace a lower contour, preferred by dogwoods. Lake impressions reward as the trail nudges toward shore. Sycamores and maples crowd the drainage where the loop closes.

Retrace the Pomperaug Trail back north to its southern junction with the Crest Trail. There, continue north with the blue/white blazes of the Crest Trail for new perspectives. You mount a rocky knoll for a limited seasonal view and descend among hemlocks. With a brief steep climb, you top the ridge above Lake Zoar. A short spur leads to a restricted lake view. Better views can be had where the trail returns to the western edge.

Descend a hemlock slope, crossing over a stone wall to a four-way trail junction with the blue/orange and blue/red trails. Here the Crest Trail continues forward to reach the Pomperaug Trail at the initial loop junction. Left on the blue/orange trail leads to the campground, and right on the blue/red trail offers an alternative return to the Pomperaug Trail.

On the Crest Trail you skirt the campground and travel wooded slope to close the loop with the Pomperaug Trail. There turn north (left) to cross the park road and backtrack the blue/yellow trail along Kettletown Brook to return to the trailhead.

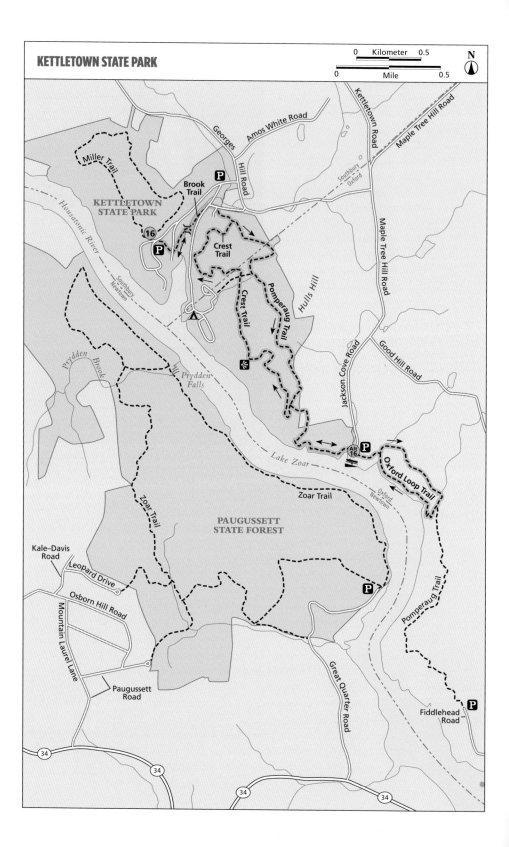

Kilometer 0 0.5

Mile 0 0.5

N

Georges

Amos White Road

Kettletown Road

Maple Tree Hill Road

Miller Trail

Hill Road

Southbury Oxford

P

Brook Trail

KETTLETOWN STATE PARK

16

P

Crest Trail

Maple Tree Hill Road

Housatonic River

Southbury Newtown

Crest Trail

Pomperaug Trail

Hulls Hill

Jackson Cove Road

Good Hill Road

Prydden Brook

Prydden Falls

Lake Zoar

Alt 16

P

Oxford Loop Trail

Zoar Trail

Oxford Newtown

Zoar Trail

PAUGUSSETT STATE FOREST

Kale–Davis Road

Leopard Drive

P

Osborn Hill Road

Pomperaug Trail

Mountain Laurel Lane

Paugussett Road

Great Quarter Road

P

Fiddlehead Road

34

34

34

34

MILES AND DIRECTIONS

0.0 Start at trailhead parking for the William Miller Trail. Follow the blue/yellow trail downslope to the park beach area and hike upstream. *Option:* You may choose to start (or end) this hike with the vistas on the William Miller Trail. Hike the Miller Trail clockwise 0.25 mile to the blue/orange spur that leads to two overlooks. Then backtrack to the trailhead (0.8 mile) or hike the full loop (2 miles).

0.3 Cross the footbridge over Kettletown Brook and continue on the blue/yellow Brook Trail.

0.5 Cross the park's campground road and follow the blue Pomperaug Trail south.

0.6 Reach the northern Pomperaug/Crest trail junction (the first loop junction). Follow the blue Pomperaug Trail south.

1.1 Reach the blue/red trail. Continue south on the blue Pomperaug Trail.

1.9 Reach the southern Pomperaug/Crest trail junction. Follow the blue Pomperaug Trail south.

2.5 Reach the Jackson Cove Recreation Area boat launch. Cross the gravel lot to resume southbound on the Pomperaug Trail.

2.6 Reach the northern Oxford Loop Trail junction. Bear left uphill along Cedar Mill Brook for the Pomperaug Trail.

3.3 Reach the southern Oxford Loop Trail junction. Turn right on the blue/white Oxford Loop Trail. *Note:* The blue Pomperaug Trail continues south, gathering Lake Zoar views in 0.9 mile and reaching Fiddlehead Road in 1.5 miles.

3.5 Cross Wells Brook.

3.9 Reach the northern Oxford Loop Trail junction. Retrace the blue Pomperaug Trail north.

4.6 Reach the southern Pomperaug/Crest trail junction. Follow the blue/white Crest Trail north.

5.1 Reach a vista.

5.6 Reach a four-way trail junction. Hike forward on the blue/white Crest Trail to return to the initial loop junction with the Pomperaug Trail. *Note:* Left on the blue/orange trail leads to the park campground; right on the blue/red trail offers an alternative return to the Pomperaug Trail.

6.3 Close the loop and turn left on the Pomperaug Trail to backtrack to the trailhead.

6.4 Cross the park road and backtrack the blue/yellow Brook Trail along Kettletown Brook.

6.9 Arrive back at the trailhead.

HIKE INFORMATION

LOCAL INFORMATION

Western Connecticut Convention and Visitors Bureau, PO Box 968, Litchfield 06759; (860) 567–4506; http://litchfieldhills.com.

LOCAL EVENTS/ATTRACTIONS

Audubon Center at Bent of the River, 185 East Flat Hill Rd., Southbury 06488; (203) 264-5098; http://bentoftheriver.audubon.org. In the village of South Britain (north off I-84, exit 14), the 660-acre Audubon Center at Bent of the River offers an environmental education center, 15 miles of trail, 2 miles of Pomperaug River frontage, and wetland, forest, field, and edge habitats, supporting 175 bird species. Grounds are open year-round, sunrise to sunset, for hiking, nature study, cross-country skiing, and snowshoeing. No pets. Audubon membership or admission fee is required.

ACCOMMODATIONS

Kettletown State Park, 1400 Georges Hill Rd., Southbury 06488; (203) 264-5678, May through Sept (call Putnam Memorial State Park, 203-938-2285, Oct through Apr); www.ct.gov/deep. This park has 56 family campsites, with camping open Memorial Day weekend through Labor Day weekend. Reservations are through ReserveAmerica, (877) 668-2267 or www.reserveamerica.com.

ORGANIZATIONS

Connecticut Forest and Park Association (CFPA), 16 Meriden Rd., Rockfall 06481; (860) 346-8733; www.ctwoodlands.org.

17 ZOAR TRAIL

On the west shore of Lake Zoar in Lower Paugussett State Forest, this blue-blazed loop celebrates lake, woods, and rolling terrain and offers a side trip to a waterfall. The Department of Environmental Protection has designated the first 2.4 miles as "scenic trail." A portion of the trail within that designation is subject to a seasonal wildlife closure for nesting raptors. The regal fliers have deemed this area suitably wild for occupation.

Start: Great Quarter Road trailhead
Distance: 7.1-mile loop (5.9-mile loop when seasonal trail closure is in effect)
Hiking time: 4 to 6 hours
Difficulty: Moderate
Elevation change: 500 feet
Trail surface: Earthen path and woods road
Best seasons: Spring through fall
Other trail users: Hunters, anglers, cross-country skiers, snowshoers
Canine compatibility: Leashed dogs permitted
Land status: State forest
Nearest town: Newtown, CT, with gas available along US 6
Fees and permits: None

Schedule: Year-round, sunrise to sunset
Maps: State forest map (available online at www.ct.gov/deep); Connecticut Forest and Park Association (CFPA) *Connecticut Walk Book, West* (available from CFPA, www.ctwoodlands.org)
Trail contact: Department of Energy and Environmental Protection, State Forests, (860) 424-3200; www.ct .gov/deep
Special considerations: Respect seasonal trail closure for wildlife. During hunting season, avoid hiking here or take necessary precautions, including wearing bright orange clothing.

FINDING THE TRAILHEAD

From I-84, take exit 11 and follow signs to CT 34. Turn east on CT 34, heading toward Monroe, Derby, and New Haven, for 4.9 miles. Turn left on Great Quarter Road and follow it northeast 1.3 miles to where it ends at a turnaround and parking area. Westbound CT 34 travelers find Great Quarter Road 0.2 mile west of the CT 34–CT 111 junction in Stevenson; turn right. Trailhead GPS: N41 24.147' / W73 11.247'

THE HIKE

From the rock barrier, follow blazes north through the shoreline hemlock-hardwood forest. Later, a steep treed slope often stands between you and sparkling Lake Zoar. Maple-leaf viburnum, fern, and sassafras decorate the understory.

After ascending and traveling the lakeside slope, the trail dips back toward the water. Tulip poplars appear, and cross-lake views find Jackson Cove Recreation Area. You also gather north–south views of this long lake impoundment on the Housatonic River.

The trail rolls along, tracing a route to what once was the settlement of Zoar before following a recessed woods road to the water's edge. Rising lake waters from the dam's completion in 1919 created several roads to nowhere. The trail grows rockier as it vacillates between 10 and 100 feet above shore. A bouldery lake slope offers cross-lake views of the steep, treed eastern rim and a plunging outcrop, a union especially pretty in autumn finery.

When next near the water, find a thin sandy beach with stump seating. Maple, oak, and ash line the shore. The trail then ascends, placing a low rise between you and the lake. After crossing a drainage, the trail bears left and before long Prydden Falls sounds below the trail.

To see the falls, delay crossing Prydden Brook and instead bear right on the side trail, following the brook downstream to a viewing spot. The falls consists of cliff and rock jumbles adorned with white streamers and weeping moss. This side path also accesses shore. Return upstream and make the crossing.

The trail continues uphill on an old road grade to a junction. The primary loop travels the footpath to the right from August 15 to April 15. Otherwise, remain on the woods road (blazed blue/white).

The blue loop traverses a hemlock-hardwood plateau to round the slope above shore. A gradual descent leads to a junction, just beyond a jut overlooking the lake. This is the end of the "scenic trail" section. Here, the Zoar Trail turns left. Avoid the path ahead that leads to private land.

The blue trail steeply sidewinds and angles upslope, topping the ridge. Passage continues in a choked hemlock stand and leafy woods. Follow the blazes. You round below a rocky knoll, keeping the knoll to your left, then veer right, descending among hemlocks to merge with the woods road of the blue/white bypass. The remainder of the hike is common to both loops.

Follow the woods road southbound on a beautiful passage framed by tulip poplar, maple, beech, oak, and birch, with mountain laurel, sweet pepperbush, and witch hazel. Shortly afterward, look for the blue blazes of the Zoar Trail to turn left off the woods road. Be alert for this turn.

Cross Prydden Brook and ascend. The hike rolls from outcrop knoll to outcrop knoll. Deer, woodpeckers, and hawks are possible sightings. From atop the rocks, Lake Zoar becomes but a distant gleam; the focus is woodland. Rock tripe and green lichen adorn the rocks, as do flecks of mica, seams of quartz, and garnet nodes. Stay with the blue blazes.

The trail descends by rolls and contours. In a wooded bottom you reach the first of two back-to-back junctions with blazed side trails. Keep to the blue Zoar Trail. Find one last ascent of a rocky rise before descending via a rock-reinforced woods road and leafy footpath. A flat outcrop extends looks across the immediate forest. Where a blue/yellow-blazed sunken grade descends to Great Quarter Road, skirting private property, take the blue Zoar Trail to the left.

This section of trail rolls through forest, passing fractured and boxy granite outcrops and crossing drainages before swinging below a picturesque rock-capped bump to reach the trailhead.

MILES AND DIRECTIONS

0.0 Start at the Great Quarter Road trailhead. Hike the blue-blazed route north along shore.

0.9 Reach a lake viewpoint.

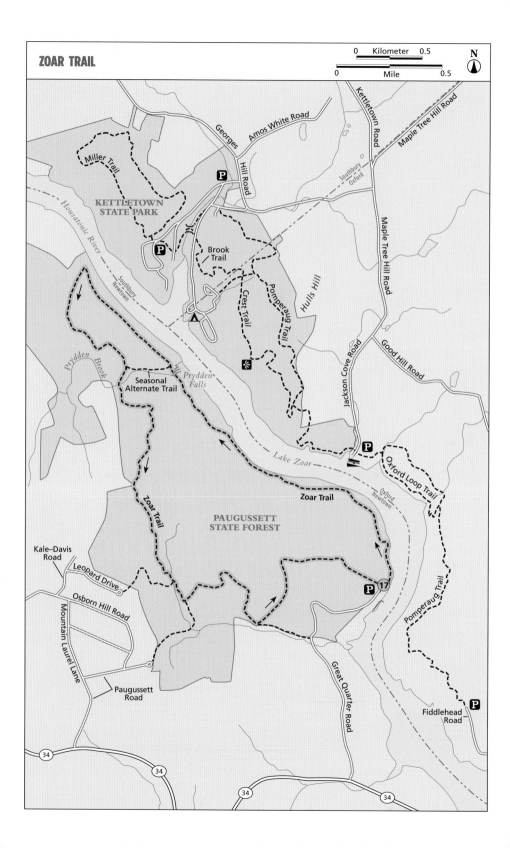

ZOAR TRAIL

0   Kilometer   0.5

0   Mile   0.5

N

Miller Trail

KETTLETOWN STATE PARK

Georges Hill Road

Amos White Road

Kettletown Road

Maple Tree Hill Road

Southbury Oxford

Housatonic River

Southbury Newtown

Brook Trail

Crest Trail

Pomperaug Trail

Hulls Hill

Maple Tree Hill Road

Prydden Brook

Seasonal Alternate Trail

Prydden Falls

Jackson Cove Road

Good Hill Road

Lake Zoar

Zoar Trail

Oxford Newtown

Oxford Loop Trail

PAUGUSSETT STATE FOREST

Zoar Trail

Kale–Davis Road

Leopard Drive

Osborn Hill Road

Mountain Laurel Lane

Paugussett Road

17

Pomperaug Trail

Great Quarter Road

Fiddlehead Road

34

34

34

34

1.2 Reach a thin beach.

1.6 Reach Prydden Brook and the falls detour. Detour right (downstream) to the waterfall viewing and shore before resuming the counterclockwise loop. *Option:* The waterfall area offers a satisfying out-and-back 3.5-mile day hike.

1.9 Reach a trail junction. Remain northbound on the blue Zoar Trail. *Note:* The seasonal-closure blue/white bypass trail heads left. Take it April 15 through August 15. It follows the woods road uphill for 0.3 mile, passing parallel to and overlooking the Prydden Brook drainage. On this truncated loop, you'd pick up the description at mile 3.6 and subtract 1.2 miles from the recorded distances.

2.6 Reach the end of the "scenic trail" section on the Zoar Trail. Turn left. *Note:* Avoid the path ahead, as it is on private land.

3.6 Reach the blue/white bypass trail junction. Continue southward on the blue trail.

3.8 Cross Prydden Brook.

5.2 Reach a trail junction with the blue/red access trail to Leopard Drive. Continue forward on the Zoar Trail.

5.4 Reach a trail junction with the blue/yellow access trail to Paugussett Road. Continue forward on the Zoar Trail.

6.2 Reach a trail junction above Great Quarter Road. Head left on the blue Zoar Trail. *Note:* The blue/yellow sunken grade ahead edges private land to reach Great Quarter Road in 0.1 mile.

7.1 Arrive back at the trailhead.

HIKE INFORMATION

LOCAL INFORMATION

Western Connecticut Convention and Visitors Bureau, PO Box 968, Litchfield 06759; (860) 567-4506; www.visitfairfieldcountyct.com.

LOCAL EVENTS/ATTRACTIONS

Derby Historical Society/David Humphreys House, 37 Elm St., Ansonia 06401; (203) 735-1908; www.derbyhistorical.org. The General David Humphreys House was both the town minister's house and the general's ancestral home. It was so named to honor the general's distinguished career as a Revolutionary War officer, diplomat, poet, and industry leader. For house tours, call for appointment.

Kellogg Environmental Center/Osborne Homestead Museum, 500 Hawthorne Ave., Derby 06418; (203) 734-2513; www.ct.gov/deep. In Osbornedale State Park, the Kellogg Environmental Center offers environmental education through workshops, hands-on activities, lectures, and exhibits and houses the collections of conservationist Frances Osborne Kellogg. The adjacent Osborne Homestead Museum, on the National Register of Historic Places, honors the life legacy of Mrs. Kellogg and holds contents of the original estate. Guided tours introduce her conservation and business accomplishments, dairy farm, and ceramic collection. The grounds, a Connecticut historical garden, encompass formal gardens, a rose garden, and ornamental shrubs and flowering trees.

Zoar Trail, Paugussett State Forest, Connecticut

ACCOMMODATIONS

Kettletown State Park, 1400 Georges Hill Rd., Southbury 06488; (203) 264-5678, May through Sept (call Putnam Memorial State Park, 203-938-2285, Oct through Apr); www.ct.gov/deep. Kettletown State Park, on the east shore of Lake Zoar, has 56 family campsites, with camping open Memorial Day weekend through Labor Day weekend. Reservations are available through ReserveAmerica, (877) 668-2267 or www.reserve america.com.

ORGANIZATIONS

Connecticut Forest and Park Association (CFPA), 16 Meriden Rd., Rockfall 06481; (860) 346-8733; www.ctwoodlands.org.

18 FARMINGTON CANAL HERITAGE TRAIL, CHESHIRE TO NEW HAVEN

This canal trail unites a story of early industry and transportation with an unfolding tale of natural beauty. Woods and swamps and the critters of each complement travel on this wide, paved linear route. Historic locks, remnant aqueducts, and a lockkeeper's house harken to the bygone era. Interpretive signs bring the past to life. The trail is ideal for shared family outings, sports training, and pure enjoyment.

Start: Cornwall Avenue in Cheshire (the northern terminus for this segment)
Distance: 6.6 miles one way
Hiking time: 3.5 to 4.5 hours
Difficulty: Easy
Elevation change: Minimal, as it traces a onetime towpath
Trail surface: Paved towpath
Best seasons: Spring through fall
Other trail users: Cyclists, joggers, skaters, wheelchair users, cross-country skiers
Canine compatibility: Leashed dogs permitted, but heed all postings and clean up after your animal
Land status: State land and town management
Nearest towns: Cheshire and Hamden, CT
Fees and permits: None

Schedule: Year-round, sunrise to sunset
Map: Canal trail map (available online from the Farmington Canal Rail-to-Trail Association, fchtrail.org)
Trail contacts: Department of Energy and Environmental Protection, State Parks, (860) 424-3200; www.ct.gov/deep. The Farmington Canal Rail-to-Trail Association, 940 Whitney Ave., Hamden 06517; fchtrail.org.
Special considerations: Keep to the narrow travel aisle to avoid straying onto private lands or encountering poison ivy. Acquaint yourself with the rules, which can change as you pass between towns. Todd Street parking has a portable toilet; drinking fountains are at Locks 12 and 14.

FINDING THE TRAILHEAD

For the northern terminus, from the junction of CT 10, CT 68, and CT 70 in Cheshire, go south on CT 10 for 0.3 mile and turn west (right) onto Cornwall Avenue. The turn is south of the green. In 0.3 mile reach the rail trail, with trailhead parking on the left. A gateway sign spans the trail. Trailhead GPS: N41 29.901' / W72 54.863'

Additional trailheads are found at regular intervals. On CT 42, find trailhead parking 1 mile west of its intersection with CT 10. There is parking at Brooksvale Park off Mount Sanford Road and on Todd Street: From the junction of Mount Carmel Road and CT 10, go 0.2 mile north on CT 10 and turn west on Todd Street to find this parking on the right.

The selected southern terminus for this hike is on Sherman Avenue. From the junction of Mount Carmel Road and CT 10, go 0.5 mile south on CT 10 and turn west on Sherman Avenue to find trailhead parking on the left in 0.1 mile. Trailhead GPS: N41 24.750' / W72 54.337'

THE HIKE

In the early 1800s, when canals were the hallmark of transportation, the Farmington Canal facilitated travel and commerce between Northampton and New Haven. Irish immigrants shoveled out the canal, locks raised and lowered the flow for travel, and mules trod the towpath pulling flat-bottomed boats. Today the linear route serves recreationists, with walking, jogging, cycling, and sometimes skiing. It is also a viable greenway for wildlife.

Southbound, the wide lane begins under open cathedral but is soon tree-framed. Bench seats allow for nature study, reading, or tying a shoelace. Road crossings partition the restful lane, marking distance and offering convenient shuttle points. Occasional distance markers also help you track progress. The corridor is part of the East Coast Greenway that will link Maine to Florida.

Ditch, woods, and swampy bottomlands vary viewing. Oaks, hickories, maples, birches, sassafras, and a few small hemlocks shape the edge community. Hummingbirds visit the jewelweed and shrubs. Wild grape, phragmites, and ferns lend texture and shape. At bridge crossings you can glimpse some of the historic construction.

Frogs, turtles, raccoons, squirrels, a choir of birds, and deer can offer encounters. Lock 12 Historical Park suggests you deviate from the main corridor to view the canal construction and operation. Reportedly, the *Amistad* slaves were transported to trial on this

Lock 12 along Farmington Canal Heritage Trail, Lock 12 Historical Park, Farmington Canal Greenway, Cheshire, Connecticut

Forest along Farmington Canal Heritage Trail, Lock 12 Historical Park, Farmington Canal Greenway, Cheshire, Connecticut

canal. A lovely swamp-footed woods then leads to the crossing of South Brooksvale Road. At times the canal still carries water.

At Mount Sanford Road, you pass beneath another gateway arch. It signals THE NEW HAVEN AND NORTH HAMPTON RAILROAD–THE CANAL LINE and your passage from Cheshire into Hamden. Interpretive signs dot this stretch. Historic advertisements, toll rates, and news items help piece together the story and romance of the canal. At 56 miles in length, the Farmington Canal was the longest canal built in New England. Twenty-eight locks, 135 bridges, 12 culverts, and a 280-foot aqueduct were among its ambitious construction.

Soon after entering Hamden, a paved spur heads right to Brooksvale Park. The park lies but a short distance, a bridge, and a couple of crosswalks away. This lawn-and-trees-and-trails community park was given to Hamden back in the late 1800s for use as a poor farm. Adjacent to the open space are the old barn and farmhouse and a small petting zoo. As the canal trail continues south, an earthen trail traces the levee on the other side of the ditch. The two later join.

Nearby residences and a utility-line corridor are hiccups in the natural corridor. A couple of big sycamores may draw attention. The Jebb Brook Nature Trail branches to the right.

After the Shepard Avenue crossing, the canal trail passes parallel and closer to CT 10. The Lock 14 Lockkeeper's House sits trailside. A drinking fountain and bike racks can be found at this charming pale-yellow cottage. Lockhouses doubled as waysides for canal travelers.

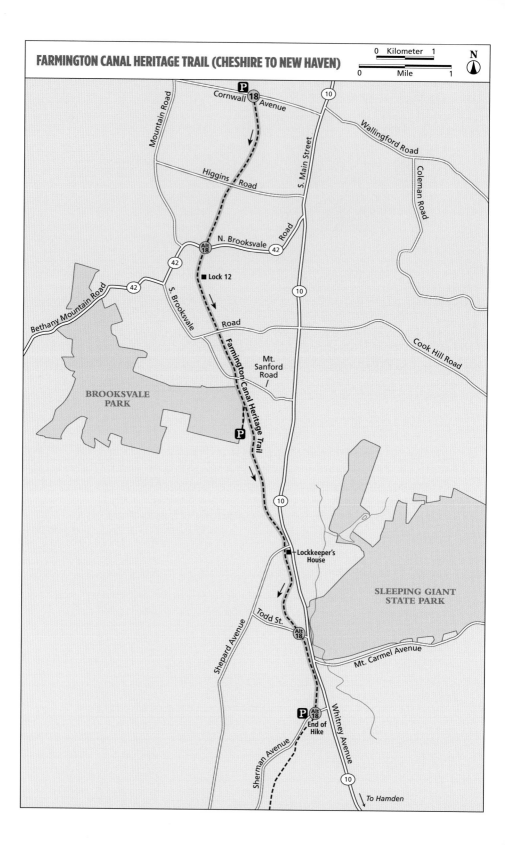

0   Kilometer   1

0   Mile   1

N

Mountain Road

P 18 Cornwall Avenue

10

Wallingford Road

Higgins Road

S. Main Street

Coleman Road

Alt 18 N. Brooksvale Road 42

42

42

Bethany Mountain Road

S. Brooksvale

■ Lock 12

10

BROOKSVALE PARK

Road

Mt. Sanford Road

Cook Hill Road

Farmington Canal Heritage Trail

P

10

■ Lockkeeper's House

SLEEPING GIANT STATE PARK

Shepard Avenue

Todd St.

Alt 18

Mt. Carmel Avenue

P Alt 18 End of Hike

Whitney Avenue

Sherman Avenue

10

To Hamden

Ahead, CT 10 businesses take this trail from natural to urban, but you can detour for a pizza slice or a gelato. Across CT 10 looms Sleeping Giant. Viburnum now favors the disturbed habitat, and side trails once again pass along and below the canal path.

Continue south, crossing Todd Street. The canal trail remains squeezed by life and business but still enjoys an attractive treed edge. It then swings out to CT 10, briefly following a sidewalk to the crosswalk at Westwoods Road. You cross, follow below a green embankment, and pass between rock cliffs. Where the trail approaches Sherman Avenue, you are traveling within the cut banks of the actual canal. Cross under Sherman Avenue and emerge at its parking lot.

MILES AND DIRECTIONS

0.0 Start at the Cornwall Avenue trailhead in Cheshire. Hike south through the gateway on paved canal trail.

1.8 Cross North Brooksvale Road.

2.1 Reach Lock 12. Continue south on the trail.

2.6 Cross Mount Sanford Road.

2.9 Reach the side spur to Brooksvale Park; the spur heads right. Keep to the canal trail.

4.2 Reach the Jebb Brook Nature Trail. It descends west from the canal trail.

4.7 Reach the Lock 14 Lockkeeper's House.

5.5 Reach Todd Street parking. Continue south.

6.6 End at Sherman Avenue parking.

HIKE INFORMATION

LOCAL INFORMATION
Central Regional Tourism District, 1 Constitution Plaza, 2nd Floor, Hartford 06103; (860) 787-9640; www.centerofct.com.

LOCAL EVENTS/ATTRACTIONS
Hubbard Park, City of Meriden; (203) 630-4259; www.meridenct.gov/city-services. Atop East Peak (elevation 976 feet), in Meriden's Hubbard Park, Castle Craig Tower lifts visitors an additional 32 feet skyward for views from the glisten of Long Island Sound to the profile of Sleeping Giant to the Berkshires of southern Massachusetts. The stone observation tower, constructed by local masons of native traprock, was dedicated in 1900. The medieval-looking tower and the 1,800-acre park that surrounds it were gifts to the people by local philanthropist businessman Walter Hubbard.

ORGANIZATIONS
The Farmington Canal Rail-to-Trail Association, 940 Whitney Ave., Hamden 06517; fchtrail.org.

19 SLEEPING GIANT STATE PARK, TOWER HIKE

At this state park, trails travel the anatomy of one of south-central Connecticut's most prominent landmarks—Sleeping Giant. Rising 700 feet and sprawling over 2 miles, the Giant serves up grand panoramas. In 1977 the entire trail system won national recreation trail distinction. Color-coded blazes identify the six east–west trails, while red geometric shapes point out the five north–south routes. Together, they suggest multiple hiking loops. This hike combines the most-walked path, the closed road to the tower, with the more demanding Blue (Quinnipiac) Trail.

Start: Park picnic area
Distance: 3.6-mile loop
Hiking time: 2.5 to 3.5 hours
Difficulty: Strenuous. Although the Tower Path is a roadway walk, the Blue Trail is strenuous, with segments of challenging descent.
Elevation change: 650 feet
Trail surface: Earthen path, woods road, outcrop/ledge
Best seasons: Spring through fall
Other trail users: Anglers, snowshoers, cross-country skiers
Canine compatibility: Leashed dogs permitted on trails and in picnic area
Land status: State park
Nearest town: Hamden, CT, with gas and services along CT 10
Fees and permits: Seasonal weekend/holiday park entrance fees for nonresidents
Schedule: Year-round, 8 a.m. to sunset
Maps: State park map (available on-site or online at www.ct.gov/

deep); Connecticut Forest and Park Association (CFPA) *Connecticut Walk Book, West* (available from CFPA www.ctwoodlands.org)
Trail contacts: Sleeping Giant State Park, 200 Mount Carmel Ave., Hamden 06518; (203) 287-5658. Department of Energy and Environmental Protection, State Parks, (860) 424-3200; www.ct.gov/deep.
Special considerations: Be attentive along rocky ledges, keeping a special eye on youngsters and pets. Expect steep grades, rocky terrain, and sections requiring hand assists. Icy conditions make ledges and cliffs too treacherous for travel. An EF-1 tornado on May 15, 2018, hit the developed trailhead area hard as well as some pockets, while lightly touching or sparing the rest of the woods.

FINDING THE TRAILHEAD

From the junction of CT 10, CT 68, and CT 70 in Cheshire, go south on CT 10 for 5.3 miles and turn left (east) on Mount Carmel Avenue. Reach the park entrance on the left in 0.3 mile. Trailhead GPS: N41 25.297' / W72 53.960'

THE HIKE

This loop combines two of the park's most popular—although leagues apart in difficulty—trails. Stay on the Tower Path for an "easy" round-trip. The Blue Trail is part of the long-distance Quinnipiac Trail, the first blue trail put on the ground. Connecticut

Summit tower, Sleeping Giant State Park, Connecticut

blues now cover more than 825 miles of countryside, and the system continues to grow. The park's stone observation tower dishes up vistas of Long Island Sound, West Rock Ridge, and the northern traprock ridges.

From the east side of picnic parking, take the wide, gravel Tower Path marked FOR PEDESTRIANS ONLY. The picnic area was heavily scoured of its trees and there was removal of hazardous trees along the Tower Path road. Elsewhere, maple, oak, hemlock, birch, beech, and dogwood weave a canopy of texture and shade above a vibrant midstory laced with mountain laurel. Chestnut oaks prefer the sunnier reaches.

At the many junctions, you will keep to the gravel tower road as it switchbacks ever higher, making a steady climb. Before a mile has gone by, you will glimpse the cliff and boulder rubble that shapes the Sleeping Giant's chin. Ahead, a monument honors a leader in preserving the park. You then cross to the other side of the mountain, which shows more boulders. Near the initial intersection with the Blue Trail, the road briefly flattens.

Where you cross the Blue Trail a second time, you top Mount Carmel, which anatomically is the Giant's left hip. It holds the attractive four-story stone tower with arched observation windows at each of its levels. Interior ramps ascend the tower. Its elevated vistas applaud the surrounding landscape: forest, storm and remedy scarring, rounded ridges, and basalt features and sweep the New Haven skyline to Long Island Sound.

You may now backtrack the Tower Path or return west, descending via the more rugged Blue Trail. Look for the first blaze of the return Blue Trail at the southwest corner of the tower. Avoid following the blue blazes that head northeast.

You travel a rocky terrain, passing through similar woods with a few azaleas in the mix. Upon crossing the Tower Path, the Blue Trail sharply ascends to and then steeply pitches from the Giant's waist. Continue to track the blue blazes. You again cross the Tower

> The building of stone towers is an architectural legacy that traces back to early civilizations. Whether a statement of pride, aspiration, affluence, or commemoration or just simply the need to see over the trees, these stately structures claim the heights of southern New England.

Path for a calmer tour along the north side of the Giant's chest, only to charge up the rocky back side of the Giant's chin, which from other vantages presents a conspicuous cliff profile.

Where the trail levels, you are treated to views. After a steep 20-foot rock descent (requiring hands and caution), a short spur leads you to an overlook of the dizzying vertical cliffs that shape the chin. Views from this perch span to the Giant's chest.

Afterward, you encounter a grueling descent through low-stature forest and over canted rock faces to skirt an abandoned quarry that provided stone for Tower Road. Road noises from CT 10 and Mount Carmel Avenue echo up the elbow, as hemlocks fill out the forest. The trail then bottoms out at the quarry. At the base of the hill, the Blue Trail follows Mill River downstream, but turns left before reaching CT 10. You close the loop at the picnic area.

MILES AND DIRECTIONS

0.0 Start at the picnic area trailhead. Follow the gated tower road (the Tower Path), ascending the Sleeping Giant.

0.8 View the Giant's chin.

1.0 Meet the Blue Trail. Keep to the Tower Path.

1.6 Reach Mount Carmel and the stone tower. Follow the Blue Trail away from the southwest corner of the tower. **Option:** For an easier 3.2-mile out-and-back, descend the Tower Path.

2.2 Cross the Tower Path.

2.5 Take in the view from the chin.

3.1 Pass a quarry.

3.6 Complete the loop back at the picnic area.

HIKE INFORMATION

LOCAL INFORMATION
Central Regional Tourism District, 1 Constitution Plaza, 2nd Floor, Hartford 06103; (860) 787-9640; www.centerofct.com.

LOCAL EVENTS/ATTRACTIONS
Quinnipiac University, 275 Mount Carmel Ave., Hamden 06518; (203) 582-8200; www.qu.edu. Across Mount Carmel Avenue from the park is the 212-acre Mount Carmel Campus of Quinnipiac University, a private university known for its election-year polling. Its attractive grounds bring together modern brick buildings, a pine grove, brick walkways, and a central clock tower.

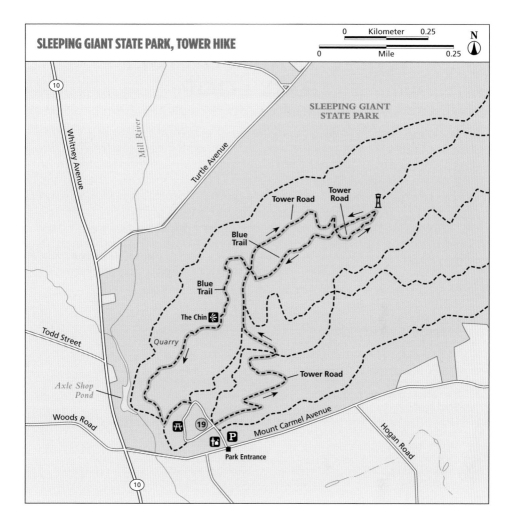

Wharton Brook State Park, east of Sleeping Giant on US 5, south of the I-91 off-ramp, is a recognized Trout Park, which receives regular weekly stocking from the state fish hatcheries. It is one of 11 such sites around the state and a good place for first fishing expeditions. This welcoming wayside park was a forerunner of the modern-day rest area. Its pond is open for fishing and swimming. Weekend and holiday fees apply for nonresidents. Contact Wharton Brook State Park c/o Sleeping Giant State Park.

ORGANIZATIONS
Sleeping Giant Park Association, www.sgpa.org.

20

SLEEPING GIANT STATE PARK, WHITE TRAIL TO VIOLET TRAIL LOOP

This hiking loop allows you to tickle the armpits of south-central Connecticut's Sleeping Giant, which stretches 2 miles long from crown to toe and heaves its chest 700 feet skyward. It is representative of the park's award-winning trail system. The loop encircles the Giant's form, traveling through mixed hardwood forest and picturesque groves of mountain laurel, the state flower. It also tops rocky outcrops for surveys of the neighborhood. Its violet and white trails are east–west trending. Red geometric trails run north–south, intersecting the loop.

Start: Park picnic area
Distance: 6-mile loop
Hiking time: 4 to 5 hours
Difficulty: Strenuous. Although the Violet Trail is relatively easy, the White Trail throws a challenging course at you.
Elevation change: 650 feet
Trail surface: Earthen path, woods road, outcrop/ledge
Best seasons: Spring through fall
Other trail users: Anglers, snowshoers, cross-country skiers
Canine compatibility: Leashed dogs permitted on trails and in picnic area
Land status: State park
Nearest town: Hamden, CT, with gas and services available along CT 10
Fees and permits: Seasonal weekend/holiday park entrance fees for nonresidents
Schedule: Year-round, 8 a.m. to sunset

Maps: State park map (available on-site or online at www.ct.gov/deep); Connecticut Forest and Park Association (CFPA) *Connecticut Walk Book, West* (available from CFPA, www.ctwoodlands.org)
Trail contacts: Sleeping Giant State Park, 200 Mount Carmel Ave., Hamden 06518; (203) 287-5658. Department of Energy and Environmental Protection, State Parks, (860) 424-3200; www.ct.gov/deep.
Special considerations: Be attentive along rocky ledges, keeping a special eye on youngsters and pets. Expect steep grades, rocky terrain, and sections requiring hand assists. Icy conditions make ledges and cliffs too treacherous for travel. An EF-1 Tornado on May 15, 2018, cleared some pine-wooded sections but most of the park was spared.

FINDING THE TRAILHEAD

From the junction of CT 10, CT 68, and CT 70 in Cheshire, go south on CT 10 for 5.3 miles and turn left (east) on Mount Carmel Avenue. Reach the park entrance on the left in 0.3 mile. Trailhead GPS: N41 25.353' / W72 54.041'

THE HIKE

For this counterclockwise hike, you begin by following the more difficult White Trail, returning along the more comfortable path of the Violet Trail. Dramatic cliffs and bald

Violet Trail, Sleeping Giant
State Park, Connecticut

outcrops shape the Sleeping Giant's anatomy. Decorating his bed are June-flowering mountain laurels. Birdsong brings cheer.

You'll find the White Trail heading north from the upper end of the picnic area loop. This trail crosses a footbridge and ascends to contour the slope. Maple, beech, American basswood, oak, and hickory frame its course. You pass below a talus slope, soon ascending the rocky base. Overhead loom dramatic reddish-brown cliffs, crags, and overhangs, partially veiled by leaves.

The White Trail crosses over the wide Tower Path to resume its twisting ascent, advancing via rock stairs and passing showy displays of mountain laurel. It then contours below the fissured cliff and breakaway blocks of the Giant's chest before topping the heaving rise. Chestnut oaks and shrubs vegetate the rises. You'll find an open view of the chin and a ledge that overlooks the campus of Quinnipiac University, before descending to contour the wooded slope.

Once across the Orange Trail, the descent steepens. Ahead, the trail contours the talus base of the right hip. Ledges provide toeholds for the scramble to the top of the hip, where you gain more views of the south-central Connecticut neighborhood.

Resume the rigorous workout, migrating down the Giant's anatomy. Cross the Red Circle Trail to ascend a rocky slope and top the right knee. You again cross the Orange Trail for a rolling passage to Hezekiah's Knob. A descent follows. You skirt an outcrop of pillow basalt and then descend the Giant's right foot.

You'll pass the Green and Yellow Trails before you reach the kiosk at the park's limited access on Chestnut Lane. In the vicinity of the kiosk, seven blazed trails radiate outward—a hiker smorgasbord of trail options and possible returns. For this hike, follow the violet blazes, returning along the left side of the Giant.

By contrast, the Violet Trail offers a sleepy woods walk. Large oaks and tulip poplars punctuate the forest. The orange-and-green blooms of the tulip tree typically go unseen in the lofty canopy, but the fallen petals may draw notice as they dot the leaf mat. Low rock walls and logs contribute to woods views. Stepping stones may keep feet dry at muddy sites. Hemlocks join the mix as hikers approach the rocky ridge of the Giant's left hand, which is showered in mountain laurel.

With a rocky descent, you hike below a similar ridge feature. You then cross the Red Circle Trail for easier undulating travel, once more in mature forest. You'll also likely hear the first drone from CT 10. Until this time the hike has been remarkably insulated. Twisted trunks characterize the mountain laurel. You next cross the Red Hexagonal Trail.

Continuing the geometric roundup, you cross the Red Diamond Trail near the abandoned quarry. View the red-rock cliff and scar to the left. A concrete shell is to the right. The trail next descends steeply along a rock wall and a second ruin, where an eroding staircase advances travel. Arches mark some of the standing walls, as poison ivy and Virginia creeper reclaim the ruins.

Follow the gravel lane away from the ruins to reach a foot trail. It contours and descends above the pond impoundment on Mill River. Cross the end of the breached dam and pursue the river downstream. The Red Diamond and Blue Trails briefly merge and depart. Now turn left, away from the river, to enter the west side of the picnic area, closing the loop.

SLEEPING GIANT STATE PARK, WHITE TRAIL TO VIOLET TRAIL LOOP

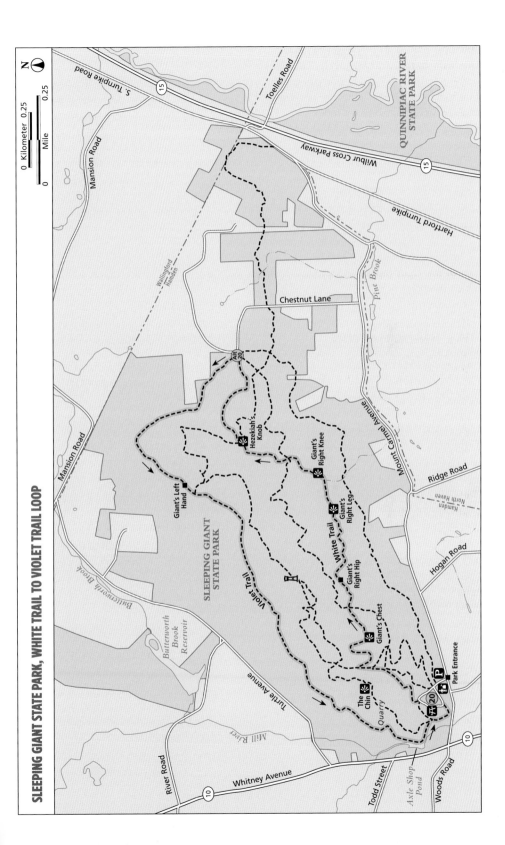

MILES AND DIRECTIONS

0.0 Start at the picnic area trailhead. Follow the White Trail from the northern (uppermost) part of the picnic area loop.

0.3 Cross over the Tower Path (a closed road).

0.6 Top the Giant's chest.

1.1 Top the right hip.

1.7 Top the right knee.

2.3 Reach Hezekiah's Knob.

2.9 Reach the trail kiosk near Chestnut Lane. Follow the Violet Trail to complete the counterclockwise loop.

3.9 Reach the rocky ridge of the Giant's left hand.

4.2 Cross the Red Circle Trail.

5.5 Cross the Red Diamond Trail near the quarry.

6.0 Close the loop at the picnic area.

HIKE INFORMATION

LOCAL INFORMATION
Central Regional Tourism District, 1 Constitution Plaza, 2nd Floor, Hartford 06103; (860) 787-9640; www.centerofct.com.

LOCAL EVENTS/ATTRACTIONS
Connecticut Vineyard and Winery Association, 433 South Main St., Suite 309, West Hartford 06110; (860) 216-6439; www.ctwine.com. Like many states across the nation, Connecticut boasts a blossoming wine industry. The Connecticut Wine Trail takes you through rolling countryside to visit two dozen wineries and vineyards, with tasting rooms for sampling the Connecticut-grown product. Several offer tours. Two of the wineries sit northeast of the park in Wallingford: **Gouveia Vineyards,** (203) 265-5526; www.gouveiavineyards.com, and **Paradise Hills Vineyard,** (203) 284-0123; www.paradisehillsvineyard.com. A Connecticut Wine Trail brochure is available.

ORGANIZATIONS
Sleeping Giant Park Association, www.sgpa.org.

21 MATTABESETT TRAIL: MILLERS POND TO COGINCHAUG CAVE; BLUFF HEAD

Casting a giant U-shaped hook through the central Connecticut countryside, the Mattabesett Trail is one of the signature long-distance trunk trails in the Connecticut blue trail system. It is also one of the Connecticut 400 Club trails, a life list of major trails in the state. Together with the Monadnock and Metacomet Trails, the Mattabesett completes the three Ms that make up the New England National Scenic Trail. The Mattabesett Trail stretches 50 miles in its entirety from the west shore of the Connecticut River on River Road in Middletown to the Metacomet Trail at US 5 (the Berlin Turnpike). This description spotlights two of its sections: Millers Pond to Coginchaug Cave and Bluff Head.

Start: Millers Pond or Bluff Head trailhead
Distance: Millers Pond to Coginchaug Cave: 9.4 miles out and back; Bluff Head: 1.4-mile loop
Hiking time: Millers Pond to Coginchaug Cave: 6 to 7 hours; Bluff Head: 1 to 2 hours
Difficulty: Millers Pond to Coginchaug Cave: strenuous; Bluff Head: moderate
Elevation change: Millers Pond to Coginchaug Cave is a rolling trail with 100 feet of elevation change and its high point at Bear Rock, 600 feet. Bluff Head has 400 feet of elevation change between the trailhead and Bluff Head (elevation 720 feet).
Trail surface: Earthen path, woods road, outcrop ledge
Best seasons: Spring through fall
Other trail users: Anglers, hunters, snowshoers, cross-country skiers
Canine compatibility: Leashed dogs permitted
Land status: State park and state forest
Nearest town: Durham or Middletown, CT
Fees and permits: None

Schedule: Year-round, sunrise to sunset
Maps: Millers Pond State Park map (available online at www.ct.gov/deep); Mattabesett Trail: Connecticut Forest and Park Association (CFPA) *Connecticut Walk Book, West* (available from CFPA, www.ctwoodlands.org)
Trail contacts: Millers Pond State Park, c/o Cockaponset State Forest, 18 Ranger Rd., Haddam 06438; (860) 345-8521. Department of Energy and Environmental Protection, State Parks, (860) 424-3200; www.ct.gov/deep
Special considerations: The Mattabesett Trail is open to foot travel only. Take necessary precautions during hunting season; learn the dates and either refrain from hiking or make yourself and your pet plainly visible. You can encounter soggy patches and stretches of difficult climb. Beware of weather conditions that can complicate travel—ice, wind, and rain—and adjust gear and hiking times accordingly. Come prepared for mosquitoes.

FINDING THE TRAILHEADS

For Millers Pond State Park Reserve, from CT 9 take exit 11 at Middletown and head west on CT 155. In 0.8 mile turn south onto Millbrook Road. Go 1.8 miles and bear left, staying on Millbrook Road for another 0.9 mile. Bear left on Foot Hills Road and in 1.2 miles turn right into the gravel parking lot. Trailhead GPS: N41 28.820' / W72 37.765'

The trailhead parking lot for Bluff Head sits west off CT 77, 4.4 miles north of its intersection with CT 80 in Guilford and 4.3 miles south of its junction with CT 17 in Durham. Trailhead GPS: N41 24.474' / W72 41.797'

THE HIKES

The Mattabesett Trail travels from the Connecticut River past reservoir lowlands, topping and traversing ledges, heights, and balds for vistas as it swings first south and then north. Tucked in between are woodland, bog, and brook. The chosen hikes illustrate the attraction.

MILLERS POND TO COGINCHAUG CAVE

You begin the hike by walking the wide access path toward Millers Pond, but then turn left on the white trail to merge with the Mattabesett Trail as it heads south along the east shore. The long, attractive, spring-fed pond is centerpiece to the minimally developed natural area. Its diverse woods and laurel shrubs dole out pond impressions; spurs offer better views.

At the grassy dam the Mattabesett Trail goes solo, hooking left to trace a higher line along shore. It then veers right, crossing the park's red trail to top the next height of ledges and fractured rock. As it descends and rolls, watch for blazes because paths web the area.

An out-of-character steep descent leads to a brook crossing and outcrop cliffs and boulders with chunky quartzite crystals and glassy mica squares. At the left side of the outcrop, you return to the ridgetop. A woods ramble follows.

Back-to-back brook crossings lead to the next rock challenge. Its ascent is via a leafy seam. Chestnut oaks, huckleberry, and pitch pines clad the heights. Outcrops shape pleasing openings for pause, but few extend views.

After a dip to a notch, you come to the Bear Rock Bypass. It heads left. Straight is Bear Rock and its western vantage of woods, fields, ridges, and notches, with migrating hawks a special treat in fall. To avoid a treacherous crevice descent on the main trail, retreat and follow the bypass.

A woodland ramble, low ridges, the crossing of Harvey Road, more rolling passage, and a brook/wet-bottomland crossing lead to Higganum Road. Cross, angling left to head south over a small brook. The trail then sashays upslope through sweet pepperbush and mountain laurel before settling on a line of travel. Bulky outcroppings, ledges, and changing forest vary impressions.

> The signature light-blue blaze of the Connecticut blue trails traces back to 1929. Reverend Edgar Laing Heermance, the first committee chair of the Connecticut Forest and Park Association, picked it from a rainbow of sample blazes because it had the best visibility when viewed under waning light.

Coginchaug Cave along Mattabesett Trail, Cockaponset State Forest, Connecticut

Watch for blazes to take the trail left in a mountain laurel tangle. You then ascend between outcrops to drier woods. Cross and follow a small brook downstream. Where its drainage becomes gorgelike, look for the trail to turn right. A rock cairn may cue this departure. Harsh light can make blaze-tracking a chore, and trail use is light here. The trail angles upslope, taking a switchback to reach the top and outcrop seating.

Past a freestanding boulder, you cross and again descend along a brook, coming to the blue/red Pine Knob spur (a right). Ignore this spur, which climbs but holds no views. Instead head for Coginchaug Cave, now within sight. It's a massive rock with a pronounced overhang and dark recess that provided shelter to early travelers. Blazes lead to the yawning gap and up its left as the trail continues to Old Blue Hills Road. For this hike, though, backtrack to Millers Pond.

BLUFF HEAD

The Bluff Head hike begins with a heave-ho, up-you-go ridge charge, advancing via braced steps and a switchback. An alternative bypass trail suggests an easier topping. For this hike, though, the bypass holds the return.

The trail then continues north along the edge. Oak, birch, maple, and witch hazel dress the hillside. Your first view is where the bypass trail tags up. You peer between treetops at the CT 77 valley below. The ridges of Broomstick rise east, and a southern haze hints at Long Island Sound.

Next up, an opening overlooks oxen-dug Myerhuber Pond, its pastoral bowl, and woodland and hills beyond. The next rise offers an outcrop vantage that spans 180-degrees east and looks directly down on the lily-donned pond. Looking into Myerhuber, the view is

Bluff Head ridge along Mattabesett Trail, New England National Scenic Trail, Connecticut

three-dimensional, with the underwater growth plainly visible. This vantage signals the turnaround.

Backtrack to follow the bypass right. It descends an attractive wooded slope, where peepers may divert attention before you follow the sunken grade of an old road to the left. The road passes below a cemetery to emerge at the parking lot.

MILES AND DIRECTIONS

MILLERS POND TO COGINCHAUG CAVE

0.0 Start at the Millers Pond trailhead. Round the gate and follow the pond access lane uphill.

0.1 Reach the white trail. Turn left, following the white blazes.

0.3 Reach the Mattabesett Trail; it merges on your left. Follow the dual blue/ white blaze south.

0.9 Reach the earthen dam. Follow the Mattabesett as it hooks back to the left. *Note:* The white trail continues across the dam to encircle Millers Pond.

2.2 Reach Bear Rock Bypass. Top Bear Rock and then return to take the bypass.

4.6 Reach the junction to Pine Knob. Forgo this spur, as there is no view. Proceed south on the blue trail.

4.7 Reach Coginchaug Cave. Backtrack to the Millers Pond trailhead. **Option:** Once you reach the dam, you can choose to return via the white trail along the west shore for new perspectives.

9.4 Arrive back at the trailhead.

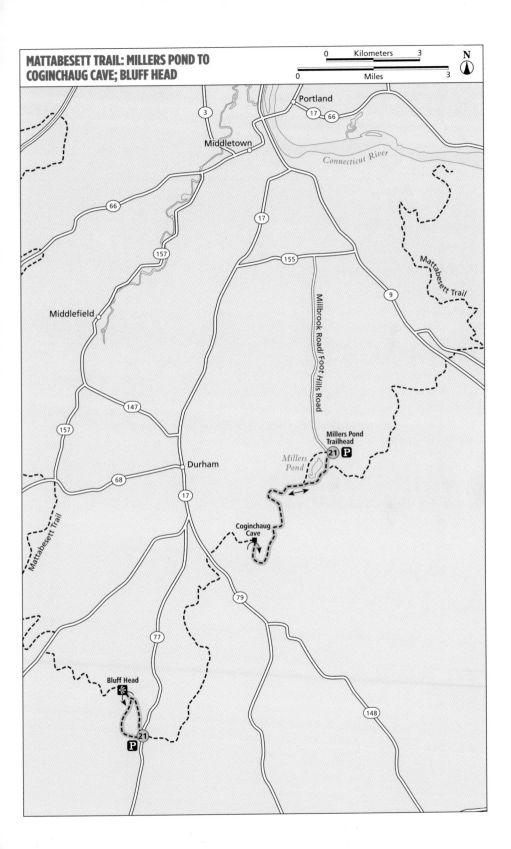

Kilometers

0   3

Miles

0   3

N

Portland

17 66

3

Middletown

Connecticut River

66

17

157

155

Mattabesett Trail

Middlefield

9

Millbrook Road/ Foot Hills Road

147

Millers Pond Trailhead

21 P

157

Millers Pond

68

Durham

Coginchaug Cave

17

Mattabesett Trail

79

77

148

Bluff Head

21

P

BLUFF HEAD

0.0 Start at the Bluff Head trailhead on CT 77. Take the steep-charging trail straight uphill. **Option:** You may instead hike south on the gentler blue/orange bypass for an easier ridge ascent, adding 0.2 mile to the distance.

0.3 Reach the ridgetop and, soon after, the junction with the blue/orange bypass. Follow the blue blazes north.

0.6 Reach the viewpoint above Myerhuber Pond. Return to the junction with blue/orange trail.

0.9 Reach the bypass trail junction. Follow the blue/orange bypass, bearing right for descent.

1.3 Pass a cemetery.

1.4 Arrive back at the trailhead.

HIKE INFORMATION

LOCAL INFORMATION

Central Regional Tourism District, 1 Constitution Plaza, 2nd Floor, Hartford 06103; (860) 787-9640; www.centerofct.com.

LOCAL EVENTS/ATTRACTIONS

Dudley Farm Museum, 2351 Durham Rd., Guilford 06437; (203) 457-0770; www .dudleyfarm.com. This museum, at the northeast corner of CT 77 and CT 80 in Guilford, rolls back the clock to the late 19th century with its restored farmhouse and barns; vegetable, herb, and flower gardens; and cropland, meadows, and woods. Farmhouse tours introduce the people, the period, and life circa 1900. Livestock contributes to the sights, sounds, and smells.

ORGANIZATIONS

Connecticut Forest and Park Association (CFPA), 16 Meriden Rd., Rockfall 06481; (860) 346-8733; www.ctwoodlands.org.

22 COCKAPONSET STATE FOREST

In south-central Connecticut, this state forest offers a tranquil woods retreat and access to Pattaconk Reservoir. The forest boasts a fine well-blazed trail system. The selected hike navigates the interlocking threads of the forest's Pattaconk, Cockaponset, and Wildwood Trails for an all-day, see-the-forest, barbell-shaped tour. You will explore pond, woods, laurel groves, and low rock ledges.

Start: Pattaconk Recreation Area trailhead
Distance: 13-mile barbell
Hiking time: 7 to 9 hours
Difficulty: Strenuous due to length
Elevation change: 300 feet
Trail surface: Earthen path and woods road
Best seasons: Spring through fall
Other trail users: Anglers, hunters, snowshoers, cross-country skiers; mountain bikers and equestrians on adjacent trails
Canine compatibility: Leashed dogs permitted
Land status: State forest
Nearest town: Killingworth, CT, with gas available along CT 81
Fees and permits: Seasonal weekend/holiday parking fee for nonresidents at Pattaconk Recreation Area
Schedule: Year-round, sunrise to sunset

Maps: State forest map (available online at www.ct.gov/deep); Connecticut Forest and Park Association (CFPA) *Connecticut Walk Book, West* (available from CFPA, www.ctwoodlands.org)
Trail contacts: Cockaponset State Forest, 18 Ranger Rd., Haddam 06438; (860) 345-8521. Department of Energy and Environmental Protection, State Forests, (860) 424-3200; www.ct.gov/deep.
Special considerations: Take necessary precautions during hunting season; be aware of the dates and either refrain from hiking or make yourself and your pet plainly visible in bright orange. Carry adequate drinking water. The Cockaponset, Pattaconk, and Wildwood Trails are for foot travel only.

FINDING THE TRAILHEAD

From CT 9, take exit 6 and go west on CT 148 for 1.7 miles. Turn right (north) on Cedar Lake Road (east of the CT 148–CT 145 junction), go 1.6 miles, and turn left at the sign for Pattaconk Lake State Recreation Area. Find large dirt parking lots on either side of the road before reaching the yellow barricade in 0.3 mile. Trailhead GPS: N41 24.446' / W72 31.520'

THE HIKE

For this ambitious hike, you round the barrier and follow the blue blazes (west) to reach the junction with the blue/red Pattaconk Trail. Turn left, following the Pattaconk south for a counterclockwise lower loop. You pass through mixed woods of beech, witch hazel, maple, oak, and mountain laurel, ascending a low ridge with a rocky crest. Mossy shelves and fern caps dress the rocks.

Cockaponset Trail,
Cockaponset State Forest,
Connecticut

On the trail's rolling descent, you cross over secondary trails and woods roads. Oaks and beeches prefer the heart of the woodland. After a drainage crossing, the trail curves left, avoiding private land. Again turn left after crossing a mossy-rock brook.

Upon crossing abandoned Filley Road (a paved road), you reach a junction. Bear left on the blue Cockaponset Trail. In the mature multistory forest, the trail is troubled by roots and rocks. From an impressive beech grove, you cross a brook to trace a low, esker-like, planed-top ridge, where tulip poplars find a niche. Deer, grouse, woodpeckers, and mice may add to sightings. On a long steady climb, the trail bed improves. Cross a faint jeep track and a rocky drainage to return to the main recreation area.

For the 13-mile barbell, you next follow the blue/red Pattaconk Trail north along the west shore of Pattaconk Reservoir, a scenic pond with an irregular shoreline. Yellow and white pond lilies spangle the shallows. Sweet pepperbush, azalea, and witch hazel add to the shore.

The trail rolls along the wooded rocky slope, drifting from the pond to cross an inlet. Past a split rock, you traverse a bouldery site and cross a second rocky inlet, leaving the reservoir. Cross rocky Pattaconk Brook. Here the blue Cockaponset Trail pinches toward the Pattaconk Trail. Keep right, following the blue/red blazes. Where the trails again meet, you follow the Cockaponset Trail north, among big-diameter trees.

Travel a wooded tier between ledges, reaching little-used Old County Road (a dirt road). Turn left on it to find the blue blazes heading north. Stay on the blue Cockaponset Trail (a footpath) as it ascends, edging or drifting into Turkey Hill Natural Area.

The Cockaponset Trail overlooks an extensive marsh of phragmites (plumed reeds) and snags. After traversing a low rock dam, it rounds the marsh in a snug green aisle of sweet pepperbush, sassafras, oak, and tangled mountain laurel. Honeycombed, folded, and fractured rock rises next enfold passage. Small clearings hint at forest management. Keep on the blue Cockaponset Trail to Jericho Road, where a plot of rare orchids sits to your right. Admire but do not touch.

The Cockaponset thrice crosses Jericho Road; this is the first crossing. At the upcoming junction with the blue/red Wildwood Trail, keep to the blue Cockaponset Trail for counterclockwise travel on the upper loop.

On the Cockaponset, you ascend and travel among outcrops, edging a standing forest of dead pines. The pole-like trunks tower above young hardwoods. Top an outcrop overlooking a wooded draw and pass the footings of an old lookout. The trail now rolls, snakes, and twists back on itself, passing from outcrop ridge to draw and back. Tall laurels create a forest within a forest. Past a clearing for an old camp, you cross Jericho Road for the third time.

A slow descent leads to the northern junction with the blue/red Wildwood Trail. Now follow the blue/red blazes to complete the upper loop. Enter an inviting hemlock grove and ascend to a woods road. Hike right along the woods road and take a quick left, returning to a foot trail to reach and travel a ridge. Again pass among pine snags and striking outcrops to close the upper loop and backtrack to the trailhead.

MILES AND DIRECTIONS

0.0 Start at the Pattaconk Recreation Area trailhead. Hike west from the barrier at the upper parking areas, following blue blazes.

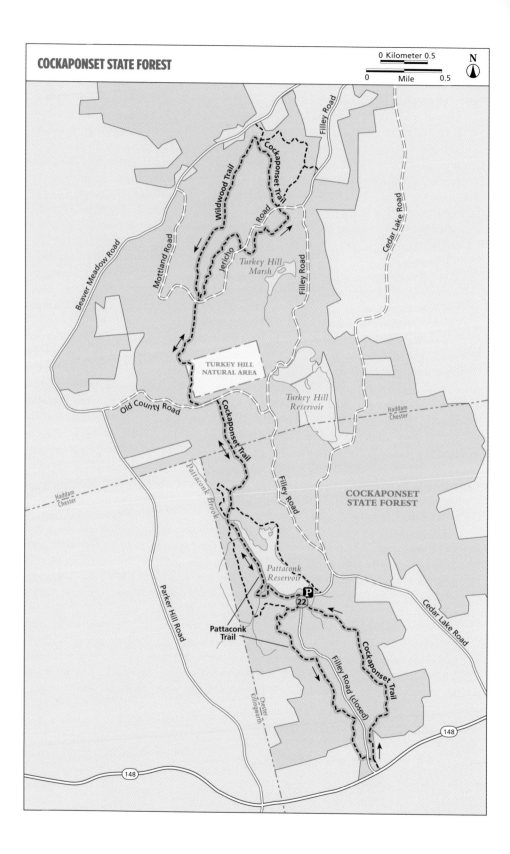

0 Kilometer 0.5

0 Mile 0.5

N

Filley Road

Cockaponset Trail

Wildwood Trail

Mottland Road

Jericho Road

Beaver Meadow Road

Turkey Hill Marsh

Filley Road

Cedar Lake Road

TURKEY HILL NATURAL AREA

Turkey Hill Reservoir

Haddam Chester

Old County Road

Cockaponset Trail

Pattaconk Brook

Haddam Chester

Filley Road

COCKAPONSET STATE FOREST

Parker Hill Road

Pattaconk Reservoir

P

22

Pattaconk Trail

Cockaponset Trail

Filley Road (closed)

Cedar Lake Road

Chester Killingworth

148

148

0.1	Turn left (south) on the blue/red Pattaconk Trail for the lower loop.
1.6	Cross abandoned Filley Road and turn left on the blue Cockaponset Trail. To the right is CT 148.
3.3	Emerge back at the recreation area. Pick up the blue/red Pattaconk Trail as it continues north along the west shore of Pattaconk Reservoir.
4.3	Cross Pattaconk Brook. Continue following the blue/red blazes.
4.5	Meet the blue/yellow trail. Continue north on the blue/red trail. **Option:** The blue/yellow trail offers a return along the reservoir's east shore for a shorter figure-eight hike.
4.6	Reach a trail junction. Follow the blue Cockaponset Trail north.
5.3	Reach Old County Road. Bear left to pick up the northbound Cockaponset Trail in just over 0.1 mile.
6.2	Reach Jericho Road. Turn right to pick up the northbound blue trail in 100 feet.
6.3	Reach the upper loop junction with the blue/red Wildwood Trail. Go counter-clockwise on the blue Cockaponset Trail.
7.3	Cross Jericho Road a second time. Turn left to resume the blue trail on the right in 50 feet.
8.1	Make a third crossing of Jericho Road.
8.8	Reach a trail junction. Follow the blue/red Wildwood Trail to complete the upper loop. **Note:** The Cockaponset Trail bears right (north) to Beaver Meadow Road.
10.0	Close the upper loop. Backtrack the Cockaponset and Pattaconk Trails to the trailhead. **Option:** Where you reach the blue/yellow trail, you can take it along the east shore for new perspectives on the reservoir.
13.0	Arrive back at the trailhead.

HIKE INFORMATION

LOCAL INFORMATION

Central Regional Tourism District, 1 Constitution Plaza, 2nd Floor, Hartford 06103; (860) 787-9640; www.centerofct.com.

LOCAL EVENTS/ATTRACTIONS

Connecticut River Museum, 67 Main St., Essex 06426; (860) 767-8269; www.ctriver museum.org. In Essex, on the Connecticut River to the southeast, you can explore the Connecticut River Museum and travel in bygone style by the **Essex Steam Train and Riverboat** (train one way, boat back) or by the **Connecticut River Tour Boat,** keeping to the water exclusively. For the paired tour, contact the Valley Railroad Company, 1 Railroad Ave., PO Box 452, Essex 06426; (860) 767-0103 or (800) 377-3987; www .essexsteamtrain.com. For the single trip, contact Connecticut River Tour Boat, www .ctriverexpeditions.org.

ACCOMMODATIONS

Hammonasset Beach State Park (on Route 1 off I-95), 1288 Boston Post Road, PO Box 271, Madison 06443; (203) 245-2785 (park office), (203) 245-1817 (campground office). Hammonasset Beach State Park, on Long Island Sound southwest of the forest, has 550 family campsites and overnight cabins, running-water restrooms, showers, and hookups. The campground operates from Memorial Day weekend through early October. Reservations are through ReserveAmerica, (877) 668-2267 or www.reserveamerica .com.

ORGANIZATIONS

Connecticut Forest and Park Association (CFPA), 16 Meriden Rd., Rockfall 06481; (860) 346-8733; www.ctwoodlands.org.

23 COLLIS P. HUNTINGTON STATE PARK

This park was a gift to the state from the Huntington family, renowned for its role in creating the nation's first transcontinental railroad and for its contributions to the art world. Anna Hyatt Huntington sculpted here, and her bear and wolf sculptures now welcome visitors to the park. The described loop offers a relaxing carriageway stroll through picturesque woodland and past outcrops, ponds, stone walls, and other remnants of history. A steep cable-line passage alone mars the loop, disrupting the reverie and the overall spirit of the trail. We suggest fashioning your own switchbacks here to ease the descent.

Start: Main park entrance
Distance: 5.9-mile loop, including cascade spur
Hiking time: 3 to 4 hours
Difficulty: Moderate, with one ridiculously steep up-and-down cable-line stretch
Elevation change: The rolling circuit has 250 feet of elevation change.
Trail surface: Carriageway and earthen path
Best seasons: Spring through fall
Other trail users: Mountain bikers, equestrians, anglers, hunters, snowshoers, cross-country skiers
Canine compatibility: Leashed dogs permitted
Land status: State park
Nearest town: Bethel, CT
Fees and permits: None
Schedule: Year-round, 8 a.m. to sunset

Map: State park map (available online at www.ct.gov/deep)
Trail contacts: Collis P. Huntington State Park, c/o Putnam Memorial State Park, 499 Black Rock Turnpike, Redding 06896; (203) 938-2285. Department of Energy and Environmental Protection, State Parks, (860) 424-3200; www.ct.gov/deep.
Special considerations: Parts of the park are open to archery-only deer hunting from Sept 15 to Dec 31. Aspetuck Valley, Huntington Ridge, and designated white trails are for foot travel only. Find toilets and a couple of picnic tables at the main parking area and at Dodgingtown Road. On carriageway stretches, markers are few, so keep a park map handy and study intersections well.

FINDING THE TRAILHEAD

From the junction of CT 302 and CT 58 in Bethel, drive 1.3 miles south on CT 58 and turn left onto Sunset Hill Road. Go 0.1 mile and bear right (south) on Sunset Hill Road. Reach the main trailhead on the left in 2.2 miles (1 mile past Old Dodgingtown Road, which holds additional trail parking). The sculpture-topped entry pillars are unmistakable. Main Trailhead GPS: N41 19.933' / W73 21.568'

THE HIKE

This clockwise loop, mostly on carriageways, follows the blue trail with a bridging white segment to South Pond.

Follow the worn track east downhill to the park's core. At the carriageway intersection, turn left to follow the blue carriageway north. Its hardened surface allows carefree strolling. Eyes roam the woodland maples and hickories and the edge tangles of ash and wild grape. Ignore side paths.

Stone walls, the glint of Lake Hopewell off to the right, stately sugar maples, a couple of giant spruce trees, and ruins harken to another life at the park, when the Huntingtons summered here. They enjoyed a casual elegance and even ran a sternwheeler on the waters. Before you reach Old Dodgingtown Road, the trail turns right. Spurs lead to area amenities.

Ahead, watch for blazes to point you left through an egress in a stone wall. You pass an old mortared foundation recessed in the slope to reach Old Dodgingtown Road. Turn right, following the road between postcard-pretty Lily Pond and West Lagoon—dark, tree-framed, still, and hypnotic. From the road's end parking, follow blue blazes northeast from a pole gate. Stone walls partition the area, and a swamp is to your right. Keep to the carriageway as it curves and ascends.

Entrance gate statue, Collis P. Huntington State Park, Connecticut

Outcrops and sporadic mountain laurel lend to the hike's visual appeal. Keep to this primary, although slimmer, thoroughfare. You cross the cable line and string past unmarked trails. Bird watching is popular. A variety of bird songs accompany footfalls.

Keep right past a series of white trails heading north to the Huntington Ridge Trail. Outcrop rims, ledges, and breakaway blocks bring interest to the woods tour, as do pockets of ferns. At a cellar depression, the blue trail swings right on a foot trail to ascend a sunken pass between outcrop ridges. Cross over the pass and wend to the notorious cable line. Follow it left. The initial pitch and rise are fiercely steep as the loop follows this undeviating line. At a dip, you cross a brook, and the cable line and blue trail part ways. Follow the blue blazes left.

The carriageway ascends with a hairpin turn. After it again crosses over the transcontinental cable line, you descend between outcrop-topped ridges. Mountain laurels favor this terrain, as do white-tailed deer. At junctions, keep to the blue trail. You enter an attractive swamp-footed woods with tulip poplars and peeling birch trunks and pass the Aspetuck Valley Trail at an information kiosk.

After a carriageway bridge, you pass the spur to Hopewell Road. At the upcoming pair of bridges, take the upstream spur before the second bridge to view a picturesque cascade below a left-bank cliff. The water spills beneath a wedged-in boulder, the size of a small cabin.

On the blue circuit, you continue the meandering ascent past a red trail to follow a ribbony brook upstream. At a triangle junction, where the blue trail ends and a red trail heads right, you now follow the white trail left, crossing a footbridge over the brook.

This trail melds into the blue trail below the grassy earthen dam of South Pond. At the spillway crossing, a blue foot trail ascends the slope and you gain views of this long rectangular pond with its lily pads and ducks. The trail next holds an uphill scramble

Blue Trail, Collis P. Huntington State Park, Connecticut

through tight shrubs. It splits and rejoins before closing the loop at the blue carriageway. Turn left and backtrack uphill to parking.

To avoid the scramble, continue forward on the wide grade, returning to the initial carriageway junction, and follow the worn track back uphill to the trailhead. This ending is more in keeping with the overall character of the trail.

MILES AND DIRECTIONS

0.0   Start at the main park entrance. Follow the worn track east downhill into the park core.

0.1   Reach a carriageway junction. Turn left for the blue trail and the clockwise loop. *Note:* The carriageway ahead is an optional return for the loop.

0.2   Reach the blue trail loop. Continue forward on the northbound carriageway. The foot trail to the right (which may go unnoticed) holds the return.

1.3   Reach the trail access at the end of Old Dodgingtown Road. Follow the blue trail northeast from the information board.

2.4   Reach the cable-line descent and passage. *Note:* After 0.1 mile, keep a sharp eye left for the blue trail's continuation.

3.4   Reach the Aspetuck Valley Trail junction. Follow the blue trail south.

3.9   Reach the Hopewell Road access. Continue forward on the blue trail.

4.0   Reach the cascade spur before crossing the second trail bridge past the Hopewell Road access. Detour upstream for viewing before resuming the loop at mile 4.1.

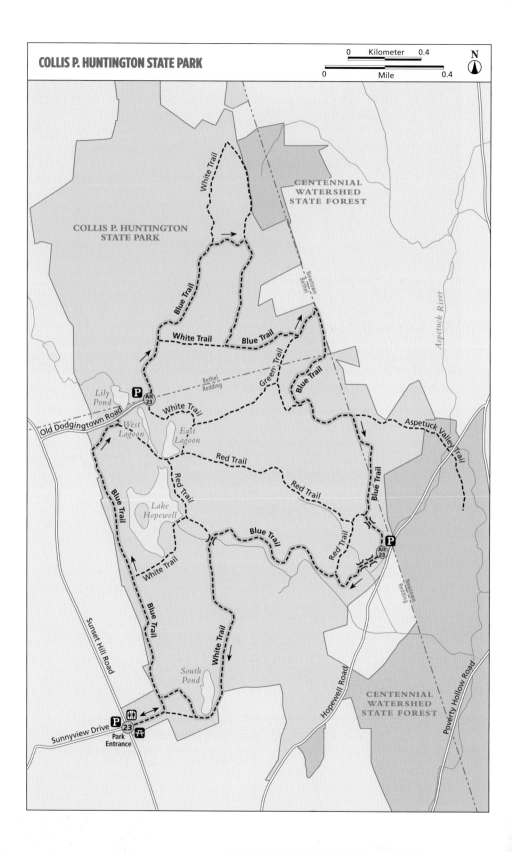

COLLIS P. HUNTINGTON STATE PARK

0 Kilometer 0.4
0 Mile 0.4

N

CENTENNIAL WATERSHED STATE FOREST

COLLIS P. HUNTINGTON STATE PARK

White Trail

Blue Trail

White Trail

Blue Trail

Newtown Bethel

Green Trail

Bethel Redding

Blue Trail

Aspetuck River

P Alt 23

Lily Pond

White Trail

Old Dodgingtown Road

Aspetuck Valley Trail

West Lagoon

East Lagoon

Red Trail

Blue Trail

Red Trail

Red Trail

Blue Trail

Lake Hopewell

P Alt 23

Blue Trail

Red Trail

White Trail

Blue Trail

Red Trail

Newtown Redding

Sunset Hill Road

Blue Trail

White Trail

South Pond

Hopewell Road

CENTENNIAL WATERSHED STATE FOREST

Poverty Hollow Road

Sunnyview Drive

P 23 A

Park Entrance

4.8 Reach a junction with the white and red trails. Follow the white trail left (south).

5.4 Reach a trail junction at the far end of South Pond dam. The blue trail resumes as an untamed foot trail that splits and joins as it strikes uphill to close the loop. *Option:* Remaining on the wide grade ascending from the pond returns you to base of the slope where you first met the blue carriageway. From there follow the worn track uphill to parking.

5.7 Close the blue trail loop. Turn left on the blue carriageway and backtrack to the start, following the worn track upslope to the trailhead.

5.9 Arrive back at the trailhead.

HIKE INFORMATION

LOCAL INFORMATION

Western Connecticut Convention and Visitors Bureau, PO Box 968, Litchfield 06759; (860) 567-4506; www.visitfairfieldcountyct.com.

LOCAL EVENTS/ATTRACTIONS

Blue Jay Orchards, 125 Plumtrees Rd., Bethel 06801; (203) 748-0119; www.bluejay orchardsct.com. This bustling 140-acre apple orchard in Bethel delights with U-pick apples, a pumpkin patch, wagon rides, and a farm market. Apple picking runs from Sept through Oct, with farm market hours Sept through Dec.

    Danbury Railway Museum, 120 White St., PO Box 90, Danbury 06813-0090; (203) 778-8337; www.danburyrailwaymuseum.org. In the old Danbury Train Station at the corner of White Street and Patriot Drive, this museum appeals to the inner rail tramp/wannabe conductor in all of us, with its vintage cars and locomotives, train sets, and train rides.

In West Rock Ridge State Park, in south-central Connecticut, this hike threads along the western escarpment rim and crest, unveiling rock outcrop, mixed woods, and mountain laurel stands and extending views. Along it, seventeenth-century English-American history is revisited at Judges Cave. West Rock Ridge is an elongated traprock mountain with plunging cliffs and a summit elevation in excess of 600 feet. Clear-day views reportedly span 200 square miles. The Regicides Trail links to the greater Quinnipiac Trail.

Start: South Overlook when gate is open for vehicle access; otherwise, start at West Rock Nature Center, 0.1 mile north of the park entrance on Wintergreen Avenue
Distance: 13.4 miles out and back from South Overlook to Sanford Feeder; 16.2 miles when starting from the nature center and hiking the park road to the overlook; 16.4 miles when taking the red trail south from the park entrance to the blue Regicides Trail at South Overlook
Hiking time: 8 to 10 hours
Difficulty: Strenuous due to length and some uneven rocky footing
Elevation change: 200 feet when starting at South Overlook; 400 feet when starting from the nature center
Trail surface: Earthen and rocky path, abandoned road
Best seasons: Spring through fall
Other trail users: Mountain bikers or equestrians on trails and routes other than the Regicides
Canine compatibility: Leashed dogs permitted on trails
Land status: State park

Nearest town: New Haven, CT
Fees and permits: None
Schedule: Year-round, 8 a.m. to sunset. Vehicle access to summit is generally only available weekends/holidays from Memorial Day weekend through the last weekend in Oct, 8 a.m. to 6 p.m.
Maps: State park map (available online at www.ct.gov/deep); Connecticut Forest and Park Association (CFPA) *Connecticut Walk Book, West* (available from CFPA, www.ctwoodlands.org)
Trail contacts: West Rock Ridge State Park, c/o Sleeping Giant State Park, 200 Mount Carmel Ave., Hamden 06518; (203) 287-5658. Department of Energy and Environmental Protection, State Parks, (860) 424-3200; www.ct.gov/deep.
Special considerations: Carry water; none is available along the trail. The blue Regicides Trail is open to foot travel only. The cliffs house peregrine falcons. Watch for their flights.

FINDING THE TRAILHEAD

From the corner of Fitch Street (CT 10) and Whalley Avenue (CT 63) in New Haven, go north on Fitch Street for 0.6 mile and turn left on Wintergreen Avenue. Brown signs for West Rock Ridge State Park mark the turn. Keep to Wintergreen Avenue, following it north and then left, staying north on it through junctions to find the state park entrance on the left in 1.2 miles. Locate West Rock Nature Center and trail parking on the right 0.1 mile farther north. Trailhead GPS: N41 20.783' / W72 58.046'. Additional parking spots sit off Wintergreen at the foot of the park.

For South Overlook, proceed into the park, following the paved park road uphill past the entrance booth, reaching the Judges Cave–South Overlook Y-junction in 0.9 mile. Turn left to reach South Overlook in another 0.4 mile. Trailhead GPS: N41 19.948' / W72 57.709'

THE HIKE

While not always easy to reach, the Regicides Trail is worth the trouble. Its loft and vantages repay tenfold. South Overlook starts you off with a 180-degree view to the east and south, looking out toward Sleeping Giant, East Rock Ridge and the Soldiers Monument, New Haven, the New Haven Lighthouse, and Long Island Sound.

The trail begins below the Civilian Conservation Corps (CCC)–constructed shelter and traces the rim edge north toward Judges Cave. Oaks, hickories, chestnuts, and tortured eastern red cedars, dry grass, and wildflowers anchor in the thin soils of the rock edge. Glimpse church steeples and New Haven neighborhoods as the trail passes below the park roadside vantages. The stonework on and along the trail likely came at the hand of the CCC as well.

Pass a blue/yellow feeder trail from a neighborhood below. The Regicides Trail rolls and ascends to emerge at the oak-shaded picnic site at Judges Cave. In this barn-size boulder-jumble with cave-like openings, overhangs, and short passages, American colonists shielded judges Edward Whalley and William Goffe. They were two of the three regicides who issued the death warrant for Charles I and became themselves fugitives with the restoration of Charles II to the British throne. They eluded royal agents for three months before escaping to Massachusetts. On nearby flat rocks, you may sleuth out later history—meticulously carved names dating to the mid-1800s.

Resume the blazed trail north at the rustic pole gate, left of the Judges Cave. Pass through similar woods to reach Buttress Gap, where you cross the land burrowed through by Wilbur Cross Parkway. Rounded outcrops present city views to the west. After a quick, steep, rocky ascent, the rest of the hike is gently rolling. Earthen segments bridge rocky stretches.

Beware of poison ivy among the outcrops, boulders, and crags of this eroded volcanic dike. The drone from Wilbur Cross Parkway echoes upslope. Drifting away from the escarpment and past an antenna, the trail briefly follows a gravel service road. Stay alert for the blazes that point out a descent to the right.

Cross forsaken Baldwin Drive (the first of six crossings) and pass three radio towers, returning to woods. Mountain laurel threads beneath the chestnut, white, and red oaks. A second parkway crossing brings a return to the western escarpment, with limited looks at marshy Konolds Pond and cross-valley views of a wooded ridge. Open views trending north occur at regular intervals.

Oak and hemlock stands alternate with mountain laurel groves. The smoother trail allows for easier walking. When next at Baldwin Drive, follow it left a few hundred

Historic inscriptions at Judges Cave, West Rock Ridge State Park, Connecticut

Civilian Conservation Corps (CCC) picnic shelter at Scenic Vista on West Rock Ridge, West Rock Ridge State Park, Connecticut

feet before returning to the rim for a partial view of Lake Dawson. Deer, owl, grouse, and woodpecker are possible wildlife sightings. More views follow, as do more parkway crossings.

Where the Regicides Trail first deviates to the east side of the ridge, you'll find an oak and rocky meadow habitat. Where it slips back west, a 180-degree view sweeps the bumpy spine of West Rock Ridge. The trail withholds an eastern perspective until late in the game, where it skirts cliffs and outcrops. Views encompass a field-rimmed pond, the city skyline, and woods.

As the trail curves away west, it tags Baldwin Drive one last time. You may turn around here or continue forward to the Sanford Feeder Trail, the selected ending. Retrace your steps to South Overlook. Tree-shaded and time-softened Baldwin Drive offers a less-demanding return. The Quinnipiac Trail continues north from the Sanford junction to points beyond.

MILES AND DIRECTIONS

0.0 Start at South Overlook. Round the CCC picnic pavilion, following the blue blazes north along the ridgeline fence. **Note:** When the summit is closed to vehicle access, start at the West Rock Nature Center parking lot or parking spots off Wintergreen. Hike into the park and up the summit road to South Overlook, adding 1.4 miles each way to the hike. The park's red trail offers another approach.

0.7 Reach Judges Cave. Hike north from the pole gate to the left of the cave.

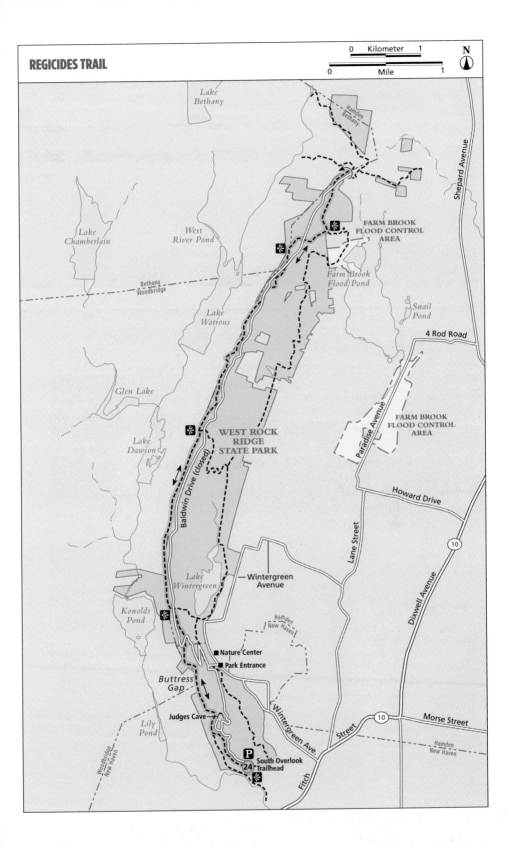

0   Kilometer   1

0   Mile   1

N

Lake Bethany

Lake Chamberlain

West River Pond

Hamden Bethany

FARM BROOK FLOOD CONTROL AREA

Farm Brook Flood Pond

Snail Pond

Bethany Woodbridge

Lake Watrous

Shepard Avenue

4 Rod Road

Glen Lake

WEST ROCK RIDGE STATE PARK

FARM BROOK FLOOD CONTROL AREA

Paradise Avenue

Lake Dawson

Baldwin Drive (closed)

Howard Drive

10

Lake Wintergreen

Wintergreen Avenue

Lane Street

Konolds Pond

Hamden New Haven

Dixwell Avenue

■ Nature Center
■ Park Entrance

Buttress Gap

Judges Cave →

Lily Pond

Woodbridge New Haven

P
24   South Overlook Trailhead

Wintergreen Ave.

Fitch Street

10   Morse Street

Hamden New Haven

1.3	Cross Buttress Gap. Several hundred feet below you is the Wilbur Cross Parkway tunnel.
1.6	Cross Baldwin Drive, the first of six crossings.
4.7	Cross under a power line.
6.0	Reach the fifth crossing of Baldwin Drive for an eastern vantage.
6.6	Cross Baldwin Drive for the last time.
6.7	Reach the junction with the blue/red Sanford Feeder Trail. Return to South Overlook.
13.4	Arrive back at South Overlook.

HIKE INFORMATION

LOCAL INFORMATION

Central Regional Tourism District, 1 Constitution Plaza, 2nd Floor, Hartford 06103; (860) 787-9640; www.centerofct.com.

LOCAL EVENTS/ATTRACTIONS

City of New Haven, (203) 946-6086 (East Rock Ranger Station) and (203) 946-8019 (Lighthouse Point Park); www.newhavenct.gov/gov/depts/parks. The city's **East Rock Park,** a mirror eastern highland attraction, extends views. Its 1812 Soldiers and Sailors Monument to New Haven's battle-fallen sons shoots 112 feet skyward. The park, open sunrise to sunset, is reached via Summit Drive off Davis Street. **New Haven Light,** another New Haven landmark, sits on the east side of the harbor at Lighthouse Point Park (a fee site). Constructed of locally quarried stone and of brick, this 1847 octagonal-design lighthouse, long gone dark, rises 97 feet above sea level. New Haven Light, also dubbed Five Mile Point Light because it stands 5 miles from the New Haven Green, is on the National Register of Historic Places.

  Beinecke Rare Book and Manuscript Library, (203) 432-2977, https://beinecke .library.yale.edu; **Peabody Museum of Natural History,** (203) 432-8987, http://peabody .yale.edu; **The Yale Art Gallery,** (203) 432-0600, https://artgallery.yale.edu. New Haven is home to prestigious **Yale University,** with its important sphere of museums and collections: the Beinecke Rare Book and Manuscript Library (121 Wall St.), the

GEOLOGY 101

Traprock ridges fashion the elongated, asymmetrical, abrupt-ridge skylines of Connecticut's Central Valley. At nearly 1,000 feet above sea level, these ridges are the product of volcanic activity and faulting, followed by centuries of erosion. They are largely basalt in composition and layered in form. Prime examples of the landmark feature are the cliffs of East Rock and West Rock, which face off across the South Central Valley at New Haven; Sleeping Giant; the Hanging Hills of Meriden; and Talcott Mountain.

  The sides of many of these ridges hold quarries where the durable rock was excavated for use in road building. Now the ridges are largely protected and recognized for their natural merit. The landform shapes microclimates for rare botanic species. Boreal plants, unusual this far south, favor the cool recesses, while other species seek the hot, dry cliff exposure.

renowned Peabody Museum of Natural History (170 Whitney Ave.), and the Yale University Art Gallery (1111 Chapel St. at York). Beinecke Library is noted for its Gutenberg Bible and original Audubon bird prints. The Peabody is celebrated for its giant dinosaur fossils, Native American artifacts, and Connecticut natural history specimens, and is a fee attraction. The Yale Art Gallery, free to the public, has grown its collection from the important seed of John Trumbull's work. It includes art objects from America, Europe, Asia, and Africa.

ORGANIZATIONS

Connecticut Forest and Park Association (CFPA), 16 Meriden Rd., Rockfall 06481; (860) 346-8733; www.ctwoodlands.org.

25 DEVIL'S DEN PRESERVE

This premier Connecticut Nature Conservancy property wears the full name Lucius Pond Ordway/Devil's Den Preserve. Its 1,756 acres in the southwest corner of the state contribute to a critical open space measuring nearly 10 square miles. Combined with adjoining town, trust, and water company lands, it provides habitat that encourages wildlife breeding and diversity. Devil's Den boasts some 20 miles of interlocking trails for a variety of hikes exploring woodland, ravines, swamp, and rock ledges.

Start: Preserve entrance trailhead
Distance: 7.2-mile loop, including vista spurs
Hiking time: 4 to 6 hours
Difficulty: Moderate
Elevation change: Travel from a trailhead elevation of 250 feet to a ledge elevation of 550 feet.
Trail surface: Earthen path, woods road, rock ledge
Best seasons: Spring through fall
Other trail users: Hunters (possibly on neighboring properties), birders, snowshoers, cross-country skiers
Canine compatibility: Dogs not permitted
Land status: Private nonprofit preserve
Nearest town: Wilton, CT, with gas along US 7
Fees and permits: None, but donation is suggested
Schedule: Year-round, sunrise to sunset, with gates locked promptly at sunset
Map: Preserve map (available on-site or online at www.nature.org; you first navigate through where they work to Connecticut, and then through the places they serve to Devil's Den)
Trail contact: Lucius Pond Ordway/Devil's Den Preserve, c/o The Nature Conservancy in Connecticut, 55 Church St., Floor 3, New Haven 06510; (203) 568-6270; www.nature.org
Special considerations: Register at the map/information board at the parking lot. No pets, no bikes, no smoking, no picnicking, no fishing, and no swimming. The preserve has its own blazing scheme: Red indicates paths open to hiking and cross-country skiing, yellow indicates foot trail, and white indicates a trail that is part of the greater Saugatuck Valley trail system. Junctions are numbered in correspondence with the map to aid in navigation and trail selection. Most junction posts also point the way back to the parking lot. Carry a map. Stay on designated trails and pack in/pack out. Because Devil's Den offers no amenities, bring drinking water and arrive bladder-empty and ready to hike.

FINDING THE TRAILHEAD

From CT 15 (the Merritt Parkway), take exit 42 and travel north on CT 57 for 5 miles. Turn right (east) on Godfrey Road, go 0.6 mile, and turn left onto Pent Road to enter the preserve. The road changes to dirt at the preserve. With Devil's Den only 35 miles from New York City, the parking lot can fill on weekends. Trailhead GPS: N41 14.226' / W73 23.759'

THE HIKE

Nomadic Native Americans hunted and camped at the Den 5,000 years ago, and the woods supplied lumber for colonial homes and fueled the production of charcoal in the

1800s. More than thirty associated burn sites and collier huts speckled what is now the preserve. Today Devil's Den provides a much needed sanctuary in a high-tech era.

The selected broad-swinging counterclockwise loop travels several named trails and has spurs to granite ledges and a bouldery ravine. Begin on the Laurel Trail, post 21. It's over your left shoulder as you look at the information board.

Slowly ascend among oak, maple, and beech. Witch hazel, mountain laurel, and sweet pepperbush fill the midstory. You step through a gap in a stone wall at post 22, turn right, and then keep right. Stone walls and large boulders dot the woods. At post 31 bear left onto the Godfrey Trail and then quickly slip left to visit the Godfrey Pond Sawmill Site, with its restored dam and historic ruins. The pond dates to the 1700s.

On the Godfrey Trail, you then round the leafy eastern pond outskirts. Keep to this trail at junctions. Towering tulip poplars and attractive beech trees complement travel. Beyond a split rock, reach a rusted steam boiler, tiger engine wheel, smokestack, and flywheel from a portable sawmill that operated here from the late 1800s to the early 1900s.

Remain on the Godfrey Trail to post 64, where the Bedford Trail (a left) next carries the loop. Keep to it, descending and contouring the base of a hill, traversing a marshy site. As the Bedford Trail curves left, be alert for an easy-to-miss, although marked, junction (post 54). Turn right here on the Deer Run Trail to reach the Den's Great Ledge and an outside neighbor, Redding Great Ledge.

The foot trail rolls and ascends, crosses through a gap in a stone wall, and bears right at the Bruzelius Trail and left at the Dayton Trail, coming to post 56. Here, bear right. You travel in sun-drenched woods to Great Ledge, a long granite ledge with a 70- to 100-foot cliff. It offers both unobstructed and filtered looks across the Saugatuck Valley woodland and distant flat ridges.

Laurel Trail, Devil's Den Preserve, Connecticut

Traverse the ledge, descend through woods, and pass the Weston-Redding town line. Keep on this trail to post 59, bear right here and again at post 60, rounding to the Redding Great Ledge view. It overlooks Saugatuck Reservoir with its treed point and islands. Twisted laurels favor this area, as do deer. Although a ledge loop is possible here, for this hike, backtrack to post 54 and the Devil's Den Loop, turning right.

Ahead, keep left for a slow ascent to a plateau of red and chestnut oaks. A gradual descent follows. At post 49 proceed forward now on the Den Trail. Round below outcrop ledges and cliffs, coming to the Ambler Gorge Trail (post 44). Descend right on it to a bouldery bowl and jumble-rock ravine with a seasonal cascade. Books of muscovite (a kind of mica) glisten in the granite. Cross the brook and ascend to two modest vistas before backtracking to the loop.

The loop descends through high-canopy forest to the confluence of Ambler and Sap Brooks and post 10, where the Pent Trail brings the loop home. The Bedford, Den, and Pent Trails are but name changes for a single arterial woods road. Keep to it. The return rolls and skirts outcrop hills. Past post 5 and sentinel tulip trees, you overlook the marshy West Branch Saugatuck River drainage at Saugatuck Refuge. End back at the parking area.

MILES AND DIRECTIONS

0.0 Start at the preserve entrance trailhead. Follow the Laurel Trail from post 21 into the preserve for counterclockwise travel.

0.4 Reach the Godfrey Trail and detour left to the Godfrey Pond Sawmill Site. Continue north on the Godfrey Trail.

1.5 Reach the portable sawmill ruins.

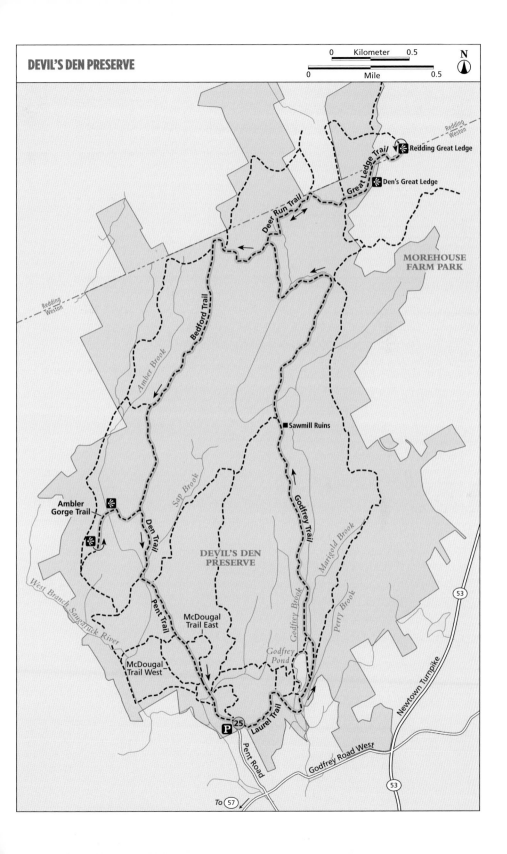

DEVIL'S DEN PRESERVE

0   Kilometer   0.5

0   Mile   0.5

N

Redding
Weston

Redding Great Ledge

Great Ledge Trail

Den's Great Ledge

Deer Run Trail

**MOREHOUSE
FARM PARK**

Bedford Trail

Amber Brook

Redding
Weston

Sawmill Ruins

Sap Brook

Godfrey Trail

**Ambler
Gorge Trail**

Den Trail

Marigold Brook

**DEVIL'S DEN
PRESERVE**

Godfrey Brook

Perry Brook

West Branch Saugatuck River

Pent Trail

McDougal
Trail East

53

McDougal
Trail West

Godfrey
Pond

P 25

Laurel Trail

Newtown Turnpike

Pent Road

Godfrey Road West

To 57

53

2.1	Reach the trail junction at post 64. Follow the Bedford Trail, bearing left.
2.6	Reach the trail junction at post 54. Take the Deer Run Trail right to gather views from the Den's Great Ledge and the Redding Great Ledge. **Option:** You may continue on the Bedford Trail for the loop alone.
3.2	Reach the Den's Great Ledge.
3.4	Reach the Redding Great Ledge. Backtrack to the Devil's Den Loop.
4.2	Return to the Devil's Den Loop at post 54. Follow the Bedford Trail right.
5.2	Reach trail junction post 49. Continue forward now on the Den Trail.
5.6	Reach the trail junction at post 44. Take the Ambler Gorge Trail for its vistas.
5.9	Reach the second Ambler Gorge view. Backtrack to the Devil's Den Loop.
6.2	Return to the loop at post 44. Turn right.
7.2	Complete the loop, arriving via the Pent Trail, at the parking area.

HIKE INFORMATION

LOCAL INFORMATION

Western Connecticut Convention and Visitors Bureau, PO Box 968, Litchfield 06759; (860) 567-4506; www.visitfairfieldcountyct.com.

LOCAL EVENTS/ATTRACTIONS

Keeler Tavern Museum, 132 Main St., Ridgefield 06877; (203) 438-5485; www.keelertavernmuseum.org. Ridgefield rolls out history with its Keeler Tavern Museum (circa 1713), complete with a 1777 British cannonball in its side. The tavern is shown by fee tour; call for schedule.

Weir Farm National Historic Site, 735 Nod Hill Rd., Wilton 06897; (203) 834-1896; www.nps.gov/wefa. Weir Farm nurtured three generations of American artists, starting with Julian Alden Weir, a leading figure in American Impressionism. His daughter, painter Dorothy Weir Young, and her husband, sculptor Mahonri Young, followed. Then New England painters Sperry and Doris Andrews took up residence. The 60-acre farm, house, and pond, along with the studios, barns, and gardens, remain.

Woodcock Nature Center, 56 Deer Run Rd., Wilton 06897; (203) 762-7280; www.woodcocknaturecenter.org. This 149-acre environmental education center on the Ridgefield-Wilton border offers easy hiking trails and boardwalk discovery, in wetland and woodland habitats. Trails are open daily, sunrise to sunset. The center has live animal exhibits and offers classes and programs.

SOUTHWEST CONNECTICUT

N. RIVER HIGHLANDS STATE PARK

This minimally developed 177-acre state park in Cromwell offers a color-coded 4-mile trail system exploring the west highland woods and Connecticut River rim. The land is rolling and once supported pasture and fields. The white trail is the one to take for river views. It puts you on the bluff, 150 feet above the water. Trails also take you down to the river past a blowhole, a place where winds whip past the cliffs, creating sound, a spiritual site for Native Americans. Park hours are 8 a.m. to sunset. Check the site map board or download a map online. Keep dogs leashed.

From the junction of CT 99 and CT 372 in Cromwell (0.7 mile north of CT 9, exit 18), go north on CT 99 for 0.6 mile to Prospect Hill Road, heading north toward Holy Apostles College and Seminary. In 0.5 mile turn right on Nooks Hill Road, and after another 0.3 mile turn left and take the single-lane underpass beneath the railroad track to stay on Nooks Hill Road. Go 0.6 mile and turn left onto Field Road. In 0.4 mile turn right into the park's gravel parking lot, adequate for eight to ten vehicles. The lot is just before Field Road crosses the railroad track. Trailhead GPS: N41 37.087' / W72 38.109'. Trail contact: River Highlands State Park, c/o Sleeping Giant State Park, 200 Mount Carmel Ave., Hamden 06518; (203) 287-5658; www.ct.gov/deep.

O. LARKIN STATE PARK TRAIL

Southwest of Waterbury and south of I-84, this rail-to-trail bridle path stretches 10 miles from its eastern terminus to Kettletown Road, encompasses 110 acres of scenic Connecticut, and runs through four towns: Middlebury, Naugatuck, Oxford, and Southbury. After a brief ascent you reach the established grade, which has a hardened surface and dusting of leaves. Initially it is sunken into the rock and wooded hillside. Woods of oak, birch, and beech shape an engaging, generally shaded travel aisle. At road crossings, rural neighborhoods briefly push aside natural impressions, but it's never a long intrusion. Hikers yield to riders, and be sure to keep dogs leashed for the safety of riders. The park is open 8 a.m. to sunset.

From I-84, take exit 17 and follow CT 63 south for 2.5 miles to reach the eastern terminus for this trail on the right (the west side of CT 63). A crescent-shaped off-road parking lot serves trail users and is long enough to accommodate horse trailers. Trail users should begin and end here because of the parking. Trailhead GPS: N41 30.723' / W73 03.906'. Trail contact: Larkin State Park Trail, c/o Putnam Memorial State Park, 499 Black Rock Turnpike, Redding 06896; (203) 938-2285; www.ct.gov/deep.

P. WADSWORTH FALLS STATE PARK

The park's namesake waterfall is the star attraction in the system of color-coded trails. A fairly level trail approaches the brink of the falls from Cherry Hill Road; trails also pass between the park core and the falls. The blue trail takes you past Little Falls en route to the orange trail, Cherry Hill Road, and the main attraction. The Coginchaug River flowing at the park's western fringe powered early industry. A remnant sluiceway hints at a onetime textile mill. At Powdermill Pond, gun powder

Wadsworth Falls, Wadsworth Falls State Park, Connecticut

was the factory production. The park is open sunrise to sunset and charges nonresidents weekend and holiday vehicle parking fees. Leashed pets are allowed on trails.

From the junction of CT 66 and CT 157 in Middletown, take CT 157 south for 1.5 miles and turn left (east) into the park. Trailhead GPS: N41 32.191' / W72 41.146'. Trail contact: Wadsworth Falls State Park, c/o Cockaponset State Forest, 18 Ranger Rd., Haddam 06438; (860) 345-8521; www.ct.gov/deep.

Q. MILLERS POND STATE PARK RESERVE

This walk-in open-space park has at its core spring-fed Millers Pond that supports both trout and bass. The pond was first dammed in the early 1700s. Later dams facilitated power at downstream mills. The park's color-coded trails include a 1.4-mile white trail circuit of the pond's shore. Other trails explore the quiet rolling woods. The park adjoins parcels of Cockaponset State Forest, broadening the field of exploration. You can craft part-day and all-day hikes. The Mattabesett Trail slips through the park, sharing the east-shore trail.

From CT 9, take exit 11 at Middletown and head west on CT 155. In 0.8 mile turn south onto Millbrook Road. Go 1.8 miles and bear left, staying on Millbrook Road for another 0.9 mile, then bear left on Foot Hills Road. In 1.2 miles turn right into the park's gravel lot. Trailhead GPS: N41 28.820' / W72 37.765'. Trail contact: Millers Pond State Park Reserve, c/o Cockaponset State Forest, 18 Ranger Rd., Haddam 06438; (860) 345-8521; www.ct.gov/deep.

R. TARRYWILE PARK

This dynamic Danbury municipal park continues to grow. Its current 722 acres enfold groomed mansion grounds, stately trees, farm and dairy settings, ponds, fields, pine stands, laurel-clad slopes, and woodland. At its core is the 1896 mansion, a shingle-sided, twenty-three-room Victorian-era American home on the National Register of Historic Places. Twenty-one miles of color-coded trails travel the property, as does the growing Ives Trail, which will run from Redding to Bennett Pond in Ridgefield. Tarrywile's trails are open free to the public from dawn to dusk, year-round (weather permitting). Keep dogs leashed and obey all park rules. The 3.2-mile Mootry Peak Lookout Hike and 3.3-mile Hearthstone Castle Hike are staff-suggested walks.

From US 7, south of I-84, take the Danbury Airport exit and turn east onto Wooster Heights Road. In 0.7 mile turn right on Southern Boulevard for Tarrywile Park and Mansion. Signs regularly mark the route. In 0.6 mile pass the entrance to the park's farm area on the right, and afterward turn right, staying on Southern Boulevard. In 0.1 mile turn right for the mansion/trails parking. Of the two parking lots, the lower lot serves trails and the environmental center. Trailhead GPS: N41 22.839' / W73 27.227'. Trail contact: Tarrywile Park and Mansion, 70 Southern Blvd., Danbury 06810; (203) 744-3130; http://tarrywile.com or www.friendsoftarrywilepark.org.

S. SAUGATUCK VALLEY AND ASPETUCK VALLEY TRAILS

These watershed areas in Easton, Newtown, Redding, and Weston represent a unique partnership among Aquarion Water Company, the Connecticut Department of Energy and Environmental Protection, and The Nature Conservancy. The cooperative allegiance meets safe-water needs while preserving open space and extending recreation. The 15,300 acres have been designated Centennial Watershed State Forest. Trails support hiking, jogging, cross-country skiing, and snowshoeing and are open daily, sunrise to sunset. A trail-use permit gives you access to all 13 miles of scenic trails; a like permit serves anglers. The trail system map serves as your permit and must be carried at all times. Maps are available online from Aquarion and the DEEP; you may also phone Aquarion to request one. Pass softly and heed all rules to protect the resource.

Saugatuck Falls Natural Area is one of several accesses to the trail network. From the junction of CT 53 and CT 107 in Redding, go north on CT 53 for 0.9 mile. Limited roadside parking is on the left next to the stone gates. Because the trail sits opposite John Read School, hikers may use school parking when school is not in session. A crosswalk links the two. Trailhead GPS: N41 18.317' / W73 24.195'. Trail contacts: Aquarion's Watershed and Environmental Office, Aquarion Water Company, 714 Black Rock Rd., Easton 06612; (203) 452-3511; www.aquarion.com. Centennial Watershed State Forest, www.ct.gov/deep.

T. CHATFIELD HOLLOW STATE PARK

Native Americans regularly hunted and fished here and wore a trail along Chatfield Hollow Brook, which threads between oak-hickory ridges. Artifacts suggest these early peoples sought refuge and held gatherings among the rock recesses and overhangs. Early settlement industries harnessed area waters for power, and centuries later the Civilian Conservation Corps planted pines and built an earth-and-stone dam to capture 7-acre Schreeder Pond. A network of color-coded interlocking trails travels the park and a neighboring parcel of Cockaponset State Forest. The trails venture past Indian caves, along ridges, past brook and ponds, through woods and lowlands. The 4.3-mile Chatfield Trail, a Connecticut Forest and Park Association blue trail, starts across the highway from the park and travels woods and boulder realms to River Road. The park charges nonresidents weekend/holiday parking fees from Memorial Day weekend to Labor Day weekend. Gates open on the second Saturday in April (opening day of trout fishing season) and close the day after Columbus Day. This is a designated Trout Park, one routinely stocked with hatchery fish.

From the circle at the intersection of CT 80 and CT 81 in Killingworth, head west on CT 80, following a sign for the state park. Drive 1.1 miles to find the state park on the right and Chatfield Trail on the left. Trailhead GPS: N41 21.865' / W72 35.044'. Trail contact: Chatfield Hollow State Park, 381 Route 80, Killingworth 06419; (860) 663-2030; www.ct.gov/deep.

U. COCKAPONSET STATE FOREST, WEBER TRACT

Named for an Indian chief, Cockaponset is the second-largest state forest in Connecticut and highly parceled. This tract adjoins Messerschmidt Pond Wildlife Management Area and has short trails exploring woods and swamp. A green trail broken by roads roughly travels the forest perimeter; an orange trail travels past Horse Pond. The forest tract is open from a half hour before sunrise to a half hour after sunset. Keep pets leashed. Trail maps are available online.

From the junction of CT 145 and CT 80, east of Killingworth, west of Winthrop and Deep River, head south on CT 145 for 1 mile and turn right into this satellite of Cockaponset State Forest. Follow the narrow gravel lane to a large gravel parking lot. Trailhead GPS: N41 20.664' / W72 29.793'. Trail contact: Cockaponset State Forest, 18 Ranger Rd., Haddam 06438; (860) 345-8521; www.ct.gov/deep.

V. ROY AND MARGOT LARSEN WILDLIFE SANCTUARY

The Larsen Sanctuary at Fairfield is one of the Audubon Society's most actively used sanctuaries. The 155-acre property features streams, ponds, wetlands, edge habitats, forest, and fields, with 7 miles of trail and boardwalks to explore the diversity and sleuth out the inhabitants. Interpretive signs aid in understanding. The 1-mile wheelchair-accessible Chiboucas Special-Use Trail is a star in the system. It visits the major habitats and has a wetland viewing platform. Sanctuary trail maps are available at the center. A nominal admission fee is collected from nonmembers of Audubon or nonresidents of Fairfield. Trails are open daily, dawn to dusk; the center and Nature Store are closed Sunday. A birds-of-prey compound and butterfly atrium are among the center attractions. No pets, no bicycles.

From Merritt Parkway/CT 15, take exit 44 to reach CT 58. Head south on CT 58 for 0.1 mile and turn right on Congress Street, following the Audubon sanctuary signs. Go 1.2 miles and turn right on Burr Street. Enter the sanctuary on the left in 1 mile. Trailhead GPS: N41 12.138' / W73 17.613'. Trail contact: Roy and Margot Larsen Wildlife Sanctuary, 2325 Burr St., Fairfield 06824; (203) 259-6305; www.ctaudubon.org.

W. GREENWICH AUDUBON SOCIETY

The Audubon Center in Greenwich boasts the nation's flagship environmental education center and 295 acres of diverse habitat probed by 7 miles of trail. A more stunning center housing than this gable-roofed, cupola-topped manor would be hard to find. Routes explore hardwood and hemlock stands, open fields, succession thickets, and lake, streams, and vernal ponds and take you past an old apple orchard and original New England homestead buildings. East Branch Byram River crosses the property and was dammed in the nineteenth century to create shallow Mead Lake. Human-made Indian Spring Pond holds water year-round. Satellite properties expand the portfolio, with 15 additional miles of trail through 686 acres. The center's Quaker Ridge Hawk Watch is one of the best observation sites in the Northeast for the fall raptor migration. Volunteers have counted more than 30,000 broad-winged hawks in a single day—a regional record unmatched even by Pennsylvania's acclaimed Hawk Mountain, north of Reading. No pets. A nominal admission fee applies if you are not an Audubon member.

From Merritt Parkway/CT 15, take exit 28 to follow Round Hill Road north. Go 1.5 miles and turn left (west) onto John Street. In 1.3 miles, at the intersection of John Street and Riversville Road, you'll find the sanctuary entrance. It angles back to the right at this intersection. Trailhead GPS: N41 05.831' / W73 41.297'. Trail contact: Audubon Greenwich, 613 Riversville Rd., Greenwich 06831; (203) 869-5272; http://greenwich .audubon.org.

X. WESTWOODS PRESERVE

This preserve's tangled trail system takes some study to navigate well, but it is also the largest recreational hiking area in Guilford. It has 40 miles of trails on 1,200 acres and a terrain diversity that entertains both boot and eye. Paths string past intriguing natural formations and cave-like recesses and overhangs, waterfalls, salt- and freshwater marshes, vantage points, and an inland tidal lake. The trails are both color and geometrically coded. Maps, a necessity, are available online. Trails cross land held by state forest, Guilford Land

Conservation Trust (GLCT), Town of Guilford, and private hands. All trails are maintained by the Westwoods Trails Committee. The White Circle Trail runs 3.5 miles long and skirts Lost Lake for nearly 0.5 mile. Its companion White Square Trail does more sightseeing and is the longest in the system. The 2-mile, cliff-traveling Yellow Circle Trail is considered the hardest and is reserved for the surefooted in fair weather. Circle trails trend north–south, with square and triangle trails marking other routes.

From the junction of CT 77 and US 1 in Guilford, go west on US 1. In 0.6 mile you pass Dunk Rock Road on the left, which provides trail access. Continuing west on US 1 for another 0.1 mile leads to Peddlers Road. Turn left here to find trailhead parking on the left past Denison Drive. This site has gravel off-road parking and a kiosk. Do not block drives. Trailhead GPS: N41 17.699' / W72 42.805'. Trail contact: Guilford Land Conservation Trust, PO Box 200, Guilford 06437; (203) 457-9253; http://guilford landtrust.org.

Y. MCKINNEY NATIONAL WILDLIFE REFUGE, SALT MEADOWS UNIT

Connecticut congressman Stewart B. McKinney advocated for this refuge that now consists of eleven units on the state's shore. The Salt Meadow Unit, in Westbrook, is the refuge cornerstone. It claims the Ester Lape estate donated for wildlife protection, with the administration center in the fieldstone house. A nature loop travels the property's coastal woods and edge habitat and offers tidal marsh overlooks. The National Audubon Society has recognized the unit as an Important Bird Area. On the Atlantic Flyway, it provides critical resting,

Menunketesuck River, Salt Meadow Unit-Stewart B. McKinney National Wildlife Refuge, Connecticut

feeding, and nesting habitat for wading birds, shorebirds, songbirds, and terns, and winter habitat for waterfowl. Experts have identified 280 species of migrating neotropical birds here. No dogs.

From I-95 between Clinton and Westbrook, take exit 64 and head south on CT 145 (Horse Mill Road) for 0.1 mile to the four-way, flashing red-light intersection. Turn left (east) onto Old Clinton Road, drive 1 mile, and turn right into the refuge at the sign. Parking is ahead in 0.1 mile at the old stone estate/headquarters. Trailhead GPS: N41 17.224' / W72 28.309'. Trail contact: Stewart B. McKinney National Wildlife Refuge, 733 Old Clinton Rd., Westbrook 06498; (860) 399-2513; www.fws.gov.

EASTERN CONNECTICUT

The retreat of the Wisconsin Glacier some 15,000 to 11,000 years ago largely shaped the state of Connecticut that we know today. The hiccoughs of advance and retreat bulldozed and deposited vast amounts of glacial debris that trapped the glacial meltwater into lakes. Glacial Lake Hitchcock claimed what is now the Connecticut River Valley. This lake stretched 200 miles northward from Connecticut all the way to Vermont. When its damming debris, near what is now Rocky Neck, gradually gave way during a centuries-long process, the breach incised the wide, north-to-south gash that is the Connecticut River. Other signatures of the glacial legacy are fertile silts, rocky deposits, eskers (low glacial debris ridges), and kettle ponds.

The major waterway of the Connecticut River effectively divides the state into two. Its sheer dominance on the landscape suggests the appropriateness that the state should wear its name. The river and its enfolding valley encouraged settlement, trade, and industry. The state's population centers continue to hug the Connecticut River, with the balance tilted toward the west. Before the arrival of the Europeans, native peoples made use of the river's bounty and transportation. *Connecticut* is an Anglicized version of their name for the river, meaning "long tidal river." Coastal influences creep up the Connecticut River as far as Enfield Rapids.

The Narragansett Indians occupied eastern Connecticut and Rhode Island, while the Mohegans lived to their south and the Pequots to their west. Native peoples fished, farmed, gathered, traded furs, and tapped sugar maple trees for sugar. The Mohawks, one of the Iroquoian Five Nations, used the Connecticut River to conduct raids on the agrarian tribes.

When the colonists arrived, they cleared forests for farms, but the rocky ground made success marginal. Small mills sprung up for the production of lumber, flour, textiles, and tools, and the Connecticut coastal shore supported maritime enterprise. But before long, modern industry and technology outpaced and replaced mill production.

Today much of the eastern state has returned to uninhabited forest. But, the name of Revolutionary War hero Nathan Hale chimes through the quiet. So, too, does the name of state heroine Prudence Crandall, the Quaker-raised schoolteacher who sparked outrage in the 1830s when she educated African-American girls in her small Canterbury school. Their shared characteristics of resolve and purpose live on in this region.

Eastern Connecticut holds a gentler terrain than its western counterpart. Its geographic features include the eastern traprock ridges, eastern uplands, and coastal lowlands. It is a landscape of mild undulations, glacier-flattened ridges, and picturesque outcrop hills. Eastern Connecticut houses the largest forest in the state, Pachaug State Forest, which spans 24,000 acres and encompasses a rare rhododendron and Atlantic white cedar swamp. This region also boasts the unheard of: an undeveloped shore along Long Island Sound. Your travels here will take you through rolling woodlands of southern hardwoods, eastern hemlock, and planted red and white pines. Mountain laurels grow with exuberance, and remote and quiet ponds reflect the sky and double the fall color fireworks.

NORTHEAST CONNECTICUT TRAILS

Northeast Connecticut unites the bounty of eastern Hartford County with that of Tolland and Windham Counties. Quiet woods and milder heights than those in the western part of the state compose this region. It's a place to lose yourself in beauty: tranquil woods, blue waters, and echoes from the past.

26 BIGELOW HOLLOW STATE PARK

Near the Massachusetts border, this eastern Connecticut state park boasts large ponds, deep woods, and tranquility. A barbell-shaped hike combines explorations of Bigelow and Breakneck Ponds. Secluded coves, peninsulas, shrubby islands, deep hemlock stands, mixed hardwood forests, and showy midstories of mountain laurel entertain glances. Nipmuck State Forest abuts the park and carries part of the hike.

Start: Bigelow Pond Trailhead at the north end of Bigelow Pond
Distance: 7.6-mile barbell
Hiking time: 4.5 to 6 hours
Difficulty: Moderate, with Breakneck Pond having the more demanding travel
Elevation change: Just over 100 feet
Trail surface: Earthen path and old logging road
Best seasons: Spring through fall
Other trail users: Hunters (in state forest only), anglers, snowshoers, snowmobilers, cross-country skiers
Canine compatibility: Leashed dogs permitted
Land status: State park and state forest
Nearest town: Sturbridge, MA, for gas and services
Fees and permits: State park seasonal weekend and holiday parking fee for nonresidents
Schedule: Year-round, 8 a.m. to sunset

Maps: State park map (available on-site or online at www.ct.gov/deep); Connecticut Forest and Park Association (CFPA) *Connecticut Walk Book, East* (available from CFPA, www.ctwoodlands.org)
Trail contacts: Bigelow Hollow State Park, c/o Shenipsit State Forest, 166 Chestnut Hill Rd., Stafford Springs 06076; (860) 684-3430. Department of Energy and Environmental Protection, State Parks, (860) 424-3200; www.ct.gov/deep.
Special considerations: Park personnel encourage all hikers to carry a current map; hikers do stray here. Selective logging can impact trail appearance and location. During hunting season take precautions to make yourself and your pet visible or hike elsewhere. Backpack campsites and lean-tos on Breakheart Pond are available by permit only (DEEP forms online).

FINDING THE TRAILHEAD

From I-84, take exit 73 for Union and go east on CT 190 for 2 miles. Turn right (east) on CT 171, go another 1.4 miles, and turn left to enter the park. Start at the Bigelow Pond Trailhead Parking Area at the north end of Bigelow Pond, about 0.75 mile into the park. Trailhead GPS: N41 59.917' / W72 07.597'

Bigelow Pond,
Bigelow Hollow State
Park, Connecticut

THE HIKE

For Bigelow Pond Loop, the lower loop in this barbell, hike west through the picnic area and cross the inlet brook. At the trail junction, keep left, following the yellow blazes for a counterclockwise shoreline tour. The blue/white Mashapaug Pond View Trail continues uphill to the right.

In the boulder-studded woods, watch your footing. Pass between a regal hemlock and a gargantuan boulder to round the west shore of the elongated pond sculpted by small islands and points. Boughs overhang the water, and mountain laurel and sweet pepper-bush crowd the shore.

At CT 171 you travel along the highway bank, which acts as a dam, to reach the east shore. Before coming to the gate on a fire lane, you turn left to resume the hike on foot trail. Hemlock and pine needles cushion footfalls. The trail travels about 15 feet above shore.

Below a wooden gate, you spur left onto a peninsula before continuing the yellow loop. This mushroom-shaped peninsula invites with a scenic outcrop, picnic table, and deep drop-off. To the north, it shapes a shallow bay. Resuming northbound, pass through the boat launch/picnic area and traverse a peninsular rise to return to the starting point.

Adding the upper (Breakneck Pond) loop, cross over the park road to the kiosk and map box on its east side and follow the white-blazed East Ridge Trail heading right. The blue/orange Ridge Trail heads left. Upon meeting a closed logging road, bear left (north) for Breakneck Pond, still following white blazes. Pass through deep hemlock woods, with interloping white pine, oak, and black cherry.

At the marshy south end of Breakneck Pond, you reach the loop junction. South Lean-to sits nearby. Go left on the Breakneck Pond View Trail (blue/white dot blaze) for a clockwise stroll. This trail hugs the west shore, traveling north among mountain laurel, conifers, and beaver-gnawed trees. You will overlook lily pad waters and gain lengthy pond views. At times the trail pinches to a logging road.

Rolling wooded ridges shape the pond basin, and shrubby islands interrupt the open water. Footing along the shore can be rugged. Kingfishers and woodpeckers may disrupt the quiet. Beyond an island-squeezed channel, view even more of this long water that stretches into Massachusetts.

You next pass below a cluster of boulders adorned in rock tripe lichen to travel a low wooded ridge where marsh spans to shore. Before the pond's outlet, you again meet the blue/orange Ridge Trail, which offers an alternative return, but for the selected hike, hold your course on the blue/white dot trail, crossing the outlet, and then bear right on a logging road to continue the shoreline hike south on the blue Nipmuck Trail.

At the Massachusetts-Connecticut state line monument, keep on the blue Nipmuck Trail. The white-blazed East Ridge Trail angles upslope. On the Nipmuck, you reach a scenic pine-shaded point overlooking the pond's aquatic mat. Bear right off the roadway, still chasing blue blazes. The trail rolls but never strays far from shore. Mountain laurels grow with abandon, and you traverse a glacial deposit of rocks and boulders.

The trail wanders past flats and East Lean-to. Buttonbush and highbush blueberry, frogs and whirligig beetles add to impressions. Cross-pond views may locate a beaver lodge. Where the Nipmuck and East Ridge Trails again meet, turn right on the white-blazed trail to close the loop and then head left to backtrack the white blazes to the Bigelow Pond picnic area.

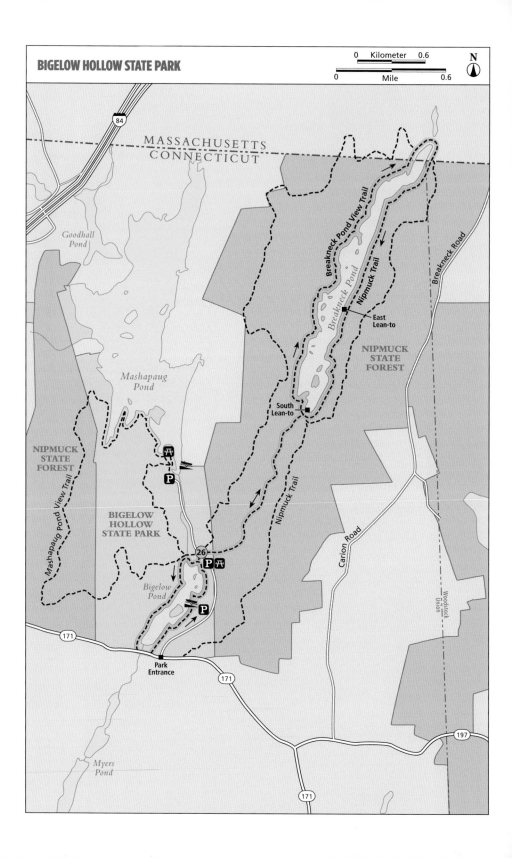

0 Kilometer 0.6

0 Mile 0.6

N

MASSACHUSETTS
CONNECTICUT

84

*Goodhall
Pond*

*Mashapaug
Pond*

Breakneck Pond View Trail

Breakneck Pond

Nipmuck Trail

East
Lean-to

NIPMUCK
STATE
FOREST

South
Lean-to

NIPMUCK
STATE
FOREST

Mashapaug Pond View Trail

Nipmuck Trail

Carion Road

Breakneck Road

Woodstock
Union

BIGELOW
HOLLOW
STATE PARK

26

*Bigelow
Pond*

171

Park
Entrance

171

197

*Myers
Pond*

171

MILES AND DIRECTIONS

0.0 Start at the Bigelow Pond Trailhead. Hike west through the picnic area to cross the inlet brook.

0.1 Reach a trail junction. Go left, following the yellow blazes counterclockwise around Bigelow Pond. **Note:** The blue/white Mashapaug Pond View Trail heads uphill to the right.

0.7 Reach CT 171. Turn left, walking the road at the south end of the pond to the east shore.

1.0 Take the peninsula spur left before resuming the yellow loop.

1.2 Resume the counterclockwise loop.

1.6 Return to the Bigelow Pond picnic area and cross over the park road to begin the Breakneck Pond loop. Follow the white-blazed East Ridge Trail to the right. **Note:** The blue/orange Ridge Trail is to your left.

2.6 Reach the loop junction at the southern marshy extent of Breakneck Pond. Go left on the Breakneck Pond View Trail (blue/white dot) for a clockwise loop. **Note:** The East Ridge Trail heads right to meet the blue Nipmuck Trail (the loop's return).

4.8 Cross the outlet. Follow the blue Nipmuck Trail south along the east shore.

6.5 Meet the white East Ridge Trail and turn right on it.

6.6 Complete the loop. Backtrack south to the trailhead.

7.6 Arrive back at the trailhead.

Option: The 5-mile Mashapaug Pond View Trail (the blue/white trail leaving the Bigelow Pond picnic area) climbs to yet another pond. At 0.1 mile reach its loop junction. Go straight to visit shore first; the return is via the wooded left fork. Be attentive to blazes throughout. After a rolling ascent you descend to cross a service road and enter the Mashapaug Pond Picnic Area. Mashapaug Pond is vast and deep, with a forested edge and a mostly private north shore. This trail travels its wild southern extreme. At 1.1 miles a spur to the right reaches a large peninsula. Here you gain a better perspective of the pond's size. The loop follows the incised bay and shore. Midway into the hike, the trail draws away from Mashapaug Pond for a pleasant hemlock-hardwood forest stroll. Pass through changing forest to close the loop and return to the trailhead.

HIKE INFORMATION

LOCAL INFORMATION

Windham Region Chamber of Commerce, 1010 Main St., PO Box 43, Willimantic 06226; (860) 423-6389; www.windhamchamber.com.

LOCAL EVENTS/ATTRACTIONS

Sturbridge Village, 1 Old Sturbridge Village Rd., Sturbridge, MA 01566; (800) 733-1830; www.osv.org. In Massachusetts, Old Sturbridge Village, an acclaimed living-history museum, depicts New England life from 1790 to 1840. Historians in period costume guide you through time among the site's antique buildings and its working farm with heritage breed animals.

ORGANIZATIONS

Connecticut Forest and Park Association (CFPA), 16 Meriden Rd., Rockfall 06481; (860) 346-8733; www.ctwoodlands.org.

27 MASHAMOQUET BROOK STATE PARK

Mashamoquet (Mushmugget) means "stream of good fishing." The namesake brook flows west to east across this nearly 1,000-acre northeast Connecticut state park composed of rolling wooded terrain, natural rock features, and picturesque swamp. A pair of interlocking colored loops explores the area. This hike combines the Blue Loop with a visit to the swamp. Stone walls web the park. An old gristmill, maintained as a museum by the Pomfret Historical Society, recalls a milling past.

Start: Picnic area trailhead
Distance: 5.1 miles for loop and side loop
Hiking time: 3 to 4 hours
Difficulty: Moderate
Elevation change: 400 feet, but rolling
Trail surface: Earthen path, woods lane, outcrop ledge, management road
Best seasons: Spring through fall
Other trail users: Anglers and birders; mountain bikers on trails north and west of Wolf Den Drive
Canine compatibility: Leashed dogs permitted in picnic areas and on hiking trails; no pets in campground, on beach, or in picnic shelter
Land status: State park
Nearest town: Dayville in Township of Killingly, CT

Fees and permits: Seasonal weekend and holiday parking fee for nonresidents; overnight fee for campers
Schedule: Year-round, 8 a.m. to sunset
Map: State park map (available online at www.ct.gov/deep)
Trail contacts: Mashamoquet Brook State Park, 147 Wolf Den Dr., Pomfret Center 06259; (860) 928-6121. Department of Energy and Environmental Protection, State Parks, (860) 424-3200; www.ct.gov/ deep.
Special considerations: The trails south and east of Wolf Den Drive are open to foot travel only. Those north and west of Wolf Den Drive allow mountain biking. Carry water. Along the trail, there is a toilet near the headquarters.

FINDING THE TRAILHEAD

At the US 44–CT 97 junction in Abington, go east on US 44 to reach Mashamoquet Brook Campground on the right in 1 mile; the main day-use entrance (and road to trailhead) on the right in 1.2 miles; and CT 101 in 2 miles, where you'd turn right, go a few yards, and turn right again onto Wolf Den Drive for the park office and Wolf Den Campground. This trail starts at the picnic area south of the old mill. Trailhead GPS: N41 51.504' / W71 58.857'

THE HIKE

Mount the steps to cross the picnic area's wide footbridge over Mashamoquet Brook. The bridge's high red-iron rails are open at the top for admiring the brook. A diversion rejoins the main flow here, and large boulders edge the tannin water. Upon crossing,

follow the yellow blazes left to reach the hiking trails. Hikers from camp arrive via the yellow blazes on the right.

At the base of the slope, you angle uphill through woods of hemlock, oak, and birch to meet the Blue Loop atop the ridge. Go left (clockwise). Sounds of nature replace the roadway hum. Follow an earthen lane, meeting the Red Trail, which swings a shorter loop. Keep left, following the shared section of trail. Snapped trees can hint at harsh weather, while scenic stone walls intersect the trail. Overhead stretches a canopy of dancing leaves. When the leaves have fallen, barren branches reveal nests.

Before long the trails separate, with the blue trail bearing left. Mountain laurel appears as the trail steadily descends to cross a footbridge over a thin tributary of Mashamoquet Brook. Find maple, hemlock, and false hellebore. The woodland relaxation invites thoughts as well as feet to wander. You next reach paved road. Turn right, following blazes toward the park office.

At the office, delay resuming the blue trail, which next follows mowed track. Instead, continue along the park road toward Wolf Den Campground to reach the Wolf Den Swamp Nature Trail (on the left) and hike its loop. It travels the shore of a snag-pierced swamp, with skunk cabbage, tufted grasses, arrowhead, cattail, and phragmites (plumed reeds). Geese, red-winged blackbirds, woodpeckers, fish, frogs, and turtles add to sightings. Insects, though, can annoy.

Back on the blue trail, hike the mowed track and pass through a gap in a 3-foot-tall stone wall, returning to hemlock-oak habitat. In places the stone wall incorporates the natural outcrop ledge. The trail rolls, topping exposed bedrock, where you can admire the woodland and wait for wildlife to come to you. Laurel again interweaves the forest.

The trail grows narrower, with rocks studding the path. You then descend from the main outcrop area to cross a footbridge over a small brook supporting false hellebore. The moist area that follows seasonally holds jack-in-the-pulpits.

Topping an outcrop, look for an arrow pointing out the ledge that holds Indian Chair, a natural rock sofa complete with back and arm rest. The seat offers a squirrel's-eye view of the woodland. Resuming clockwise, you traverse woods with a fuller midstory, and the Red Trail returns to share the course at a drainage boardwalk, where marsh marigolds complement the dark water. Now climb steeply to Wolf Den. Its rock ledges shape a boxy opening leading to a crawlspace, 30 feet long. In 1742 Israel Putnum crept into this den and shot a wolf that had troubled area farmers.

At a three-pronged junction, a 200-foot spur leads right to Table Rock—an elevated 10-by-20-foot natural slab. The Red Trail heads straight, and the Blue Loop heads left, passing through dense laurel to rustic Wolf Den State Park Picnic Area. Hike out its graveled access road to Wolf Den Drive and look right to locate the blue trail as it heads north off this road. Enjoy a similar woods setting with dense laurel where the road brings added light. Follow the blazes for a mildly descending stroll. Close the loop and retrace the yellow trail to the picnic area bridge.

MILES AND DIRECTIONS

0.0 Start at the picnic area trailhead. Cross the footbridge and follow the yellow trail left. **Note:** The brook campground is reached to your right.

0.2 Reach the Blue Loop. Hike this blazed route left (clockwise).

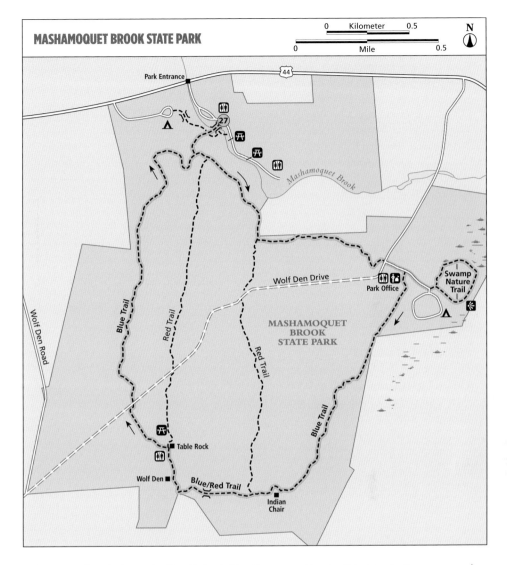

0   Kilometer   0.5

0   Mile   0.5

N

Park Entrance

44

27

Mashamoquet Brook

Wolf Den Drive

Park Office

Swamp
Nature
Trail

MASHAMOQUET
BROOK
STATE PARK

Blue Trail

Red Trail

Wolf Den Road

Red Trail

Blue Trail

Table Rock

Wolf Den

Blue/Red Trail

Indian
Chair

1.2 Reach the park office. Delay taking the mowed track of the blue trail. Instead, follow the road southeast toward Wolf Den Campground to locate the start of the Wolf Den Swamp Nature Trail (on the left) and walk its loop.

1.9 Resume clockwise travel on the Blue Loop near the park office.

2.8 Reach Indian Chair. Proceed on the blue trail.

3.2 Reach Wolf Den. Proceed on the blue trail.

3.4 Reach the Wolf Den Picnic Area. Follow the gravel entry road out to Wolf Den Drive and look right to pick up the blue trail as it heads north away from the road.

4.9 Complete the Blue Loop. Retrace the yellow trail to the trailhead.

5.1 Arrive back at the trailhead.

HIKE INFORMATION

LOCAL INFORMATION

Northeastern Connecticut Chamber of Commerce, 210 Westcott Rd., Danielson 06239; (860) 774-8001; http://nectchamber.com.

LOCAL EVENTS/ATTRACTIONS

The Center at Pomfret (Lois Orswell Grassland Bird Conservation Center), 218 Day Rd., Pomfret Center 06259; (860) 928-4948; www.ctaudubon.org. The Connecticut Audubon's Center at Pomfret opened in 2011 with the ambitious mission to engage children in nature. The center offers wildlife displays, guided walks, and lectures. Adjoining Bafflin Sanctuary, it is surrounded by trails, traversing fields, woods, and edge habitats.

Roseland Cottage, 556 Route 169, PO Box 186, Woodstock 06281; (860) 928-4074; www.historicnewengland.org/historic-properties/homes. The 1846 Gothic Revival–style Bowen House, dubbed Roseland Cottage, is a National Historic Landmark open for touring (admission charged). It sits across from the Woodstock town common. Its dressy gabled architecture, English landscaping, carriage barn, and detailed Victorian interior encapsulate the era of the successful and well-connected Bowen family, who entertained presidents here.

ACCOMMODATIONS

This park has two campgrounds open Memorial Day weekend through Labor Day weekend. **Mashamoquet Brook Campground** offers 18 wooded camping sites; **Wolf Den Campground** has 35 campsites. Reservations are available through ReserveAmerica, (877) 668-2267 or www.reserveamerica.com.

28 CASE MOUNTAIN RECREATION AREA, WHITE CARRIAGEWAY LOOP

This 640-acre metropolitan open space rolls out a pleasant wooded welcome mat and has more than 10 miles of well-marked carriageways and foot trails exploring its limits. Benches encourage a leisurely pace, reflection, and nature study. The relaxing loop of the white-blazed carriageway takes you to the park's heights for a fine view of the central Connecticut River Valley. The loop also passes picturesque outcrops and the quiet of elongated Upper Case Pond. All but the final foot trail link is on carriageway.

Start: Case Mountain Recreation Area trailhead
Distance: 3.5-mile lollipop
Hiking time: 2.5 to 3 hours
Difficulty: Easy, but a steady climb from the trailhead
Elevation change: Travel between a trailhead elevation of 450 feet and the Lookout Mountain overlook elevation of 744 feet.
Trail surface: Carriageway and earthen path
Best seasons: Spring through fall
Other trail users: Mountain bikers, joggers, snowshoers, cross-country skiers
Canine compatibility: Leashed dogs permitted
Land status: Metropolitan watershed open space
Nearest town: Manchester, CT
Fees and permits: None

Schedule: Year-round, sunrise to sunset
Map: Connecticut Forest and Park Association (CFPA) *Connecticut Walk Book, East* (available from CFPA, www.ctwoodlands.org)
Trail contact: Case Mountain Recreation Area, c/o Town of Manchester, Center Springs Park Lodge (Main Office), 39 Lodge Dr., Manchester 06040; (860) 647-3084; http://recreation.townofmanchester .org
Special considerations: There are no amenities at the site. Bring drinking water for the hike. Be sure to keep to the marked trail at Upper Case Pond to avoid straying onto private land. Rattlesnakes and copperheads, although rarely seen, do find habitat here.

FINDING THE TRAILHEAD

From I-384, take exit 4. Eastbound travelers turn right on Wyllys Street/Spring Street and continue right (west) on Spring Street, crossing the one-lane stone bridge at a waterfall. Trailhead parking is on the left at 0.2 mile, just after the bridge, as Spring Street enters a bend. Westbound travelers turn right on Highland Street and then right on Wyllys Street, keeping right for westbound travel on Spring Street. Parking is signed for Case Mountain–Spring Street. Trailhead GPS: N41 45.679' / W72 29.408'

THE HIKE

A long, steady climb on a paved grade that later becomes gravel carries you into the recreation area. Birch, chestnut oak, and hickory edge the route. Color-coded and unblazed trails branch from this arterial, but the white blazes are reliably spaced for carefree travel.

At the loop junction, continue forward on the carriageway for counterclockwise travel, saving the foot-trail segment for the return. Hemlocks, maples, and mountain laurel vary the woods mix. Benches along the loop welcome pause and reflection. These pleasing woods give up few clues that they were heavily harvested in the 1900s for the production of charcoal to fuel Case Mills. Keen-eyed detectives, though, might spy the hint of charcoal mounds.

The carriageway climbs and wends to Lookout Mountain, emerging from the low-tree cover. You may continue forward toward the vista bench seating, staying on the white trail, or veer left up the summit outcrop to win a higher perspective. An attractive shapely white pine with tiered boughs contributes to the shared western view that looks out over the bridges and wooded expanse of the Connecticut River and across Hartford's city skyline to the ridges vanishing west in the morning fog or afternoon haze. The big, broad summit can accommodate many viewers. The white, pink, and yellow trails all converge here.

By tracing a crescent course south and a bit west over the top, you rejoin the white carriageway that continued forward from the benches below. You now enter full woods contouring the upper slope of Lookout Mountain. Layered outcrops and ledges punctuate the woods. Again keep to the white carriageway. Junctions are mostly well labeled. The trail crews do a good job here.

Case Pond, Case Mountain Recreation Area, Manchester, Connecticut

As you continue the swinging descent, you crisscross the Shenipsit Trail, a Connecticut blue trail. Ledge shelves and outcrop cliffs rise to your left. Whale-like boulders, split rocks, and jumbles rise in their midst. Fallen leaves, lichen, moss, and splashes of fern add to their charm. Swamp maples and hemlocks grow in the wetter conditions on the right.

Across the East the production of charcoal to fuel the manufacturing furnaces of the eighteenth and early nineteenth centuries gobbled up great expanses of woodland. Colliers would tend the slow-burning wigwam-shaped hearths that produced the prized resource.

Pass between slopes and later glimpse a few houses off to the right as you approach the Case Pond parking access. Keep in the woods, following the carriageway left and skirting the basin of Case Pond. White pines and hemlocks replace the hardwoods. Arrive at the granite marker for Upper Case Pond and a mossy stone wall that borders the travel lane. Upper Case Pond feeds from the marshy upper drainage to open water, with still-water reflections of the rimming trees. A few small private structures front the pond.

Keep alert for the loop's foot-trail return, which heads left off the carriageway. It is marked by a post and blazes. The carriageway ahead enters private property. The foot trail, although rooted at times, still offers comfortable travel and widens as it climbs. Benches are found here as well. After a casual woods meander, a short boardwalk spans a wet-bottomed area and the trail passes a leaf-dappled pond.

Close the loop at the main carriageway and turn right for the descent back to the trailhead. At the trailhead you might want to walk over to view the marriage of stonework and water at the bridge and waterfall, but you will need to be on the road to best see the terraced spill, the stone-banked channel, and the repeating arches of the bridge. With the bending road, narrow road bridge, and hurried drivers, stay alert to traffic and forgo this viewing during commute times.

MILES AND DIRECTIONS

0.0 Start at the Case Mountain Recreation Area trailhead. Ascend the paved service lane/carriageway into the recreation area.

0.3 Reach the loop junction. Continue forward on the white carriageway.

0.8 Reach the Lookout Mountain overlook. Ascend the outcrop for the highest vantage, or proceed forward to the viewing benches. Both paths meet at the far end of the vista clearing.

2.2 Reach Upper Case Pond. Continue southwest along shore.

2.5 Turn left off the carriageway, following the marked foot trail uphill. **Note:** The carriageway ahead enters private property.

3.2 Close the loop. Turn right, backtracking the paved lane to the trailhead.

3.5 Arrive back at the trailhead.

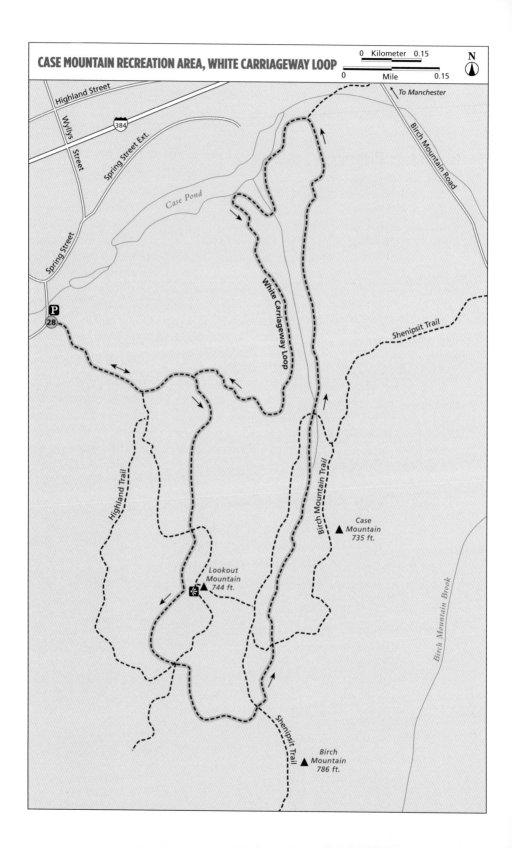

0   Kilometer   0.15

0   Mile   0.15

N

Highland Street

Wyllys Street

Spring Street Ext.

384

Case Pond

Spring Street

To Manchester

Birch Mountain Road

White Carriageway Loop

Shenipsit Trail

P
28

Highland Trail

Birch Mountain Trail

Case
Mountain
735 ft.

Birch Mountain Brook

Lookout
Mountain
744 ft.

Shenipsit Trail

Birch
Mountain
786 ft.

HIKE INFORMATION

LOCAL INFORMATION

Central Regional Tourism District, 1 Constitution Plaza, 2nd Floor, Hartford 06103; (860) 787-9640; www.centerofct.com.

LOCAL EVENTS/ATTRACTIONS

Nathan Hale Homestead, 2299 South St., Coventry 06238; (860) 742-6917; www .ctlandmarks.org. This property holds and honors the 1776 family home of Connecticut state hero Nathan Hale. Nathan and five of his brothers served in the patriot army. Nathan was caught and hanged as a spy, but his last words live on: "I only regret that I have but one life to lose for my country." The Georgian-style home became a Connecticut Landmark in 1940. The house is furnished with Hale-family pieces and period antiques, and is surrounded by Nathan Hale State Forest.

Wickham Park, 1329 West Middle Turnpike, Manchester 06040; (860) 528-0856; www.wickhampark.org. This private foundation park in Manchester and East Hartford encompasses 250 rolling acres of themed gardens, open fields, woodlands, ponds, walking paths, and picnic areas. An admission is charged.

ORGANIZATIONS

Connecticut Forest and Park Association (CFPA), 16 Meriden Rd., Rockfall 06481; (860) 346-8733; www.ctwoodlands.org.

29 NIPMUCK TRAIL, FENTON RIVER

This section of the Nipmuck Trail, one of the classic trunk-line trails of the Connecticut Forest and Park Association (CFPA) blue trail system, dishes up one of the best and closest river walks in the state. It runs between Mansfield Hollow State Park and Gurleyville Grist Mill. The trail twice crosses repurposed steel bridges and tops 50-Foot Cliff for a survey of the forest-and-swamp mosaic of the immediate neighborhood.

Start: Picnic area trailhead at Mansfield Hollow State Park
Distance: 11.2 miles out and back
Hiking time: 7 to 8 hours
Difficulty: Moderate, but can be strenuous when heavy rain swamps bottomlands
Elevation change: 300 feet
Trail surface: Earthen path, woods road, pipeline corridor
Best seasons: Spring through fall
Other trail users: Anglers, bow hunters, snowshoers, cross-country skiers; mountain bikers and equestrians on adjacent trails
Canine compatibility: Leashed dogs permitted
Land status: State park, wildlife area, town open space, land trust
Nearest town: Willimantic, CT
Fees and permits: None

Schedule: Year-round, 8 a.m. to sunset (for park trailhead)
Maps: State park map (available online at www.ct.gov/deep); Connecticut Forest and Park Association (CFPA) *Connecticut Walk Book, East* (available from CFPA, www.ctwoodlands.org)
Trail contacts: Mansfield Hollow State Park, c/o Mashamoquet Brook State Park, 147 Wolf Den Dr., Pomfret Center 06259; (860) 928-6121. Department of Energy and Environmental Protection, State Parks, (860) 424-3200; www.ct.gov/deep.
Special considerations: The blue Nipmuck Trail and the blue/white Fenton Trail are for foot travel only. Other colored routes are open to nonvehicle multiuse. Bring drinking water.

FINDING THE TRAILHEAD

From US 6 at Willimantic, take the exit for CT 195 and the University of Connecticut at Storrs and go north on CT 195 for 2.1 miles. Turn right (east) on Bassett Bridge Road at Mansfield Center. Continue 0.9 mile, turn left into the park, and go 0.3 mile more to the picnic area/trailhead. Trailhead GPS: N41 45.889' / W72 10.722'

THE HIKE

Mansfield Hollow traces its origin to the hurricanes of the 1930s, with the dammed lake and surrounding open space a direct response to the uncontrolled flooding. A secondary benefit is the recreation this undeveloped land sponsors.

Follow the blue East Branch Nipmuck Trail, heading north in white pine–hardwood forest on rooted path. The lake is but glare beyond the trees. Although this

Fenton River along Nipmuck Trail, Mansfield Hollow Wildlife Area, Connecticut

hike barely snares a brushing glance at Mansfield Hollow Lake, once it pairs with the Fenton River, you are treated to a great water show.

Nearing CT 89, travel is on woods roads, and yellow blazes share the way. You skirt a ball field in Mansfield's Southeast Park, following the treed edge and entry road to the CT 89 crossing. The trail then dips into forest, passing umbrella-branched maples, crossing a paved lane, and crossing a footbridge below the rock levee and culvert of the road.

Study blazes where you navigate woods roads and sort through meetings with other trails. Follow the shared blue and yellow course over South Iron Bridge. This repurposed 1901 bridge saves history and serves up early Fenton River views. Downstream holds scalloped banks, draping boughs, and riffles. Upstream is glassy, parting brushy banks.

Now, turn left upstream on a trampled-grass and sometimes soggy path, leaving behind the yellow trail. A thick riparian growth isolates the Fenton River, and just a few iron posts confirm the way. Ahead you traverse an esker-like ridge between the river and an eastern swamp. Descend from the ridge, and at the next ascent look for a foot trail to take you left over North Iron Bridge. Continue north upstream. Blue/white blazes head downstream.

The narrow Fenton River is a classic tannin-colored water with alternating smooth flows and small riffles, with an attractive shading woodland. Its quiet charm may blunt your willingness to turn away for the Chaffeeville Road crossing, but there will be more viewing farther north.

But, first, blazes lead you away from the river to 50-Foot Cliff for an overlook of the Fenton River neighborhood. The trail rolls through changing woods, crosses a brook, and climbs a rise of layered ledges. Traverse the summit's thin-trunked woods to the edge vista, which overlooks the rolling Connecticut wooded expanse to the south-southeast, with its different textures and heights. Fall leaf-seekers gather here.

In the nineteenth century the Berlin Iron Bridge Company of East Berlin was Connecticut's only large-scale fabricator of iron-truss bridges, producing upwards of 1,000 bridges. Most were used in the Northeast, with hundreds in Connecticut, but few remain. Two have been repurposed for the Nipmuck Trail.

From the vantage, the trail hooks back through similar woods. Where it crosses the pipeline corridor, you reach the junction of the two branches of the Nipmuck Trail. Bear right, northbound, descending woods road along a stone wall and past wolf trees before turning left to follow the shrubby pipeline's edge to gravel Bousa Road.

Cross and briefly descend along the pipeline's right edge before turning right into woods. You trace a section of built-up levee. At its breach, follow the blazes along shore and upslope to cross the river on the bridge structure just below Chaffeeville Road. You then return to the levee. Rockwork ditches and an old millpond hint at the area's past.

At times the trail is so close to the river that only a few roots hold in place the bank. Other times you are on floodplain, with its logs, snags, trickles, and standing water. The clear river holds brookies and brown trout. Chaffeeville Road is above to the east, reached by an occasional spur.

At dirt Stone Mill Road, head left to Gurleyville Grist Mill. For this hike, it signals the turnaround. The Nipmuck, however, continues north over Stone Mill Bridge. Large cutstone blocks and twelve-pane windows fashion the classic mill built into the riverbank. Owned by Joshua's Trust (Joshua's Tract Conservation and Historic Trust), the mill is seasonally open and contains the complete system of historic mill equipment.

MILES AND DIRECTIONS

- **0.0** Start at Mansfield Hollow State Park, at the picnic area trailhead. Descend to the trailhead kiosk and follow the blue blazes heading north.
- **1.3** Reach the CT 89 crossing. Follow the blue blazes descending the roadside slope.
- **1.7** Meet the southern end of the blue/white Fenton Trail at a Y-junction on woods road. Turn right to keep to the Nipmuck Trail, following the blue/yellow blazes.
- **1.9** Cross South Iron Bridge. Follow the blue trail, turning left (upstream) on a trampled-grass path that can be muddy. **Note:** The yellow trail continues forward on woods road.
- **2.4** Cross North Iron Bridge. Continue north (upstream) on the blue trail. **Note:** The blue/white Fenton Trail heads downstream, suggesting a return option.
- **2.9** Cross Chaffeeville Road.
- **3.5** Reach the 50-Foot Cliff overlook.
- **4.2** Cross Bousa Road. Trace the right (east) edge of pipeline corridor to pick up the trail heading right into woods.
- **5.6** Reach Gurleyville Grist Mill on Stone Mill Road. Backtrack to the trailhead.
- **11.2** Arrive back at the trailhead.

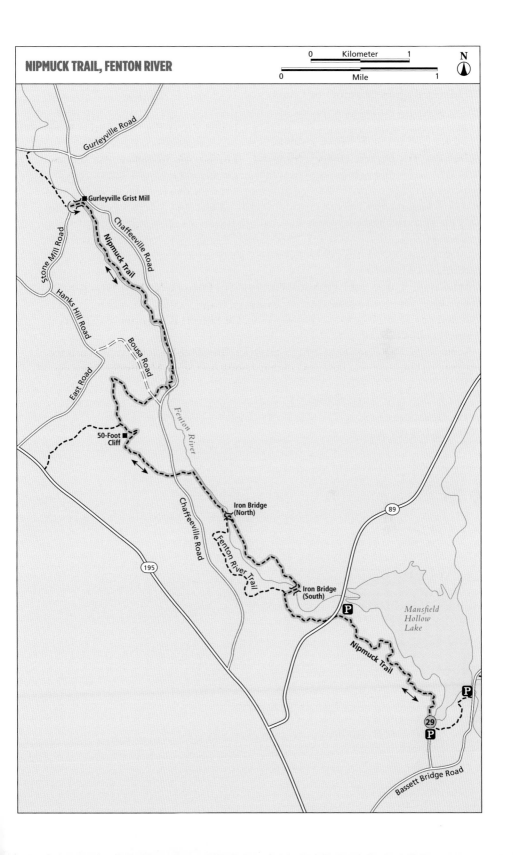

HIKE INFORMATION

LOCAL INFORMATION

Windham Region Chamber of Commerce, 1010 Main St., PO Box 43, Willimantic 06226; (860) 423-6389; www.windhamchamber.com.

LOCAL EVENTS/ATTRACTIONS

Windham Textile and History Museum, 411 Main St., Willimantic 06226; (860) 456-2178; www.millmuseum.org. The Windham Textile and History Museum preserves the story of this important industry that helped shape the development of Connecticut and New England from colonial times forward. Its exhibits and collections introduce not only the industry but the inventors and craftspeople and the social trends the enterprise sponsored.

ORGANIZATIONS

Connecticut Forest and Park Association (CFPA), 16 Meriden Rd., Rockfall 06481; (860) 346-8733; www.ctwoodlands.org.

30 JAMES L. GOODWIN STATE FOREST

Abutting 13,000-acre Natchaug State Forest, this 2,171-acre (3-square-mile) forest contributes to a vital northeast Connecticut open space and wildlife habitat. Ponds, swamps, rolling hardwood forests, meadows, tree plantations, and an abandoned rail line fashion its habitat mosaic. The featured broad-swinging loop on foot trail and woods road takes you through forest and plantation to explore Pine Acres Pond and Swamp and visit Black Spruce Pond. This loop incorporates part of the long-distance Natchaug Trail.

Start: Pine Acres Pond trailhead
Distance: 5.9-mile loop
Hiking time: 4 to 5 hours
Difficulty: Moderate
Elevation change: 200 feet
Trail surface: Earthen path and woods road
Best seasons: Spring through fall
Other trail users: Anglers, birders, mountain bikers, equestrians, snowshoers, cross-country skiers
Canine compatibility: Leashed dogs permitted (maximum 7-foot leash)
Land status: State forest
Nearest town: Chaplin, CT, with gas available along US 6
Fees and permits: None
Schedule: Year-round, a half hour before sunrise to a half hour after sunset

Maps: State forest map (available online at www.ct.gov/deep); Connecticut Forest and Park Association (CFPA) *Connecticut Walk Book, East* (available from CFPA, www.ctwoodlands.org)
Trail contacts: James L. Goodwin State Forest, 23 Potter Rd., Hampton 06247; (860) 455-9534. Department of Energy and Environmental Protection, State Parks, (860) 424-3200; www.ct.gov/deep.
Special considerations: The blue Natchaug Trail is open to foot travel only; all other state forest trails are open to multiple-use, nonmotorized travel. Bring drinking water.

FINDING THE TRAILHEAD

From the junction of US 6 and CT 169 in Brooklyn Center, go west on US 6 for 7.3 miles and turn right (north) on Potter Road for the state forest. Arriving from the west, go 3 miles east on US 6 from its junction with CT 198 in South Chaplin and turn left on Potter Road. Parking is on the right in 0.2 mile. Trailhead GPS: N41 46.537' / W72 04.934'

THE HIKE

Hike the access road toward the boat launch to follow the blue/yellow blazes along the southern end of Pine Acres Pond, a 135-acre lake built by James L. Goodwin in 1933, with the damming of Cedar Swamp Brook. Planted white pine and Norway spruce, red maple, rhododendron, bramble, and jewelweed frame travel. The whole forest reveals management practices implemented by Goodwin, an early Yale-trained forester and a trail-blazing state conservationist.

Pine Acres Pond, James L Goodwin
State Forest, Connecticut

At the dam, follow the blue/white Pine Acres Pond Trail, turning left (north) to cross the dam and spillway footbridges. The yellow Brown Hill Marsh Trail slips farther from shore, as it too swings north. Enjoy open looks at the dark-water pond, with its mats of pond lily, arrowhead, and rimming trees. Continue north along the pond's east shore, passing through spruce plantation and hardwood forest. Sweet pepperbush, azalea, and highbush blueberry favor the shore, while tall ferns favor the woods.

The trail is mostly flat and somewhat root-bound. A gap in the shore cover reveals the snag-pierced impound, a watery "bed of nails." You typically will spy evidence of beaver activity, geese, ducks, herons, and maybe a cormorant drying its wings. Past a beech-clad rise, view the pond's lily pad surface, treed islands, and a cattail swamp stretching north.

Where you reach a four-way junction with a red trail, spur left on it to Governor's Island. You follow an attractive levee edged by small pines and dense herbs and forbs, fragrant in early summer, to reach the island's viewing platform. It overlooks the surrounding bog.

North on the loop, thick woods severely limit swamp views, as a woods road conducts travel away from the upper swamp of Pine Acres Pond. The hike parallels a stone wall through pine plantation before passing through a breach in the wall to reach Estabrooks Road. Angle right to resume northbound travel on a scenic recessed woods road.

Past a spruce stand, view the abandoned rail line of the Air Line Trail before crossing over it. A lovely hardwood forest graced by ferns next advances the hike. Cross 11th Section Road and follow the blue/white blazes south along the east shore of Black Spruce Pond. The dense shrub border denies views and the trail can be rocky or muddy, but the area azalea, mountain laurel, and sheep laurel are attractive. Where the trail is on leaf-littered woods road, you might glimpse the snag-filled water.

In a stand of pines, you meet the blue-blazed woods road of the Natchaug Trail and follow it left (south) for the loop. However, a short detour right on the Natchaug leads to the earthen dam for an open look at Black Spruce Pond, its beaver lodge, lily pads, and many snags.

Ascend south and bear right at the fork onto narrower woods road. Grasses invade the bed and ferns dress the shoulder as the Natchaug Trail parts hardwood forest and conifer plantation. Because blazing has been infrequent here in the past, keep alert for where the Natchaug turns left on foot trail. It traverses a conifer plantation with dispersed deciduous trees and crosses stone walls. On paved Cannon Road, turn left to again pick up the southbound trail.

A similar trek leads back to 11th Section Road, where you angle right across the road, descending once more through conifer plantation. Unruly bramble may grab at your legs. Then, meet the Air Line Trail, following it briefly right. Interpretive panels on the Air Line relate area history. You then turn left, touring soggy woodland and nearing Pine Acres Pond. Visit another viewing site and close the loop back at trailhead parking.

MILES AND DIRECTIONS

0.0 Start at the Pine Acres Pond trailhead. Descend the boat launch road to follow the blue/yellow blazes, rounding the south end of the pond to the dam.

0.2 Follow the blue/white blazes left. *Option:* The yellow Brown Hill Marsh Trail leads north and east to another impoundment pond.

1.5 Reach a four-way junction with a red trail. Spur left to Governor's Island before proceeding north on the loop. *Option:* By taking the red trail to the right, you can fashion a shorter loop back to the trailhead.

1.8 Return to the four-way junction and take the blue/white trail north.

2.5 Cross Estabrooks Road. Continue north, following blue/white blazes.

2.7 Cross the Air Line Trail/East Coast Greenway Trail (a rail trail).

3.2 Cross 11th Section Road. Follow the blue/white trail south along the east shore of Black Spruce Pond.

3.8 Reach the blue Natchaug Trail. Turn left, following its blazes south. *Option:* A detour right leads to the dam and an open pond view in 250 feet.

4.7 Angle left across Cannon Road.

5.3 Reach the Air Line Trail. Turn right, sharing its route.

5.5 Turn left off the Air Line Trail.

5.8 Reach a viewing site.

5.9 Arrive back at the trailhead.

HIKE INFORMATION

LOCAL INFORMATION

Windham Region Chamber of Commerce, 1010 Main St., PO Box 43, Willimantic 06226; (860) 423-6389; www.windhamchamber.com.

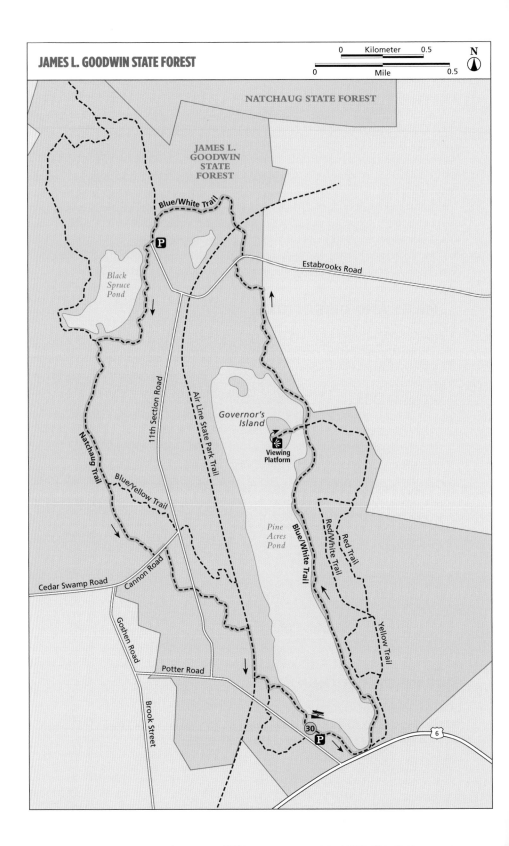

JAMES L. GOODWIN STATE FOREST

0 Kilometer 0.5

0 Mile 0.5

N

NATCHAUG STATE FOREST

JAMES L. GOODWIN STATE FOREST

Blue/White Trail

P

Estabrooks Road

Black Spruce Pond

Natchaug Trail

11th Section Road

Air Line State Park Trail

Governor's Island

Viewing Platform

Blue/Yellow Trail

Cedar Swamp Road

Cannon Road

Pine Acres Pond

Blue/White Trail

Red/White Trail

Red Trail

Yellow Trail

Goshen Road

Potter Road

Brook Street

30

P

6

LOCAL EVENTS/ATTRACTIONS

The adjacent **Goodwin Conservation Center,** with its interpretive museum and native plant gardens, focuses on natural history and forestry in its exhibits, workshops, and field tours. It is a joint project of the DEEP and Connecticut Forest and Park Association. Friends of Goodwin Forest, 23 Potter Road, Hampton 06247.

Prudence Crandall Museum, 1 South Canterbury Rd., Canterbury 06331; (860) 546-7800; www.cultureandtourism.org. This museum honors New England's first academy for African-American women (1833–1834) and the state heroine who founded it. View changing exhibits and period furnishings. This National Historic Landmark is on both the Connecticut Freedom Trail and the Connecticut Women's Heritage Trail.

ORGANIZATIONS

Connecticut Forest and Park Association (CFPA), 16 Meriden Rd., Rockfall 06481; (860) 346-8733; www.ctwoodlands.org.

Friends of Goodwin Forest, 23 Potter Rd., Hampton 06247.

HONORABLE MENTIONS
NORTHEAST CONNECTICUT

Z. SHENIPSIT TRAIL, SOAPSTONE MOUNTAIN

In Shenipsit State Forest, this popular 1.2-mile section of the Shenipsit Trail offers a satisfying woodland climb from the lower trailhead to an overlook platform surveying the wooded expanse of northern and eastern Connecticut and southeastern Massachusetts. Longer hikes can be fashioned by extending your travel on the blue Shenipsit Trail or by following the color-coded trails of the state forest or the white-circle-blazed counterclockwise trail of a running club.

In Stafford Springs at the junction of CT 190 and CT 140, drive west on CT 140 for 5 miles and turn right (north) on Burbank Road, which later becomes Gulf Road. Stay on it for 1.7 miles and turn left into Shenipsit State Forest, reaching the lower trailhead parking. Trailhead GPS: N41 57.695' / W72 24.565'. Weekends and holidays, the ample lot can fill. The paved forest road then climbs another 0.9 mile to the summit trailhead parking. Trailhead GPS: N41 57.490' / W72 24.809'. Trail contact: Shenipsit State Forest, 166 Chestnut Hill Rd. (CT 190), Stafford Springs 06067; (860) 684-3430; www.ct.gov/deep.

AA. MAJOR MICHAEL DONNELLY LAND PRESERVE

This 115-acre South Windsor preserve shows even small places can hold pleasing rambles. Protecting watershed and honoring a local-hero advocate for veterans, the preserve's pond, wetland, field, and woodland mosaic offers changing settings and varied wildlife. The foot trail and rustic boardwalks can be off-limits during wet periods, or mosquitoes can chase you back, but generally the site offers a tranquil visit. A gazebo, fishing platform, wildlife blinds, and benches allow wildlife to come to you. Before hiking, study the kiosk map.

From the junction of CT 30 and CT 194 in Wapping, head northwest on CT 194 (Sullivan Avenue) and stay on it, passing CT 74. In 1 mile turn left for the signed park and large off-road parking area. Trailhead GPS: N41 50.449' / W72 33.558'. Trail contact: Town of South Windsor, 1540 Sullivan Ave., South Windsor 06074; (860) 644-2511; www.southwindsor.org.

AB. RISLEY POND

At this Manchester-protected watershed and water-supply source, a 2.6-mile hiking loop rings the shore and outskirts of Risley Pond that straddle the Vernon-Bolton town line. Passing through field and woods, the loop allows limited access for pond viewing, but no fishing, swimming, or other water activity. Sections of this rocky, brook-crossing trail are difficult to complete under wet conditions. You may spy white-tailed deer and wild turkey while hiking. Connecticut Forest and Park Association (CFPA) volunteers maintain the trail.

At the junction of US 6, CT 85, and Cider Mill Road (north of I-384, exit 5), drive north on Cider Mill Road for 0.6 mile, turn right on Lake Street, and continue 0.8 mile more to find off-road parking for a dozen vehicles on the right, at the north end of Risley Pond. Trailhead GPS: N41 48.131' / W72 28.232'. Trail contacts: Recreation, Town of Manchester, 39 Lodge Dr., Manchester 06040; (860) 647-3084; http://recreation .townofmanchester.org. CFPA, 16 Meriden Rd., Rockfall 06481; (860) 346-8733; www .ctwoodlands.org.

AC. HOP RIVER STATE PARK TRAIL

Repurposing 20 miles of the passenger and freight line between Providence and Waterbury, this attractive surfaced recreational rail trail extends linear travel east across the state through woods, field, and riparian habitats. You can discover both nature and history, the engineering of the grade, and the commerce and prosperity of the region. The rail line carried everything from crops to quarried stone. When plotting a course from the old depot station at Vernon Parks and Recreation, Valley Falls Park is just over 4 miles away.

From Vernon at the junction of CT 83 and CT 30/Hartford Turnpike, go northeast on CT 30 for 0.4 mile, turning right (south) on Dobson Road and crossing over I-84, where the name changes to Washington Street. In another 0.4 mile, turn left on Church Street to reach the western trailhead parking lot on the left in 0.2 mile. Trailhead GPS: N41 49.317' / W72 28.822'. For the easternmost trailhead, from the junction of US 6 and CT 87, head east on US 6 for 2.2 miles and turn left (north) onto Hop River Road. Continue 0.3 mile to trailhead parking on the left. Or, from the junction of US 6 and CT 66, head west on US 6 for 1.5 miles and turn right (north) on Hop River Road to reach the trailhead in 0.3 mile. Trailhead GPS: N41 43.806' / W72 18.395'. Trail contact: Hop River State Park Trail, c/o Connecticut Department of Energy and Environmental Protection, Eastern District, 209 Hebron Rd., Marlborough 06447; (860) 295-9523; www.ct.gov/deep.

AD. TRAIL WOOD, EDWIN WAY TEALE MEMORIAL SANCTUARY

This Audubon sanctuary holds the retreat of the Pulitzer Prize–winning author of the American Seasons series and *A Naturalist Buys an Old Farm*. Eleven named trails and keyed discoveries guide you across the property. Maps are available at the information shed. Field, woods, brook, and stone walls contribute to the site's inspiration. The grounds are open dawn to dusk. Tours of the writing cabin and museum are by appointment. Donations are suggested.

In Hampton, go north on CT 97 for 1.1 miles and turn left on Kenyon Road. Stay on it for 0.2 mile, turning left into the sanctuary. Visitor parking is reached on the left before the house. From US 44 in Abington, you'd drive 5.3 miles south on CT 97 and turn right on Kenyon Road to reach the sanctuary turn in 0.2 mile. Trailhead GPS: N41 48.533' / W72 03.706'. Trail contact: Connecticut Audubon Society, Center at Trail Wood, 93 Kenyon Rd., Hampton 06259; (860) 928-4948; www.ctaudubon.org.

AE. BAFFLIN NATURE SANCTUARY

At this Connecticut Audubon Society (CAS) property, multiple trailheads access its 8 miles of nature trail and the state Air Line Trail. You'll explore a patchwork of fields and woods, riparian area and rise. Hikes follow mowed tracks and footpaths, with the trails open daylight hours. Birding is popular.

In the town of Pomfret, you'll reach trail parking east off CT 169, north of its junction with CT 101 and south of its junction with US 44. Parking is near picturesque long barns of stone and red-painted wood. Trailhead GPS: N41 51.764' / W71 57.540'. For the Grassland Bird Conservation Center and trailhead, from the junction of CT 169 and Day Road (1 mile north of the CT 101–CT 169 junction), turn right (east) on Day Road and keep right at Needles Eye Road to reach the uphill turn to the center. Trailhead GPS: N41 51.764' / W71 57.540'. Trail contact: Center at Pomfret Grassland Bird Conservation Center, 218 Day Road, Pomfret Center 06259; (860) 928-4948; www .ctaudubon.org.

AF. GAY CITY STATE PARK

Within this park's 1,500 acres, you will explore peaceful woods, the Blackledge River, swamps and ponds, and the historic remains of an eighteenth-century settlement, Gay City. Started in 1796 by an isolationist religious sect, Gay City's early success centered around its mill—originally a sawmill, later a woolen and paper mill. The blockades in the War of 1812, the Civil War deaths of the town's young men, and fire all played a role in the demise of Gay City. The 2.6-mile Pond Loop and

Park pond, Gay City State Park, Connecticut

the 5-mile Outer Loop uncover mill ruins, ditches, cellar holes, a cemetery, and stone walls. The Shenipsit Trail also passes through the park.

The park sits 3 miles south of Bolton off CT 85. From I-384 eastbound, take exit 5 and go south on CT 85 for 4.5 miles, turning right (west) into the park. Both trails start at the westbound gated woods road in 0.3 mile. Parking fees are collected from nonresidents weekends and holidays. Park opens the third Saturday in April and closes Columbus Day weekend, hours: 8 a.m. to sunset. Trailhead GPS: N41 43.224' / W72 26.496'. Trail contact: Gay City State Park, 435 North St., Hebron 06248; (860) 295-9523; www.ct .gov/deep.

AG. MANSFIELD HOLLOW STATE PARK

This open space owing its origin to flood control holds a variety of hiking opportunities. The Nipmuck Trail, featured earlier in the book, was just the beginning. Color-coded routes web the woods, and the flood-control levee offers a fine walk on the level.

From US 6 at Willimantic, take the exit for CT 195 and the University of Connecticut at Storrs and go north on CT 195 for 2.1 miles. Turn right (east) on Bassett Bridge Road at Mansfield Center. Continue 0.9 mile, turn left into the park, and go 0.3 mile more to the picnic area/trailhead. Trailhead GPS: N41 45.889' / W72 10.722'. You can also continue on Bassett Bridge Road to the boat launch. Trail contact: Mansfield Hollow State Park, c/o Mashamoquet Brook State Park, 147 Wolf Den Dr., Pomfret Center 06259; (860) 928-6121; www.ct.gov/deep.

SOUTHEAST CONNECTICUT TRAILS

Completing the Connecticut puzzle, Southeast Connecticut brings together the natural and historic offerings of Middlesex and New London Counties. The region stretches east from the Connecticut River estuary and includes the state's historic shipbuilding maritime coast. Swamp lowlands, rolling woods, and copious mountain laurel enchant foot travelers.

31 AIR LINE NATIONAL RECREATION TRAIL, EAST HAMPTON TO COLUMBIA

This trail trends east–west across the region, and, contrary to its name, owes its start to railroading. "Air Line" refers to the rail designers' intent for its arrow-straight travel, as if by air, between Boston and New York City. Nature, though, had a different concept. Despite its inherent narrowness, the scenery is top-notch and you have the fun of uncovering clues to a vibrant railroading past. Railroads were the essential link between producing farms and mills and urban markets. This stretch carries you over two buried trestles (viaducts). When the trains became too heavy for the leggy spans, the ground was raised to bridge the travel gap and bear the load.

Start: East Hampton trailhead
Distance: 13.8 miles one way from East Hampton to Chesbro Bridge Road, but trail extends to Windham
Hiking time: 8 to 10 hours
Difficulty: Moderate due to distance
Elevation change: 250 feet of modest gradient due to its original purpose
Trail surface: Hardened-surface railroad bed
Best seasons: Spring through fall
Other trail users: Mountain bikers, equestrians, joggers, birders, cross-country skiers
Canine compatibility: Leashed dogs permitted
Land status: State park, state forest, wildlife management area, town parks
Nearest towns: East Hampton and Willimantic, CT

Fees and permits: None
Schedule: Year-round, 8 a.m. to sunset
Map: Air Line State Park Trail brochure and park map (available online at www.ct.gov/deep)
Trail contacts: East Hampton Parks and Recreation, 20 East High St., East Hampton 06424; (860) 267-7300. Department of Energy and Environmental Protection, Eastern District Headquarters, 209 Hebron Rd., Marlborough 06447; (860) 295-9523; or DEEP main office, (860) 424-3200; www.ct.gov/deep.
Special considerations: Respect adjacent private land. During spring and fall hunting seasons, dress in bright colors. There is a breach in rail trail travel at CT 2.

FINDING THE TRAILHEAD

From the junction of CT 66 and CT 196 in East Hampton, head south on CT 196 for 0.4 mile and turn left (east) on Flanders Road, following signs for the trail. Go 0.2 mile and turn right on Smith Street to reach parking on the left in 0.1 mile. Trailhead GPS: N41 34.740' / W72 29.495'

For this hike's eastern trailhead, from the intersection of CT 66 and CT 87 in Columbia, drive 1 mile west on CT 66 and turn left on Pine Street. Where Pine Street turns right, bear left on Chesbro Bridge Road to reach the Chesbro Bridge Road parking, just before Tobacco Street (2.5 miles off CT 66). Trailhead GPS: N41 39.773' / W72 17.412'

THE HIKE

This hike explores part of the 22-mile southern segment of the Air Line State Park Trail. The northern segment is 21 miles and stretches from Windham to Pomfret. This 1870s-built railroad served as an artery of commerce and a connector of communities. Its intended arrow-straight course butted heads with the reality of Connecticut's ridge and valley terrain, and the expensive need to cut and fill. Local politics, too, troubled the railroad's inception. Still, its attractive aisle and mastery of engineering win you over.

This hike begins in East Hampton, known for its bell production, and continues east-northeast to Chesbro Bridge Road in Columbia, west of Willimantic. Regularly spaced road crossings, many with limited parking, allow you to see the route in smaller bites.

Railroad bridge, Air Line State Park Trail, Salmon River State Forest, Connecticut

Air Line Trail, Air Line State Park, Connecticut

You'll travel in woods of various mix, along meadow and marsh, across streams and roads, and past the curious gazes of neighboring farm animals. Earliest views are of Cranberry Bog. Its crop of native cranberries spawned a commercial enterprise in the 1920s and 1930s. Today it attracts wildlife.

The linear route has a hard-surfaced bed and is ideal for exercise and see-the-countryside walks. Oak, hickory, maple, birch, and conifer—all the usual players—make up the framing woods. Openings offer looks at the neighboring habitats and ridges. The

GROWING A GREENWAY

Connecticut's Air Line Trail and Farmington Canal Heritage Trail and Rhode Island's Blackstone and East Bay Bike Paths are segments of the greater East Coast Greenway Trail, linking Key West, Florida, to Calais, Maine, at the Canadian border. The goal for the completed 3,000-mile route is to provide a traffic-free passage from border to border. The pedestrian/cyclist through-way will pass through fifteen states, the District of Columbia, twenty-five major cities, and untold smaller communities and showcase the habitats and histories of the places it travels.

The East Coast Greenway is part of a burgeoning concept in national transportation that provides nonmotorized recreational and commuting opportunities to millions of Americans. It reclaims abandoned transportation lines that once linked the communities and markets. About 25 percent of the greenway is complete, but the trail already has a following of End-to-Enders who have completed the route, despite the traffic. The East Coast Greenway Alliance is the guiding group behind the ambitious pathway. To learn more, contact the alliance at 5826 Fayetteville Road, Suite 210, Durham, NC 27713; (919) 797-0619; info@greenway.org; www.greenway.org.

New England Limited carried passengers until 1902. Freight ran here until the combined punch of the 1955 flooding and the 1960s opening of the interstate system spelled its demise.

An early structural attraction is Rapallo Viaduct at Flat Brook. The trestle crossing was built in 1873 to span the nearly 0.25-mile gap, the longest of the two viaduct spans. In 1913, in answer to the increasing weight of freight trains, engineers had the 60-foot-tall trestle towers underfilled to support the weight. For twenty months, sand and cinder surfacing materials were hauled to the project. Now the raised-earth passage invites admiration and pause, with bench seats and marsh overlooks.

Farther east, Lyman Viaduct stands twice as tall above Dickinson Creek. You might hear the gurgle of the creek as it flows through a culvert in the rocky span. At the viaducts you also may spy the underlying construction—heavy block supports or iron artifacts.

A sunken grade blasted through rock slope leads to Bull Hill Road. Beyond its parking, you traverse part of Salmon River State Forest. This 6,000-acre forest protects watershed woodland critical to the recovery of the Atlantic salmon. At its River Road, you cross one of several historic brownstone bridges built to advance the rail line.

At CT 2 you are diverted briefly off the old line, past the commuter parking lot and back onto the trail at Old Hartford Road, where the aisle's treed tunnel is a familiar, welcoming sight. At Grayville Road tall thin trees frame the travel aisle as the trail heads south toward another parcel of Salmon River State Forest. The trail is well used and family friendly. Its length ensures times of solitude.

You pass the Colchester Railroad grade, which stretches south. It served the Hayward Rubber Complex. At Raymond Brook Marsh, view wetland habitats and watch for wildlife. Waders, paddlers, hawks, and songbirds may be spied. Deer, too, are common.

Where the trail crosses CT 85 (modern Amston), Turnerville Station once served passengers and a silk mill's shipping. After the route crosses CT 207 to travel the area north of Lake Williams, you might notice a spur used as a switching station for passing trains. This hike comes to an end at Chesbro Bridge Road. But, for those who wish to continue, the grade continues northeast toward CT 87 to reach Windham (at Willimantic) in 5.7 miles. You'll find additional parking along this segment.

MILES AND DIRECTIONS

0.0 Start at the East Hampton trailhead. Pass through the trail gateway, heading east.

1.4 Reach Rapallo Viaduct.

2.5 Reach Lyman Viaduct.

3.0 Cross Bull Hill Road.

5.3 Cross the brownstone bridge spanning River Road.

6.3 Follow the Air Line reroute around CT 2.

6.5 Resume eastbound travel at Old Hartford Road.

8.5 Cross Grayville Road.

10.0 Pass the southbound Colchester Railroad grade.

10.8 Cross CT 207.

13.8 End at Chesbro Bridge Road.

AIR LINE NATIONAL RECREATION TRAIL, EAST HAMPTON TO COLUMBIA

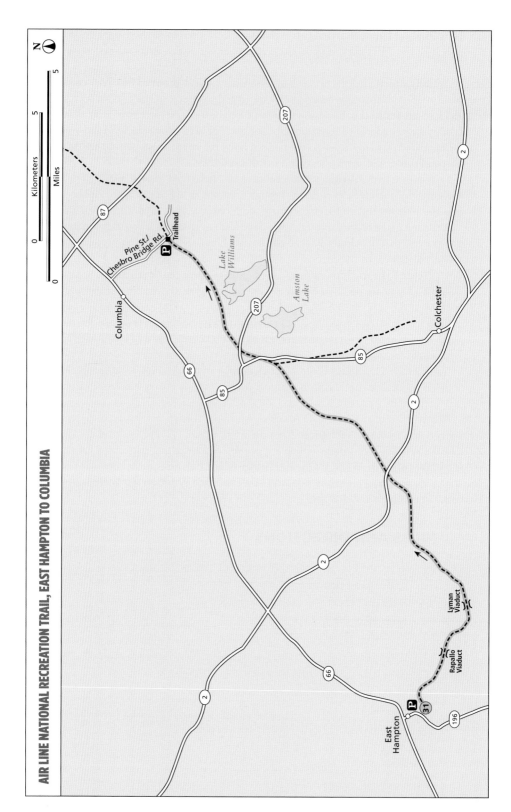

HIKE INFORMATION

LOCAL INFORMATION

Windham Region Chamber of Commerce, 1010 Main St., PO Box 43, Willimantic 06226; (860) 423-6389; www.windhamchamber.com.

ORGANIZATIONS

Rails-to-Trails Conservancy, The Duke Ellington Building, 2121 Ward Ct. NW, 5th Floor, Washington, DC 20037; (202) 331-9696; www.railstotrails.org.

32 SALMON RIVER TRAIL

Entirely on state land, this lasso-shaped hike explores Salmon River State Forest and Day Pond State Park. Its highlights include the old Comstock covered bridge (refurbished in 2011), limited Salmon River access and viewing, the reflective beauty of Day Pond, rock walls and cellar ruins, and an unexpected waterfall find.

Start: Comstock covered bridge trailhead
Distance: 7.3-mile lollipop with waterfall spur
Hiking time: 5 to 6 hours
Difficulty: Moderate
Elevation change: 350 feet
Trail surface: Earthen path and woods road
Best seasons: Spring through fall
Other trail users: Anglers, hunters (in parts of the state forest), snowshoers, cross-country skiers
Canine compatibility: Leashed dogs permitted on trails and in picnic areas
Land status: State park and forest
Nearest town: Colchester, CT, with gas available in East Hampton or Westchester along CT 16
Fees and permits: Seasonal weekend/ holiday parking fee for nonresidents at Day Pond State Park
Schedule: Salmon River State Forest is open year-round. Forest recreation areas are open 8 a.m. to sunset, with the rest of the forest open a half hour before sunrise to a half hour after sunset. Day Pond State Park is open 8 a.m. to sunset from the third Sat in Apr through Columbus Day weekend.
Maps: State park and forest maps (available online at www.ct.gov/deep); Connecticut Forest and Park Association (CFPA) *Connecticut Walk Book, East* (available from CFPA, www.ctwoodlands.org)
Trail contacts: Salmon River State Forest and Day Pond State Park, c/o Eastern District Headquarters, 209 Hebron Rd., Marlborough 06447; (860) 295-9523. Department of Energy and Environmental Protection, State Parks, (860) 424-3200; www.ct.gov/deep.
Special considerations: The blue-blazed Salmon River Trail and the blue/red Day Pond Brook spur are for foot travel only. Other trails allow nonmotorized multiuse. Carry drinking water.

FINDING THE TRAILHEAD

From the junction of CT 16 and CT 196 (south of East Hampton), proceed east on CT 16 for 3.6 miles and turn left on Comstock Bridge Road to reach trail parking on the right at the covered bridge. Trailhead GPS: N41 33.186' / W72 26.981'

THE HIKE

This is a Connecticut blue trail, marked by the signature blaze. It begins with your passing through the historic covered bridge that dates to 1791 and spans the shallow Salmon River. Upon crossing, the trail swings left.

Sycamores contribute to the river's shore. This attractive, slow-moving, rocky-bottomed river supports juvenile Atlantic salmon, a species decimated by industrial pollution at the turn of the twentieth century. The state forest protects the river watershed and species dependent on the river.

Day Pond Brook Falls, Salmon River
State Forest, Connecticut

Full shade graces travel. The woodland enfolding the trail holds maple, hemlock, oak, and witch hazel. Keep watch for the trail to turn uphill away from the Salmon River. A fishing path continues upstream. Because the trail now zigzags between woods roads as it climbs, remain attentive to blazes.

At a Y-junction bear right to come upon a river view spanning a steep meadow of goldenrod. The full forest of the opposite slope is especially pretty when in fall attire. Where the trail flattens atop the rise, American beech trees have a strong presence, as do pockets of young trees. Before reaching a utility corridor, the trail turns right uphill through a full forest with mountain laurel in its midlevel. The trail then tops out and begins a slow descent as it meanders along the ridge.

As the trail rolls out its relaxing sojourn, you'll discover a rock wall ornamented in lichen. More rock walls add to travel. At the Salmon River Loop junction, turn right for counterclockwise exploration on the Salmon River Trail (south loop). The setting is characteristic Connecticut forest.

After you pass a 15-foot-high boulder (a glacial erratic) on the right, the trail enters a comfortable descent, crosses a woods road, and arrives at Day Pond State Park, with its picnic area, rustic facilities, and parking. The pond may bid delay, with its sandy beach and attractive lily mats.

Follow the blazed Salmon River Trail left, crossing the rock dam of Day Pond on the gravel park road, and immediately reenter the forest on the left, now back on the Salmon River Trail (north loop). Cross a woods road, bearing slightly left, and soon after pursue Day Pond Brook downstream. An abundance of ferns and the song of the brook add to the hike's tranquility. At a junction, the Salmon River Trail heads right upslope and crosses a utility-line corridor.

The trail then passes over a forested knob before resuming its meandering course. Outcrops coated with lichen and moss vary viewing. Eventually the trail pairs with a drainage, heading downslope. Cross the drainage past an old dam site to arrive at a homestead ruin, marked by cellar holes and rock walls.

Where the trail comes to a T-junction with a woods road, turn left for the loop and shortly after turn right, coming to the junction with the Day Pond Brook waterfall spur. On this blue/red spur, you follow the narrow footpath blazed by an Eagle Scout across the forested drainage slope and downstream to waterfall viewing. The waterfall is a surprise, all the better after recent rain. It shows a sequence of cascades spilling over and through ledges on Day Pond Brook. The upper falls and pool are a charming launch to the lower cascades and slide.

Return to the loop and turn right, passing more rock walls, remnant foundations, and cellar depressions. Cross the bridge over Day Pond Brook and head uphill. Hemlocks are well-represented. After passing through a utility corridor, you complete the loop. Turn right to backtrack to Comstock Bridge.

MILES AND DIRECTIONS

0.0 Start at the Comstock covered bridge trailhead. Cross through and follow the blue blazes left.

0.2 Reach a junction. Head uphill away from the Salmon River. Avoid the path upstream.

SALMON RIVER TRAIL

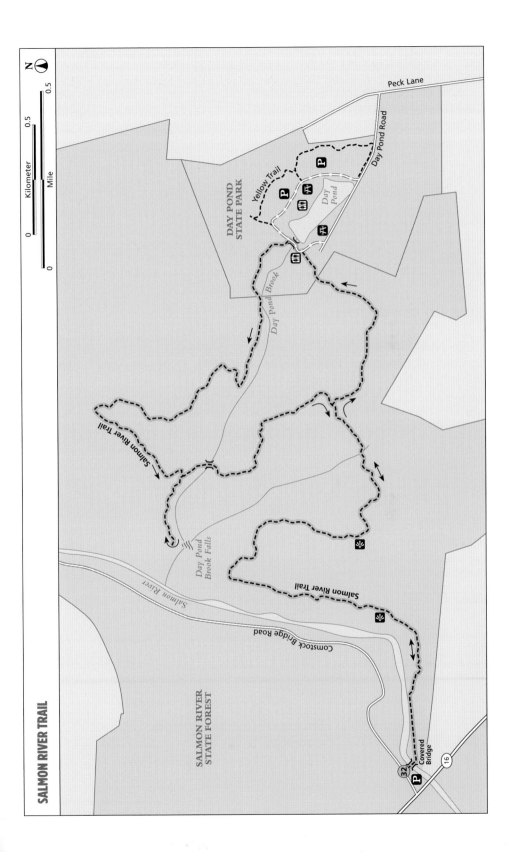

0.5	Bear right at a Y-junction.
2.0	Reach the Salmon River Loop and turn right.
2.6	Enter Day Pond State Park. Cross the dam to continue loop travel.
3.1	Reach a junction. Head right, up the hill.
3.4	Top a forested knob.
4.0	Pass an old homestead site.
4.2	Reach a T-junction with a woods road and turn left.
4.3	Turn right, coming to the marked Day Pond Brook Spur Trail. Follow the blue/red blazes right, downstream, to waterfall viewing (4.5).
4.7	Return to the loop and turn right.
4.8	Cross the bridge over Day Pond Brook and continue uphill.
5.3	Close the loop and backtrack right to the trailhead.
7.3	Arrive back at the trailhead.

HIKE INFORMATION

ORGANIZATIONS

Connecticut Forest and Park Association (CFPA), 16 Meriden Rd., Rockfall 06481; (860) 346-8733; www.ctwoodlands.org.

33 PACHAUG STATE FOREST, PACHAUG-QUINEBAUG LOOP

In southeast Connecticut abutting Rhode Island, Pachaug State Forest represents the largest state-held forest in Connecticut, covering more than 26,000 acres. The featured hike originates from the Chapman/headquarters area and incorporates parts of two long-distance trails: the Pachaug and the Quinebaug. This combined loop explores hardwood forest and conifer plantation and travels along brook and pond for a most-of-the-day excursion. If time allows, consider taking the forest's short trail through a rare rhododendron-white cedar swamp for a visual treat. Another short hike tops the area high point, Mount Misery (summit elevation 441 feet), for a vista.

Start: Civilian Conservation Corps (CCC) Monument trailhead
Distance: 13.2-mile lollipop
Hiking time: 8 to 9 hours
Difficulty: Strenuous due to length
Elevation change: 280 feet
Trail surface: Earthen path, woods road, management road
Best seasons: Spring through fall
Other trail users: Hunters (in parts of the state forest), snowshoers, cross-country skiers; mountain bikers, equestrians, ATVers, and snowmobilers on designated routes only; motorists at forest road crossings
Canine compatibility: Leashed dogs permitted
Land status: State forest
Nearest town: Jewett City in Township of Griswold, CT
Fees and permits: None for day-use parking or hiking, but overnight campground fees apply

Schedule: Year-round, with recreation areas open 8 a.m. to sunset; all other forest areas open a half hour before sunrise to a half hour after sunset
Maps: State forest map (available online at www.ct.gov/deep); Connecticut Forest and Park Association (CFPA) *Connecticut Walk Book, East* (available from CFPA, www.ctwoodlands.org)
Trail contacts: Pachaug State Forest, Route 49, PO Box 5, Voluntown 06384; (860) 376-4075. Department of Energy and Environmental Protection, State Parks and Forests, (860) 424-3200; www.ct.gov/deep.
Special considerations: The blue, blue/red, yellow, and white trails are open to foot travel only. The forest has designated trails for mountain bikes, horses, ATVs, and snowmobiles; consult maps.

FINDING THE TRAILHEAD

From I-395, take exit 85 and go east on CT 138 to Voluntown, 5.8 miles. Continue east on CT 138/CT 165 for 0.8 mile and turn north on CT 49. Go 0.6 mile on CT 49 and turn left (west) on Headquarters Road. At the road fork in 0.7 mile, turn right to reach the CCC Monument trailhead on the right. Trailhead GPS: N41 35.605' / W71 51.922'

THE HIKE

From the monument to the men of Company 179 and the historic flagpole in the CCC area, follow the blue blazes east up the grassy slope. Enter the pines, reaching

Lowden Brook, Pachaug State Forest,
Connecticut

the Nehantic/Pachaug trail junction, and turn left (north) on the Pachaug Trail. The Pachaug contours the wooded slope east of Trail 1 Road. Look for deer, raccoons, and woodpeckers and be ready for quick direction changes wherever the trail meets woods roads.

Near an old ruin, you meet a woods road and turn left for a birch-lined passage ending at a boulder barrier. Pass through the barrier gap and hike left, reaching Trail 1 Road south of Lowden Brook Picnic Area. Turn right and pass between the boulders on the right to resume the Pachaug Trail.

Hike northeast past some picnic tables. The rocky footpath leads through mixed woods of maple, hickory, ash, beech, pine, hemlock, and birch, following Lowden Brook upstream. Mountain laurel and sweet pepperbush favor the drainage. Lowden Brook shows dark mossy boulders and sparkling cascades. Muddy sites record recent wildlife visits.

Veer upslope from the brook, passing stone walls, before swinging left and finding easier footing. You then return streamside to cross the brook and enter a spruce plantation. Next, angle right across Gardner Road, following a gated woods road. Grasses push up through the roadbed, while ferns shower the shoulders.

Be alert as the trail zigzags among woods roads. Past a stone foundation, the Pachaug tours a plantation forest. At the loop junction with the blue/red cut-across trail, keep north on the Pachaug for a counterclockwise loop.

The hike alternates between hardwood forest and conifer plantation, passing a spring and catch basin on the right. Angle right across paved Hell Hollow Road to pass through a spruce grove. Left on Hell Hollow Road is the pond. Stone walls partition the plantations. At a fork bear right for the Pachaug Trail, contouring a rocky slope. At the junction with the yellow trail, follow the yellow-blazed Pachaug-Quinebaug crossover trail left for the loop.

Follow yellow blazes downhill to contour an oak and birch hillside, with sassafras, chestnut, and huckleberry weaving an understory. Where the trail traverses a wooded plateau, there is a scenic beech grove. Turn left on dirt Flat Rock Road (closed to vehicles here), chasing yellow blazes to the blue-blazed Quinebaug Trail. Upon meeting it, turn left (west) along Flat Rock Road for the loop.

Pass Devils Den, an assemblage of rocks, on the left. Descend and look for the trail to bear left off Flat Rock Road onto a narrower woods road. Here the rolling tour temporarily regains its country lane charm, with draping branches of dogwood, ash, maple, birch, and beech. Beyond a pine plantation, the trail is more scarred. Next round a gate and angle right across Hell Hollow Road.

Descend in hardwoods, soon passing a stand of mature white pines on this engaging stretch of the Quinebaug Trail. Meander pine plantation and mixed forest, slowly descending. Where you glimpse a red maple swamp, it clues you're nearing the site of marsh-reclaimed Phillips Pond. You depart the Quinebaug Trail at the former pond.

Cross the earthen dam and footbridge, viewing remnant standing water, vegetated islands, and aquatic plants. You pass through the picnic area and follow the blue/red crossover east toward the Pachaug Trail. From the barrier, you tour maple-draped trail.

At the Pachaug Trail, you then turn right to backtrack the trail south to the trailhead.

Phillips Pond, Pachaug State Forest,
Connecticut

MILES AND DIRECTIONS

0.0 Start at the CCC Monument trailhead. Hike east up the grassy slope.

0.1 Reach a blue-trail junction in the pines. Turn left, following the Pachaug Trail north. *Note:* The Nehantic Trail turns right, continuing south to Beachdale Pond Picnic Area in 0.9 mile.

1.3 Pass Lowden Brook Picnic Area.

2.3 Cross Lowden Brook.

2.7 Cross Gardner Road.

3.0 Reach the loop junction. Continue forward on the Pachaug Trail for counter-clockwise travel. The loop's return is via the blue/red crossover.

4.2 Cross Hell Hollow Road. *Note:* Left on the road is Hell Hollow Pond.

5.1 Reach a junction with the yellow trail. Follow the yellow connector left to the Quinebaug Trail.

6.0 Meet the blue Quinebaug Trail. Follow it left along Flat Rock Road. *Option:* A detour right (north) on the Quinebaug Trail finds Lockes Meadow Pond, a wetland meadow and popular birding site, in about 0.5 mile.

6.5 Turn south off Flat Rock Road.

7.7 Cross Hell Hollow Road.

9.5 Reach the dam at a marsh-reclaimed pond. Cross and follow the blue/red crossover east to the Pachaug Trail.

10.2 Close the loop at the Pachaug Trail. Turn right to backtrack south to the trailhead.

13.2 Arrive back at the CCC trailhead.

Options: The 0.5-mile Rhododendron Sanctuary Walk starts north off Cutoff Road, opposite Mount Misery Campground. On cushiony trail, pass into a wooded area, bearing right to round an island of trees. Azalea, mountain laurel, sweet pepperbush, highbush blueberry, and red maple announce the swamp. Here you travel a levee through the wetland forest of cedar, sphagnum moss, bog grass, and junglelike rhododendron, reaching 40 feet tall, sporting 8-inch leaves, and, in July, brandishing glorious floral pompoms. Twisting skyward through the cedar and hemlock canopy, the rhododendrons shape a brief, exciting passageway of texture and shape. The walk ends with a small loop, but high water can make it impassable.

The hike to Mount Misery begins south off the Cutoff Road, west of the Rhododendron Sanctuary. You follow the blue Nehantic Trail uphill to the forest's high point. This trail climbs 0.8 mile and gains 170 feet in elevation. Hemlock, pine, oak, and mountain laurel frame this well-marked, well-traveled trail that advances by switchbacks. Pockets of fern, some rock studding, and sheep laurel bring visual interest. Top a rise and round over an outcrop, encountering oaks, twisted pine, and a more open cathedral, with limited outward looks. Snags reach skyward with imploring arms. The summit outcrop holds a 180-degree perspective of glacier-planed ridges and lowland forest, with pines towering above the leafy crowns. Return as you came.

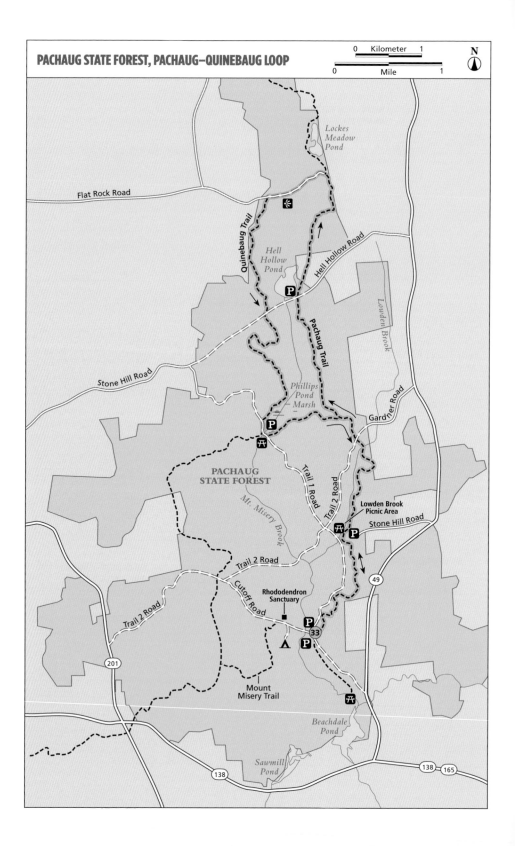

0   Kilometer   1

0   Mile   1

N

Lockes Meadow Pond

Flat Rock Road

Quinebaug Trail

Hell Hollow Pond

Hell Hollow Road

Lowden Brook

Pachaug Trail

Stone Hill Road

Phillips Pond Marsh

Gardner Road

PACHAUG STATE FOREST

Mt. Misery Brook

Trail 1 Road

Trail 2 Road

Lowden Brook Picnic Area

Stone Hill Road

Trail 2 Road

Trail 2 Road

Cutoff Road

Rhododendron Sanctuary

49

201

33

Mount Misery Trail

Beachdale Pond

Sawmill Pond

138

138 — 165

ALL HAIL THE CCC!

Without question, one of the nation's greatest programs ever for the advancement of recreation has to be the establishment and operation of the Civilian Conservation Corps (1933–1942), part of Franklin D. Roosevelt's New Deal.

In the face of despair and joblessness, Roosevelt responded with the CCC. This program mobilized the nation's surplus of idle young men, organizing them into a noncombative military machine that stormed the nation sea to sea, taking on improvement projects that had to come together in a hurry. Forests, agricultural lands, parks, swamps, roads, trails, and water improvements were the ideal targets, requiring muscle and number.

It is said the CCC brought together two wasted national resources: land and young men. But even its founders could not have anticipated what a recipe for success it would become or how far-reaching and lasting the impact.

The CCC gave national, state, and local parks their footing. Across Connecticut and Rhode Island and across the nation, CCC camps built park roads, trails, lodges, promontories, lookout towers, swimming holes, picnic areas, and campgrounds. They also laid trails and roads into the nation's remote reaches and deep into forests. The men battled flood, fire, and insect infestation, and they improved fisheries and wildlife lands.

The CCC left its imprint on society, too. It improved the general health, education, skill sets, and family stability of its enrollees, and helped families and businesses back home. Records show the average enrollee gained twelve pounds, despite the hard work. Enrollees received eye and dental care, had access to classes, and learned trades.

The model for this successful federal program traces to an earlier Connecticut state program initiated by Robert Ross, a Connecticut Forest and Park Association forester from 1929 to 1935. His plan put the state's youth to work in the Connecticut forest in 1930.

The CCC, "Roosevelt's Tree Army," began with an ambitious rollout of 275,000 men and by its wartime end had processed 3 million enrollees. Both Connecticut and Rhode Island were among the initial rollout, with Connecticut hosting fourteen camps and Rhode Island, three. The number of camps increased as the program matured.

The CCC arrived on the scene after the forests in both of these states had suffered from fire and a general disregard and when marginal agricultural lands were being forfeited to the states. During the CCC tenure, Connecticut saw its forest expanse triple. In that same period, Rhode Island nearly doubled its forest.

It would be difficult to throw a dart at a map and hit a site wholly untouched by the CCC. This is true in Connecticut and Rhode Island, and for just about any state in the nation.

In Connecticut the handiwork of the CCC can be found at such state forests as Peoples, Cockaponset, Mohawk, Pachaug, Shenipsit, and Tunxis. Squantz Pond, Black Rock, Macedonia Brook, West Rock Ridge, and Wooster Mountain were among the state parks where the men sweated and toiled. Rhode Island's vast George Washington and Arcadia Management Areas and Burlingame State Park prospered under CCC labor.

The Depression and the CCC came together in the perfect storm for the advancement of recreation. Nationwide, by the numbers, the CCC planted 3 billion trees and built 711 new state parks, 3,470 fire towers, and 97,000 miles of fire road, with 52,000 acres developed into public campgrounds—a legacy to honor.

HIKE INFORMATION

LOCAL INFORMATION

Chamber of Commerce of Eastern Connecticut, 914 Hartford Turnpike, Suite 206, Waterford 06385; (860) 701-9113; www.chamberect.com.

ACCOMMODATIONS

The state forest's **Mount Misery Campground** has 22 campsites, reservations needed. Water, fireplaces, and pit toilets are provided. Its **Frog Hollow Horse Camp Area** offers 18 campsites on a first-come, first-served basis. The campgrounds are open seasonally beginning mid-Apr (Mount Misery Campground) and Memorial Day weekend (Frog Hollow Horse Camp). Both campgrounds close on Labor Day.

ORGANIZATIONS

Connecticut Forest and Park Association (CFPA), 16 Meriden Rd., Rockfall 06481; (860) 346-8733; www.ctwoodlands.org.

34 DEVIL'S HOPYARD STATE PARK

At the heart of this 860-acre state park, find the tumbling streamers and dark-rock escarpment of 60-foot Chapman Falls. The park name traces either to the growing of hops (an ingredient for beer) or to a charming myth that explains the potholes at the foot of the waterfall as the Devil's hoofprints, burned into place as he danced about to evade the falling water. Brook-size Eightmile River, a charming covered footbridge, and loop trails through mature and varied forest complete the park's invitation.

Start: Upper picnic area trailhead, near the covered bridge
Distance: 2.6-mile loop with spurs
Hiking time: 1.5 to 2 hours
Difficulty: Easy
Elevation change: 300 feet
Trail surface: Earthen path
Best seasons: Spring through fall
Other trail users: Birders and anglers
Canine compatibility: Leashed dogs permitted in picnic areas and on hiking trails; no pets allowed in the campground
Land status: State park
Nearest town: Salem, CT, with gas at the junction of CT 82 and CT 85

Fees and permits: None for day-use parking or hiking, but overnight campground fees apply
Schedule: Year-round, 8 a.m. to sunset
Map: State park map (available online at www.ct.gov/deep)
Trail contacts: Devil's Hopyard State Park, 366 Hopyard Rd., East Haddam 06423; (860) 526-2336. Department of Energy and Environmental Protection, State Parks, (860) 424-3200; www.ct.gov/deep.
Special considerations: Despite the short nature of the trails, hiking boots are recommended because of areas of roots and rocks. The park trails are for foot travel only.

FINDING THE TRAILHEAD

From the small village of Millington (6 miles east of East Haddam), go east on Haywardville Road, following signs for the park. In 0.7 mile turn right (south) on CT 434 (Hopyard Road). In 0.75 mile turn left for the falls, or go another 0.25 mile south, turning left for the picnic area trailheads. Trailhead GPS: N41 28.938' / W72 20.488'

THE HIKE

This hike combines the walk to Chapman Falls with a section of the Vista Trail, paying tribute to the Eightmile Wild and Scenic River, one of only two federally recognized waters in the state. The other is the Farmington. Currently, in all of New England, there are only ten federal wild and scenic rivers. More than 25 miles of this river's main stem and feeder waters are protected.

From the end of the park road, follow the unblazed trail north toward Chapman Falls to view this tumble on Eightmile River. Just a short upstream walk leads to the waterfall and its outcrop and boulder shore, where you can admire the three-tiered 60-foot drop. The lacy water curves around and over the escarpment of reddish-hued Scotland schist.

Forest along Witch Hazel Trail,
Devil's Hopyard State Park, Connecticut

CONNECTICUT'S EIGHTMILE RIVER, A RIVER OF CLASS

In 1968, a banner year for recreation, Congress passed both the National Scenic Trails Act and the National Wild and Scenic Rivers Act. The rivers act defined three classifications of water: wild (unrestricted flows in pristine, natural settings); scenic (unrestricted flows in lightly touched settings, accessible by road); and recreational (flows that are accessible and minimally developed with high recreational merit). For Connecticut's Eightmile River, 25.3 miles of its main stem and major tributaries received federal recognition as scenic water in 2008.

The Eightmile River, which empties into the lower Connecticut River, drains a sweeping rural watershed that encompasses areas of unfragmented habitat and supports rare and diverse wildlife. The water is considered of high quality, and the stream flow is unrestrained. Because of that, the river has played a crucial role in the state's salmon restoration process.

Stepped ledges, eroded potholes, a dark plunge pool, and the attractive enfolding woods contribute to viewing.

The potholes, eroded cylindrical holes ranging from a few inches deep to feet in diameter and depth, are among the finest of their kind in New England. Contrary to myth, the burrowing is caused by the persistent abrasion of stones caught and swirled by the stream's eddies.

Return downstream to the covered bridge to begin the orange-blazed Vista Trail. Pass through this pedestrian bridge that spans Eightmile River. The bridge shows rustic wood siding and has beam-framed windows for viewing the waterway's rich hemlock drainage and leafy drape.

On the east shore, turn right (downstream) following orange blazes for the selected counterclockwise loop. The return is via the white trail. You soon meet the Blue Trail; it turns left for a shorter interior loop. The wide-surfaced Vista Trail travels among mature hemlocks, white pines, and mixed hardwoods. Laurel and azalea edge the brook-size river.

Where the orange trail forks, keep right (riverside). The trail ahead narrows to a footpath, rolling up and over the rocks of the lower slope to tag the riverbank. Ferns and moss complement the tannin-darkened water.

A short spur left leads to Devil's Oven, an eroded cave-like hollow in the park's Brimfield Formation of schist and gneiss. After the oven spur the main trail draws above the river and veers left for a steep climb to gain the ridge. Ledge overhangs draw notice. Round to the top of the ridge and the vista spur junction. Turn right, descending to the vantage. Framed in mountain laurel, it offers an open look at the surrounding forested hills and a pasture and pond. Back at the loop, turn right.

On the ridge flat, hemlock snags pierce the leafy woods, while ferns, grasses, and wildflowers penetrate the duff. Find a moderate descent, hugging the line of the slope and crossing small drainages announced by mountain laurel and skunk cabbage. Deer feed on the fungi. Where the orange Vista Trail turns left to close its loop, keep right now following the white trail.

In a choked hemlock grove, a side path to the right leads past an old oak to a youth group camp. Keep to the loop, which descends among picturesque beech trees and white pines, crossing a rocky drainage. At a four-way junction, a blue/white connector descends left to cross a brook and meet the Blue Loop. The spur to the right heads toward the

Covered Bridge, Devil's Hopyard
State Park, Connecticut

youth group camps and Foxtown Road. For the chosen loop proceed forward on the white trail. More spurs branch to the road as you follow the narrow brook downstream.

Where the white trail forks, follow the left fork southbound toward the covered bridge and flume. Side spurs to the right lead to views of a seasonal falls and the shore of broad-ened Eightmile River. Unseen, Chapman Falls sounds upstream. Close the loop at the bridge.

MILES AND DIRECTIONS

0.0 Start at the upper picnic area trailhead. From the end of the park road, hike the unblazed trail north (upstream) toward Chapman Falls.

0.1 Reach Chapman Falls viewing. Return downstream to the covered bridge.

0.2 Pass through the bridge and turn right on the orange Vista Trail for a coun-terclockwise park loop. The return is via the white trail.

0.3 Reach the junction with the Blue Trail. Proceed forward (downstream) on the orange trail. **Option:** The 0.5-mile blue trail swings an interior woodland hill loop.

0.4 Reach the orange loop junction. Keep right.

0.6 Reach the Devil's Oven spur. Turn left to view this cave-like opening in a ledge.

0.7 Resume hiking downstream on the orange trail.

1.1 Reach the ridgetop and vista spur junction. Turn right for the view.

1.3 Return to the loop and turn right.

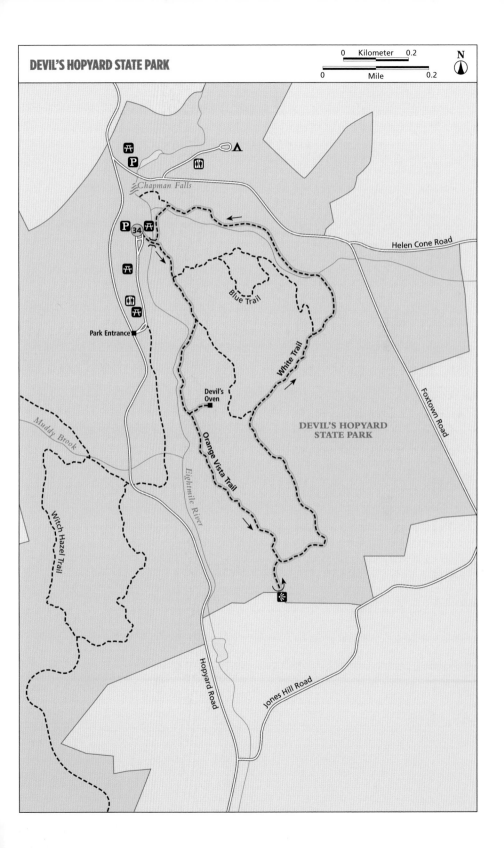

DEVIL'S HOPYARD STATE PARK

0   Kilometer   0.2

0   Mile   0.2

N

Chapman Falls

Helen Cone Road

Blue Trail

White Trail

Foxtown Road

Park Entrance

Devil's
Oven

DEVIL'S HOPYARD
STATE PARK

Muddy Brook

Orange Vista Trail

Eightmile River

Witch Hazel Trail

Hopyard Road

Jones Hill Road

1.8 Reach the loop return for the orange trail. Keep right following the white blazes for the chosen loop. *Option:* The orange Vista Trail offers an alternative loop return to the park core and trailhead.

1.9 Reach a right spur to youth group camps. Keep to the white trail.

2.2 Reach a four-way junction. Continue forward on the white trail. *Note:* The blue/white spur to the left meets the Blue Loop, and the spur to the right leads toward the youth group camps and Foxtown Road.

2.5 Reach the white trail fork and go left (southward) toward the covered bridge.

2.6 Complete the loop at the bridge.

Option: The 2.2-mile out-and-back (3.7-mile when adding pond spur) Millington to Witch Hazel Loop visits the southwest corner of the park above Muddy Brook. It begins at the southernmost picnic area, on the gated woods road near the entrance. Follow red blazes downstream along Eightmile River, passing eastern hemlock, towering oak, maple, dogwood, and mountain laurel. Across the Muddy Brook footbridge, the lane narrows and bears right to cross CT 434 (Hopyard Road). On the west side of CT 434, you reach the yellow loop. Counterclockwise, follow the yellow/red blazes, hiking upstream on a woods road along the hemlock-filled drainage of Muddy Brook. A few big birches accent the woods. Stay with the yellow blazes. Where the path places you closer to the brook, glimpse Baby Falls, a ledge drop with a pretty 3-foot cascade. Notice the woodland canopy and understory changes, with hardwoods, ferns, huge boulders, 10-foot-tall mountain laurel, and huckleberry. Where a southbound spur leads to a pond, stay on the loop. Close the loop, and return to the picnic area via the red trail.

HIKE INFORMATION

LOCAL INFORMATION
Chamber of Commerce of Eastern Connecticut, 914 Hartford Turnpike, Suite 206, Waterford 06385; (860) 701-9113; www.chamberect.com.

ACCOMMODATIONS
Devil's Hopyard Campground offers 21 family campsites in a wooded setting, from mid-Apr through Labor Day. Reservations are through ReserveAmerica, (877) 668-2267 or www.reserveamerica.com.

35 GREEN FALL POND, NARRAGANSETT-NEHANTIC-PACHAUG HIKE

This out-of-the-way unit of Pachaug State Forest is worth seeking out for its picturesque lake marked by treed islands and peninsulas, its tranquil forest, and its jaw-dropping mountain laurel. Who cares if there are spring and summer mosquitoes? With so much beauty at stake, just carry the bug armor, and keep the camera handy.

Start: Green Fall Pond trailhead across from the campground
Distance: 5.8-mile loop
Hiking time: 4 to 5 hours
Difficulty: Moderate, with strenuous rocky stretch on the Nehantic Trail
Elevation change: 200 feet, but rolling
Trail surface: Earthen path, rocky bed, woods road
Best seasons: Spring through fall
Other trail users: Anglers and hunters; mountain bikers and equestrians where the Pachaug Multiuse Trail crosses the northern loop
Canine compatibility: Leashed dogs permitted
Land status: State forest
Nearest town: Jewett City in Township of Griswold, CT
Fees and permits: Seasonal weekend/holiday parking fee for nonresidents; overnight campground fees
Schedule: Year-round, with recreation areas open 8 a.m. to sunset; all other forest areas open a half hour before sunrise to a half hour after sunset
Maps: State forest map (available online at www.ct.gov/deep); Connecticut Forest and Park Association (CFPA) *Connecticut Walk Book, East* (available from CFPA, www.ctwoodlands.org)
Trail contacts: Pachaug State Forest, Route 49, PO Box 5, Voluntown 06384; (860) 376-4075. Department of Energy and Environmental Protection, State Parks and Forests, (860) 424-3200; www.ct.gov/deep.
Special considerations: Carry adequate drinking water for your trail time away from the recreation area. When the water system is up, you do have a chance to resupply between the two lobes of travel. Take precautions during hunting season. The blue, blue/orange, blue/red, and blue/yellow trails are all foot traffic only.

FINDING THE TRAILHEAD

From the junction of CT 138, CT 165, and CT 49 in Voluntown, head south off CT 138 onto CT 165W/CT 49S and take an immediate left turn onto Pendleton Hill Road to follow CT 49S toward Westerly. In 2 miles turn left onto gravel Fish Road. Go another mile and bear right on Green Falls Road, passing the entry station. Reach the campground and Green Fall Pond trailhead at the end of the developed area in 2 miles. Trailhead GPS: N41 32.212' / W71 48.577'

THE HIKE

Hike the blue/orange trail south beneath an umbrella of mountain laurel and an upper canopy of oaks, maples, birches, and beeches. A boulder and ledge hilltop rises to the

east. A tanglewood of laurel separates the trail from the pond's edge. Sassafras, sweet pepperbush, and huckleberry variously fill out the midstory. Where you scramble over pond-side rocks, spurs break to shore.

Meet the blue Narragansett Trail, which arrives from the left to share travel south. The trail improves soon afterward. Rocks afford pond views with cross-pond looks at an island and the even-height basin woods. Ducks may protest your nearness. More spurs access shore as you round the deep-set coves of Green Fall Pond.

Hike across the earthen dike and pass through a hemlock-darkened woods threaded by old stone walls. At the Green Fall River dam and spillway falls, you cross the dam and footbridge, remaining on the blue/orange pond loop. The Narragansett breaks away to follow the river downstream.

The loop hugs the shore, affording looks at the pond, the island, and a rocky-footed peninsula that shapes a narrow inlet cove. Tiny rock islands pierce the mirror stillness. Step across a trickling brook to round onto the peninsula for shore access. You then head uphill on the log-braced steps, reaching Green Falls Road where it is paved. Turn right, following the road to close the Pond Loop or to add the upper (Nehantic-Pachaug) loop.

Adding the upper loop, look for the marked Nehantic Trail to turn north off the forest road. This short stretch is the most rugged of the whole hike, scrambling over boulder and brook. The path is less worn, so watch for the blue blazing. Cross Green Falls Road, round the gate, and descend on woods road. You quickly enter a pine stand to the right as the woods road enters a bend.

The trail rolls from big pines to oak-maple woods to young pines. Stone walls that have survived centuries of winter storms and tree falls stand stalwart in the woods. Find sweet pepperbush and cinnamon ferns at drainage crossings. In places planks help keep feet dry. Climb from bottomland to outcrop slope for a squirrel's eye view of this classic Connecticut woodland.

You then meander down to a series of brook crossings as the trail weaves through choked young pines with a few bigger trees. Approaching Fish Road, keep alert for the junction with the blue/red crossover. It takes the loop east. The blue Nehantic Trail continues north.

Cross Green Falls Road at the rock and flower divide and enter the opposite woods. Ascend to a mountain laurel plateau for stunning, brushing passage. A more impressive showing of the state flower would be difficult to imagine. Sweet pepperbush and huckleberry alternately interrupt or mingle in the bonanza.

As the trail worms through laurel thicket, soggy spots may require creative footing. A network of stone walls webs the woods. Coming to a T-junction at a woods lane, turn right. Left is the blue/yellow Laurel Loop. Ahead, meet the Pachaug Trail and continue straight (south) on the laurel-squeezed lane, now tracking blue blazes.

While on this woods lane, don't get too complacent because the trail turns right to follow foot trail through a more open woodland. Although the laurel is not gone, glacial rocks vary the visuals. Pass between boulders, viewing the woods below as well as the trailside trees. The trail rolls and swings between outcrops. Low pitch pines and chestnut oaks favor the outcrops.

The trail then pitches and climbs between drainage crossings. Quartzite veins the streamside rock. You next squeeze through the zigzag slot of Split Rock and briefly climb to set up the final descent to the trailhead. Emerge near the campground.

MILES AND DIRECTIONS

0.0 Start at the Green Fall Pond trailhead across from the campground. Follow the blue/orange trail, heading south along the east shore of Green Fall Pond for a clockwise loop.

0.3 Meet and follow the blue Narragansett Trail south along shore. *Note:* The left fork carries the Narragansett east to the Connecticut–Rhode Island border.

0.9 Reach the dam and Green Fall River spillway. Cross the dam, following the blue/orange blazes of the pond loop. *Note:* The Narragansett Trail heads south, downstream along the river.

1.6 Reach Green Falls Road. Turn right, following it into the forest recreation area.

1.8 Turn left (north) off Green Falls Road, following the signed and blue-blazed Nehantic Trail.

2.1 Cross Green Falls Road and round a gate to descend on woods road.

3.7 Turn right on the blue/red trail as you approach Fish Road. *Note:* The Nehantic Trail continues northbound.

3.8 Cross Green Falls Road near the entrance booth divide. Continue eastward, following the blue/red blaze.

4.9 Reach the blue Pachaug Trail. Follow it right to continue clockwise travel on the upper loop.

5.8 Arrive back at the trailhead, descending the slope above the campground.

Options: The adjoining Laurel Ridge property to the north extends travel options, as do explorations on any of the long-distance blue trails.

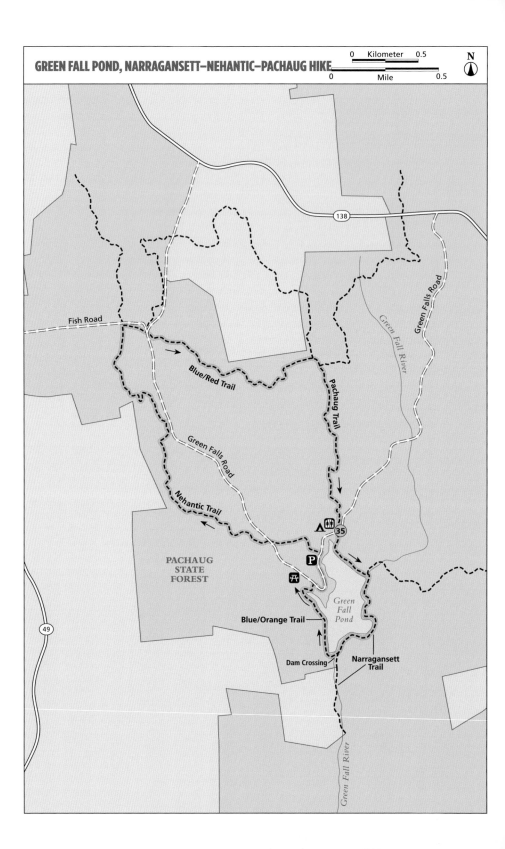

0   Kilometer   0.5

0   Mile   0.5

N

138

Fish Road

Blue/Red Trail

Pachaug Trail

Green Fall River

Green Falls Road

Green Falls Road

Nehantic Trail

PACHAUG
STATE
FOREST

49

35

P

Green
Fall
Pond

Blue/Orange Trail

Dam Crossing

Narragansett
Trail

Green Fall River

HIKE INFORMATION

LOCAL INFORMATION

Chamber of Commerce of Eastern Connecticut, 914 Hartford Turnpike, Suite 206, Waterford 06385; (860) 701-9113; www.chamberect.com.

ACCOMMODATIONS

Green Falls Campground has 18 wooded campsites available from mid-Apr until Labor Day. Reservations must be made through ReserveAmerica, (877) 668-2267 or www.reserveamerica.com.

ORGANIZATIONS

Connecticut Forest and Park Association (CFPA), 16 Meriden Rd., Rockfall 06481; (860) 346-8733; www.ctwoodlands.org.

36 HARTMAN RECREATIONAL PARK, HERITAGE TRAIL

At this 302-acre open space find north–south trending ridges separated by attractive wooded valleys and wetlands. Across the property a dotting of stone ruins and miles of stone walls recall a thriving colonial settlement. Remnant foot trails and cart roads from that early community contribute to the interlocking color-coded pathways of today. Other paths link to the trails of Nehantic State Forest.

Start: Entrance trailhead
Distance: 3-mile lollipop
Hiking time: 1.5 to 2.5 hours
Difficulty: Moderate
Elevation change: 200 feet, but rolling
Trail surface: Earthen path and cart trails
Best seasons: Spring through fall
Other trail users: Mountain bikers, equestrians, snowshoers, cross-country skiers
Canine compatibility: Leashed dogs permitted (keep animals controlled and clean up after them)
Land status: Town recreational park
Nearest town: Salem, CT, with gas at the junction of CT 82 and CT 85

Fees and permits: None
Schedule: Year-round, sunrise to sunset
Map: Regional park map (available online at www.lymelandtrust.org)
Trail contact: Lyme Land Conservation Trust, PO Box 1002, Lyme 06371; (860) 434-5051; www.lymelandtrust.org
Special considerations: No motor vehicles, hunting, fires, or collecting. In this color-coded trail system, yellow blazes indicate a connector trail, white blazes a foot trail only; carry a park map. Bring water and beware of poison ivy, which is abundant throughout the park.

FINDING THE TRAILHEAD

From the junction of CT 82 and CT 156, east of Hadlyme, drive south on CT 156E for 1.7 miles and turn left (east) onto Beaver Brook Road in North Lyme. Go 2.6 miles on Beaver Brook Road and turn left (north) on Gungy/Grassy Hill Road. Go 1 mile on Gungy Road, finding trailhead parking on the right. Trailhead GPS: N41 25.580' / W72 17.257'

THE HIKE

The park's interlocking trails lay out a variety of hiking options, suitable for most any schedule. The longest is the 3-mile orange-blazed Heritage Trail, featured here. It strings past the cultural ruins of farm, mill, and early enterprise and seventeenth-, eighteenth-, and nineteenth-century stone walls and foundations. It also shows off the rolling park terrain and changing habitats.

From the gated dirt management road (the purple arterial trail), you follow the orange-blazed Heritage Trail left through young forest of maple, beech, and oak. Sweet pepperbush favors moist areas. You soon glimpse the snag-edged and lily pad-decorated mill

Birch trunks along Heritage Trail,
Hartman Park, Old Lyme, Connecticut

pond at the crossing of a small footbridge at the old sawmill site. Afterward you enter the picnic area/open-air classroom with its information board.

Cross the park road and head uphill for a counterclockwise loop. You hike past the north end of the green trail, which heads right, back to trailhead parking, and soon after cross a yellow-blazed one. In springtime dogwoods lend bloom to this stretch.

The first well-preserved foundation of an old barn (Lee Barn) calls you aside. Shortly afterward the orange trail briefly follows the park road north. At a cellar hole and rock foundation recalling the Lee Farmhouse, the Heritage Trail ascends right through old fields overgrown with cedar and encroached upon by oaks and maples.

Where another yellow connector heads left, bear right for the "Big Scramble," a switchbacking climb through mountain laurel, topping Chapman Ridge. The trail now journeys north, skirting the various stonework of the Chapman Farm.

Hike past the Hartman Park blue trail on your left to traverse the shrub thicket of a power-line corridor. A spur to the right tops some rocks for a western vantage looking out the corridor. Watch for vultures and hawks before reentering woods at a scenic beech grove.

Transmitted by a deer-tick bite, Lyme Disease was first diagnosed in 1975 in Lyme, Connecticut, following an inexplicable outbreak of arthritis-like symptoms among area children. Joint pain is a late-stage symptom. After any hiking, do a head-to-toe search for and removal of any ticks. With fine-point tweezers or one of the tick scoops now on the market, grip at the head or mouthparts and give a steady backward tug until the tick is removed. Clean the site, and monitor for redness. Always see a doctor if any redness, weakness, or illness occurs.

Descend Chapman Ridge, again finding abundant mountain laurel and passing a stone fireplace, to hike the park road to the right. Pass beneath aspen and tulip poplar, viewing stonework that recalls another old farm. As you bear left from the road, a telltale circular depression hints at an old charcoal kiln.

From fern-filled glen, you round below a huge boulder outcrop and again ascend. The Hartman Park red trail, (formerly dubbed the Nubble and Ridges Trail for its outward character) arrives on the right as the Heritage Trail tackles Three Chimneys Ridge. A compound of rock work, including three small fireplaces, suggests the ridge name. The Heritage Trail then descends past an enormous boulder against which a barn/sheep shed once stood.

Woody grapevines drape between trees. Stay with the orange blazes for rolling travel of Jumble Ridge. Hike past a yellow blazed connector heading left (south) toward the blue trail and another heading north. A circular trench marks another nineteenth-century charcoal kiln. Ahead find more ruins and a second pass through a power-line corridor.

Cross a drainage at the old flume site, and continue on the orange Heritage Trail, bearing right on the park road to complete the loop. Up ahead, you then backtrack right, passing through the classroom/picnic site to return to the trailhead.

MILES AND DIRECTIONS

0.0 Start at the entrance trailhead. Walk up the gated park road and turn left to follow the orange Heritage Trail.

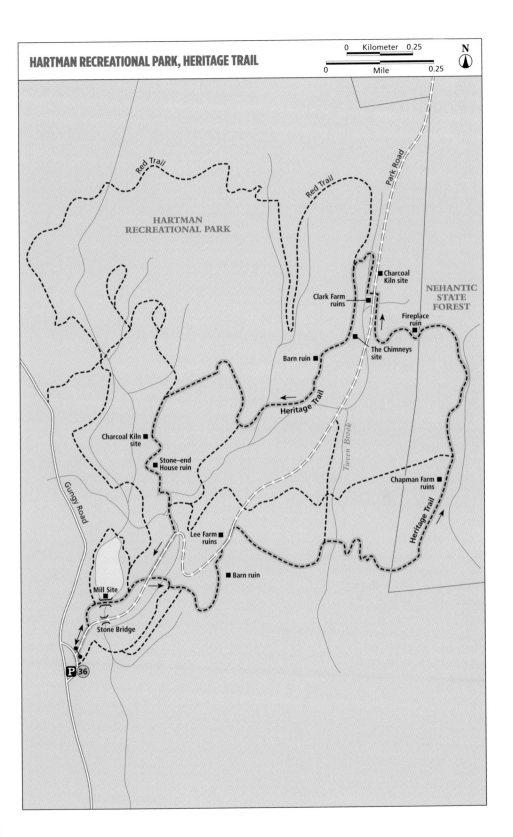

HARTMAN RECREATIONAL PARK, HERITAGE TRAIL

0   Kilometer   0.25

0   Mile   0.25

N

Red Trail

Red Trail

Park Road

HARTMAN
RECREATIONAL PARK

Charcoal
Kiln site

Clark Farm
ruins

NEHANTIC
STATE
FOREST

Fireplace
ruin

The Chimneys
site

Barn ruin

Heritage Trail

Tween Brook

Charcoal Kiln
site

Chapman Farm
ruins

Stone–end
House ruin

Heritage Trail

Gungy Road

Lee Farm
ruins

Barn ruin

Mill Site

Stone Bridge

P 36

0.2 Reach the picnic area/open-air classroom. Follow the orange blazes across the park road for a counterclockwise loop.

0.5 Reach an old barn foundation.

0.8 Top Chapman Ridge.

1.0 Pass the Hartman Park blue trail to travel a shrubby power-line corridor.

1.7 Meet the Hartman Park red trail on Three Chimneys Ridge.

2.0 Reach Jumble Ridge.

2.7 Bear right on the park road, keeping to the orange loop.

2.8 Close the loop at the picnic area and return to the trailhead.

3.0 Arrive back at the trailhead.

Option: The park's red trail rolls from ridge to ridge, tagging interesting cliff and rock features. It fashions a 2.5-mile loop with a 200-foot elevation change. From the picnic area/open-air classroom, it heads north. It then passes Hartman Field, Cave Cliff, and Three Chimneys Ridge before returning to the start. Rocks of quartzite, schist, and gneiss characterize the tour, including a broken overhang dubbed Snout Rock. Find the trail rolling, generally forested, and bursting with beautiful pockets of laurel.

HIKE INFORMATION

LOCAL INFORMATION

East Haddam, Connecticut, Town Office Building, 1 Plains Rd., PO Box 385, Moodus 06469; (860) 873-5020; www.easthaddam.org.

LOCAL EVENTS/ATTRACTIONS

Gillette Castle State Park, 67 River Rd., East Haddam 06423; (860) 526-2336; www.ct.gov/deep. The Castle, an East Haddam landmark overlooking the Connecticut River, is a bastion out of time and place. This medieval fieldstone fortress (circa 1919) atop Seventh Sister was the vision and retreat of actor, playwright, and noted Sherlock Holmes portrayer William Hooker Gillette (1853–1937). The park preserves the castle and grounds for sightseeing and recreation.

Goodspeed Opera House, 6 Main St., PO Box A, East Haddam 06423-0281; (860) 873-8664 (administration) or (860) 873-8668 (box office); http://goodspeed.org. The 1876 Goodspeed Opera House, on the other hand, is the charming belle of the Connecticut River. Built to satisfy banker William H. Goodspeed's love of theater, it again houses musical theater today. In between performances, it lived out a rich, diverse history from militia to mercantile.

ORGANIZATIONS

Lyme Land Conservation Trust, PO Box 1002, Lyme 06371; www.lymelandtrust.org.

37 NAYANTAQUIT TRAIL/ UNCAS POND

In Nehantic State Forest, southeast of Hadlyme, this rolling loop passes through a gentle terrain of low ridges and mixed forest, serving up solitude and relaxation. Wildlife sightings, historic stone walls and old foundations, and the forest's many color shades and shapes are the hike's beguilements. Midway, a side trip to the deep clear waters of Uncas Pond beckons a picnic lunch or a quick swim.

Start: Keeny Road trailhead at the forest's north boundary
Distance: 5.4-mile lollipop with an out-and-back spur
Hiking time: 3 to 4 hours
Difficulty: Moderate
Elevation change: The trail has 400 feet of elevation change between the low point at Uncas Pond and the high point at Nickerson Hill.
Trail surface: Earthen path, woods road, management road
Best seasons: Spring through fall
Other trail users: Anglers and birders; mountain bikers and equestrians on unblazed trails or roads
Canine compatibility: Leashed dogs permitted
Land status: State forest
Nearest town: Old Lyme, CT
Fees and permits: None
Schedule: Year-round, with recreation areas open 8 a.m. to sunset; all other forest areas open a half hour before sunrise to a half hour after sunset
Maps: State forest map (available online at www.ct.gov/deep); Connecticut Forest and Park Association (CFPA) *Connecticut Walk Book, East* (available from CFPA, www.ctwoodlands.org)
Trail contacts: Nehantic State Forest, c/o Rocky Neck State Park, 244 West Main St., Niantic 06357; (860) 739-5471. Department of Energy and Environmental Protection, State Parks and Forests, (860) 424-3200; www.ct.gov/deep.
Special considerations: Swimming is at your own risk. Because periodic logging is part of forestry management, during such times the trail can be closed for safety concerns. The Nayantaquit, the blue/yellow crossover, and the blue/green Uncas Pond connector are all open to foot travel only. Bring drinking water.

FINDING THE TRAILHEAD

From the junction of CT 82 and CT 156 (east of Hadlyme, west of North Plain), go south on CT 156E for 1.7 miles, reaching North Lyme. Turn east on Beaver Brook Road, drive 1.9 miles, and turn right (south) on Keeny Road. Reach trailhead parking on the right in 1.3 miles. The final 0.3 mile is on dirt road. Trailhead GPS: N41 23.761' / W72 18.430'

THE HIKE

Named for an Indian tribe that hunted in this part of Nehantic State Forest, this loop wins you over with its relaxing familiarity. From the parking area, hike in on a gated dirt road, taking an immediate left, following blue blazes and locating a trail sign.

A young and varied forest of oak, maple, birch, dogwood, sassafras, shadbush, and hazelnut welcomes you. The understory holds huckleberry and sarsaparilla. You cross a scenic

Uncas Pond, Nehantic State Forest, Connecticut

rock wall and pass a huge boulder on the left to come to the loop junction. Turn left (clockwise), following a narrow path with a mild incline.

The trail levels off near the edge of a plateau. Boulders and the occasional stump dot the forest, which, although young, provides a full leafy umbrella. A sometimes-steep descent takes you into a mature oak-hickory complex. As the trail weaves and rolls among the boulder outcrops, it gathers different visuals and generates different moods. Cross a thin drainage, pass a regal 4-foot-diameter tulip poplar, and cross a rock wall.

Atop Brown Hill, in a small transition meadow, find a junction. The loop continues left, while the blue/yellow crossover heads right for a shorter hike. On the crossover, stone walls and foundations recall the land's domestic history as pasture and farmland. Keep left for the full loop, quickly reaching the blue/green spur to Uncas Pond. The spur heads left; the loop turns right.

Choosing to go left for Uncas Pond, pass quietly because wild turkey or deer may be spied. You descend past a doghouse-size rock shelter to travel in tall mixed deciduous woods. The trail then rolls up and over the next outcrop rise, reaching a dirt forest road (Keeny Road).

Look for the blue/green trail across the road. This short segment rolls over a small wooded rise to emerge at a post barricade on the picnic area entrance road. The improved beach access is at the picnic area's south end.

Wooden beams terrace the slope, and sand greets the water. You can expect company in summer and a change of volume from the forest quiet. Sparkling blue, the deep waters of Uncas Pond are mostly rimmed by forest, with a couple of houses visible. Pond lilies dot the water's edge.

After backtracking to the loop, resume clockwise travel by heading straight. You will track the blazes through a couple of quick direction changes to walk a tranquil country lane bathed in filtered light. Beyond a stone wall shaded by a gnarly oak, the lane yields to a logging road. Bear right, cross a drainage culvert, and continue tracking blazes.

Ascending via footpath through woods of oak, hickory, and beech, you top a small hill. After crossing a stone wall, you travel the summit of Nickerson Hill, tagging the hike's high point (elevation 452 feet). Large round boulders dot a sloping outcrop, which offers limited views across the tall foreground forest. Filling out the area are spiny armed snags, young deciduous trees, and cedars.

Keep on the blazed loop. In the leafy canopy, insects create the sound of high-tension wires. Next find a series of crossings over woods roads, a brook, and a secondary trail. As the blue/yellow crossover tags up, continue forward.

With a steady descent, cross the width of a long meadow swath, brimming with wild berry, sumac, herbs, and forbs. Be alert for poison ivy. Cross a small brook into a wetter maple woodland and pass through a goldenrod opening to close the loop and return to the trailhead.

MILES AND DIRECTIONS

0.0 Start at the Keeny Road trailhead at the forest's north boundary. Follow the gated forest road, taking an immediate left on the blue-blazed Nayantaquit Trail.

0.2 Reach the loop junction. Go left (clockwise).

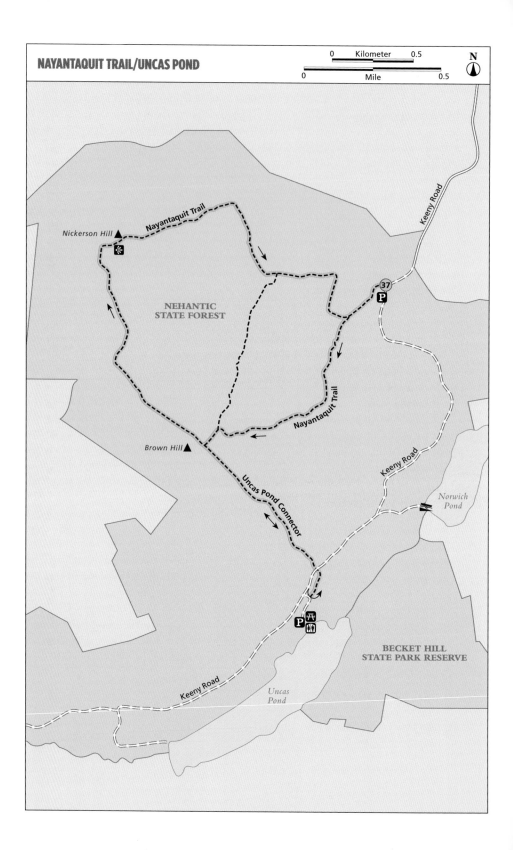

Kilometer

0   0.5

Mile

0   0.5

N

Keeny Road

Nickerson Hill ▲

Nayantaquit Trail

NEHANTIC
STATE FOREST

37
P

Nayantaquit Trail

Brown Hill ▲

Uncas Pond Connector

Keeny Road

Norwich
Pond

P

BECKET HILL
STATE PARK RESERVE

Keeny Road

Uncas
Pond

1.0	Reach the blue/yellow crossover atop Brown Hill. Stay with the blue blazes.
1.1	Reach the blue/green Uncas Pond Connector. Follow the blue/green trail left to Uncas Pond.
2.1	Reach Uncas Pond. Backtrack the blue/green trail to Brown Hill and the loop.
3.1	Reach the loop junction. Continue forward (clockwise) on the blue loop, heading northwest to complete the circuit.
4.0	Top Nickerson Hill.
4.8	Reach the blue/yellow crossover. Continue forward on the blue trail.
5.2	Complete the loop. Backtrack left to the trailhead.
5.4	Arrive back at the trailhead.

HIKE INFORMATION

LOCAL INFORMATION

Chamber of Commerce of Eastern Connecticut, 914 Hartford Turnpike, Suite 206, Waterford 06385; (860) 701-9113; www.chamberect.com.

LOCAL EVENTS/ATTRACTIONS

East Lyme Historical Society, 228 West Main St. (Route 156), PO Box 112, East Lyme 06333; (860) 739-6070; www.eastlymehistoricalsociety.org. At East Lyme's Thomas Lee House and Little Boston School, you can view one of Connecticut's oldest wood-frame houses (circa 1660), the first district school (circa 1734), a barn, and period gardens. You also learn about a Lee descendant, Ezra Lee, who in 1776 volunteered to operate the one-man "Turtle," America's first submarine, against the British *Eagle* moored in New York Harbor. The sites are open Wed through Sun afternoons in July and Aug, or by appointment.

Florence Griswold Museum, 96 Lyme St., Old Lyme 06371; (860) 434-5542; https://florencegriswoldmuseum.org. In Old Lyme the Florence Griswold Museum provides a look into the life and the context behind the work of early 20th-century artists. View paintings, stroll the grounds, and spy the inspiration.

ORGANIZATIONS

Connecticut Forest and Park Association (CFPA), 16 Meriden Rd., Rockfall 06481; (860) 346-8733; www.ctwoodlands.org.

Uncas Pond Connector Trail bridge, Nehantic State Forest, Connecticut

38 BLUFF POINT STATE PARK AND COASTAL RESERVE

This hike explores Connecticut's last vestige of undeveloped coast—an 800-acre wooded peninsula that extends into Long Island Sound and is bounded by the Poquonnock River and Mumford Cove. Its sandy spit offers coastal and bay discovery. The varied wild supports deer, raccoons, and sea, shore, and woodland birds. Designated a coastal reserve, site facilities are few. An easy loop on closed dirt roads and shore introduces the coastal woodland, spit, and bluff and gives nod to the 1700s homesite of Governor Winthrop.

Start: Picnic area trailhead
Distance: 5-mile loop with out-and-back spur
Hiking time: 3 to 4 hours
Difficulty: Easy
Elevation change: 100 feet
Trail surface: Woods road and sandy beach
Best seasons: Spring through fall
Other trail users: Anglers, birders, mountain bikers
Canine compatibility: Leashed dogs permitted. Apr 1 to Sept 1, no dogs allowed on beach.
Land status: State park
Nearest town: Groton, CT, with gas available along US 1
Fees and permits: None

Schedule: Year-round, 8 a.m. to sunset
Map: State park map (available online at www.ct.gov/deep)
Trail contacts: Bluff Point State Park and Coastal Reserve, c/o Fort Trumbull State Park, 90 Walbach St., New London 06320; (860) 444-7591. Department of Energy and Environmental Protection, State Parks, (860) 424-3200; www.ct.gov/deep.
Special considerations: Bring drinking water because there is none at the park. Summer beachgoers swell numbers. Be alert to the tide, when walking the beach.

FINDING THE TRAILHEAD

From I-95, take exit 88, go 1 mile south on CT 117, and turn west on US 1. In 0.3 mile turn south on Depot Road at a sign for park. Go 0.3 mile and bear right to pass under the railroad tracks. Reach the gravel parking lot, picnic area, and trail in 0.4 mile. Trailhead GPS: N41 20.125' / W72 01.995'

THE HIKE

This hike focuses on the western loop. It can be extended or shortened according to your interests or time constraints.

From the center of the picnic area, head south on the gated woods road, passing parallel to the Poquonnock River on its flow seaward. Swans may ply the bay. Often anglers line the riprap shore, while sea kayakers dig their way to Long Island Sound. Across the river sits the small Groton–New London Airport.

On this hike you travel at the perimeter of a mixed oak-hickory woods, with sassafras, hawthorn, cherry, and the occasional eastern red cedar. Greenbrier, wild grape, and bramble contribute to the understory tangle. At the loop junction, head right for a

Poquonnock River estuary, Bluff Point
State Park, Connecticut

counterclockwise loop. You will find periodic looks at the gravelly Poquonnock shore, its width dependent on tide. In spring a pair of ospreys (sea hawks) may settle atop an offshore nesting platform.

The trail opens up as it skirts a grassy tidal marsh with cattails at one end. In open areas native beach plum, beach pea, and red and white shore roses grow. The main woods road passes between a bouldery forested hill and the tight tangle of the bayward woods. A semi-overgrown colonial rock wall adds interest and charm.

Ahead, keep to the woods road. The lesser trail to the left offers a cutoff to the Governor Winthrop site to shorten the hike. At a Poquonnock River spur, you overlook the tidal grass plain and bay of this coastal river. The productive 100-acre salt marsh attracts resident and migratory birds.

Later, a footpath to the left offers a cutoff to Bluff Point. Keep to the wide travel lane, to arrive at the beach below Bluff Point. Tide-pool rocks string off the point, while pebbles, cobbles, and sun-bleached shells make up the coastal shore. Views sweep Long Island Sound from Groton Heights to Bluff Point and take in New York's Fisher's Island and Rhode Island's Watch Hill.

An attractive 200-foot-wide tombolo beach (the spit) arcs west to Bushy Point. Journeying west along it, you view both the sound and Poquonnock River bay shore. Wading and seabirds may detain glances.

The seashore's tide-deposited strings of seaweed, sea lettuce, bladder-floated algae, skate egg-cases, periwinkles, horseshoe crabs or their shells, and flotsam and jetsam entice beachcombers to their knees. At about two-thirds of the way, stable sands replace the shifting gravels. At low tide, Bushy Point signals the turnaround (be sure to allow adequate time for a safe return). At high tide, it becomes a vegetated rock island and you

Shells on Brushy Point Beach, Bluff Point State Park, Connecticut

are turned back by the tide. Pine Island sits farther offshore, while a scenic brick lighthouse blinks to the west.

Back at Bluff Point, resume the loop atop the 20-foot bluff. Views broaden and strain east. You continue rounding the point to overlook the mouth of Mumford Cove and pass Sunset Rock. A dwarfed woods and dense, thorny understory enfold the gravel road/trail, which mildly climbs. Cardinals, blue jays, hawks, and vultures can all draw eyes skyward.

At a four-way junction, look across the rock wall to the right to discover the ruins—a stone foundation, chunks of red brick, and a hard-to-see well now filled with stones. Here stood the home of Governor Fitzjohn Winthrop (grandson of the famous Massachusetts Bay governor). Circa 1700, the Winthrop house had a 300-foot tunnel connecting it to the barn, a safeguard against Indian attacks. Beware of poison ivy in the historic area.

Keep north on the main woods road to complete the western loop. The smaller track to the right offers a longer return to the picnic area trailhead. Tall forest enfolds the hike as you complete the loop and return to parking.

MILES AND DIRECTIONS

0.0 Start at the picnic area trailhead. Follow the gravel road south. *Option:* A second grade heads east, allowing you to fashion an eastern loop or visit Mumford Cove.

0.1 Reach the the hike's loop junction. Go right.

0.9 Reach the cut-across to the site of Governor Winthrop's house. Continue forward (south).

1.0 Reach and follow right the side spur to a Poquonnock River cove view. Backtrack to the loop.

1.2 Resume counterclockwise travel.

1.4 Reach a trail fork. Bear right to visit the spit and Bushy Point. *Option:* The trail straight ahead is a shortcut to Bluff Point.

2.2 Reach Bushy Point or the high-tide turnaround. Return east along the spit to resume the counterclockwise loop atop Bluff Point.

3.0 Reach the Bluff Point viewpoint. Continue counterclockwise on the loop, rounding the bluff and passing between the coastal reserve and the natural preserve that spans east to Mumford Cove.

3.6 Pass Sunset Rock.

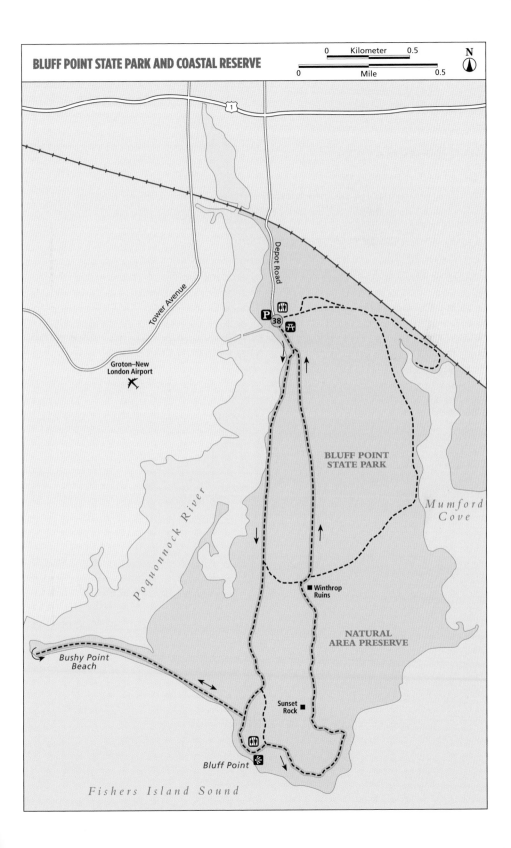

BLUFF POINT STATE PARK AND COASTAL RESERVE

0   Kilometer   0.5

0   Mile   0.5

N

1

Tower Avenue

Depot Road

Groton–New London Airport

P 38

Poquonnock River

BLUFF POINT STATE PARK

Mumford Cove

Winthrop Ruins

NATURAL AREA PRESERVE

Bushy Point Beach

Sunset Rock

Bluff Point

Fishers Island Sound

4.0 Reach the Winthrop house ruins. Follow the gravel road north to complete the loop. ***Option:*** By taking the trail to the right, you can lengthen the hike, with the return leg passing closer to Mumford Cove.

4.9 Close the loop. Backtrack to the trailhead.

5.0 Arrive back at the trailhead.

HIKE INFORMATION

LOCAL INFORMATION

Mystic & Shoreline Visitor Information Center, 27 Coogan Blvd., Building 1-D, Olde Mistick Village, Mystic 06355; (860) 536-1641; http://mysticinfocenter.com.

LOCAL EVENTS/ATTRACTIONS

Fort Griswold State Park and **Fort Trumbull State Park** take you back in time. Fort Griswold (Groton) keeps sacred the Revolutionary War site overtaken in 1781 by British forces led by Benedict Arnold. Nearly half the fort's defenders died in the assault. Fort Trumbull (New London) preserves the Thames River fort (1839–1852) that served as part of the nation's coastal defense system. For both, contact Fort Trumbull State Park, 90 Walbach St., New London 06320; (860) 444-7591; www.ct.gov/deep. Fort Griswold, (860) 449-6877 (seasonal).

39 BARN ISLAND WILDLIFE MANAGEMENT AREA

Before the Europeans arrived, much of Connecticut was swampland. This hike allows you to view this nearly vanquished habitat. Tidal marsh, estuary channels and ponds, a coastal river, upland woods, and coastal grasslands characterize the wildlife management area (WMA). Egrets dot white to open spaces, while hawks soar the sky and songbirds animate branch and wind. Old dikes, mosquito ditches (early 1900s attempts to remove mosquito breeding habitat), and former roads partition the area. A historic cemetery speaks of the past.

Start: Louis Bayer monument trailhead
Distance: 4.2-mile lollipop with cemetery spur
Hiking time: About 3 hours
Difficulty: Easy
Elevation change: Less than 100 feet
Trail surface: Earthen or grassy path, dike, woods road
Best seasons: Spring through fall
Other trail users: Birders, mountain bikers, equestrians, hunters, snowshoers, cross-country skiers
Canine compatibility: Leashed dogs permitted (maximum leash length 7 feet to protect wildlife), exceptions for active hunts
Land status: State wildlife management area
Nearest town: Stonington or Pawcatuck, CT, with gas available along US 1
Fees and permits: None

Schedule: Year-round, sunrise to sunset
Maps: WMA trail map (on-site map board only); online hunting map, available at www.ct.gov/deep
Trail contact: Barn Island WMA, Connecticut Department of Energy and Environmental Protection, Wildlife Division, Eastern District, 209 Hebron Rd., Marlborough 06447; (860) 295-9523; www.ct.gov/deep
Special considerations: Bring drinking water for the hike. Take precautions, including wearing bright-colored clothing, during hunting season, Sept through Feb. The peak hunting period for small game and deer takes place from mid-Oct through Dec. No hunting is allowed on Sun. Boat launch parking is for boaters only.

FINDING THE TRAILHEAD

From US 1 (5.6 miles northeast of Mystic and 2.6 miles southwest of Westerly and the Rhode Island border), turn southeast (toward the coast) onto Greenhaven Road. In 0.1 mile turn right on Palmer Neck Road, signed for Barn Island and the boat launch. Enter the WMA in 1.2 miles and reach trailhead parking in 1.4 miles. The boat launch is at road's end, 0.2 mile farther. Trailhead GPS: N41 20.378' / W71 52.658'

THE HIKE

Start at the stone monument honoring Louis Bayer, an advocate for this tidal marsh declared by noted botanist, educator, and conservationist William A. Niering to be "the finest coastal wild in Connecticut." The WMA's 1,000-acre mosaic has earned global recognition as an Important Bird Area. Gulls, ospreys, ibises, herons, vireos, catbirds, and more engage binoculars.

Quickly you come upon the site's native plant demonstration garden and an elevated view of the swamp. Here you can learn some of the commonplace plants in the coastal environment, as well as study the landscape: the high-low marsh, the beach, the 1900s-dug mosquito ditches, the impoundment dikes and ponds, and the upland coastal forest.

Pass among oak–maple mixed woods and thicket to reach the swamp, a textured sea of salt grasses, dark pools, and thin drainages. Insect chirrs, white flights of egrets, and diving cormorants enliven the scene.

Upon returning to woods, you reach both a junction and the "You are here" board. Take a moment to study the map before continuing forward on the woods road. You'll skirt an old cellar hole on the left. Centuries ago the land was used for farm and pasture.

At the next marsh opening, your views stretch to the horizon of Little Narragansett Bay. The coastal salt spray and swamp methane may tweak your nostrils. Global warming studies have been conducted in the swamp for the past few years, and you might see evidence of past or present studies.

Back in woods, you reach the next junction. Here the main track (the loop) curves left, but first take the track less traveled to the right to visit the historic cemetery. It skirts marsh and adds broad views of the WMA. Later, travel again flips from marsh to woods, and the road is more defined. Keen eyes might detect more sunlight where Hurricane

Salt water marsh, Barn Island Wildlife Management Area, Connecticut

Cemetery, Barn Island Wildlife Management Area, Connecticut

Irene toppled trees in 2011. An old stone well in the woods and stone walls again hint at previous uses of the land.

As you approach stone entry gates, the cemetery sits across the stone wall to your right. It contains slate headstones from different eras, the oldest dating back to the 1790s. Buried here are Veterans of the War of 1812. You might notice the different scripts, weathering gothic designs, or unadorned remembrances. There are twenty or more markers plainly visible among the natural vegetation that now adds to the quiet sleep. Beware poison ivy and pass respectfully.

READING THE STONES

Colonial burial grounds, forgotten and preserved, are treasuries of the past. Each tells a story. The earliest burial grounds had fieldstone or wooden markers. In the seventeenth and eighteenth centuries, the markers were typically thin slate slabs, 30 inches tall. For many the carved headstones face west, the footstones east. This was done to protect the grave and to orient the departed toward the sunrise of Judgment Day.

Some of the earliest stones reflect the stern sensibility of the Puritans, in verse and motif. Grim mortality symbols—skulls, coffins, scythes, and hourglasses—reflect a Puritan influence. Winged faces, angels, and trees of life were the more hopeful symbols of the eighteenth century. Urns and willows were other later choices. The stone engravings of ornament, border, and script offer clues to the carvers, the artists of the day. Inscriptions may indicate the departed's station in life, relationships, or cause of death.

By following the woods road through the stone gateway, you have a pleasant woods walk that dead-ends at the WMA's boundary gate. For this hike, though, turn around to resume the counterclockwise loop at the last junction.

A woodland ramble follows. Keep to the main woods road, ignoring side paths. Where you reach a Y-junction, bear left for the loop. The path to the right is another dead end. Enjoy a rustling canopy. When leaves are shed, the trail holds different moods and discoveries. Cinnamon ferns, sarsaparilla, stone walls, and an undulating and sashaying course characterize travel. Again keep to the main trail, as secondary trails branch to its sides.

Where you again come to a woods road junction, bear left to continue the loop. To the right leads toward Palmer Neck Road. The chosen woodland ramble continues trending back toward the salt marsh. Where the marsh is glimpsed beyond the trees, a stone monument notes the bequest that prompted the 2004 extension of the marsh.

Tall thicket enfolds the grassy travel lane as you edge impounds and stroll out of woods, returning to the loop junction and the "You are here" board. Turn right to return to the trailhead. For added discovery, you may cross over Palmer Neck Road and trace the short spur to marsh viewing.

MILES AND DIRECTIONS

0.0 Start at the Louis Bayer monument trailhead. Round the barrier and follow the woods road east into the swamp. **Option:** The woods road heading west off Palmer Neck Road leads to a cove/bay overlook in 0.1 mile.

0.1 Reach and trace the dike.

0.3 Reach the first junction (the loop junction) and "You are here" board. Continue forward on the earthen woods road. **Note:** The grassy lane to the left is the loop's return.

0.8 Reach the cemetery spur, where the main woods road bends left. Follow the spur's grassy track to the right, edging marsh.

1.5 Reach the cemetery at a stone gateway and then backtrack to the loop. **Option:** Passing through the gateway, you have a nice woodland walk that dead-ends at a boundary gate.

2.2 Resume the counterclockwise loop, now turning right.

2.5 Reach a Y-junction. Bear left for the loop. The path to the right is another dead end.

3.5 Reach a woods road junction. Bear left for the loop. **Note:** The right leads toward Palmer Neck Road.

3.9 Close the loop at the "You are here" board. Turn right to return to the trailhead.

4.2 Arrive back at the trailhead.

HIKE INFORMATION

LOCAL INFORMATION

Mystic & Shoreline Visitor Information Center, 27 Coogan Blvd., Building 1-D, Olde Mistick Village, Mystic 06355; (860) 536-1641; http://mysticinfocenter.com.

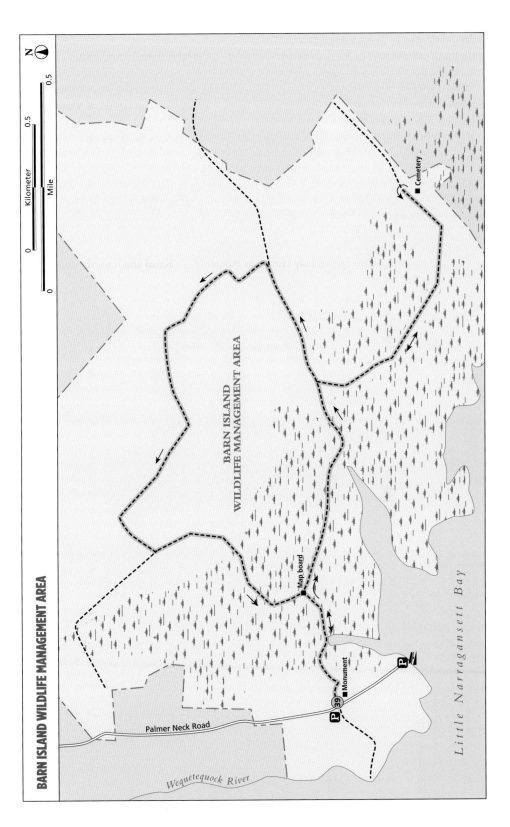

BARN ISLAND WILDLIFE MANAGEMENT AREA

BARN ISLAND
WILDLIFE MANAGEMENT AREA

Palmer Neck Road

Wequetequock River

Little Narragansett Bay

Cemetery

Map board

Monument

N

Kilometer
0   0.5

Mile
0   0.5

LOCAL EVENTS/ATTRACTIONS

The **town of Mystic,** home to Mystic Aquarium and Mystic Seaport, embodies the maritime story of coastal Connecticut.

Mystic Aquarium, 55 Coogan Blvd., Mystic 06355; (860) 572-5955; www.mystic aquarium.org. This aquarium is among the nation's best for viewing, appreciating, and understanding ocean life.

Mystic Seaport Museum, 75 Greenmanville Ave., Mystic 06355; (860) 572-0711; www.mysticseaport.org. This popular attraction includes a re-created 19th-century coastal village, historic ships, working shipyards, and exhibits.

Denison Pequotsepos Nature Center, 109 Pequotsepos Rd., Mystic 06355; (860) 536-1216; www.dpnc.org. Another Mystic offering is the Denison Pequotsepos Nature Center with its adjacent 300-acre preserve, 10 miles of hiking trail, and nature study.

HONORABLE MENTIONS
SOUTHEAST CONNECTICUT

AH. SHENIPSIT TRAIL, GREAT HILL HIKE

North of Cobalt, this 0.6-mile out-and-back hike to Great Hill introduces the southern reach of the now 50-mile-long Shenipsit Trail, which journeys north from Meshomasic State Forest through Shenipsit State Forest toward Massachusetts. You'll find outcrop vistas, mixed woods, and dressy accents of mountain laurel. Atop Great Hill ridge, the white-blazed vista spur descends to a quartzite outcrop and 90-degree southwestern view. For longer hikes, continue north with the blue blazes.

From the junction of CT 66 and CT 151 in Cobalt, head north on Depot Hill Road and stay on it for 0.8 mile. Turn right onto Great Hill Road/Gadpouch Road, which changes to dirt, and proceed 0.5 mile to reach the trailhead on the left, with a parking turnout on the right. Another turnout sits just beyond. Trailhead GPS: N41 34.588' / W72 33.068'. Trail contact: Meshomasic State Forest, Connecticut Department of Energy and Environmental Protection, 79 Elm St., Hartford 06106; (860) 424-3200; www.ct.gov/deep.

AI. HURD AND GEORGE DUDLEY SEYMOUR STATE PARKS

These adjoining state park properties offer woodland and bluff travel above the Connecticut River and fishing access on the river floodplain. Together they protect 2.5 miles of river shore and encompass 1,200 acres. A variety of trails show off the area and present views. The River Trail offers steep access, and Split-Rock has an aptly named feature. Park hours are 8 a.m. to sunset.

From the junction of CT 151 and CT 149 in Moodus, go north on CT 151 for 5.4 miles and take the hard left turn for Hurd State Park. There is trailhead parking at the intersection. Continue 0.6 mile to enter Hurd State Park on the right. Trailhead GPS: N41 31.576' / W72 33.005'. Trail contact: Hurd and Seymour State Parks, c/o Eastern District Headquarters, 209 Hebron Rd., Marlborough 06447; (860) 295-9523; www.ct .gov/deep.

AJ. **MACHIMOODUS STATE PARK**

At this minimally developed park that was once a farm, trails take you past pond, wetland, field, and forest and along the bluff rim for restricted vantages overlooking the Connecticut River. Its Lower and Upper Vista Trails shape loop travel. The park terrain has some roll to it, and the old farm roads now serve as trails.

Pond, Machimoodus State Park, Connecticut

From the junction of CT 151 and CT 149 in Moodus, go north on CT 151 for 1.3 miles and turn left into the parking lot. Trailhead GPS: N41 30.126' / W72 28.643'. Trail contact: Machimoodus State Park, c/o Gillette Castle State Park, 67 River Rd., East Haddam 06423; (860) 526-2336; www.ct.gov/deep.

AK. **POQUETANUCK COVE PRESERVE**

A property of The Nature Conservancy, this 234-acre preserve offers a 1.5-mile hiking loop that travels in rolling beech-oak woodland and dips along a hemlock-darkened drainage cut to visit the Thames River shore. It arrives where the river broadens into Poquetanuck Cove, which shows tidal influence. Peninsulas and islands add to cove viewing. Old stone walls and stately maples hint at a past use of the land for farming. Native Americans gathered at the tidal bay to harvest shellfish. The preserve is open daylight hours. Heed all conservancy rules.

From CT 2A in Poquetanuck (west of its junction with CT 117), turn south on Cider Mill Road, which later becomes Avery Hill Road. Drive 0.8 mile, reaching preserve parking on the right. It's signed. Be careful of rock studding in the lot. Trailhead GPS: N41 28.484' / W72 02.628'. Trail contact: The Nature Conservancy in Connecticut, 55 Church St., Floor 3, New Haven 06510; (203) 568-6270; www.nature.org.

AL. **GILLETTE CASTLE STATE PARK**

On the eastern highland bluff overlooking the Connecticut River, this park is best known for its medieval-looking stone castle, but the land also has a fine network of foot trails exploring the property ponds, lawns, and woods and following the line of a miniature railroad that once ran here. Trails run between the river shore and the park high line.

From the junction of CT 151 and CT 82 in East Haddam, follow CT 82E southward for 1.3 miles, turning right on River Road, following signs. Continue another 1.6 miles and turn right to enter the park from 8 a.m. to sunset. Reach the main parking at the visitor center in 0.6 mile. Trailhead GPS: N41 25.416' / W72 25.616'. Trail contact: Gillette Castle State Park, 67 River Road, East Haddam 06423; (860) 526-2336; www .ct.gov/deep.

AM. SELDEN CREEK PRESERVE

This property of The Nature Conservancy over-looks the Connecticut River at Selden Neck. Here, Selden Creek slips between the preserve and state park–held Selden Neck. The site trail offers a peace-ful coastal woodland ramble. Find a map displayed at the site kiosk, where you also learn that this is one of the most biologically significant areas on the lower Connecticut River. This upland helps protect the freshwater marsh of Selden Creek. Marshes far-ther south tend to be brackish. Bald eagles winter in the area. Hours are dawn to dusk. Across the road is the Ravine Trail on trust lands, another exam-ple of the cooperative efforts to preserve the state tidelands.

Club moss, Selden Creek Preserve, Connecticut

From the junction of CT 148 and CT 82 in Had-lyme, head west toward the river and ferry on CT 148. Go 0.6 mile and turn left onto Joshuatown Road. Continue 1.4 miles to reach the sanctuary and off-road parking on the right. Watch the odometer because signs are set back from the road. Trailhead GPS: N41 24.486' / W72 23.879'. Trail contact: The Nature Conservancy in Connecti-cut, 55 Church St., Floor 3, New Haven 06510; (203) 568-6270; www.nature.org.

AN. THE OSWEGATCHIE HILLS NATURE PRESERVE

West of the Niantic River, this 457-acre preserve encompasses north-south trending ridges, glacier-scoured ravine lowlands, and Clark Pond, built to supply ice for area fish-ing fleets in the 1900s. The site's 7 miles of marked trails show off woods and waters, pass ledge and quarry, and take you to the preserve high point Mt. Tabor (elevation 280 feet). Birding and photography popularly pair with hiking.

In Niantic, at the intersection of CT 161/Pennsylvania Avenue and Oswegatchie Hills Road, drive north on Memorial Park Drive to Veterans Memorial Field. Find parking near the ballfields. Trailhead GPS: N41 20.057'/ W72 11.903'. Trail contact: Friends of the Oswegatchie Hills Nature Preserve, PO Box 163, Niantic 06357; www.oswhills.org.

AO. HALEY FARM STATE PARK

Caleb Haley, a fish-market dealer, owned this farm from 1869 to 1924 and erected 3 miles of stone walls. The Groton Open Space Association helped save and grow this park, which offers charming strolls in pastoral settings with all those stone walls.

From the junction of CT 117 and US 1 (south of I-95, exit 88), head east on US 1 for 0.9 mile and turn south on CT 215/Groton Long Point Road. Go 1.2 miles and turn right on Brook Street for 0.3 mile. Turn left on Haley Farm Lane to reach parking for the state park in 0.1 mile. Trailhead GPS: N41 19.933' / W72 00.343'. Trail contact: Haley Farm State Park, c/o Fort Trumbull State Park, 90 Walbach St., New London 06320; (860) 444-7591; www.ct.gov/deep.

RHODE ISLAND

Rhode Island, formally the State of Rhode Island and Providence Plantations, informally the Ocean State, represents the marriage of two colonial provinces well fractured by water. The smallest state in the Union, Rhode Island is probably best associated with blue seas, billowing sails, and popular sandy beaches—and rightfully so. But don't let the state's size, lack of nosebleed elevations, and ocean character mislead you. Rhode Island has some class-act hiking and natural spaces. It may be 14 percent water, but the other 86 percent is land and 60 percent of that land is forest, northeastern coastal forest.

The face of Rhode Island is the product of ice-mass advances and retreats during the last ice age and the emptying of moraine-dammed glacial Lake Narragansett that gouged out the bay that today shares the Narragansett name and empties into Rhode Island Sound. The terrain consists of Narragansett lowlands adjacent the bay and western state uplands. Block Island, with its sea cliffs, wooded uplands, and sandy beaches, sits 12 miles off the Rhode Island mainland.

Covering 150 square miles, Narragansett Bay is the largest natural estuary in New England and a natural shipping aisle. It served as an early tribal boundary, keeping the Narragansett Indians to the west and the Wampanoag Indians to the east. As you travel Rhode Island, you will discover rivers and places that still wear the musical native names that trip up modern tongues.

Like Connecticut, Rhode Island has a humid continental climate marked by warm, rainy summers and brisk winters. The flora and fauna of these neighboring states also share similarity. In Rhode Island, though, you can expect the ocean influences to slip farther inland. Sea spray influences both the species and the growth of trees and plants.

Rhode Island has a history of independent thought and a strong compass of purpose that traces to its colonial founding in 1636 under Roger Williams. This was a breakaway society sponsoring freedom of religion from political thought. Rhode Island was the first colony to denounce British rule and the last to ratify the Constitution, holding out for the assurance of a forthcoming bill of rights. It also was the first state to answer Lincoln's call to arms.

During its settlement, Rhode Island can point to a rare compatible association with the native peoples. In the post–world war era, the state became a melting pot for Anglo, European, and Mediterranean immigrants.

Variously farming, dairying, fishing, shipping, lumbering, and manufacturing have sustained the state. Rhode Island was at the forefront of the American Industrial Revolution, with its textile manufacturing along the Blackstone River. Today manufacturing here, like elsewhere in the factory belt, has taken a backseat to service businesses and tourism. State population centers continue to cling to the rivers that fueled the state's early industry.

Stone walls, pens, cellars, and forgotten cemeteries hint at a time when the forest was tilled and partitioned for pasture. Retired military bases now serve as surprisingly vital wildlife lands. The reclaimed runways shape recreational paths, while gulls use the hard tarmac surfaces to break open shellfish. Reclaimed rail and canal routes offer superb linear pathways. Altogether, state rambles introduce peaceful woodlands, rocky realms, meadows, ponds, and swamps. Rhode Island offers first-rate bird watching, from tiny songbirds to seabirds to the bald eagles and ospreys that soar the sky. And, let's not forget those nautical attractions. They have hiker appeal as well.

40 GEORGE WASHINGTON MANAGEMENT AREA, WALKABOUT TRAIL

In northwest Rhode Island, this extensive management area incorporates George Washington Memorial State Forest and the adjoining Casimir Pulaski Memorial State Park. It holds a color-coded trail system, with the Walkabout Trail and Angell Loop (to an Indian grave) being prized examples. The featured Walkabout Trail leads you through lakeshore, woodland, and wetland settings and offers solitude and wildlife discovery. It gives nod to the aboriginal concept of walking for the sake of walking. The trail's interlocking colored links allow you to customize hike length.

Start: Bowdish Reservoir beach trailhead in George Washington State Forest
Distance: 8-mile loop, with options to shorten to a 2- or a 6-mile loop or lengthen, adding the 1.2-mile out-and-back Peck Pond spur
Hiking time: 5 to 6 hours
Difficulty: Moderate
Elevation change: 200 feet
Trail surface: Earthen path, woods road, boardwalk segments, management road
Best seasons: Spring through fall
Other trail users: Mountain bikers, equestrians, hunters, snowshoers, cross-country skiers
Canine compatibility: Leashed dogs permitted
Land status: State management area

Nearest town: Chepachet in Township of Glocester, RI
Fees and permits: Either a day-use parking fee or overnight campground fee required
Schedule: Year-round, sunrise to sunset
Maps: George Washington Management Area and Pulaski Recreation Area maps (available online at www.exploreri.org)
Trail contact: George Washington Management Area, 2185 Putnam Pike, Chepachet 02814; (401) 568-2085; www.riparks.com
Special considerations: In spring and following rains, wet conditions on the Walkabout Trail can increase its difficulty.

FINDING THE TRAILHEAD

From the junction of RI 100, RI 102, and US 44 in Chepachet, go west on US 44 for 4.2 miles and turn north for George Washington Memorial State Forest and its campground. (This turn is 0.8 mile east of the intersection of US 44 and RI 94.) Pass through the entry gate into the campground, finding the Walkabout trailhead on the northeast shore of Bowdish Reservoir near the picnic area, beach, and boat launch (0.4 mile). Trailhead GPS: N41 55.423' / W71 45.486'

THE HIKE

Built by Australian sailors awaiting repair of their ship, the HMAS *Perth*, the Walkabout Trail traces its name and intent to the Aborigines of the sailors' homeland. It refers to the tribal people's compelling need to wander, to "walkabout."

Walkabout Trail, George Washington
Management Area, Rhode Island

Heading west from the marked trailhead, you skirt the northern shore of Bowdish Reservoir in hemlock-hardwood forest. The tricolor blazing is intact at the start. Stay blue for the 2-mile loop, red for the 6-mile loop, and orange for the full 8-mile loop. Each is a clockwise journey.

Canada geese may ply the water or plod along shore. Rocks and tangled roots erupt in the trail. Find soggy drainages and frag-ments of boardwalk. Before turning away from the reservoir, a flattish granite outcrop serves up a farewell view.

Walkabout Trail plaque, George Washington Management Area, Rhode Island

The meandering, wooded Walkabout skirts a private campground on Wilbur Pond. Where the blue trail takes a turn for home, proceed forward for the longer hikes, con-tinuing along the forest rim. Branches deny pond views, but the mountain laurel engages. Later, large boulders and 50 feet of open shore provide pond viewing. Ahead stretches a merry chase across the spreading inlet drainages. Some may require ingenuity to craft dry crossings.

While the blazing may appear excessive during the main hiking season, once the leaves drop the marking is necessary. With a final look at a scenic reflecting bay-water, ascend away from Wilbur Pond. The hike is now in deciduous forest with a few pines. Where the red trail splits off, follow the orange blazes.

Fewer obstacles riddle the trail, allowing for mind and feet to ramble. Changes in light-ing, birdsong, and a whispering breeze lend to the soothing message. Cross a drivable dirt road (Cold Spring Trail), then cross a grassy woods road and a second dirt road with a trailside bench. As you trace a time-healed woods road through a dark hemlock grove, you'll find a sign and red arrows for Pulaski Park. You may now continue forward on the orange loop or go sightseeing, following the red arrows.

On the detour left to Pulaski Park, Peck Pond, and the Pulaski Park trail system, you ascend through rich forest, with cushiony footfalls on the wood-chip-softened lane to come out at a pine-shaded picnic spot above Peck Pond. Pass through the park to the open beach and park amenities. There are flush toilets and water during summer months. Multicolored blazings hint at other hiking options. The size of the parking lot suggests

AN ANCIENT CALLING

"Walkabout" is a European-coined term for an Australian aboriginal custom that traces back thousands of years. It is the act of simply getting up and walking off solo into the desert. What to the uninformed eye appears to be aimless wandering is actually quite purposeful, driven by a walker's desire to connect to the environment to reestablish ties to the past. The Aborigine con-sider themselves keepers of the land, so establishing this connection is both a responsibility and a necessity. Walking leads to spiritual centeredness. Seekers tend to travel ancient paths or songlines—verbal maps encrypted into their song, lore, and ceremony. A walkabout, although ancient, is contemporary in need.

Bowdish Reservoir, George Washington Management Area, Rhode Island

the place hums in summer, but off-season visitors share the area with wildlife. Upon backtracking to the Walkabout, bear left to resume the orange loop.

You pass beneath beautiful pines and over a hemlock-edged brook. At the upcoming junction, the Walkabout Trail turns right, while the red arrows ahead lead back to Pulaski Park. The loop takes you across a skunk cabbage bog on boardwalk and the dirt road of the Inner Border Trail. The woods remain wet.

At the Richardson Trail (a road) crossing, you find another bench seat. You then round a snag-riddled wildlife pond and marsh, cross the earthen dam, and ascend away through woods. Soon orange-loop travel merges with the returning red trail. The meeting comes where snags open the forest to mountain laurel.

Cross the Center Trail road and travel rustic corduroy through a marshy site before meeting up with the blue loop. You end the hike, returning to Bowdish Reservoir along the access road to the boat launch.

MILES AND DIRECTIONS

0.0   Start at Bowdish Reservoir's beach trailhead. Follow the tricolor blazing west into woods at a monument rock and signboard for the Walkabout Trail. Orange marks the full loop.

0.8   Continue forward where the blue loop splits away on forest road for its clockwise return.

1.0   Reach the shore of Wilbur Pond. Continue following the orange and red blazes.

1.5   Ascend away from Wilbur Pond.

2.0   Follow the orange blazes as the red trail splits off.

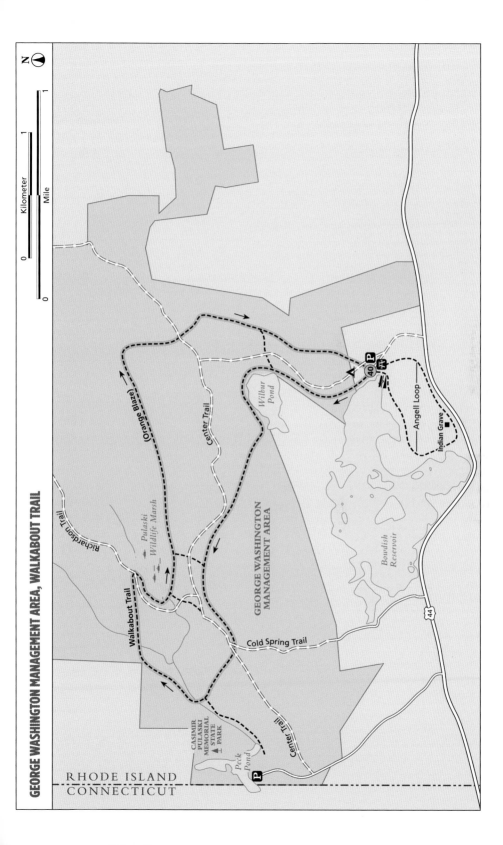

GEORGE WASHINGTON MANAGEMENT AREA, WALKABOUT TRAIL

N

0   Kilometer   1

0   Mile   1

RHODE ISLAND
CONNECTICUT

CASIMIR
PULASKI
MEMORIAL
STATE
PARK

Peck
Pond

Center Trail

Walkabout Trail

Richardson Trail

(Orange Blaze)

Pulaski
Wildlife Marsh

Cold Spring Trail

Center Trail

GEORGE WASHINGTON
MANAGEMENT AREA

Wilbur
Pond

Bowdish
Reservoir

Angell Loop

Indian Grave

40

44

2.9 Cross a dirt road (Cold Spring Trail). Remain on the orange loop.

3.5 Reach the Peck Pond/Pulaski Park trail junction. For the Walkabout, continue forward with the orange blazes. ***Option:*** To add the 1.2-mile out-and-back spur to Peck Pond and the developed park, head left, following the red-arrow blaze.

3.8 Reach a trail junction. Turn right, following orange. ***Note:*** Straight leads to Pulaski Park.

4.3 Cross the dirt road of the Inner Border Trail. Follow the orange blazes.

5.7 Meet the red loop. Follow the orange and red blazes, keeping left, to return to the trailhead.

7.3 Meet the blue loop. Follow the tricolor blazing back to the trailhead.

8.0 End back at Bowdish Reservoir (9.2 if you added Peck Pond spur).

Option: The easy 1.4-mile Angell Loop starts south of the launch and travels to an Indian grave midway. White-blazed, it rounds along the south shore of the boat launch cove, passing among eastern hemlock, mountain laurel, white pine, oak, birch, and beech. In 300 feet at the loop junction, bear right. Cross a small boggy inlet to find gaps in the tree cover for viewing big Bowdish Reservoir, with its irregular shoreline. After you turn away from shore into pine-oak woods, watch for the 30-foot spur heading left to the Indian grave. Only a faded wooden sign and arranged stones mark the site. Your forest return is gently rolling on old woods road and footpath.

HIKE INFORMATION

LOCAL INFORMATION

Blackstone Bikeway and Visitor's Center, I-295 North, Cumberland; c/o Lincoln Woods State Park, 2 Manchester Print Works Road, Lincoln 02865; (401) 723-7892; www.riparks.com.

ACCOMMODATIONS

George Washington Camping Area, (401) 568-6700 (seasonal) or (401) 568-2085. The Management Area campground has 45 campsites in the woods above Bowdish Reservoir, with the sites open from the opening day for trout (the second Sat in Apr) until the Mon of Columbus Day weekend. Reservations are through ReserveAmerica, (877) 742-2675 or www.reserveamerica.com.

41 GEORGE B. PARKER WOODLAND

This Audubon Society of Rhode Island woodland and wildlife refuge holds rich hardwood forest, moist bottomland, peaceful brooks, and early American history. On its grounds, old foundations, stone walls, quarry sites, and inexplicable cairns harken to the past. As legend has it, the site's Biscuit Hill traces its name to the Revolutionary War, when a food wagon of biscuits overturned en route to General Rochambeau's troops. The Paul Cook and Milton A. Gowdey Memorial Trails, two loops stitched by a connecting trail, travel the site's Coventry and Foster Tracts.

Start: Main entrance trailhead
Distance: 7-mile barbell
Hiking time: 4 to 5 hours
Difficulty: Moderate
Elevation change: 200 feet
Trail surface: Earthen path, boardwalk, woods road
Best seasons: Spring through fall
Other trail users: Birders
Canine compatibility: No dogs permitted
Land status: Private nonprofit sanctuary woodland
Nearest town: Coventry Center, RI
Fees and permits: None, but consider an Audubon membership or donation

Schedule: Year-round, sunrise to sunset
Map: George B. Parker Woodland map (available online at www.asri .org or www.exploreri.org)
Trail contact: George B. Parker Woodland, c/o Audubon Society of RI, 12 Sanderson Rd., Smithfield 02917; (401) 949-5454 or (401) 295-8283 (Parker Woodland); www.asri .org
Special considerations: This is a private Audubon sanctuary. Obey all posted rules: no picnicking, no bicycles, no pets, no smoking, and no collecting. With no on-site facilities, come prepared and bring drinking water.

FINDING THE TRAILHEAD

From I-95, take exit 5, go north on RI 102 for 8.3 miles, and turn right (east) on Maple Valley Road. Go 0.2 mile to find the main entrance parking for Parker Woodland on the left. Trailhead GPS: N41 43.017' / W71 41.881'

THE HIKE

For this color-coded trail system, blue marks the loops; orange, the access trail; and yellow, the connectors. Head north for a gentle descent from the parking kiosk into a mixed woods of red cedar, pine, beech, birch, oak, maple, dogwood, and hickory. The groundcover variously reveals Virginia creeper, Canada mayflower, club moss, poison ivy, and hog peanut.

Farther along, a half-dozen fern varieties decorate a moist bottomland, along with sweet pepperbush, azalea, trillium, wood lily, and nettles. Attractive boardwalk spans the soggier reaches, and a footbridge crosses over Turkey Meadow Brook, a slow, thin waterway beneath drooping boughs. A sawmill once operated along this brook.

Tiger lily, George Parker Woodland Audubon Sanctuary, Rhode Island

You then reach Paul Cook Memorial Trail and turn left for a clockwise tour of the Coventry Tract. Stones stud the trail, rock walls grace travel, and oaks and hickories are the "big guys" of the woods. Sassafras, highbush blueberry, and huckleberry fill the midstory.

Cross Biscuit Hill Road, a grassy, narrow woods road. On either side are ruins from the Vaughn farm site. Spy the dry-laid fieldstone foundations, the cellar to a central-chimney colonial home, stairs, and a stone-lined well with capstone. The buildings here dated to the mid-eighteenth century. Now trees grow up through the cellar floor. A sign interprets the lay of the farm.

A slow ascent follows, passing among pines and crossing a lichen-mottled outcropping. Where the trail descends, be sure to duck at a protruding rock. You cross an unnamed woods road and continue descending. In the mixed hardwoods, outcrop and boulders suggest high-stepping.

The Cook Memorial Trail then rolls to a four-way junction. To the left leads to the Milton A. Gowdey Memorial Trail and the Foster Tract; to the right lies Biscuit Hill Road. Straight continues the 3-mile Paul Cook Memorial Trail.

For the full 7-mile hike, turn left, following the rocky connecting trail through beech-hardwood forest. Past a monstrous big boulder, you follow Pine Swamp Brook upstream, contouring the slope 20 feet above the drainage before crossing its footbridge.

A foot trail ribbed by roots then ascends to the Gowdey Trail; go left (clockwise) and watch out for poison ivy. A gentle incline allows for a relaxing stroll. You then descend back toward Pine Swamp Brook, ushered by sweet pepperbush. After pulling away from the brook, you find another historical farmstead. Rock walls, stone pens, and a 5-foot-deep foundation mark this site. You next descend a low rise to cross Pig Hill Road.

Where the trail passes between offset rock walls, you enter a boulder-dotted landscape. On the right a disturbed area with displaced rock and reclaiming vegetation signals an old

GEORGE B. PARKER WOODLAND

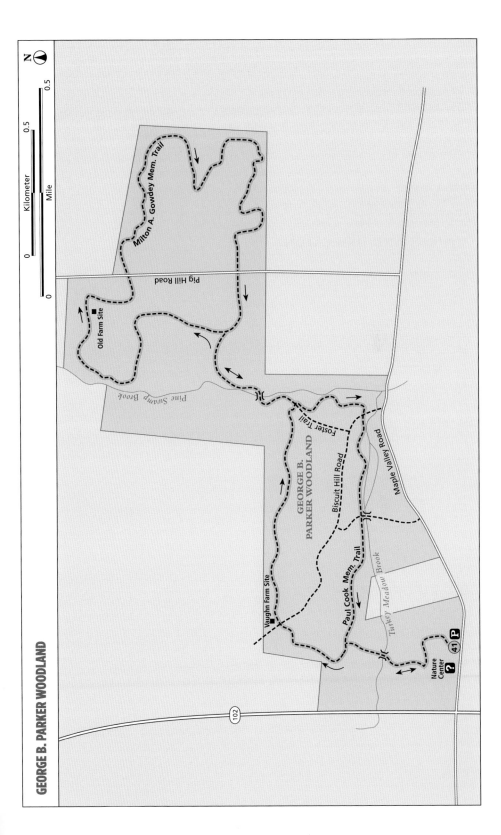

Milton A. Gowdey Mem. Trail

Pig Hill Road

Old Farm Site

Pine Swamp Brook

Foster Trail

GEORGE B.
PARKER WOODLAND

Biscuit Hill Road

Vaughn Farm Site

Paul Cook Mem. Trail

Maple Valley Road

Turkey Meadow Brook

Nature
Center

41

102

N

Kilometer

Mile

0   0.5   0.5

0   0.5

quarry site. The trail advances by long, sleepy undulations to cross Pig Hill Road a second time. It then passes through a (usually gated) parking lot. Again, watch out for poison ivy. After you close the Gowdey loop, backtrack along the connector to the Coventry Tract to resume clockwise travel (a left) on the Paul Cook Memorial Trail.

You descend among outcrops, briefly passing near Pine Swamp Brook. Find showings of mountain laurel, pass another foundation on the left, and cross Biscuit Hill Road to contour above Turkey Meadow Brook. At a four-way junction, continue forward on the blue-blazed Cook Trail, where you'll find cairns, some 4 feet tall, others broad and squat. Their origins are unknown. One theory attributes them to colonial field clearing. Another suggests they are sacred precolonial Celtic or Narragansett Indian monuments. Close the loop and turn left uphill to the trailhead.

MILES AND DIRECTIONS

0.0 Start at the main entrance trailhead. Hike north into the woodland from the kiosk shelter.

0.4 Cross the footbridge over Turkey Meadow Brook.

0.5 Reach the Paul Cook Memorial Trail. Follow the blue blazes left (clockwise).

1.0 Cross Biscuit Hill Road.

2.0 Reach a four-way junction. Follow the yellow connector left to Foster Tract and the Gowdey Trail. **Note:** Forward continues the blue-blazed Cook Trail; right leads to Biscuit Hill Road.

2.2 Cross the Pine Swamp Brook footbridge.

2.4 Reach the Milton A. Gowdey Memorial Trail. Follow the blue blazes left.

3.2 Reach a historical farmstead site.

3.5 Cross Pig Hill Road.

5.0 Close the Gowdey loop. Backtrack the yellow connector to the 2-mile junction and resume clockwise travel on the Cook Trail.

6.1 Reach a four-way junction. Continue forward, following the blue blazes.

6.5 Complete the Cook loop. Turn left to return to the trailhead.

7.0 Arrive back at the trailhead.

HIKE INFORMATION

LOCAL INFORMATION

Central Rhode Island Chamber of Commerce, 3288 Post Rd., Warwick 02886; (401) 732-1100; www.centralrichamber.com.

Visit Warwick, Rhode Island, City of Warwick Department of Tourism, Culture and Development, 3275 Post Rd., Warwick 02886; (401) 738-2014; www.visitwarwickri .com.

42 TILLINGHAST POND MANAGEMENT AREA

At this out-of-the-way property of The Nature Conservancy (TNC), a trio of interlocking trails explore around and outward from the jigsaw shore of lovely cobalt Tillinghast Pond. Quiet woods, open hayfields, boulder realms, pond overlooks, and a historic cemetery compose both place and the site's story. Peninsulas, picturesque coves, mats of pond lily, and marshy edges add to the charm of Tillinghast Pond. Additional trails probe adjacent open spaces.

Start: Pond trailhead
Distance: 3.9-mile loop with spur
Hiking time: 2.5 to 3 hours
Difficulty: Easy
Elevation change: 100 feet
Trail surface: Earthen path, mowed track, woods road
Best seasons: Spring through fall
Other trail users: Hunters, birders, anglers, snowshoers, cross-country skiers
Canine compatibility: No dogs permitted
Land status: Private nonprofit preserve
Nearest town: West Greenwich, RI, with gas available off I-95
Fees and permits: None
Schedule: Year-round, sunrise to sunset

Map: Tillinghast Pond Management Area map (at the on-site map board and available online at www.nature .org or www.exploreri.org)
Trail contact: Tillinghast Pond Management Area, TNC, Borderlands Preserves, Providence Office, 159 Waterman St., Providence 02906; (401) 331-7110; www.nature.org
Special considerations: During the allowed hunting seasons in Rhode Island, wear the required fluorescent orange. Because some private land edges this property, be sure to keep to the designated trails, pack in/pack out, and use your best trail manners. Be careful when crossing any wet planks. There are no facilities at the site, so attend to personal needs before your arrival. Bring drinking water.

FINDING THE TRAILHEAD

From I-95, exit 5B, head north on RI 102 for 3.1 miles and turn left on Plain Meetinghouse Road. Remain on Plain Meetinghouse Road for 3.9 miles to its junction with Plain Road, then turn right on Plain Road to reach the trailhead on the right in 0.5 mile. Trailhead GPS: N41 38.697' / W71 45.404'

THE HIKE

This hike stitches together the white Pond and the yellow Flintlock Loops for a single big clockwise loop. Map posts at key junctions help you track course.

On the opposite side of the parking lot from the kiosk, follow the white trail as it travels the pine-oak-maple shoreline. Although you pass close to the pond, you gather only branch-filtered impressions. Plain Road is close but lightly traveled. The orange Coney Brook Trail heads left.

Where the shoreline pitch steepens, you gain the first open look at the pond and its basin. As the trail switches left, a side trail travels onto a peninsula for additional viewing.

Water lilies at Tillinghast Pond, Tillinghast Pond Management Area, Rhode Island

The deep coves, lily mosaics, and conifer skylines create a picturesque water-and-woods postcard image. You then cross the outlet on Plain Road before returning to shore.

The trail next traces an elevated bench of land between field and pond before rounding the next cove. Where it nears working fields, keep to the thin line of the trail and its paired planks at soggy reaches. Classic white pines tower above shore.

Past a seating bench, the trail alternates between woods and field edge. The hayfields are part of the site's management, and their continuation honors the historic perspective of the area. In a cooperative effort, TNC, the town, and Rhode Island DEM are keeping the historic working landscape. A local farmer leases the crop.

Keep watch to your right for the spur to the viewing dock. This platform extends into the pond for a closer look at the pond vegetation and aquatic life and a better overall sense of place. A rolling woodland passage with picturesque mossy boulders, rock walls, pond glimpses, and beaver-gnawed trunks and raised waters leads to the next seating. You'll likely want to pause here for a farewell look at the pond and its narrow arm.

The trail then draws above and away from the pond to meet the yellow Flintlock Loop. Follow it left, hiking in predominantly oak woodland with sassafras and huckleberry. Insect buzzing or the hoot of an owl may give voice to the woods.

At the North–South junction, although the North Fork is pleasant enough, take the slightly longer south fork to travel West and East Boulder Gardens. Where the forks again meet, the Flintlock continues eastward, descending and wending to Narrow Lane. When taking the south fork, you'd bear right. From the north fork, it's a left.

Turn right on Narrow Lane (a woods road). The blue trail here fashions a 4-mile loop through neighboring Wickaboxet Management Area. Look for the return of the blue loop a bit farther ahead.

The hike's arrow-straight, tree-framed aisle again showcases tall white pines. Before long an unmarked spur leads left to a side pond. You may view the large, round lily pond, but its marshy edge urges you keep your distance. Bear left upon return.

Hike through tighter, younger pines, pass a wolf tree, and enter a wild pasture skirting its edge. Babbling precedes your arrival at a stone bridge, where the upstream pool drains over a weir into the flowing brook. Here the trail curves right, traveling alongside a wall of big boulders. You continue in semi-open transition habitat to skirt the remains of an old residence and a set of stairs (Ellis Homestead).

Track the blazes along a trammeled field-path, and turn left into woods. An old cemetery rimmed by stone walls is on your left. It holds a few tilted dark-stone markers, faint from time and weathering. Several indicate November 1821, perhaps a hard winter, an accident, or disease—a secret now kept by the oaks.

A pine-oak woods enfolds the return to Tillinghast Pond. Upon meeting the white-blazed Pond Loop, keep left to return to the trailhead. Plaques may identify scarlet oak and red maple. You'll once again glimpse Tillinghast Pond at some intersecting stone walls before ending the hike at the trailhead.

MILES AND DIRECTIONS

0.0 Start at the pond trailhead. Take the white path, heading left (clockwise) along shore.

0.3 Cross the outlet on the road and resume hiking the shoreline trail.

1.6 Reach the Flintlock Trail. Follow the yellow blazes left. **Note:** The white blazes continue the Pond Loop to the right.

TILLINGHAST POND MANAGEMENT AREA

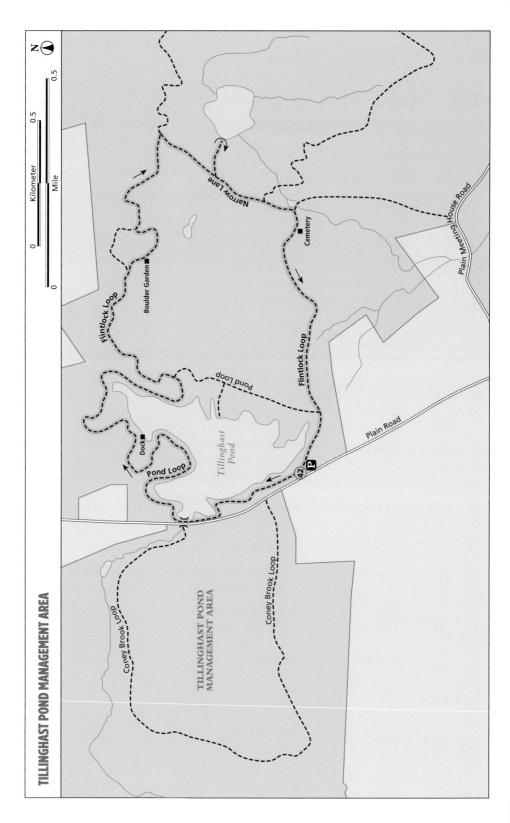

N

0   0.5   Kilometer
0   0.5   Mile

Flintlock Loop

Boulder Garden

Narrow Lane

Pond Loop

Dock

Pond Loop

Tillinghast Pond

Flintlock Loop

Cemetery

Coney Brook Loop

Coney Brook Loop

42

P

Plain Road

TILLINGHAST POND
MANAGEMENT AREA

Plain Meeting House Road

2.0 Reach the western North–South junction; either fork works. Take the south spur to wander among picturesque boulder rubble.

2.2 Reach the eastern North–South junction. Continue eastward on the Flintlock Loop.

2.6 Reach Narrow Lane. Turn right. *Note:* The blue-blazed Wickaboxet Loop journeys from here through the state's Wickaboxet Management Area, which sits to the east. You'll pass the blue loop's return farther along on the Flint-lock Loop.

2.8 Reach a pond spur. Detour left 0.1 mile to view the pond, and on return, turn left for the loop.

3.2 Hike past the remains of a house.

3.3 Turn left into woods, passing a cemetery.

3.7 Meet the white-blazed Pond Loop. Bear left for the trailhead.

3.9 Arrive back at the trailhead.

Option: The orange-blazed 2.2-mile Coney Brook Loop explores field and woods edge on the opposite side of Plain Road.

HIKE INFORMATION

LOCAL INFORMATION

Central Rhode Island Chamber of Commerce, 3288 Post Rd., Warwick 02886; (401) 732-1100; www.centralrichamber.com.

Visit Warwick, Rhode Island, City of Warwick Department of Tourism, Culture and Development, 3275 Post Rd., Warwick 02886; (401) 738-2014; www.visitwarwickri .com.

43 EAST BAY BIKE PATH

Voted one of the nation's best rail trails and in the Rails-to-Trails Hall of Fame, the East Bay Bike Path is worth seeking out. With its close pairing to Narragansett Bay, sparkling waters are a frequent companion. Although bicycling is popular, pedestrian travel rivals it. The treed greenway strings from historic Bristol through Warren and Barrington and onward to the heights of East Providence. Corridor towns and parks suggest stops for amenities and services. Sights include an Audubon swamp and picturesque Pomham Rocks Light.

Start: Independence Park trailhead in Bristol (the southern terminus)
Distance: 13 miles one way from Bristol to East Providence
Hiking time: Depending on segment, anywhere from all day to an hour or two
Difficulty: Easy, with the northern stretch in East Providence showing more gradient and difficulty (Cyclists find afternoon winds on that final leg especially challenging.)
Elevation change: Less than 100 feet
Trail surface: Paved railroad bed with street crossings
Best seasons: Spring through fall
Other trail users: Cyclists, wheelchair and stroller users, joggers, birders, anglers, snowshoers, and cross-country skiers, with motorists at intersections only
Canine compatibility: Leashed dogs permitted; no dogs at Audubon property
Land status: Town, state park, and private, nonprofit sanctuary
Nearest towns: Bristol, Warren, Barrington, and East Providence, RI
Fees and permits: None (If, however, you choose to access the Audubon nature center, an Audubon membership or daily fee is required.)
Schedule: Year-round, sunrise to sunset
Map: East Bay Bike Path map (available online at www.dot.ri.gov/community/bikeri)
Trail contacts: East Bay Bike Path, Rails-to-Trails Conservancy, The Duke Ellington Building, 2121 Ward Ct. NW, 5th Floor, Washington, DC 20037; (202) 331-9696; www.railstotrails .org. Rhode Island Department of Environmental Management (which manages the trail), (401) 667-6200.
Special considerations: Public restrooms are available at the southern terminus and at Haines Memorial Park. Businesses along the route have restrooms for customer use. Food services sit conveniently near and along the route. The bike path has nearly 50 road crossings, all well marked. Trail users yield to traffic. Plan to carry a supply of drinking water. Because the trail hums with activity, take a moment to note the rules for travel and passing on this shared-use trail.

FINDING THE TRAILHEAD

In Bristol, start along the bay at Independence Park (the southern terminus). It's at the intersection of Thames Street and Oliver Street. Trailhead GPS: N41 40.512' / W71 16.747'

The chosen northern terminus is at East Providence's Fort Hill overlook parking, west off Veterans Memorial Highway, 0.5 mile south of I-195, exit 4. Trailhead GPS: N41 48.793' / W71 23.302'

THE HIKE

Ideal for pedaling, jogging, strolling, and sharing with family and friends, the East Bay Bike Path traces part of what was the Providence and Bristol Railroad. Today's businesses invite you aside to purchase a slice, bite into a donut, or slurp on soft frozen lemonade.

On a northbound hike, images of Bristol Harbor first pair with the wide, paved passage. The broken shells on the lane betray where gulls have cracked open recent dinners. From the moored boats of the harbor, views switch to marshy-edged Mill Pond with its dotting ducks and skulking herons. Lining the trail are tall phragmites, sumacs, and an occasional rail fence. Because water images dominate the first mile, trail neighborhoods go unnoticed.

After crossing the entrance road to Colt State Park, the trail funnels through low mixed woods entangled with grape, viburnum, and creeper. Cross narrow, quiet neighborhood streets and pass Bristol Highlands Private Beach, snaring looks at the choppy open water and filled sails. At Aaron Avenue bench seating suggests a longer appreciation.

At the Audubon sanctuary a boardwalk bids you to detour left into the swamp to view the habitat and its plopping residents. The walk ends at a Narragansett Bay beach-and-wrack overlook. A pea-soup of duckweed, plumed phragmites, and cattails characterize the swamp. More of this habitat at Jacobs Point Salt Marsh Restoration pairs with the bike path as it continues north, crossing from Bristol into Warren.

Warren, too, rolls out quiet neighborhoods and small streets, with Warren River glimpses. After passing through the Lester M. DeRiso Bike Path Tunnel, bigger trees frame travel. The trail passes a sports park and a market and makes its first major road crossing at RI 114 (Main Street at Campbell), a lighted intersection.

Snag at Jacobs Point Salt Marsh, East Bay Bike Path State Park, Rhode Island

Pomham Rocks Lighthouse,
East Bay Bike Path State Park,
Rhode Island

From the park-and-ride at Franklin Street, you travel through the Warren Historic District on a more urban greenway. You'll pass the municipal buildings and Town Hall, a clock tower, and steeples. Soon after, you overlook the broadened water of the Warren River, where egrets, swans, cormorants, ducks, and geese gather.

At the Palmer and Barrington River railroad bridges, anglers cast for stripers and other catches. Views are of the waters or the attractive arched highway bridge. Interpretive boards tell of native peoples, area families, industries, and rail stations. The surprisingly natural-appearing Brickyard Pond is a flooded clay pit excavated for the building of Providence. Beyond it, the marshy Little Echo pond produced ice for the oyster industry.

Picturesque Haines Park was state-purchased early on from the estate of its physician owner who touted the benefits of nature and relaxation. From its shady rest, you pass fields, woods, and shoreline along Barrington Cove. Where the trail passes between two big ponds, look for cormorants on the pipeline.

At the lighted intersection at Riverside Square, you can salute a World War II monument and flag. You then pass an old depot station and cross under a highway to again tour along lapping bay where cliffs meet the water. View the isolated, classic Pomham Rocks Light Station—white painted and red roofed, atop a scenic rock, with a black catwalk around the beacon.

A mesh-fence-enclosed industrial plant jars the spell briefly, but watery views again put everything right. Shipping and recreational boats ply the river harbor, and abandoned rails hint at the corridor's past life. At Boyden Heights Conservation Area, a foot trail leads to a marsh viewing deck.

After more impressions of the rocky shore, the marsh pond, a mansion-topped point, and the industrial river with its diamond-spangled water, the grade pushes north, making the rise to the East Providence overlook parking and trail terminus. Swans favor the

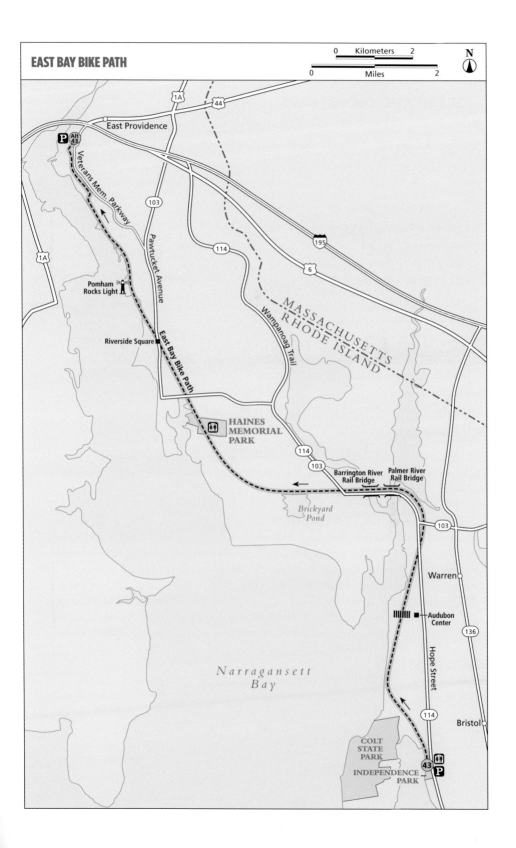

EAST BAY BIKE PATH

0 — Kilometers — 2

0 — Miles — 2

N

1A

44

East Providence

P Alt 43

Veterans Mem. Parkway

103

Pawtucket Avenue

114

195

6

1A

Pomham Rocks Light

Riverside Square

East Bay Bike Path

Wampanoag Trail

MASSACHUSETTS
RHODE ISLAND

HAINES MEMORIAL PARK

114

103

Barrington River Rail Bridge

Palmer River Rail Bridge

Brickyard Pond

103

Warren

Audubon Center

136

Hope Street

Narragansett Bay

114

Bristol

COLT STATE PARK

INDEPENDENCE PARK

43 P

inland ponds created by the railroad causeway. Views of Providence and the Providence River and Harbor sign off the journey.

MILES AND DIRECTIONS

0.0 Start in Bristol at the Independence Park trailhead. Follow the paved bicycle path north along Bristol Harbor.

0.9 Cross the entry road to Colt State Park.

2.5 Reach the Audubon swamp and nature center boardwalks. *Note:* Right leads to the center (a fee site with amenities; no pets or bicycles); left leads into the swamp to a bay viewpoint (again no pets, no bikes).

4.0 Pass the municipal buildings in the Warren Historic District.

4.8 Cross the Palmer River rail bridge.

5.2 Cross the Barrington River rail bridge.

6.4 Pass Brickyard Pond.

8.0 Reach Haines Park.

9.5 Reach Riverside Square.

10.0 View Pomham Rocks Light.

11.0 Reach Boyden Heights Conservation Area.

13.0 End at the northern trailhead in East Providence at the bluff overlook parking lot.

HIKE INFORMATION

LOCAL INFORMATION
Discover Newport, 23 America's Cup Ave., Newport 02840; (401) 849-8048 or (800) 326-6030; www.discovernewport.org.

LOCAL EVENTS/ATTRACTIONS
Blithewold Mansion, Gardens and Arboretum, 101 Ferry Rd. (Route 114), Bristol 02809; (401) 253-2707; www.blithewold.org. The Blithewold garden estate in Bristol is one of the finest public gardens in all of New England. The 45-room English manor sets the stage for the magnificent tree and flower collection.

   Coggeshall Farm Museum, 1 Colt Drive, Bristol 02809; (401) 253-9062; www.coggeshallfarm.org. Another Bristol attraction, the Coggeshall Farm Museum, allows you to observe and experience preindustrial farm life in a working farm environment.

ORGANIZATIONS
Rails-to-Trails Conservancy, The Duke Ellington Building, 2121 Ward Ct. NW, 5th Floor, Washington, DC 20037; (202) 331-9696; www.railstotrails.org.

44 BREAKHEART POND–MOUNT TOM LOOP, WITH BEN UTTER SPUR

This ambitious see–Arcadia Management Area woodland loop unites several named trails, visiting Breakheart Pond, and traversing the rocky ridge of Mount Tom. It begins beside the Wood River, what scientists consider the wildest river in Rhode Island, and swings past its feeding waters. A side trip on the Ben Utter Trail takes you upstream along the Falls River past onetime mill sites and through laurel to the stair-stepped cascades of Stepstone Falls, a winner by any measure.

Start: Wood River canoe access/check station trailhead
Distance: 16.1-mile loop, including the Ben Utter side trail
Hiking time: 10 to 12 hours
Difficulty: Strenuous
Elevation change: 250 feet
Trail surface: Earthen path, woods road, management road
Best seasons: Late spring through early fall (summer is preferred for its long daylight)
Other trail users: Anglers and hunters, mountain bikers and equestrians on management roads
Canine compatibility: Leashed dogs permitted
Land status: State management area
Nearest town: Wyoming or West Greenwich, RI, with gas available off I-95
Fees and permits: None; for backpacking camping, reserve in advance, with all written permits secured in person at the Arcadia Management Area Headquarters

Schedule: Year-round, sunrise to sunset
Map: None. Arcadia Management Area trail list (request from headquarters)
Trail contact: Arcadia Management Area Headquarters, 260 Arcadia Rd., Hope Valley 02823; (401) 539-2356; www.dem.ri.gov.
Special considerations: Expect wet, rough spots and difficult footing much of way. Keep all dogs leashed from Apr 1 through Aug 15; hunting dogs may be off leash Aug 16 through Mar 30. On Mount Tom, keep to the trail to avoid straying onto private lands. Oct through Feb all hikers must wear a fluorescent orange hat or vest in accordance with Rhode Island regulations. Keep track of blazes and your time. This area, with its light management and no recent map, requires strong navigation skills.

FINDING THE TRAILHEAD

From the RI 3–RI 165 junction (0.3 mile east of I-95), go west on RI 165 for 3.5 miles and turn left (south) into the Wood River canoe access/check station trailhead parking lot. Trailhead GPS: N41 34.374' / W71 43.294'

THE HIKE

Counterclockwise, you follow white blazes out to RI 165, turn east to cross the Wood River, and resume via foot trail on the river's east shore. The trail trends east in pine-oak woods, passing parallel to but away from RI 165. Sheep laurel lines a small brook that you cross.

Breakheart Brook,
Arcadia Management Area,
Rhode Island

After an ascent the trail dips to cross Summit Road. Hike alongside a stone wall and walk past the North–South and Dove Trails. A wetter rock-studded woods houses travel to the Arcadia Trail, which you follow left. Where you come out at a roadside turnout, angle right across RI 165 to the John B. Hudson Trail.

Follow the Hudson Trail's yellow blaze north through richly mixed leafy and piney woods. In June the midstory mountain laurel enchants. Cross a small brook and the woods road of the Tripp Trail, keeping to the Hudson Trail.

You descend along and crisscross a small brook to reach fast-flowing Breakheart Brook. Even hopscotching from rock to root, you can still end up muddy, but the sweet pepperbush and skunk cabbage delight. Continue upstream to the dam and spillway of Breakheart Pond. A deciduous rim and backset pines enfold the circular water, lily pad mosaic, and eerie morning mist.

Track the yellow blazes along the dirt road to the right and turn left into woodland, passing to the east of Breakheart Pond. After a while, you'll cross the Breakheart Brook footbridge between beaver-dammed pools and bear right, still following yellow blazes. Make a slow ascent to cross Matteson Plain Road.

Enter another weaving rocky descent to the footbridge crossing of the dark East Fork Flat River. Follow the blazes left on overgrown track. Pass through pine plantation and mixed woods, coming to what was a rickety footbridge at the West Fork Flat River. If absent or unsafe, you must wade.

Keeping to the blazed route, ascend and cross the shoulder of Penny Hill, with its outcrops and oak-huckleberry complex. Descend through semi-open woods, with pitch pine and aspen, to cross Austin Farm Road. After quick direction changes, you meet this road a second time. Follow it left, crossing the Falls River.

The yellow Ben Utter Trail here is worthwhile if time and legs allow. It follows the Falls River upstream, swinging a lasso around Stepstone Falls, before backtracking downstream. It is joined by the blue North–South Trail. Past a mill site on a rise, spy the telltale water diversions. At the lasso fork, turn right, following the white-blazed River Trail across the river footbridge and past impressive boulder slabs. Cross the top of Stepstone Falls on Falls River Road and then return downstream on the yellow Ben Utter Trail, viewing the sequential cascades. At a cabin-style shelter, be alert. You take the immediate sharp left downhill from the cabin to return to the lasso fork and backtrack downstream.

Resuming the loop, turn right on Austin Farm Road and then left on the white Escoheag Trail. The blue North–South Trail briefly merges. In mature pine plantation, the Escoheag Trail ascends right.

Leaves don't simply fall. Modern botany explains that, in an act of preservation, trees send chemical messages for abscission cells to form at the leaf connections. Like unwanted sponging relatives, the leaves are cut off from support, left to the whims of the fall wind.

At Barber Road the loop heads left on the white-blazed Mount Tom Trail. Traverse a scenic flat ridge with small-diameter trees and arbors of laurel. At a fork bear right, descending to angle left across RI 165. Tracking white, ascend to the outcrop-and-ledge reaches of Mount Tom Ridge. Interspersed low oaks filter views. An open view southwest sweeps the opposite ridge and marshy woodland basin.

Stepstone Falls, Arcadia
Management Area, Rhode Island

Descend past balanced boulders with fern seams to cross Mount Tom Road, just north of Parris Brook. You then follow the brook's tannin water downstream and head left (north) on the Blitzkrieg Trail (a dirt road). White blazes next point you through hot, dry pine plantation (be careful of ant mounds) before returning you to the Wood River parking lot.

MILES AND DIRECTIONS

0.0 Start at the Wood River canoe access/field check station trailhead. Follow the white blazes from the parking lot to RI 165, turn east to cross the Wood River road bridge, and pick up the trail on the opposite shore.

1.1 Cross Summit Road.

1.7 Reach the Arcadia Trail and follow it left.

2.0 Reach the John B. Hudson Trail. Follow it north and keep to its yellow-blazed trail.

3.0 Reach Breakheart Brook.

3.5 Reach Breakheart Pond. Hike the dirt road to the right for 0.2 mile before turning left, still following yellow blazes.

5.3 Cross Matteson Plain Road.

6.1 Cross a footbridge over the East Fork Flat River. Follow blazes left.

6.6 Cross the West Fork Flat River.

8.3 Cross Austin Farm Road.

8.9 Reach Austin Farm Road. Follow it left, crossing the Falls River road bridge.

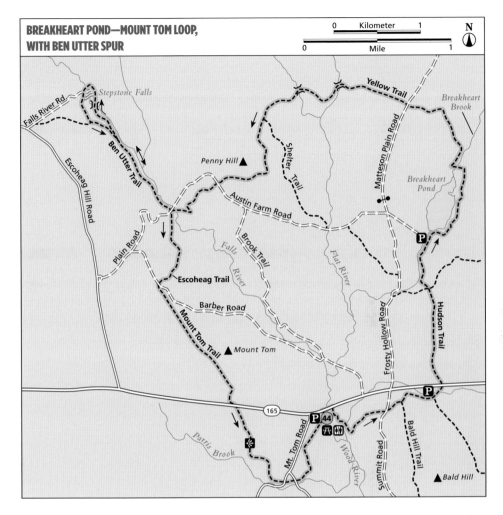

0   Kilometer   1

0   Mile   1

N

Stepstone Falls

Falls River Rd.

Yellow Trail

Breakheart Brook

Escoheag Hill Road

Ben Utter Trail

Penny Hill ▲

Shelter Trail

Matteson Plain Road

Breakheart Pond

Austin Farm Road

P

Plain Road

Brook Trail

Falls River

Flat River

Escoheag Trail

Barber Road

Mount Tom Trail ▲ Mount Tom

Frosty Hollow Road

Hudson Trail

P

165

P

Parris Brook

Mt. Tom Road

Wood River

Summit Road

Bald Hill Trail

▲ Bald Hill

9.0 Turn right upstream on the 2.6-mile out-and-back yellow Ben Utter Trail. *Option:* For the loop alone, continue forward on Austin Farm Road to pick up the Escoheag Trail.

10.0 Reach the lasso fork on the Ben Utter Trail. Head right on the white trail.

10.2 Reach the Stepstone Falls boxy outcrop. Continue upstream, round the head of Stepstone Falls on Falls River Road, and resume downstream on the yellow Ben Utter Trail.

11.6 Return to the management area loop. Turn right on Austin Farm Road, hiking 200 feet to pick up the white Escoheag Trail, which is briefly joined by the blue North–South Trail.

12.5 Reach Barber Road. Turn left, now following the white Mount Tom Trail. *Note:* The Escoheag Trail bears right here.

13.5 Reach a fork. Bear right, descending to the road cut of RI 165.

13.7 Angle left across RI 165 to Mount Tom.

14.4 Reach the southwestern view.

15.0 Cross paved Mount Tom Road just north of Parris Brook. Follow Parris Brook downstream to take the Blitzkrieg Trail left.

16.1 Arrive back at the Wood River trailhead.

HIKE INFORMATION

LOCAL INFORMATION

Central Rhode Island Chamber of Commerce, 3288 Post Rd., Warwick 02886; (401) 732-1100; www.centralrichamber.com.

Visit Warwick, Rhode Island, City of Warwick Department of Tourism, Culture and Development, 3275 Post Rd., Warwick 02886; (401) 738-2014; www.visitwarwickri .com.

LOCAL EVENTS/ATTRACTIONS

Tomaquag Museum, 390A Summit Rd., Exeter 02822; (401) 491-9063; www .tomaquagmuseum.org. Begun by anthropologist Eva Butler and run by Native Americans, this museum educates visitors with its more than 20,000 artifacts and thousands of archives on the indigenous peoples of Rhode Island and New England, their culture, tradition, art, and past. Phone for information on tours, classes, and hours.

ORGANIZATIONS

Appalachian Mountain Club (AMC), 10 City Square, Boston 02129; (617) 523-0636; www.outdoors.org.

45 GREAT SWAMP MANAGEMENT AREA

This relaxing loop on woods roads travels through upland and wet-footed woods, past fields, and alongside open and vegetated waters—the habitats of pond turtle and croaking frog, patrolling kingfisher and dive-bombing osprey. Covering nearly 3,400 acres, with a 138-acre impound, Great Swamp is one of the most extensive freshwater swamps in the region. Spring migration swells bird counts and species sightings.

Start: Management area trailhead
Distance: 4.4-mile lollipop
Hiking time: 2.5 to 3 hours
Difficulty: Easy
Elevation change: 100 feet
Trail surface: Gravel and grass management road, levee
Best seasons: Spring through fall
Other trail users: Equestrians, hunters, anglers, snowshoers, cross-country skiers
Canine compatibility: Leashed dogs permitted
Land status: State management area
Nearest town: West Kingston, RI
Fees and permits: None
Schedule: Year-round, sunrise to sunset

Map: State management area map (request copy from management office, specify your interest in hiking trails)
Trail contact: Great Swamp Management Area, 277 Great Neck Rd., West Kingston 02892; (401) 789-0281; www.dem.ri.gov.
Special considerations: With much of the hike being open-cathedral, carry drinking water, use sunscreen, and wear a hat. Keep all dogs leashed from Mar 15 through Aug 15; hunting dogs may be off leash Aug 16 through Mar 14. Oct through Feb all hikers must wear a fluorescent orange hat or vest in accordance with Rhode Island regulations.

FINDING THE TRAILHEAD

 From RI 138 in West Kingston, turn south onto Liberty Lane at the sign for the management area. The turn is just west of the RI 138–RI 110 intersection. In 0.8 mile the road changes to gravel and bends left, becoming Great Neck Road. Trailhead parking is at road's end in another mile. Trailhead GPS: N41 28.12' / W71 34.781'

THE HIKE

Following the management road south, you don't have to walk far before you see the wet-footed forest and undergrowth. Snags pierce the thicket, and power lines open views. You may pause to observe the lily pad–capped black-water pools, aquatic mammal scent mounds, and sunning baby turtles, or listen to the screech of a fish hawk.

The travel corridor alternates between partial shade and sun exposure, and the marsh visuals are richly textured and colored. Buzzing dragonflies, sometimes–menacing mosquitoes, and plopping residents can all draw notice. At the initial management-road fork, where a midway granite slab denotes Dr. John H. Mulleedy memorial trails, bear right to continue toward the swamp loop.

The grade mildly ascends and wends left as secondary tracks branch right. Keep to the primary track, edging a tall grass and goldenrod field on the right. Trees border the road's left shoulder. The hike has a country-lane meander about it. In a wildflower-shrub passage, you may encounter sulphur butterflies and percolating grasshoppers.

The trail alternates from wooded to open before passing into a power line corridor and following at its side. Although detractive, this utility-line opening clears the way for southern viewing toward the core swamp. Where the trail returns to woods, the grassy track on your right is the loop's return. Continue forward for the clockwise loop.

You might spy the remains of a few old stone walls, now nearly vanished in the woods debris, or a lonely bluebird box in a goldenrod field, where orange butterflies flit. Where this primary track forks, follow the right fork for a pleasant woods walk. Side tracks branch from it, but hold your line as the track descends and trends toward the swamp.

At the base of the slope, as the track swings left, you reach the Great Swamp impoundment. A granite seat invites pause for the view. A levee path then takes you around the swamp, with its open water mirroring the sky. Mottling the wetland are arrowleaf, lily pads, cattails, and shrubs. As you walk the levee, the open marsh is to your right; a red maple swamp is to your left. Looking across the swamp, you'll likely spy the heavy nests erected by ospreys atop power poles.

Poison ivy grows spotty at the levee's edge. Other impressions are the splashes of jumping fish or the knocking of woodpeckers. Seasonally, shriveled leathery shells and shallow

Trail entrance board, Great Swamp Management Area, Rhode Island

depressions reveal where turtles nested on the levee. Small islands with trees and mats of vegetation vary the look of the swamp. Herons, kingfishers, and darting swallows may pierce the swamp sky.

Travel is flat, carefree, and muggy. Be sure to carry adequate water. From the eastern shore you round to the swamp's south shore, still tracing the impound levee but gaining new perspectives on the swamp. You next follow the open-water channel where builders excavated the levee fill.

You then return to a gravel track wending uphill through woods. The rustling canopy is a nice reprieve from the hothouse of the open swamp. Close the loop and retrace the management road left and north to the trailhead parking lot.

MILES AND DIRECTIONS

0.0 Start at the management area trailhead. Follow the closed road south into the management area.

0.4 Bear right at the road fork to reach the swamp loop.

0.8 Reach the swamp loop junction past the power line corridor. Continue forward (clockwise). *Note:* The grassy track on your right is the return.

1.5 Reach a fork in the management road. Bear right.

1.9 Reach the open water of Great Swamp. Follow the levee rounding the swamp.

3.4 Reach the end of the levee. Continue forward on woods road.

3.6 Complete the loop. Backtrack the management road left (north) to the trailhead.

4.4 Arrive back at the trailhead.

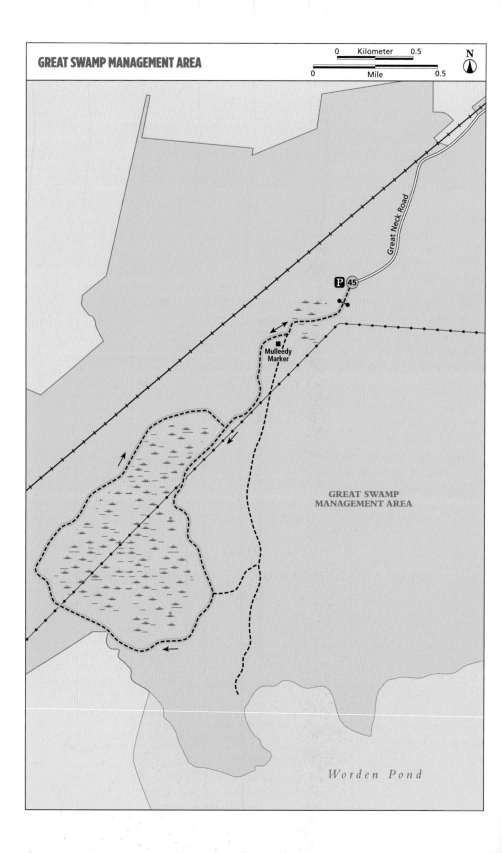

GREAT SWAMP MANAGEMENT AREA

0 Kilometer 0.5

0 Mile 0.5

N

Great Neck Road

P 45

Mulleedy Marker

GREAT SWAMP
MANAGEMENT AREA

Worden Pond

HIKE INFORMATION

LOCAL INFORMATION
South Kingstown Chamber of Commerce and Industry, 230 Old Tower Hill Rd., Wakefield 02879; (401) 783-2801; www.srichamber.com.

LOCAL EVENTS/ATTRACTIONS
Gilbert Stuart Birthplace and Museum, 815 Gilbert Stuart Rd., Saunderstown 02874; (401) 294-3001; www.gilbertstuartmuseum.org. This site provides an amazing look back at 18th-century Rhode Island life and industry, as well as a peek into life and art of this renowned American portraitist. It encompasses the 1750 birthplace of Gilbert Stuart, waterwheels, a snuff mill (the first such mill in the American colonies), a gristmill, a fish ladder, a colonial herb garden, and nature trails at Carr Pond. The birthplace is a National Historic Landmark.

    The South County (William C. O'Neill) Bike Path stretches 8 miles long. From the Kingston train station, it follows the old Narragansett Pier Railroad, passing through the villages of Peace Dale and Wakefield, to the town of Narragansett and the South County Museum at the coast. You cross this trail en route to the trailhead. Friends of William C. O'Neill Bike Path, 481 Post Rd., Wakefield 02879; (401) 783-8886; http://southcountybikepath.org. Or www.dot.ri.gov/bikeri.

46 SACHUEST POINT NATIONAL WILDLIFE REFUGE

At this 242-acre former naval communications station, a simple trail travels the jagged rocky peninsula overlooking Sachuest Bay, the broad Sakonnet River mouth, and the open waters of Rhode Island Sound. From October to mid-April, wintering harlequin ducks in striking plumage captivate spectators. Stormy seas can herd dozens of the birds onto shoreline rocks. September flocks of tree swallows feeding on bayberry, fall migrating ospreys and hawks, snowy owls hunting winter rodents, and spring songbirds suggest repeat tours. Occasionally, harbor seals haul out on the rocks.

Start: Refuge headquarters/visitor center trailhead
Distance: 2.5-mile loop
Hiking time: 1.5 to 2 hours
Difficulty: Easy
Elevation change: Virtually flat
Trail surface: Earthen path
Best seasons: Spring through fall
Other trail users: Birders and anglers
Canine compatibility: No dogs permitted
Land status: National wildlife refuge
Nearest town: Newport, RI
Fees and permits: None
Schedule: Year-round; grounds sunrise to sunset; visitor center: 10 a.m. to 4 p.m.

Map: Refuge trail map (available at visitor center during hours or online at www.fws.gov/refuge/sachuest_ point)
Trail contact: Sachuest Point National Wildlife Refuge, Rhode Island National Wildlife Refuge Complex, 50 Bend Rd., Charlestown 02813; (401) 364-9124 or (401) 619-2680 (Sachuest Visitor Center); www .fws.gov/refuge/sachuest_point
Special considerations: Beware of poison ivy, and bring repellent for biting insects.

FINDING THE TRAILHEAD

From the junction of RI 138A (Aquidneck Avenue) and Green End Avenue in Middletown, go east on Green End Avenue for 1.5 miles. Turn right on Third Beach Road and stay on it for 1.8 miles, bearing right at 1.5 miles. Turn left (south) on Sachuest Point Road to reach the visitor center and parking lot in 0.7 mile. Trailhead GPS: N41 28.779' / W71 14.614'

THE HIKE

An easy perimeter loop combines the site's two named trails to travel the shoreline and upland habitat of this boot-shaped peninsula. The trail visits both Sachuest and Flint Points, with bird and wildlife watching, rocky shores, coastal vistas, spring–flowering shrubs, and surf fishing as enticements. If time is limited, either point satisfies curiosity.

Counterclockwise, you begin west of the visitor center and stroll the Ocean View Loop south toward Sachuest Point and to overlook Sachuest Bay. From the bluff, views sweep the rocky refuge shore, the cliffs and historic buildings of Middletown, and the mansions of Newport across the way. Beach plum, bayberry, poison ivy, shore rose, and

tangled vines weave a dense rich border, while daisy and clover lend accents. In early summer a fragrant intermingling of sweet and salt air envelops your passage.

Where the bluff flattens, you can access the rocky shore, but use only the prescribed access points on the refuge map and beware of poison ivy. The shore consists of huge gray rockweed–clad boulders with quartz seams. Look for mussels, crabs, barnacles, and starfish within the jumble.

For the perimeter hike, keep to the bluff edge. Views to your left showcase the shrubs and plants of the upland habitat. This untamed tangled-shrub and grassland area can seclude red fox, weasel, and eastern cottontail. Interpretive plaques enhance understanding.

At Sachuest Point, views include a lighthouse island off Sakonnet Point. At times you'll see surf fishermen cast from the nearby rocks for blacks, blues, and stripers (bass). An unexpected wave slapping at the point reasserts the area's wildness.

The bluff stroll now carries you north away from Sachuest Point. You pass at the edge a field, snaring coastal glimpses over the top of thick seaward shrubs. A side trail overlooks Price Neck, a small scenic cove with rocky tongues extending into the water. Ahead, birdhouses may dot the field to the left. Bench seats welcome leisurely appreciation of life and sea. November through March offers the best viewing of ducks.

Coastal views now come rapid-fire. View the scalloped shore, sun-bleached spits, straggled rocks, and dark water gliding to shore. The junction ahead is the Flint Point Loop; the mowed

Wrinkled rose, Sachuest Point National Wildlife Refuge, Rhode Island

swath inland leads to the visitor center. For the full perimeter loop, continue hiking along the peninsula rim.

View offshore fishing boats as well as Island Rocks—long, low, gray outcrops piercing the water close to shore. An observation platform lifts you above the obstacle of the tall bordering shrubs.

On Flint Point take the spur to the right to a single-story platform overlooking a Sakonnet River cove and Third Beach. Looks across the neck of the peninsula find Second Beach on Sachuest Bay. Cormorants may crowd the tiny rock island between Flint Point and Third Beach, capping the view.

From Flint Point the perimeter loop swings southwest, returning to the central path to the visitor center. As you pass through a shrub corridor and a shrub-field complex, yellow warblers and swallows contribute to the finale. Before the visitor center, one last observation platform bids a visit. You end back at the parking lot.

MILES AND DIRECTIONS

0.0 Start at the visitor center. Hike west from the center to follow Ocean View Loop south along shore for a counterclockwise circling of the peninsula.

0.6 Reach Sachuest Point.

1.3 Reach the Flint Point Loop junction. Continue forward along the rim. *Option:* Following the mowed swath inland leads to the visitor center for a 1.5-mile loop.

1.9 Reach Flint Point.

2.5 Arrive back at the parking lot.

HIKE INFORMATION

LOCAL INFORMATION
Discover Newport, 23 America's Cup Ave., Newport 02840; (401) 849-8048 or (800) 326-6030; www.discovernewport.org.

LOCAL EVENTS/ATTRACTIONS
Old Colony and Newport Railway, 19 Americas Cup Ave., Newport 02840; (401) 295-1203; http://trainsri.com/old-colony-newport. This attraction offers an 1864

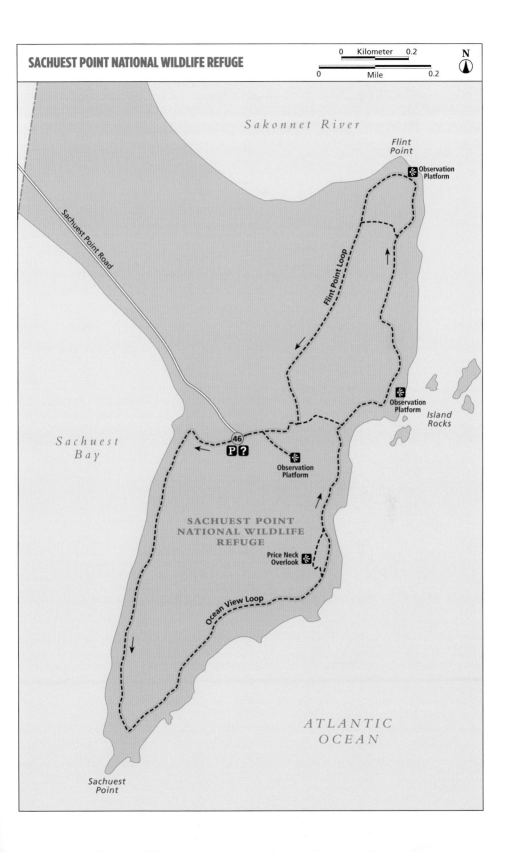

SACHUEST POINT NATIONAL WILDLIFE REFUGE

0   Kilometer   0.2

0   Mile   0.2

N

Sakonnet River

Flint
Point

Observation
Platform

Flint Point Loop

Observation
Platform

Island
Rocks

*Sachuest
Bay*

46

P ?

Observation
Platform

SACHUEST POINT
NATIONAL WILDLIFE
REFUGE

Price Neck
Overlook

Ocean View Loop

*ATLANTIC
OCEAN*

Sachuest
Point

railway look at Narragansett Bay, with its blue waters, white ships, romantic shores, and wildlife, as well as the area's naval history. Ride in parlor car elegance or in the camaraderie of coach.

The Preservation Society of Newport County, 424 Bellevue Ave., Newport 02840; (401) 847-1000; www.newportmansions.org. This Society recommends another **bluff walk** that takes you past the grand Newport mansions that pair elegantly with the sea.

47 VIN GORMLEY TRAIL

This "yellow trail" circuit travels the outlying forest, wetland, and rock habitat enfolding Watchaug Pond, with views of the pond reserved for the hike's end. You initially follow public roadway before surrendering to trail. Points of interest include Burlingame State Park and Kimball Wildlife Refuge, a property of the Audubon Society of Rhode Island. In places the state's North–South through-trail, blazed in blue, shares the way.

Start: Burlingame State Park day-use trailhead
Distance: 8.5-mile loop
Hiking time: 5 to 7 hours
Difficulty: Moderate
Elevation change: 150 feet
Trail surface: Earthen path, boardwalk, woods road, public roadway
Best seasons: Spring through fall
Other trail users: Mountain bikers, birders, motorists (on roadway stretch), snowshoers, cross-country skiers
Canine compatibility: No dogs permitted

Land status: State park and private nonprofit sanctuary
Nearest town: Charlestown, RI
Fees and permits: Day-use parking fee
Schedule: Year-round, 8 a.m. to sunset
Map: Vin Gormley Trail map, available at the fee station or at the campground office (west of Prosser Trail off US 1)
Trail contact: Burlingame State Park, 1 Burlingame State Park Rd., Charlestown 02813; (401) 322-8910; www.riparks.com
Special considerations: Expect some muddy, wet stretches in spring.

FINDING THE TRAILHEAD

Access is only off US 1 South. From the junction of RI 2/RI 112 and US 1 in Charlestown, go west on US 1 South for 2.4 miles and turn right (north) on Prosser Trail for Burlingame State Park Picnic Area and Beach. On US 1 North, go 3.4 miles east from RI 216, take the formal U-turn onto US 1 South, and turn north on Prosser Trail in 0.4 mile. Reach day-use parking on the left in 0.7 mile. Trailhead GPS: N41 22.816′ / W71 40.634′

THE HIKE

Named for John Vincent Gormley, a dedicated trail-smith, this 8.5-mile hiker circuit offers a relaxing woodland stroll at the outskirts of Watchaug Pond. Mixed woodland, bog, and brook settings host travel. Flowering shrubs recommend spring passage. Yellow paint and plastic cards blaze the route, with the occasional distance marker to cheer you on.

Counterclockwise, the first mile is logged on road and paced off fast. From the day-use fee station, you follow the blazes east out the access road and north (left) on the Prosser Trail, a tree-lined, two-lane, lightly trafficked road. At Kings Factory Road you turn left and hike another quarter mile or so to where the trail turns left into woods for the natural tour. Birch, pine, cherry, and chestnut, white, red, and black oaks enfold the trail. Be alert for poison ivy.

Watchaug Pond dawn, Burlingame
State Park, Rhode Island

Along this 4-foot-wide meandering trail, wildflowers, club moss, sassafras, huckleberry, and ferns variously make up the understory vegetation. Deer, toads, or foxes may snare attention. After the trail angles right across a quiet paved lane, you enter a moist habitat with thick shrubs, including sweet pepperbush, azalea, highbush blueberry, and green-brier. The shrub abundance leads you to the crossing of an inlet.

The comfortable, obstacle-free trail welcomes mindless travel. Below a lichen-etched outcrop, mountain laurel thrives. From a clearing, you turn right onto an attractive, narrow woods road draped in hemlock-hardwood forest.

Heed the blazes and arrow markers signaling direction changes. Birdsong fills the leafy canopy, while Indian pipes push up through the forest duff. Small footbridges span a pair of slightly larger brooks. After crossing a dirt road, you again tour bog habitat on a rustic boardwalk of hewn logs. Beyond the boardwalk the trail turns left, traversing a flat outcrop.

Where the trail next rolls up and over rock outcrops, you find 15- to 20-foot cliffs with showy fern seams. Past the rocky area, you again travel among low shrubs, especially pretty when the sheep laurel bushes parade dark pink blooms.

Turn left on Buckeye Brook Road to cross the bridge over the scenic wide, slow water, accented by pond lilies and arrowhead. The hike resumes on the left. Oak, tall sassafras, and pitch pine next frame the narrow woods path. Find stone walls and patchy shade.

Poison ivy is more prevalent in the open woods. On old woods road you pass alongside a brook that is screened from view. At its footbridge crossing, view a big maple. Afterward, you reach more of the boardwalk laid by Vin Gormley.

Cross through the Perry Healy Brook covered bridge. The brook is meandering, tannin-tinted, and accented by lush grasses, ferns, and branches and enlivened by dragonflies and frogs. Bog boardwalks continue in red maple swamp. Skunk cabbage and wetland shrubs dress the swamp.

Watch for a couple of direction changes before entering the state park campground, where restrooms and water are available. Hike through the open campground, tracking blazes, for a sunny walk. Past the playground but before the camp store, you descend along the edge of a field to enter woods. This hardwood forest ushers you to Kimball Wildlife Refuge; obey rules.

At the refuge, side trails branch left to Watchaug Pond, as blazed paths from the Audubon trail system arrive and depart on the right. Keep to the yellow Vin Gormley Trail. From the refuge, you hike left on dirt road past lakeshore residences. At the Watchaug Pond Fishing Access, you'll find open viewing of the huge recreational water. Not long afterward, you complete the loop.

MILES AND DIRECTIONS

- **0.0** Start at the Burlingame State Park day-use trailhead. Follow Prosser Trail/ Kings Factory Road north from the parking lot.
- **0.9** Take the yellow-blazed foot trail west (left) off Kings Factory Road.
- **2.6** Travel a boggy area on rustic boardwalk.
- **3.7** Cross the Buckeye Brook Road bridge.
- **5.9** Cross through the Perry Healy Brook covered bridge.
- **7.0** Enter the state park campground.

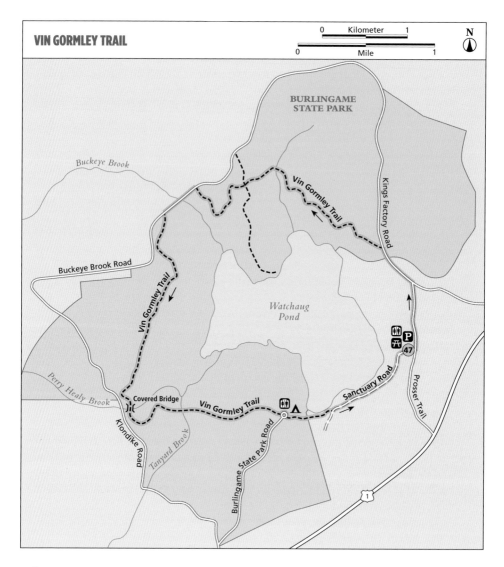

0   Kilometer   1

0   Mile   1

N

BURLINGAME
STATE PARK

Buckeye Brook

Vin Gormley Trail

Kings Factory Road

Buckeye Brook Road

Vin Gormley Trail

Watchaug
Pond

Perry Healy Brook

47

P

Covered Bridge

Vin Gormley Trail

Sanctuary Road

Prosser Trail

Klondike Road

Tanyard Brook

Burlingame State Park Road

1

7.7   Enter Kimball Wildlife Refuge.

8.3   Reach the Watchaug Pond Fishing Access.

8.5   Arrive back at the day-use trailhead.

HIKE INFORMATION

LOCAL INFORMATION

Charlestown Chamber of Commerce, 4945 Old Post Rd., Charlestown 02813; (401) 364-3878; www.charlestownrichamber.com.

Vin Gormley Trail, Burlingame State Park, Rhode Island

ACCOMMODATIONS

Burlingame State Park, 1 Burlingame State Park Rd., Charlestown 02813; (401) 322-7337. Burlingame State Park has more than 700 family campsites and is open mid-Apr through early Oct. Reservations are available through ReserveAmerica, (877) 742-2675 or www.reserveamerica.com.

ORGANIZATIONS

Appalachian Mountain Club (AMC), 10 City Square, Boston 02129; (617) 523-0636; www.outdoors.org.

48 NINIGRET CONSERVATION AREA, EAST BEACH HIKE

Reclaiming a US Naval Air Station on the coast of Block Island Sound, the adjoining properties of this state beach conservation area, a Charlestown town beach, and a 400-acre federal wildlife refuge forge an uncommon coastal open space benefitting wildlife and humans. The modern wild encompasses upland grassland, shrubland, and woodland; marsh and pond habitats; and barrier-beach dunes, swale, and shore. The diversity supports native and migrant species.

Start: Blue Shutters Town Beach parking area
Distance: 7 miles out and back
Hiking time: 3.5 to 5 hours
Difficulty: Easy
Elevation change: Flat
Trail surface: Sandy strand
Best seasons: Apr through mid-Sept
Other trail users: Birders, swimmers, sunbathers
Canine compatibility: No dogs permitted
Land status: State beach conservation area
Nearest town: Charlestown, RI
Fees and permits: Summer season parking fees at both the town beach and the beach conservation area, which offers an alternative starting point, reducing the total hike distance by 0.4 mile
Schedule: Year-round; Ninigret Conservation Area: 8 a.m. to sunset; Blue Shutters Town Beach parking area: 8 a.m. (weekends)/9 a.m. (weekdays) to 5 p.m. (during beach season), otherwise no gate
Maps: None needed
Trail contact: East Beach, Ninigret Conservation Area, c/o Burlingame State Park, 1 Burlingame State Park Rd., Charlestown 02813; (401) 322-8910; www.riparks.com
Special considerations: Blue Shutters Town Beach has a bathhouse/restroom; chemical toilets serve the conservation area. Bring drinking water. Dune crossings are restricted to designated accesses. Respect closures for nesting piping plovers and for habitat protection. Bring insect repellent, and beware of poison ivy and ticks in the upland areas.

FINDING THE TRAILHEAD

From the US 1–RI 216 junction in Charlestown, go 0.8 mile east on US 1 North and turn right onto East Beach Road, following it to the beach and the parking areas at Blue Shutters Town Beach and Ninigret Conservation Area. Trailhead GPS: N41 20.500′ / W71 41.689′

THE HIKE

This barrier beach welcomes with crystalline sands. Eastbound you pass from popular bathing beach to wilderness strand of open sand and adjoining upland. You may view nesting piping plovers (April through August), inland woodcock courtships at dusk (mid-March through June), and wintering waterfowl. Because the upland and dune covers serve deer, fox, rabbit, and red squirrel, as well as a variety of songbirds, keep your binoculars handy.

East Beach, Ninigret
Conservation Area,
Rhode Island

This hike also takes you past Rhode Island's largest coastal pond, Ninigret Pond, a 1,700-acre brackish pond breached to the ocean. Beach pea and poison ivy grow along its shore. A scull may slice the open water, while gulls clamor atop the rocks and colored buoys mark crab pots.

For the full East Beach hike, start at Blue Shutters Town Beach and head east. The coconut-oiled masses do not venture far from the beach facilities. Be sure to bring plenty of drinking water because the tendency is to dally.

As you pace east the strand grows more and more wild. Before long you enter Ninigret Conservation Area. Capped by dune grass and beach pea, 4-foot-high sand dunes back the strand. Behind the dunes, primitive camping areas serve self-contained four-wheel-drive vehicles. Although the camp disperses a few more beachgoers, the beach rolls out ample solitude.

A gentle cant greets the close-breaking waves, and orange flecks contribute to the beauty of the sand. Dips in the dunes reveal a shoreline swale and Ninigret Pond to the north. Black, purple, and green seaweed, whelk and skate egg cases, pebble patches, and scattered shells complement the clean strand. The call to dig your toes into the sand or kick at the surf is strong.

Offshore views include the long, flat profile of Block Island and the bobbing fishing and leisure boats. After a mile, find the first of several regularly spaced designated dune accesses between camp and beach. These crossings broaden perspective on the area.

At the toe of the seaward dune, piping plovers commonly nest. Grant the tiny birds a wide safety margin. The jetty of Charlestown Breachway, which opens Ninigret Pond to the ocean, becomes more obvious. Drift fences help preserve the dune as the beach walk takes you from conservation land to national wildlife refuge. East of the refuge, private parcels back the beach, so keep toward the ocean shore.

NINIGRET CONSERVATION AREA, EAST BEACH HIKE

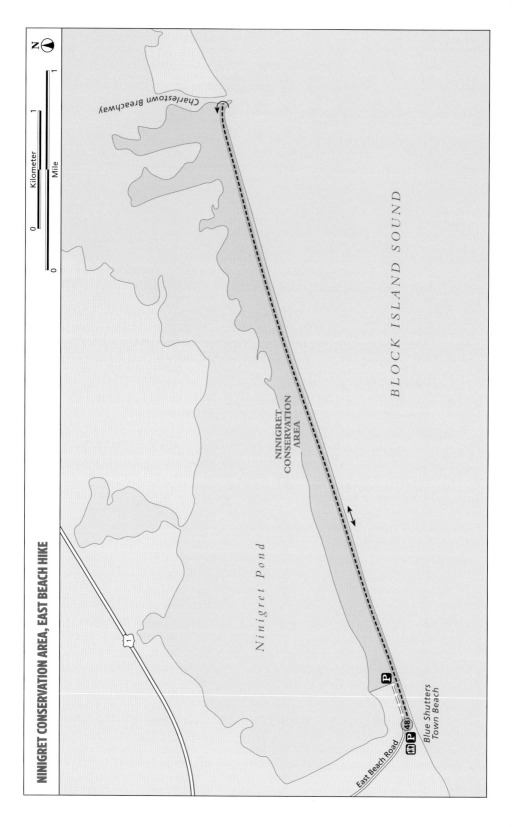

Reach the riprap channel of Charlestown Breachway, where aqua-green water surges in and out of Ninigret Pond. A screech may sound an osprey's presence. Views sweep Block Island Sound, the breachway, Ninigret Pond, and the far marshy shore. A low estuarine island, brushy points, and jungles of phragmites contribute to the pond imagery, as do the plumes of egrets and cormorants. Seasonally, seaweed can overwhelm the waves curling to shore. When ready, turn back for a fine recap.

MILES AND DIRECTIONS

0.0 Start at Blue Shutters Beach. Hike the beach east.

0.2 Enter Ninigret Conservation Area. Continue east along the beach.

1.2 Reach the first of the designated dune accesses. *Note:* Accesses are found at 1.5, 2.2, 2.5, 2.8, and 3.5 miles.

2.8 Enter Ninigret National Wildlife Refuge. Again, continue east along the beach.

3.5 Reach Charlestown Breachway, the hike's turnaround point. Backtrack west.

7.0 Arrive back at Blue Shutters Town Beach.

HIKE INFORMATION

LOCAL INFORMATION
Charlestown Chamber of Commerce, 4945 Old Post Rd., Charlestown 02813; (401) 364-3878; www.charlestownrichamber.com.

LOCAL EVENTS/ATTRACTIONS
Watch Hill Carousel and Beach, (401) 348-6007; http://watchhillbeachandcarousel .com. Watch Hill's Flying Horse Carousel, on Bay Street in Westerly, is the oldest carousel in America and the last of its kind. The free-flying hand-carved wooden horses still delight little ones in summer.

The 1856 **Watch Hill Lighthouse** stands 45 feet tall and attracts with the romance of the sea and maritime history. You must walk to this light. Viewing is from the lighthouse grounds 8 a.m. to sunset; check webpage for the museum's limited hours. Watch Hill Lighthouse Keepers Association, 14 Lighthouse Rd., Watch Hill 02891; www.watchhill lighthousekeepers.org.

ACCOMMODATIONS
Burlingame State Park, 1 Burlingame State Park Rd., Charlestown 02813; (401) 322-7337. Burlingame State Park (north of East Beach across US 1) has more than 700 family campsites and is open mid-Apr through early Oct. Reservations are available through ReserveAmerica, (877) 742-2675 or www.reserveamerica.com.

49 TRUSTOM POND NATIONAL WILDLIFE REFUGE

This federal wildlife refuge/onetime farm offers up images pastoral, wooded, and coastal. Open fields, salt and freshwater ponds, vegetated islands, marshy and thickety shores, and quiet, low-canopy woods shape its mosaic. The big blue centerpiece is 160-acre Trustom Pond, the only undeveloped coastal salt pond in Rhode Island. A host of birds populate and visit the property. This is one for slow touring, binoculars, and breathing deep.

Start: Refuge trailhead
Distance: 2.8-mile lollipop with spurs
Hiking time: 2 to 2.5 hours
Difficulty: Easy
Elevation change: Virtually flat
Trail surface: Earthen or cinder path, boardwalk, mowed track
Best seasons: Spring through fall
Other trail users: Birders
Canine compatibility: No dogs permitted
Land status: National wildlife refuge
Nearest town: Charlestown or Narragansett, RI
Fees and permits: None
Schedule: Year-round, sunrise to sunset

Map: Refuge map (available online at www.fws.gov/refuge/trustom_pond)
Trail contact: Trustom Pond National Wildlife Refuge, Rhode Island National Wildlife Refuge Complex, 1040 Matunuck Schoolhouse Rd., South Kingstown 02879; (401) 364-9124; www.fws.gov/refuge/trustom_pond
Special considerations: Bring drinking water, and keep to the trails to protect habitats and wildlife. Seasonally, you may need insect repellent and be alert for poison ivy. The parking lot can fill on summer weekends.

FINDING THE TRAILHEAD

From the junction of US 1 and RI 2/212 in Charlestown, go east on US 1 North for 3.5 miles and turn right (south) onto Moonstone Beach Road, following signs for the refuge. Go 1 mile and turn right on Matunuck Schoolhouse Road, continue 0.7 mile, and turn left into the refuge, reaching parking in 0.1 mile. Trailhead GPS: N41 22.998' / W71 35.116'

THE HIKE

This refuge has grown to its present 787-acre size from the initial generous 365-acre donation of Mrs. Ann Kenyon Morse in 1974 and the 1982 Audubon barrier beach addition for the protection of nesting piping plovers. The varied habitats provide rich viewing and shape critical niches for 300 bird species, 40 mammal species, and a host of reptiles, amphibians, and insects. As seasons change, so do sightings.

This hike combines the refuge's short, flat, easy trails into a single foot journey that welcomes slow study. Interpretive boards and benches also slow the pace. From the contact station, you head south through coastal thicket to reach the loop junction at a field of goldenrod, milkweed, Queen Anne's lace, and mixed shrubs. By hiking clockwise on the

Trailhead mapboard, Trustom Pond National Wildlife Refuge, Rhode Island

Farm Field Loop, you round first to Otter Point and then to Osprey Point, the refuge's two prized overlooks.

Much of the refuge was former farm/sheep pasture. Native grasses—big and little bluestem, switchgrass, and Indian grass—are being reestablished in the large meadow edged by trail. The return of the grasses creates habitat for eastern bluebirds, bobolinks, and northern harriers. Many of the grasses are head-high and have a wonderful dancing movement in the wind.

Back-to-back Farm Pond viewing sites draw you aside to overlook the long dark-water pond, its lily pad cap and piercing wetland grasses, and the aquatic insect movements that ripple the surface. Wild grape entangles the rimming red maples. Cattails, frogs, and fishes divert glances.

Where the Farm Field Loop heads right on mowed track, continue forward on the cinder path toward Otter Point. Junctions are well signed for sorting out travel. You then hike past the Red Maple Swamp Trail (the loop's continuation) to visit Otter Point.

The trek to the point offers looks out to Trustom Pond and Block Island Sound. Trustom is an enormous salt pond with swans and snapping turtles among its tenants. Islands, edging marsh grass, and a wooded shore add to its impression. Trailside trees creak and crack in the wind. The observation platform has bi-level spotting scopes and interpretive boards to help in bird identification. Because the grassy trail beyond the platform doesn't significantly improve upon the view, backtrack to the Red Maple Swamp Trail to resume the clockwise loop.

On the Red Maple Swamp Trail, sweet pepperbush and cinnamon fern contribute to the lush swamp growth; a boardwalk spans open water. The remains of a windmill

and stone walls harken to the farm era. Goldenrod dominates clearings, and an arresting wolf tree clears its own gallery. White-tailed deer might flee. Biologists are studying their impact here.

At the Osprey Point Trail, turn left to visit the overlook. Right holds the loop's return. Warblers, flycatchers, and nuthatches may draw attention as the trail traces the narrow, wooded pond peninsula. Pass benches and a low platform before reaching the viewing deck that allows looks at the barrier beach with breaches that extend looks to Block Island Sound. The surf's crush carries to the trail, but Trustom Pond is the immediate attention-grabber. The telescope allows you to pinpoint a lighthouse or better focus on wildlife.

When ready, retrace the peninsula walk and continue forward on the Osprey Point Trail, past the Red Maple Swamp Trail, to find new discovery. Even a slight change in elevation results in cosmetic changes to the forest. Geese, voles, and rabbits may be spied along the mowed track as you return to the more-open setting of the hike's start. The Farm Field Loop arrives on right, sharing the return to the initial loop junction. Close the loop and backtrack left to the trailhead.

MILES AND DIRECTIONS

0.0 Start at the refuge trailhead. Hike the access lane south past the contact station into the refuge.

0.1 Reach the loop junction. Turn left (clockwise), following the Farm Field Loop.

0.3 Reach both the Red Maple Swamp Trail (the loop's continuation) and the spur to Otter Point. Proceed forward to visit the Otter Point Observation Platform.

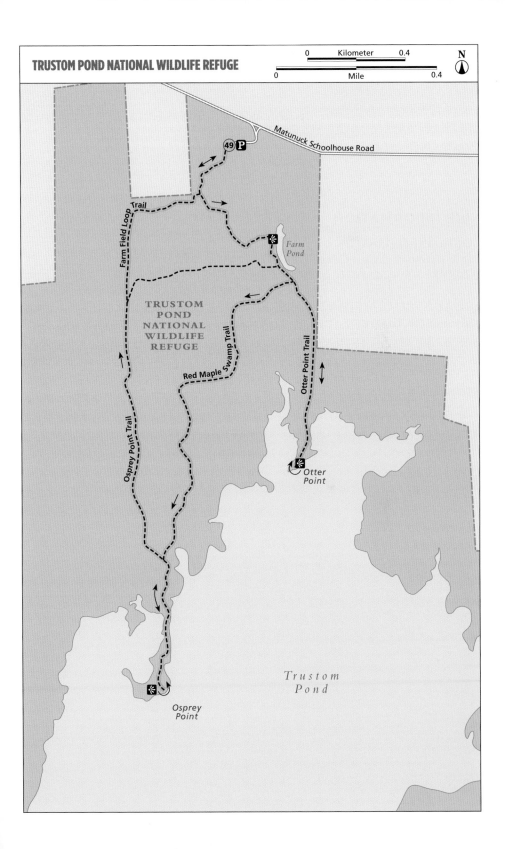

TRUSTOM POND NATIONAL WILDLIFE REFUGE

Kilometer

Mile

N

Matunuck Schoolhouse Road

49 P

Farm Field Loop Trail

Farm Pond

TRUSTOM POND NATIONAL WILDLIFE REFUGE

Red Maple Swamp Trail

Otter Point Trail

Osprey Point Trail

Otter Point

Trustom Pond

Osprey Point

0.7	Reach Otter Point. Backtrack to the Red Maple Swamp Trail.
1.1	Turn left on the Red Maple Swamp Trail.
1.7	Reach the Osprey Point Trail. Turn left to visit the point.
1.9	Reach Osprey Point. Backtrack to the loop.
2.1	Continue forward on the Osprey Point Trail. **Note:** Before long the Farm Field Loop arrives on the right to share the return.
2.7	Close the loop. Backtrack left to the trailhead.
2.8	Arrive back at the refuge trailhead.

HIKE INFORMATION

LOCAL INFORMATION

South County Tourism Council, 4160 Old Post Rd., Charlestown 02813; (401) 789-4422; (800) 548-4662; www.southcountyri.com.

LOCAL EVENTS/ATTRACTIONS

Narragansett Towers, 35 Ocean Road, Narragansett 02882; (401) 782-2597; www.thetowersri.com. In Narragansett, The Towers span Ocean Road (Route 1A). They are the remnant structures of the Narragansett Pier Casino, part of the stylish resort community that flourished here from the late 19th century through the turn of the 20th century. Today the great hall above the archway hosts special events.

ACCOMMODATIONS

Burlingame State Park, 1 Burlingame State Park Rd., Charlestown 02813; (401) 322-7337. Burlingame State Park (west of the refuge, north off US 1) has more than 700 family campsites and is open mid-Apr through early Oct. Reservations are available through ReserveAmerica, (877) 742-2675 or www.reserveamerica.com.

50 BLOCK ISLAND, NORTH ISLAND HIKING

The north end of Block Island rolls out trails of history and discovery, tracing beach, bluff, and inland habitat. With fair weather and tide, virtually the entire island beach perimeter is open to walking. North Light is the signature landmark of the northern shore. The Bluff Trail provides an elevated vantage on the sculpted shore of Block Island North, while the beach below puts you up close with the eroded cliffs, rock and sand shore, and the gulls that gather there. This particular hike visits all three, with an island taxi ride and low tide making it possible.

Start: The Nature Conservancy's Clay Head Preserve trailhead
Distance: 7.9 miles one way with taxi shuttle to start
Hiking time: All day, first ferry to last ferry
Difficulty: Strenuous
Elevation change: 80 feet
Trail surface: Beach, earthen path, mowed track, island road
Best seasons: Late spring through early fall (for more daylight)
Other trail users: Birders; cyclists and motorists on island road system
Canine compatibility: Leave dogs at home
Land status: Town beaches, private nonprofit lands, private land
Nearest towns: New Shoreham on Block Island, Narragansett on mainland
Fees and permits: Ferry and taxi fares; North Light Interpretive Center (seasonally open) admission fee

Schedule: Year-round, daylight hours
Map: Block Island tourism map (available at the hospitality center listed below)
Trail contact: Block Island Hospitality Center, 1 Water St., New Shoreham 02807; (401) 466-2982; www.blockislandchamber.com
Special considerations: Because of the hike's length and the ferry schedules, using a taxi allows you to see as much as possible in a day. Bring drinking water and protection against the sun. Amenities are few. There are restrooms at the ferry landing and at the town beaches in season. Come prepared for insects, and be alert for poison ivy and ticks. Away from the developed beaches, there is no swimming due to dangerous riptides. In right-of-ways, keep to the trail or road to avoid trespass. Check tides before starting, and revise your hike accordingly.

FINDING THE TRAILHEAD

Take the Block Island Ferry from Point Judith in Galilee (GPS: N41 22.784' / W71 30.664') to the Block Island Old Harbor Ferry Landing (GPS: N41 10.388' / W71 33.463') and then take an island taxi to the Nature Conservancy's Clay Head Preserve trailhead. Trailhead GPS: N41 12.515' / W71 33.719'

THE HIKE

This hike requires a brisk pace to complete before the last ferry. Diversions are many, and not all of the beach is easy to walk. If you expect that either time or will may run short, focus on a piece of the hike instead.

The Clay Head Trail launches you into upland habitat as you skirt the big inland water of Clay Head Swamp. Birders seek songbird in the scrub and waterfowl on the ponds. As the trail drifts seaward, the sand underfoot betrays this was once shifting dune, now stabilized by vegetation.

The bluff walk north extends frequent views and elevated perspectives on island, shore, and sound. Keep right as mowed tracks branch inland to Corn Neck Road and a maze of passages. Glances south overlook Clay Head Swamp to Old Harbor. An early view features a strong cove curvature, cliff rim, and nearshore boulders. Birders say to watch for peregrine falcons.

You next skirt a smaller marshy pond. Where the trail slips inland, edging untamed fields, you travel in vegetated aisles or tunnels of low coastal trees. Erosion has whittled the bluff cliffs, adding bulges, cuts, and dips, but no beach access. Goldenrod complements views. Plovers and gulls flock on shore, and buoys bob in the near waters, with sail and fishing boats farther out.

Where the bluff footpath meets a two-track, follow it right (north) along a stone wall to descend left on a dirt driveway (a courtesy right-of-way) to Corn Neck Road. There, turn right, briefly hiking at road's edge, to take a narrow footpath onto the beach and turn north. Cobbles often inspire beach artisans to fashion balanced cairns or totems.

At North Light parking, Settlers' Rock may call you aside. Placed in 1911, it commemorated the 250th anniversary of the 1661 purchase and settlement of Block Island. A rededication occurred in 1961. North Light and Sandy Point bid you forward. The beach north typically holds cobbles and loose sand. You may notice lots of quartz, bits of shell, seaweed, and feathers as you pace off the distance to the rhythmic beat of the surf.

Settlers' Rock monument (left), Block Island North Lighthouse (right), Block Island National Wildlife Refuge, Block Island, Rhode Island

A curved loose-sand track at the upper beach leads to the 1867 North Light. The picturesque stone building, white tower, and black beacon ringed by a catwalk sit among the rolling dunes. Lichens paint the tiny outbuildings. Wild beach rose and coastal shrubs and grasses mottle the heaving sands, while national wildlife refuge stretches beyond the drift fences.

From the grounds of the light, take the dune egress to the beach. Arriving among drift logs, you turn right (north) to round Sandy Point, where gulls commonly congregate. Upon rounding Sandy Point, you then begin the long trek south, following the island's perimeter shore to Old Harbor.

On this journey (low tides allowing), you will travel wilderness strand and public recreation beach for a low-road perspective on the framing bluffs and scalloped shore. You'll trace the arc of Cow Cove, pass Grove Point, and glimpse offshore rocks as you round beneath the bluffs. Offshore, a history of shipwrecks belongs to the immediate sea. Cobbles and seabirds remain companions.

You round below Clay Head and Balls Points. Past Jerrys Point you start to encounter beachgoers and sun seekers, but the fine sand beach is welcome underfoot. To the south sits Old Harbor at the distant end of a long beach curvature.

Mansion Beach blends into Scotch Beach, which slides into Block Island Municipal Beach. The latter has a formal bathhouse. Where riprap and tide push you up onto the road for your continuation into town, stroll past benches and a monument citing an original settler and presettlement landings and clashes. Ferries add to closing views. You then follow Water Street through the charming waterfront of Old Harbor to return to the landing.

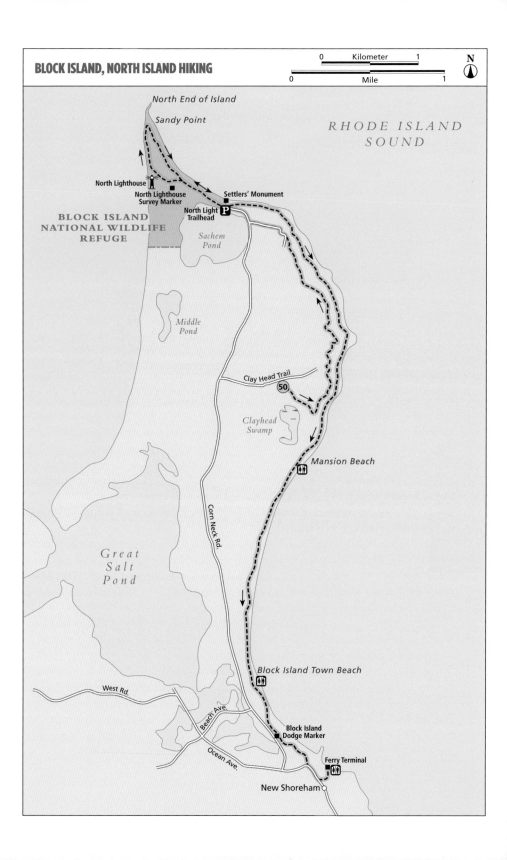

0   Kilometer   1

0   Mile   1

N

North End of Island

Sandy Point

RHODE ISLAND
SOUND

North Lighthouse

North Lighthouse
Survey Marker

Settlers' Monument

North Light
Trailhead

P

BLOCK ISLAND
NATIONAL WILDLIFE
REFUGE

Sachem
Pond

Middle
Pond

Clay Head Trail

50

Clayhead
Swamp

Mansion Beach

Corn Neck Rd.

Great
Salt
Pond

Block Island Town Beach

West Rd.

Beach Ave.

Block Island
Dodge Marker

Ferry Terminal

Ocean Ave.

New Shoreham

MILES AND DIRECTIONS

0.0 Start at the TNC Clay Head Preserve trailhead. Hike the Clay Head Trail toward the bluff.

0.4 Reach the bluff. Hike north along the bluff edge, ignoring mowed tracks to the island interior.

1.9 Reach the dirt access road. Turn left. (Keep to this drive to avoid trespass onto private land.)

2.1 Reach Corn Neck Road. Turn right, following the road's edge for 100 yards to take the footpath onto the beach. There, turn left, hiking the beach north.

2.2 Pass North Light parking and Settlers' Monument. Proceed north for the lighthouse.

2.5 Veer left on the loose-sand track at the upper beach to visit North Light.

2.6 Reach North Light. Take the marked egress through the dunes to the beach.

2.7 Reach the beach. Turn right (north) to round Sandy Point.

2.9 Reach Sandy Point. Hike the beach south to the Old Harbor Ferry Landing.

5.8 Reach Mansion Beach.

7.1 Reach the town beach bathhouse.

7.7 Reach Water Street and follow it into Old Harbor.

7.9 End at the Old Harbor Ferry Landing.

Options: South Block Island, with its beach and light, or The Nature Conservancy's Rodman Hollow open space offer additional hiking and wildlife-watching opportunities.

HIKE INFORMATION

LOCAL INFORMATION
Block Island Hospitality Center, 1 Water St., New Shoreham 02807; (401) 466-2982; www.blockislandchamber.com.

LOCAL EVENTS/ATTRACTIONS
The last weekend in Sept or first weekend in Oct, the Audubon Society of Rhode Island hosts **Birding Weekend on Block Island** to coincide with the return of the migrant species. Audubon Society of Rhode Island, 12 Sanderson Rd., Smithfield 02917; (401) 949-5454; www.asri.org.

ACCOMMODATIONS
Fishermen's Memorial State Park, 1011 Point Judith Rd., Narragansett 02882; (401) 789-8374; www.riparks.com. This park near Point Judith has 182 family campsites and is open mid-Apr through Oct. Reservations are through ReserveAmerica, (877) 742-2675 or www.reserveamerica.com.

HONORABLE MENTIONS
RHODE ISLAND

AP. BLACKSTONE RIVER BIKEWAY

Part of the greater 48-mile John H. Chafee Blackstone River Valley National Heritage Corridor between Providence, Rhode Island, and Worcester, Massachusetts, this growing 11.5-mile paved bikeway between Woonsocket and Valley Falls, Rhode Island, celebrates the Industrial Revolution that changed the nation from an agrarian economy of family farms to a manufacturing one of urban centers. The Blackstone River both powered manufacturing and moved raw material to and finished products from the region's eighteenth- and nineteenth-century mills. The canal operated from 1828 to 1848, when it was superseded by railroads. The bikeway salutes some of the best-preserved sections of the historic canal and takes you past historic towns, river structures, and modern parks.

In Woonsocket, start at the River's Edge Recreation Complex, taking Davison Avenue south off RI 126N/RI 122. Trailhead GPS: N42 00.026' / W71 29.907'. Trail contact: Blackstone Heritage Corridor, 670 Linwood Ave., Whitinsville 01588; (508) 234-4242; blackstoneheritagecorridor.org.

AQ. LIME ROCK PRESERVE (AUST FAMILY PRESERVE AT LIME ROCK)

In the town of Lincoln, this 130-acre preserve along the Moshassuck River and Manton Reservoir is known for its marble ledges and the unique flora that favors this calcium-rich environment. Water, woods, marsh, and, of course, the ledges are visited by the site's short trail system (2.5 miles). Footpath and a retired electric rail bed lead you through the area. Poison ivy and a respect for the area's sensitive habitats will encourage you to keep to the trail.

From the junction RI 123 and RI 246, 0.2 mile west of RI 146, go north on RI 246 for 1.6 miles and turn west on Wilbur Road to find the trailhead turnout (parking for one or two vehicles) on the right in 0.7 mile. Trailhead GPS: N41 54.418' / W71 24.060'. Trail contact: The Nature Conservancy, Rhode Island Chapter, 159 Waterman St., Providence, 02906; (401) 331-7110; www.nature.org.

AR. PACHAUG TRAIL

At the Connecticut border, this 7-mile out-and-back sampling of the blue Pachaug Trail strings between Beach Pond Trailhead and a boat launch in Connecticut. It shares its start with the yellow Tippecansett Trail, heading north from RI 165. It then solos left to overlook Beach Pond and tag its sculpted shore. You also will pass among scenic boulder jumbles, marked by overhangs, shelters, and short passageways, and travel in mixed woods and soggy reaches. Lush mountain laurel, sweet pepperbush, and highbush blueberry favor shore. Keep to the path to avoid private property.

Start at Beach Pond parking (a fee site), on the north side of RI 165. From the junction of RI 3 and RI 165 (0.3 mile east of I-95), go west on RI 165 for 6.6 miles to trail parking. From Voluntown, Connecticut: From the junction of CT 49 and 138/165, go east on CT 165/RI 165 for 4.3 miles. Trailhead GPS: N41 34.439' / W71 47.182'. Trail contacts: Arcadia Management Area Headquarters, 260 Arcadia Rd., Hope Valley 02823; (401) 539-2356. Parks and Recreation, 1100 Tower Hill Rd., North Kingstown 02852; (401) 667-6200; www.riparks.com.

AS. BROWNING MILL POND

In Arcadia Management Area, Browning Mill Pond is one of the launch points to the area's extensive trail network. From here you can fashion a variety of hikes, circuits, and distance walks. From the yellow Roaring Brook Trail, you can navigate an easy 1.5-mile pond perimeter hike.

From the junction of RI 3 and RI 165, east of I-95, head west on RI 165, crossing under the interstate. In 1.5 miles turn left (south) on Arcadia Road, signed for the management area and Tomaquag Museum. Continue south another 1.6 miles to this trail's dirt parking lot on the right. Trailhead GPS: N41 33.361' / W71 41.130'. Trail contacts: Arcadia Management Area Headquarters, 260 Arcadia Rd., Hope Valley 02823; (401) 539-2356. Parks and Recreation, 1100 Tower Hill Rd., North Kingstown 02852; (401) 667-6200; www.riparks.com.

AT. CHAFEE NATURE PRESERVE

At this 230-acre waterfront preserve, short nature trails explore the grounds, with Rome Point the destination. Once considered for a nuclear power plant, Rome Point's history has been nuclear from the start, from its purchase from the Narragansett Indians to its confiscation by the state in 1775 from its Tory-leaning landowner George Rome. Donated by Narragansett Electric Company to Rhode Island, the preserve honors the late US senator John H. Chafee, a champion of open space. The primary trail is an old road that takes you from the parking lot to the Narragansett Bay shore, where you hike the beach north to walk the peninsula out to Rome Point. Views are of Narragansett Bay and the preserve marsh, estuary, swamp woodland, and beach. In winter, seals commonly haul out on the bay rocks.

From the junction of RI 138 and RI 1A, west of the Jamestown Bridge, go north on RI 1A for 1 mile to reach the preserve and turnout parking on the right. A map kiosk shows the trails. Trailhead GPS: N41 32.227' / W71 26.233'. Trail contact: John H. Chafee Nature Preserve, c/o Goddard Memorial State Park, (401) 884-2010, State of Rhode Island Department of Environmental Management, Division of Parks and Recreation, 1100 Tower Hill Rd., North Kingstown 02852; (401) 667-6200; www.riparks .com.

AU. NORMAN BIRD SANCTUARY

At 325 acres, this privately held Aquidneck Island sanctuary offers 7 miles of trail. You will find north–south trending craggy ridges and puddingstone outcrop parted by linear marshes, abandoned pasture, rich woodland, and inland freshwater ponds. Views sweep the dramatic rocky coastline to Rhode Island Sound, as well as preserve features. To get you started, consider the easy 1.1-mile Woodland Trail loop, the 2-mile out-and-back Hanging Rock Trail, or the 2-mile out-and-back Gray Craig Trail. Gain your bearings at the visitor center barn. A trail fee is charged, and no pets allowed. The sanctuary is open daily (except major holidays), 9 a.m. to 5 p.m.

From the junction of RI 138A (Aquidneck Avenue) and Green End Avenue in Middletown, go east on Green End Avenue for 1.5 miles and turn right on Third Beach Road. Go 0.7 mile to enter the sanctuary on the right. Trailhead GPS: N41 29.975' / W71 15.056'. Trail contact: Norman Bird Sanctuary, 583 Third Beach Rd., Middletown 02842; (401) 846-2577; www.normanbirdsanctuary.org.

AV. CAROLINA MANAGEMENT AREA

At this Rhode Island Fish and Wildlife Area in Richmond, management roads and mowed tracks explore the management parcels that total more than 2,300 acres. From the trailhead described below, you can craft a counterclockwise southern loop across the property bounded by Meadow Brook and the Pawcatuck River. It's about a 3-mile hike, with a 0.2-mile return along Pine Hill Road. The habitat mosaic is conifer-hardwood forest, field, and wetland. As you turn away from the river, you pass a historic cemetery. Birding walks are popular here. Hunting safety rules apply from the third Saturday in October through February and from April 25 through the end of May.

From US 1 at Charlestown, follow RI 112/RI 2 north for 3 miles to the RI 2 split-off and continue north on RI 112 for 2.8 miles more. Turn left west on Pine Hill Road, reaching the primary trailhead parking lot on the left in 1.5 miles. Trailhead GPS: N41 27.980' / W71 41.306'. Trail contact:

Woods road, Carolina Management Area, Rhode Island

Carolina Management Area, Rhode Island Division of Fish and Wildlife, Great Swamp Field Headquarters, 277 Great Neck Rd., West Kingston 02892; (401) 789-0281; www .dem.ri.gov.

AW. FRANCIS C. CARTER MEMORIAL PRESERVE

This attractive 840-acre preserve of The Nature Conservancy, the second largest in the state, has a 6.6-mile network of interlocking color-coded trails that explore upland pitch pine and scrub oak woods, a terrain of 12,000-year-old glacier-deposited boulders, and the Pawcatuck River floodplain. A vernal pool with an overlook deck and a 35-acre grassland contribute to the flora and fauna wealth. Stone walls speak to a former era. The preserve is open daylight hours. Heed all rules, practicing no-trace travel. At times RI 112 is a noisy neighbor.

From US 1 at Charlestown, follow RI 112/RI 2 north for 3 miles to the RI 2 split-off and continue north on RI 112 for 1 mile to find limited trail parking on the left. Be careful of the sharp road edge when turning off RI 112. Trailhead GPS: N41 38.696' / W71 45.406'. Trail contact: The Nature Conservancy, Rhode Island Chapter, 159 Waterman St., Providence 02906; (401) 331-7110; www.nature.org.

AX. NINIGRET NATIONAL WILDLIFE REFUGE

On the coast of Block Island Sound at Charlestown, this federal wildlife refuge has parcels on both sides of US 1. On the north side, you'll find the Kettle Pond Visitor Center, an observation deck, and nature trails that link to the longer hiking trails at Watchaug Pond. The southern parcel offers two nature trails in separate areas: the 1-mile Foster Cove Loop (the western trail) and the 1.4-mile out-and-back Grassy Point trails (the eastern trail plus spurs, visiting Ninigret Pond, a 1,700-acre brackish coastal pond breached to the ocean). Refuge habitats include upland grassland, shrubland, woodland, marsh, and pond. When hiking, carry insect repellent and beware of poison ivy and ticks. Leave pets at home. Trails are open year-round, sunrise to sunset.

At Charlestown, the Kettle Pond Visitor Center has access off US 1 South only, while Foster Cove and Grassy Point have their accesses off US 1 North. U-turn lanes allow visits to each site. The Kettle Pond Visitor Center on Bend Road is north off US 1 South, 1 mile west of Prosser Trail. Trailhead GPS: N41 22.047' / W71 41.118'. For Foster Cove and Grassy Point, from the US 1–RI 216 junction, go east on US 1 North, reaching the right-hand turn for the Foster Cove Trail in 2.6 miles (Trailhead GPS: N41 22.086' / W71 40.325') and the right turn for RI 1A, the turnoff for the Grassy Point Trail, in 2.8 miles. Once on RI 1A, drive 0.4 mile to Ninigret Park and follow signs past the nature center to access the eastern refuge and Grassy Point trailhead (Trailhead GPS: N41 21.891' / W71 39.371'). Trail contact: Ninigret National Wildlife Refuge, Refuge Headquarters, 50 Bend Rd., Charlestown 02813; (401) 364-9124; www.fws.gov/refuge/ninigret.

CLUBS & TRAIL GROUPS

Appalachian Mountain Club (AMC), the nation's oldest outdoor recreation and conservation organization (active since 1876), promotes the protection, enjoyment, and wise use of mountains, rivers, and trails in the Appalachian region. Appalachian Mountain Club, Main Office, 10 City Square, Boston 02129; (617) 523-0636; www.outdoors.org.

Appalachian Trail Conservancy (ATC), formerly known as the Appalachian Trail Conference, is a volunteer-based, private nonprofit organization dedicated to the conservation of the 2,190-mile Appalachian National Scenic Trail (AT) and its 250,000-acre greenway extending from Maine to Georgia. The ATC has done so since 1925 and also provides AT information and education. It works in unison with the National Park Service, thirty maintaining clubs, and a host of partners and volunteers. Appalachian Trail Conservancy, PO Box 807, 799 Washington St., Harpers Ferry, WV 25425-0807; (304) 535-6331; www.appalachiantrail.org.

Connecticut Forest and Park Association (CFPA), established in 1895 to conserve land and promote trails, has been the guiding light and steward of the Connecticut blue trail system since the system's conception in 1929. Each year its members contribute 25,000 volunteer hours, keeping 825 miles of trail open, maintained, and growing. The association also compiles and updates the *Connecticut Walk Book,* a hikers' resource. Connecticut Forest and Park Association, 16 Meriden Rd., Rockfall, CT 06481; (860) 346-8733; www.ctwoodlands.org.

New York–New Jersey Trail Conference is a federation of member clubs and individuals that takes a leadership role in building, maintaining, marking, and promoting trails and advocating for open space in the New York–New Jersey region. The network's handiwork touches 2,150 miles of foot trails; you'll enter their reach in the Taconic Mountains at the northwest corner of Connecticut. New York–New Jersey Trail Conference, 600 Ramapo Valley Rd. (Route 202), Mahwah, NJ 07430; (201) 512-9348; www.nynjtc.org.

Rails-to-Trails Conservancy is the nonprofit group spearheading the reclamation of the nation's abandoned rail corridors for recreation. Rails-to-Trails Conservancy, The Duke Ellington Building, 2121 Ward Ct. NW, 5th Floor, Washington, DC 20037; (202) 331-9696; www.railstotrails.org.

ABOUT THE AUTHORS

They're back! Again. Who says you can never go home again? And, again?

This Oregon-based duo, George, born and raised in Connecticut, and Rhonda, a Montana-convert to the New England way of things, truly do have the trails of Connecticut and Rhode Island tattooed on their boots, and they continue to find reasons to keep coming back.

The two have been hiking together for more than thirty years, and have covered the contiguous United States from corner to corner, with forays into Mexico and Canada. They are avid enthusiasts of all kinds of habitats and mindful of all the feet that have passed before theirs in this rich and historic region. This is their fourth round of looking at this region's trails—professionally, that is. Personally, they've scoured the trails dozens of times.

Rhonda (a writer) and George (a photographer) have collaborated on more than twenty of outdoor guide and travel/photography books and produced thousands of articles on nature, travel, and outdoor recreation, as well as calendars, postcards, and brochures. Other titles by the two include *Hiking New York, Fourth Edition,* and *Camping Oregon, Third Edition* (both FalconGuides), *California State Parks: A Complete Recreation Guide, Second Edition,* and *Best Short Hikes in Northwest Oregon,* as well as the photographic celebrations, *Our Oregon* and *Our Washington.*